Atlanta

The Making of a World Class City

Produced in cooperation with the
Metro Atlanta Chamber of Commerce

Atlanta

The Making of a World Class City

By **David Black**
Corporate Profiles by **Pam Baker** and **Virginia Parker**
Featuring the photography of **Ron Sherman**
Special Introduction by **Billy Payne**

ATLANTA

The Making of a World Class City

By David Black
Corporate Profiles by Pam Baker and Virginia Parker
Featuring the photography of Ron Sherman

Special introduction by William Payne

Produced in cooperation with the Metro Atlanta Chamber of Commerce

Staff for *Atlanta: The Making of a World Class City*

Publisher's Sales Associates	**Bill Koons, John Lorenzo, John Tew, Robbie Wills, Tom Carter**
Acquisitions	**Henry S. Beers**
Executive Editor	**James E. Turner**
Managing Editor	**Wendi L. Lewis**
Profile Editors	**Lenita Gilreath & Mary Catherine Richardson**
Design Director	**Scott Phillips**
Production Artists	**Ramona Davis & Lenita Gilreath**
Photo Editors	**Scott Phillips and Wendi L. Lewis**
Production Manager	**Jarrod Stiff**
Contract Manager	**Christi Stevens**
Editorial Assistant	**Amanda J. Burbank**
National Sales Manager	**John Hecker**
Sales Assistant	**Annette Lozier**
Proofreader	**Angela Mann**
Accounting Services	**Sara Ann Turner**
Printing Production	**Gary G. Pulliam/DC Graphics**
Pre-press & separations	**Artcraft Graphic Productions**

CCI

Community Communications, Inc.
Montgomery, Alabama

James E. Turner, Chairman of the Board
Ronald P. Beers, President
Daniel S. Chambliss, Vice President

PREFACE

Atlanta is barely 150 years old, but it has enough history for a city three times its age—slavery, war, utter destruction, occupation, natural disaster, civil disobedience, tragedy, and triumph.

Despite this abundance, Atlantans are often indicted as ignorant, if not contemptuous, of their history, all too willing to erase or tear down the past in favor of whatever is new. There is some truth to that charge—particularly when it comes to fine old buildings—but the other side of the coin is that Atlantans have always been willing to embrace the future, particularly when it comes to commerce.

Atlantans were early embracers of the railroad, the telephone, the automobile, and the airplane. Thanks to Henry Grady, Atlanta was the first city to hit on the idea of promoting itself as a destination for the ambitious entrepreneur. Later it became the first city to advertise itself to the rest of the country as a good place to do business, a practice that quickly became commonplace. In the edgy 1960s, it was the city's business community that forced change in race relations.

Today, Atlantans continue to enthusiastically embrace the newest technology. Entrepreneurship continues to flourish. And the challenges of the new millennium—suburban sprawl, traffic, air and water pollution—are drawing the attention of the newest generation of business leaders.

Atlantans have a tradition of making big things happen, from the grand expositions of the late 1800s to the 1996 Olympics. Expect that tradition to continue well into the next millennium.

David Black, *Author*

The Making of a World Class City

A SPECIAL INTRODUCTION

by
William Porter Payne

I grew up in Atlanta during the 1950s and '60s and remember being vividly aware of what seemed to be a small-town environment located in the middle of a large metropolitan area that had no physical limitations. For some reason, I noticed, the atmosphere always seemed electrically charged as people constantly talked about Atlanta's growth and impending emergence as one of America's truly great cities. I can even distinctly remember a slogan adopted by the Atlanta Chamber of Commerce during that period which proclaimed Atlanta as "the world's next great city." I remember thinking at the time that this particular slogan was a bit adventuresome and yet it did set a target that appeared to be the possible result of the infectious enthusiasm that has always been a part of the population and personality of Atlanta.

During these same years and particularly in the 1960s and '70s, we seemed shocked to discover that the growth and prosperity of our community brought with it complicated infrastructure and

social issues. No, it would not be an easy job to marshal and perpetuate Atlanta's growth and prosperity in a manner that to the fullest extent possible preserved the small-town feeling and the sense of neighborhood which we all cherish. After all, how could any city proclaim itself the capital city of the South unless it could also preserve and demonstrate every single day the warmth and friendliness of its people—true Southern hospitality.

As we struggled with this growth and prosperity, we were amazingly surprised to discover that other people on the outside looking in seemed to love Atlanta as much as we did. Atlanta was increasingly becoming a corporate or regional headquarters for so many fine American companies. Atlanta became almost a required stopover for corporate executives as they worked their way up the ladder of their corporate hierarchy. But unlike so many other cities similarly blessed with growth and prosperity, something was different about Atlanta. It had a magical, inexplicable allure, and countless numbers of these corporate executives refused to leave Atlanta when their companies attempted to transfer them to their next career move. A consensus was beginning to develop that Atlanta truly represented the best place in America to live, work, and to raise a family.

Was it then possible as we looked toward the new millennium that Atlanta could indeed become the measure of its historical rhetoric and emerge as "the world's next great city"?

Atlanta's personality and eternal optimism surfaced again in 1987 when a small group of dedicated volunteers proclaimed to a disbelieving world that they believed the combination of the friendliness of Atlanta and the compelling power of the Olympic Movement would be a wonderful partnership. Atlanta would become a candidate for the Olympic Games—not just any Olympic Games but the centennial celebration of this wonderful international movement.

When my former football coach at the University of Georgia, Vince Dooley, first heard of the idea he responded by saying, "I guess I let Billy play too many games without his helmet!"

Others were equally shocked and disbelieving as Atlanta's candidacy gained momentum and as the world began to see and ultimately to realize what Atlanta offered to the Olympic Movement. The atmosphere in Atlanta was once again electric as the entire community gradually joined in the advancement of this preposterous idea and began having a positive effect on the world's sporting community as they introduced Atlanta.

Citizens of Atlanta began asking themselves if this crazy idea could be the beginning of the fulfillment of our designation as "the world's next great city." During the three-and-one-half years of the campaign and the resulting election of Atlanta as the Host City of the 1996 Centennial Olympic Games, the world received a major dose of Southern hospitality. The world was introduced to Atlanta and, more importantly, the world came to know the people of Atlanta. Once again, Atlanta's greatest asset proved to be the sincerity and the friendliness of its citizens. It was a compelling message that reverberated throughout the entire world and that, against all odds, prevailed over the candidacies of other formidable cities.

The celebration of the Centennial Olympic Games in the summer of 1996 represented Atlanta's crowning achievement and I believe the fulfillment of our goal and objective to welcome the world as if they were members of our own family. Once again it was the friendliness of our people, the infectious smiles on their faces and the sincerity of their welcome to our five-and-one-half million visitors that forged Atlanta's place in Olympic history. There was a sense of oneness within our community that seemingly diminished and made altogether unimportant our differences, which otherwise seem to divide us at other times. I said repeatedly during the Games that we, the people of Atlanta, looked into a mirror...and we were beautiful. For the first time in our community's history, we experienced and celebrated that which we share in common—an affection for each other and a shared pride in our city.

Many have attempted to define the legacy of our Olympic Games in the context of the $500 million of facilities the Organizing Committee built and then gave away to various municipalities or universities, the $5 billion positive economic impact it had on

CHAPTER ONE
Atlanta Today

For all its colorful history, the story of Atlanta is primarily one of business. What's most surprising about the story is that Atlanta has so few of the advantages once believed essential to a great business city.

One Atlantic Center and the Woodruff Arts Center.
Photo by Ron Sherman

Where most of America's great business cities were either seaports or located alongside navigable rivers, Atlanta at first was nothing more than the stake pounded into the ground at the end of a railroad line.

When the early pioneers had nevertheless raised Atlanta to a thriving regional crossroads and manufacturing center, the city was completely leveled by war, conquered and occupied by the Union Army.

When, after prodigious effort, Atlanta rebuilt itself physically and emerged again as a regional capital, it was one of the poorest and least developed regions of the country, a condition that persisted well into the latter half of the century.

Through it all, Atlanta has persevered and thrived. The South is now the fastest-growing region of the country and Atlanta remains its leading city.

Why?

◄ Atlanta was at first nothing more than the stake pounded into the ground at the end of a railroad line. Photo courtesy of the Atlanta History Center

◄ When, in the early 1800s, city fathers invited the state capital to move from Milledgeville to Atlanta, the offer was laughed at. Atlanta was little more than a muddy intersection. But city fathers persevered, and eventually the Legislature accepted the offer, even after Atlanta was burned. Photo by Ron Sherman

Because Atlanta has always been a hard-working town. No, not in the old blue-collar, punching-a-time-clock, three-shift-a-day formula, but in a white-collar, networking way. And with the arrival of the Information Age, Atlanta's business culture—with its emphasis on marketing and business services—is right in step with the times.

Because Atlanta has always been a town of dreamers. Perhaps the greatest dreamer of them all was Alexander Stephens who, in 1839, looked out over the uninhabited, heavily forested ridges of present-day Atlanta and predicted that a "magnificent inland city will at no distant date be built here." Stephens later was elected governor and witnessed the truth of his prophecy.

Just a few years later, the city fathers invited the state capital to move from Milledgeville to Atlanta, at the time little more than a muddy intersection. The offer was laughed at. What kind of nerve did these people possess? The city fathers were undeterred and kept the invitation open. They kept inviting even after Sherman burned the city. Just as oddly, the Legislature accepted the offer to move to a ruined town. Who was the greater dreamer?

Atlanta has always been a savvy town when it comes to appearances. It is a city as insecure and sensitive and boastful as a gawky teenager, to be sure, and displays an attitude that infuriates its critics. But it has an innate understanding and belief in the power of marketing and promoting itself as what it wants to be tomorrow, not what it is today. It's no coincidence that seventy years ago

Atlanta became the first city to nationally advertise itself to businessmen, urging them to come and be part of it all.

Because for most of its history, the Atlanta business community and local government have been barely distinguishable. The cozy arrangement has had its critics but also its triumphs. During the 1950s and '60s, Atlanta should have been ground zero for the violent tensions of the civil rights movement. But thanks to two extraordinarily capable and sensitive mayors—William Hartsfield and Ivan Allen Jr.—it was other American cities that burned, not Atlanta.

For these reasons and many others, Atlanta has been a boomtown during the majority of its years. The Civil War, the Great Depression, and the economically stagnant 1970s all slowed the momentum somewhat, but when economic conditions in the country are good generally, Atlanta performs spectacularly.

Witness the last two decades. The middle years of the 1980s became known as the "Golden Years" because of the convergence of Sun Belt migration and a booming national economy. All types of construction—commercial and residential—surged to record levels, as did new job creation. For many cities, this would be a once-in-a-lifetime event to be remembered fondly. But after a brief lull to change decades, the 1990s brought Atlanta more of the same, erasing many of the growth benchmarks set in the 1980s.

Between 1992 and 1997, the metro Atlanta economy created more than 450,000 new jobs, leading the country in net job growth in 1992, 1993, 1994, and 1996. The metro population

▶ As was true of most early Southern cities, agriculture was the economic mainstay. Atlanta farmers produced peaches, for which the area would be known for the "Georgia Peach," and cotton. Photos courtesy Georgia Department of Archives and History

increased by 100,000 annually, driving the metro population from just under 3 million in 1990 to 3.65 million in 1997.

The flocking of the young and ambitious to Atlanta is a key part of the city's story. But over the last twenty years the rewards of successful entrepreneurism have grown to a previously unimagined magnitude. In 1980, Home Depot was just an idea in the head of two men cast off by their previous employer. Less than twenty years later, Home Depot was the largest public company in Georgia, a national retailing powerhouse with annual sales of more than $24 billion a year.

In the late 1960s, Ted Turner was a firey young man who owned a billboard company and a forlorn television station. Only a decade later, Turner was a sports magnate, a world-class sailor, and the godfather of cable television. Ten years after that, Turner is an international celebrity and media mogul of the first rank.

Today Atlanta is full of entrepreneurs with an idea they want to turn into a company, small companies that want to be big, and big companies that want to be global. There are more than twenty-three thousand black-owned businesses in Atlanta, and more than eighty-three thousand owned by women.

Atlanta's economy in the beginning was based on its central location and transportation links. Today the railroads are still here and busy as ever. So are the three interstate highways built to accommodate the automobile. When commercial aviation was invented, Atlanta hopped on board early thanks to Mayor Hartsfield. Today, 68 million passengers use Hartsfield Atlanta International Airport each year, making it one of the busiest airports in the world. The telecommunications industry can take advantage of the intersection of two massive fiber optic trunk routes in Atlanta. And the metro area still boasts the largest toll-free calling zone in the U.S., more than 7,000 square miles.

Thanks to Ted Turner, the national and international prominence of Cable News Network projected Atlanta's name to the far corners of the globe, giving Atlanta cachet among international business circles. While it wasn't until the 1980s that international business operations began to take serious root in Atlanta, there are nearly 1,000 international facilities in Atlanta—a quarter of them national headquarters—all drawn by the low costs, convenient transportation links, and pleasant environment that attract their U.S. peers.

Ever since the 1920s, when Atlanta first went trolling for the attention of the national business community, it has been attractive destination to the Fortune 500.

As far back as the 1880s, observers have noted that Atlanta's hustle and bustle distinguished it from other Southern cities. That made Atlanta a comfortable choice for Northern corporations establishing regional offices. Of the current Fortune 1000, seven

▲ The 1980s and 1990s have been golden years for Atlanta's growth, bringing a wealth of new commercial and residential development, and a boom in new job creation. Photo by Ron Sherman

29

hundred have operations in Atlanta, while twenty-eight are head-quartered here. Of the Fortune 500, thirteen call Atlanta home.

Some, like utility company Southern Co., are homegrown enterprises. Others, like Georgia-Pacific Corp. and United Parcel Service, are recent transplants. Coca-Cola, of course, is one of the first multi-national corporations, but it is also nearly as much a cultural icon as it is a business. All of them, new or old, local or transplant, share a commitment to civic and charitable involvement that is one of corporate Atlanta's unique features.

But the issue in American business isn't just who is big today but who is growing and will be big tomorrow. Atlanta is positioning itself to take better advantage of the emergence of knowledge-based businesses and the metro area's sixty colleges, universities, and technical schools. The state sponsors business incubators in high technology and telecommunications and is organizing similar biotechnology incubators. Increasing the size and number of local venture capital firms, vital to the financing of new business ideas, is also a high priority. More than 166,000 Atlantans now work in high-tech jobs, and projections put Atlanta in the top three cities for technology job growth in the future.

Physically, Atlanta long ago outgrew the city limits. For a while, it was thought that Interstate 285 would be the new defining line,

but the explosive growth of the suburbs was barely slowed. With nothing in the way of physical barriers to growth and a steady influx of new citizens, the metropolitan area has burst out in all directions—particularly to the north—until it covers twenty counties and more than 6,000 square miles.

As Atlanta faces the next millennium, it will have to overcome problems with transportation, water, suburban sprawl, and air quality spawned by the economic growth of the last thirty years. The problems are difficult and alleviating them may be painful and expensive, but who would be willing to look at Atlanta and its history and bet against it? ❧

▶ **Atlanta is a city with a rich history and tradition, but which nonetheless is unafraid to step boldly into the future.** Photo by Ron Sherman

▶ **Physically, Atlanta long ago outgrew the city limits, bursting out in all directions until it covers twenty counties and more than six thousand square miles.** Photo by Ron Sherman

MORRISON MANAGEMENT SPECIALISTS

While most of Atlanta is just waking up, Glenn Davenport, Chairman and CEO of Morrison Management Specialists, is already in the office. As he has his second cup of coffee, the Morrison team has already prepared a breakfast for hundreds of thousands of hospital patients, retirement community residents, employees, and visitors Morrison serves across the country.

When eating right was more important than eating fast, Morrison Cafeterias were the place for a great tasting meal. The company's commitment to serving hospitals goes back 45 years. Their experience in retirement communities is equally broad. Glenn Davenport is one of the reasons the Morrison heritage remains strong. Glenn joined the company fresh from college and has been with Morrison ever since.

Today, Morrison Management Specialists is the largest independent company specializing in food, nutrition, and dining services for healthcare and senior living. The company is proud to call Atlanta home, and Davenport appreciates the city's virtues every day. Here, Morrison continues to add to its history of success.

◄ **Some of Atlanta's youngest residents find joy in the simple pleasures.** Photo by Ron Sherman

◄ **Chastain Park is the site for concerts ranging from jazz to classical, modern rock to rhythm and blues. This laid-back venue invites concert-goers to bring a picnic and add a little elegance to the evening.** Photo by Ron Sherman

GEORGIA POWER COMPANY

From the 1880s, Georgia Power and its predecessor companies have been at the heart of Georgia's modernization. Both the company and the state have been historically bound to a common future.

Georgia Power serves customers in 57,000 of the state's 59,000 square miles, for a total of more than 1.8 million customers in all but 6 of Georgia's 159 counties. One of the state's largest taxpayers, Georgia Power pays taxes to city, county, state, and federal agencies totaling nearly $710 million. Nearly 40 plants across the state generate energy to power Georgia's homes and businesses.

The Georgia Resource Center is only one example of how Georgia Power helps to build industry in Georgia. Located in downtown Atlanta and operated as a public/private partnership for economic development, the center is used by other statewide allies to provide prospective companies with a high-tech, high-impact presentation of Georgia's business infrastructure.

For those new to Atlanta and Georgia, the center provides 52 overview videos in six languages. More detailed visual tours of communities, buildings, and sites are accessed through interactive databases featuring extensive and current information on 260 communities, 600 industrial parks, 450 available industrial buildings in the state, and 2,800 industrial, commercial, and office buildings in the metro Atlanta area.

BANK OF AMERICA

At the peak of the Great Depression, when more than 1,800 U.S. banks failed, Citizens & Southern National Bank celebrated the grand opening of its seven-story Mitchell Street office in Atlanta. As is typical of Atlanta companies, it continued to grow at a phenomenal rate. By 1987, the bank's centennial year, it had billions in assets and 466 branches in three states. In 1992, it merged with North Carolina National Bank to become one of the largest banks in the country: NationsBank.

In 1998, the bank merged with BankAmerica to form the country's first truly nationwide bank. The name changed once again, to Bank of America.

Despite the tremendous growth and the ever-increasing national clout, the bank retained its hometown Atlanta feel. Many of the tellers who work at Bank of America also worked there when it was C&S. Many of the loan officers are also familiar faces, and customers are still greeted by name.

YANCEY BROS. CO.

In downtown Atlanta on Peachtree Street, two brothers opened a small family business. The year was 1914; among their fledgling distinctions was the appointment as the nation's first dealer for Adams mule graders. The mule-drawn grader was a modern advancement and an innovative addition to the Yancey Brothers line of hardware, picks, shovels, and prison uniforms.

Today, Yancey Bros. Co. is the nation's oldest Caterpillar dealer and is renowned as a leader in the construction equipment industry, as it has been for more than 85 years now. Through all the growth, and the modern advancements and technological achievements, Yancey Bros. Co. has always been based in Atlanta, as much a part of the historic cityscape as Peachtree Street itself.

▼ **A variety of housing choices are available in and around the Atlanta and Fulton County area, from relaxed and elegant estate homes to apartment homes and townhouses in the heart of the city.** Photos by Ron Sherman

NORTEL NETWORKS

Nortel Networks has Unified Network solutions operations in more than 150 countries and territories worldwide, with offices and facilities in North America, Europe, Asia/Pacific, Caribbean and Latin America, the Middle East, and Africa. This global representation encompasses more than 50 native languages and 55 national origins.

Atlanta has several advantages that help Nortel Networks achieve global dominance. For example, access to an international airport is essential, especially for the sales and marketing teams. Hartsfield International Airport offers the convenience and efficiency of numerous direct, daily flights to most of Nortel Networks' major markets worldwide.

Atlanta is also an attractive culture to many of the types of people Nortel Networks recruits and hires, most of whom are innovative, dynamic individuals seeking diverse and stimulating life experiences.

Further, graduates from Georgia Tech, one of the nation's best engineering schools, are actively recruited to fill many of the sales, development, and engineering positions available at Nortel Networks' Alpharetta campus and other company locations. A constant supply of highly trained and versatile workforce members is the lifeblood of Nortel Networks.

SOUTHERN COMPANY

The name Southern Company is becoming known throughout the energy world, standing as an icon for superb service and true Southern pride. The company, based in Atlanta, is an international energy provider with more than $35 billion in assets through regional utilities and foreign operations.

Through its international subsidiaries and affiliates, Southern Company provides electricity in ten countries including China, England, Germany, the Philippines, and Brazil, and parts of the United States outside its traditional service territory. Of course, Southern Company keeps the home lights burning, too, through its five U.S. electric utilities: Alabama Power, Georgia Power, Gulf Power, Mississippi Power, and Savannah Electric. Other subsidiaries include Southern Energy Inc., Southern Nuclear, Southern Communications Services, Southern Company Energy Solutions, and Southern Company Services.

Like many Atlanta-based companies, Southern Company began as a good idea nearly a century ago. Back then, Atlanta was a good place to live and work. Since then, the company has become a stalwart in the city, in the Southeast, and now in other regions of North America and in growing markets internationally. It is fitting that the city and Southern Company, who have shared a wealth of history, now share the prospects of a prosperous future.

▶ **Atlanta boasts beautiful vistas both in town and in the country. It's easy to see why early settlers chose to build their city in the rich Georgia landscape.** Photos by Ron Sherman

EQUIFAX

Atlanta and Equifax have come a long way together. And, together they have a long way to go. Today, Equifax is preeminent among Atlanta's companies that have surpassed the 100-year milestone, while remaining firmly established on the solid foundation built by this city. With the advent of the new millennium, this partnership of city and company will meet new challenges as they continue to build and move confidently forward into the 21st century.

Atlanta was a city of 89,000 people in 1899, when Equifax first opened the doors of its local credit reporting business. Over the past 100 years, the growth of both the city and company has been extraordinary. Atlanta is now a city with a commanding international presence and a population of nearly three million. And, Equifax—while still "at home" in Atlanta—is a global corporation with annual revenues of more than $1.7 billion, 13,000 employees in 17 countries, and customers in nearly 50 more.

Through its information, transaction processing, and knowledge-based businesses, Equifax serves banking, finance, retail, credit card, telecommunications/utilities, automotive, information technology, healthcare and new media industries, and government. Global operations include consumer and commercial credit information, check authorization, card processing, card processing software, modeling, analytics, consulting, and direct-to-consumer services.

THE COCA-COLA COMPANY

The Coca-Cola Company is the world's largest manufacturer, marketer, and distributor of soft-drink and non-carbonated beverage concentrates and syrups.

Coca-Cola is the world's favorite soft drink, enjoyed over a billion times a day in nearly 200 countries all over the globe. The familiar shape of its bottle and the flowing script of its trademark are the most widely recognized trademarks in the world.

John Stith Pemberton, an Atlanta pharmacist, concocted the refreshing beverage in May of 1886, and sold it for five cents a glass at Jacob's Pharmacy in downtown Atlanta. The Company's headquarters are still in downtown Atlanta, close to its humble beginnings. An anchor in the revitalized inner city, the Company has, for over a century, impacted the community and supported its hometown.

The genesis of The Coca-Cola Company's philanthropic involvement in Atlanta was the generosity of Robert W. Woodruff, who became president of the Company in 1923 and guided it into the 1980s. Mr. Woodruff's contributions to Atlanta's educational, civic, and cultural communities amounted to hundreds of millions of dollars and continue to touch and improve the lives of countless people. The Coca-Cola Company and The Coca-Cola Foundation continue that tradition of support throughout metro Atlanta, the United States, and the world.

◄ **A number of golf courses in the Atlanta area attract world-class competition, as well as the weekend duffer.** Photo by Ron Sherman

The Esthetic Dental Practice of
GOLDSTEIN, GARBER, SALAMA & GRIBBLE
Located in Atlanta, But Perhaps More Known Throughout The World!

The dental practice of Goldstein, Garber, Salama & Gribble has long been considered one of the world's leading resources for cosmetic dentistry. The finest clinical expertise and technology available today are presented in an ambience of beauty and comfort. The internationally known doctors, who are also professors at six major universities and authors of several dental textbooks, are regularly sought after by the news media when a dental expert is needed.

Founded over 70 years ago, this group practice is now headed by Dr. Ronald Goldstein, author, lecturer, and practitioner. One of many unique aspects of this practice is that it may be the only dental practice in the world that includes three dual-specialists—including periodontics, prosthodontics, and orthodontics and implants. Another special feature is their in-house state-of-the-art dental laboratory, with internationally-known technicians and ceramists.

Visionaries and teachers of cosmetic dentistry, they utilize the latest technology available in dentistry—all designed to diagnose, communicate, and treat the patient in the most comfortable setting possible. Nowhere else in Atlanta—or perhaps the world—can this be found or duplicated!

▼ The Atlanta Braves, who have won seven straight divisional titles and more games than any other team in the 1990s, make their home at the new Turner Field. Constructed for the 1996 Centennial Olympic Games, the stadium was converted into the Braves' permanent home in 1997 and named for team owner and media mogul Ted Turner. Also on site is the Ivan Allen Jr. Braves Museum and Hall of Fame. Photo by Ron Sherman

LOCKHEED MARTIN
AERONAUTICAL SYSTEMS

When Americans think of aviation, the name Lockheed Martin comes to mind as easily as the Wright Brothers. After all, the company is one of the oldest and most respected names in the business.

The Marietta plant fed the U.S. Air Force with planes and the Atlanta workforce with groceries. Bell Aircraft opened the Marietta plant to build the 668 Boeing-designed Superfortresses as part of the B-29 production pool during World War II. All contracts were canceled the day after VJ-Day in 1945; the plant closed down and did not reopen until the Air Force asked Lockheed to reopen the Marietta plant in 1950. It was a time that was hard on everyone, but the flying, fighting machines made it a little easier to survive.

Today, Lockheed Martin builds a variety of planes, parts, and other aerial equipment for use during war and during peace. It is a mainstay in Atlanta's employment figures and fuels the aeronautical and engineering fields that lead to many of the country's advancements.

◄ **The Atlanta Steeplechase is an elegant and colorful tradition.** Photo by Ron Sherman

GEORGIA STATE UNIVERSITY

Birthed in Atlanta in 1913, Georgia State University has added much to the Atlanta scene. It anchors downtown as no other entity could. Students mingle throughout the streets and energize the inner city.

But, Georgia State is also a major research institution. It seeks real-life solutions to real-life problems on many urban-oriented issues. The university identifies and defines the challenges of the day, and of the future.

Within its walls visionaries chase cures, corrections, correlations, commonalities, clarifications, and conclusions. From these detailed and grueling investigations come the answers vibrant cities need to thrive, and stifled cities need to simply survive.

AT&T

AT&T Corp., formerly American Telephone and Telegraph Company, was incorporated in 1885 to manage and expand long-distance service. Based in Atlanta, it continued as a long-distance company until it became the parent company of the Bell System in 1899. It divested itself of the Bell companies in 1984. In 1995, it split into three distinct companies: a new AT&T, Lucent Technologies, and NCR Corp. But essentially, many still think of AT&T as "the" long-distance company.

In Atlanta, AT&T is often thought of as one of the city's best business successes. Seen as somewhat of an upstart organization in the early days, no one in today's world could imagine working and living without long-distance communication.

Though AT&T has become a worldly mega-giant, no longer pinned to a single geographic position, the company is true to its hometown roots and is a big supporter of Atlanta and Atlanta businesses.

▶ **A balloon rally fills Atlanta's sky with firey color.** Photo by Ron Sherman

▶ **The Chattahoochee River has long been an integral part of the Atlanta landscape, whether for travel, as a food source, or as a popular recreational destination.** Photo by Ron Sherman

FEDERAL HOME LOAN BANK

The rigors of the Great Depression seem far removed from the prosperous Atlanta of today. Our nation and our region have since experienced a resurgence fueled by the strongest economy the world has ever seen.

A significant contribution to that resurgence was the Federal Home Loan Bank Act, a landmark piece of legislation that created the Federal Home Loan Bank System. The Fourth District Federal Home Loan Bank, created in 1932 and now known as the Federal Home Loan Bank of Atlanta, was physically moved to Atlanta in 1972. Though Atlanta was farther from the geographic center of the bank's eight-state District, it was a thriving city and had become a major financial and transportation hub.

Today, The Federal Home Loan Bank of Atlanta is a $50 billion wholesale bank providing a wide variety of credit and correspondent banking services to enhance the profitability of financial institutions active in residential mortgage lending.

Federally chartered and stock-holder owned, the Bank is one of 12 independent district banks that constitute the Federal Home Loan Bank System. The Bank is a leader in the Federal Home Loan Bank System, with more than one thousand members.

UNITED PARCEL SERVICE

Every day, UPS delivers 12 million letters, packages, and parcels worldwide. The global UPS system reaches more than 4 billion of the Earth's approximately 6 billion people.

The UPS air fleet is one of the ten largest in the world with 216 company-owned jet cargo planes and 302 chartered aircraft making more than 1,500 flights each day to 610 airports around the globe.

Competing internationally requires an outstanding communications system, and UPS is an industry leader in information technology development and application. For example, the UPS global telecommunications network links 250,000 users in 70 international locations, making UPS the largest user of cellular technology in the world.

Given the massive logistics involved in operating on such a scale, Atlanta is a perfect choice for UPS headquarters. Atlanta, with its world-league Hartsfield airport, major highway networks, and its Olympic-sized electronic network, is a perfect match for companies like UPS that require the best in infrastructure and the brightest of workforces.

But initially, UPS chose Atlanta because of more personal issues. The beautiful weather, lots of green space, and unsurpassed quality of life features attracted 96 percent of the managers at UPS…as they attract thousands today.

▲ The night is alive in Atlanta, with a wide variety of cutting-edge restaurants as well as clubs, bars, and gathering spots offering a diverse selection of themes and entertainment. Photo by Ron Sherman

◄ Atlanta is a great place to play, whether your pleasure is a rousing game of basketball in one of the city's many parks, or an activity for the younger members of the family. Photos by Ron Sherman

▶ The expression of art can be found throughout the Atlanta area, from its vast offering of festivals, hands-on activities, and museums to expressive murals that are a part of the city's daily landscape.

Photos by Ron Sherman

PRICEWATERHOUSECOOPERS LLP

The merger that created PricewaterhouseCoopers brought together 140,000 professionals, creating a world that offers unlimited resources, unparalleled knowledge, and innovative solutions.

PricewaterhouseCoopers (www.pwcglobal.com) is the largest professional services organization, nearly the largest recruiter of people, and one of the biggest investors in technology. But, there is more to PricewaterhouseCoopers than just its size. The Firm's global presence provides access to information and skills that facilitate delivery of premium service and superior capabilities.

The image of a vessel symbolizes the intersection of people, knowledge, and worlds. The vessel represents a union of these three fundamental principals of the Firm's global identity.

Atlanta, a city that embraces diversity and international culture, is home to the enlightened ranks who hope to understand and create a new future. PricewaterhouseCoopers salutes Atlanta.

KAISER PERMANENTE

Kaiser Permanente pioneered the coordinated approach to health care more than 50 years ago. As a non-profit health care provider, the organization's goal is to continue to provide Atlanta and Georgia with convenient and affordable, quality medical care.

Kaiser Permanente has been consistently rated by independent surveys as Atlanta's premier health plan for member satisfaction and overall value. Indeed, members enjoy a wide range of benefits featuring quality care and exceptional service. It's no wonder members make up one of the happiest and healthiest communities in Atlanta.

There are nine KP medical centers located all over Atlanta and a growing list of Affiliated Community Physicians practicing throughout the area. Headquarters for the Georgia region are also located in Atlanta.

All told, there are more than 250,000 Georgians enrolled in Kaiser Permanente. Kaiser Permanente chose Metro Atlanta because of the city's reputation for excellence and advancements. Kaiser Permanente is proud to be a part of such a thriving region.

ALSTON & BIRD LLP

Alston & Bird's roots in the Atlanta community and the legal profession reach back into the 19th century when Atlanta was emerging as the transportation and commercial center of the New South. Two years after Robert Cotton Alston founded the firm in 1893, he and his partner, Judge Henry B. Tompkins, played a pivotal role in Atlanta in the foreclosure and reorganization of the Savannah & Western Railroad, the old Central Railroad, and other lines. Such involvement—which combined legal skills with the leading technology of the day—has evolved into Alston & Bird's blueprint for strategic growth.

Counseling its clients in the context of what has grown from a local to a regional, national, and now a global economic environment, the firm has overlaid its broad range of legal skills and business knowledge with a commitment to innovation and technology. This commitment enables Alston & Bird to provide superior client service and facilitate its clients' success.

With offices in Atlanta, Washington, D.C.; Charlotte, and the Research Triangle area in Raleigh, North Carolina, Alston & Bird today has over 450 attorneys practicing in more than 30 areas. Following in Robert Alston's footsteps, the firm's attorneys are helping clients in Atlanta and around the world form global joint ventures and alliances, negotiate licensing and advance pricing agreements, handle technology outsourcing and electronic commerce issues, and achieve their most ambitious business goals.

AKZO NOBEL

Akzo Nobel, based in Arhem, The Netherlands, serves customers throughout the world with healthcare products, coatings, chemicals, and fibers. The company currently employs approximately 86,000 people in more than 70 countries.

Eka Chemicals, a leading supplier of bleaching and paper chemicals, is the Pulp and Paper Chemicals business unit of Akzo Nobel. Car Refinishes, a leading manufacturer of high-quality products for collision repair, is a business unit of Akzo Nobel Coatings.

Atlanta is a strong business hub and essential to North American operations, from transportation and technology, to workforce recruitment and customer expediency, to geographic convenience among multiple locations. Which is why Eka Chemicals Inc. and Akzo Nobel Coatings Inc., Car Refinishes selected Atlanta for their corporate headquarters.

▲ **Atlanta welcomes the energy of her youthful population, who can try their hand at "extreme sports" like skateboarding or refuse to get lost in the crowd at one of the city's many organized entertainment events.**
Photos by Ron Sherman

◄ **An afternoon is easily spent in peaceful meditation, a quiet walk, or a friendly chat at waterside.**
Photo by Ron Sherman

TRAMMELL CROW

The Trammell Crow Company is one of the largest providers of diversified commercial real estate services in the United States and Canada, managing more than 415 million square feet of property. Through its 150 offices, the company delivers a comprehensive range of services within its five core lines of business: property management and leasing, brokerage, infrastructure management, development and construction, and retail.

The relationships that the Trammell Crow Company has forged throughout its history are extensive and include more than 550 investor/owner clients and 16,200 tenants nationwide. The longevity of many of these relationships has proved the company's ability to provide important competitive advantages. This is also why Trammell Crow came to Atlanta.

Representing hundreds of investors, it was prudent to have a continuous presence in booming Atlanta. The city was, and is, a good source for sound real estate investments and developments. Through the years, Trammell Crow has been substantially involved in many of the city's corporate and industrial deals.

WORLDSPAN®

Atlanta has long been known as a premier hub for travel and commerce. And certainly, much of the world travels through the gates of metro Atlanta. Because of WORLDSPAN's exceptional ability to facilitate both, it was logical for the company to base its world headquarters in Atlanta.

In an era of unprecedented technological change, WORLDSPAN has emerged as one of the leading providers of travel-related technology. The Atlanta-based electronic commerce company provides global communications and electronic distribution of information for the world's leading travel service providers, including airlines, hotel and car companies, cruise lines, and tour services. With a strong foray into the Internet arena, WORLDSPAN has also become a leading processor of Internet-travel bookings.

WORLDSPAN is rooted in Atlanta, as is one of its owners—Delta Air Lines. Founded February 7, 1990, WORLDSPAN is owned by three of the world's leading air carriers: Delta Air Lines, Northwest Airlines, and Trans World Airlines. The partnership is based on a commitment to provide high quality, efficient travel-information services.

WORLDSPAN is proud to be a part of Atlanta's unparalleled reputation as a center of opportunity, growth, and innovation.

▶ **Just steps away from the towering skyscrapers of downtown, Atlantans find a peaceful respite.**
Photos by Ron Sherman

▶ **Atlanta is a great place to live, work, and raise a family.** Photos by Ron Sherman

AGL RESOURCES INC.

AGL Resources and its major subsidiary—Atlanta Gas Light Company (AGLC)—have been proud to serve customers for more than 140 years with natural gas service.

The AGLC was chartered on February 16, 1856, to serve the city of Atlanta. Since then, the company has grown to serve nearly 1.5 million residential, commercial, and industrial customers in 243 communities throughout Georgia and southeastern Tennessee. AGL Resources, an Atlanta-based, NYSE-listed utility holding company, is a regional energy company with operations in six southeastern states.

Through it all, Atlanta has been home and headquarters. The emergence of the city as a world leader occurred alongside the company's emergence as the eighth largest natural gas distribution utility in the United States, and the largest in the Southeast. Throughout the combined history, only two things remained constant in both stories—change and growth. No matter what other changes lie ahead in the next millennium, both Atlanta and AGL Resources will continue to grow together.

JONES, DAY, REAVIS & POGUE

Tracing its origins to 1893, Jones, Day, Reavis & Pogue is one of the world's largest and most geographically diverse law firms in the world with more than 1,200 lawyers resident in 22 offices in major business and finance centers around the world.

Jones Day has long recognized Atlanta's role as the South's premier city and a city of growing importance internationally. The opening in 1989 of a Jones Day office in Atlanta enabled the Firm to complete its goal of establishing a presence in each of the leading U.S. financial and business centers.

Jones Day's Atlanta office includes approximately 100 lawyers, supported by a highly qualified staff and state-of-the-art communication and computer systems. As an integral part of an international law firm that spans four continents and has locations in ten major U.S. cities, Jones Day's Atlanta office offers valuable expertise in local and regional matters as well as issues of national and international scope.

MARTA

As the nation's seventh largest public transit system, MARTA is as busy as the people it serves. Some 560,000 riders travel comfortably and efficiently throughout metropolitan Atlanta daily; 30,000 of them passing through MARTA's busiest rail station, Five Points.

Designated as the first ever "Official Provider of Public Transportation" for the Olympic Games, MARTA proved it had the capacity and finesse to serve the world. During the Centennial Olympic Games, MARTA transported more than 1.5 million riders daily, offering 24-hour rail service.

Positioned and ready for our region's future needs, MARTA continues to expand service and develop transit projects for Atlanta—The World Class City.

TROUTMAN SANDERS LLP

Tracing its origin to 1897, Troutman Sanders is one of Atlanta's oldest and largest law firms, with nearly 300 lawyers. It is the largest international law practice headquartered in the city of Atlanta.

The firm has an established reputation for excellence. Experienced in virtually every aspect of commercial law and public policy, the firm is progressive, proactive, and continually expanding its resources.

Troutman Sanders is not only known for its dedication to clients, but also for its commitment to the community. The firm believes this long-standing support helps make a difference at home and around the world.

◄ **The Chattahoochee River is no stolid monument to a city's history, but still a vital part of the daily life of Atlanta.** Photos by Ron Sherman

GEORGIA-PACIFIC CORPORATION

Though an international giant in the paper industry, Georgia-Pacific is proud to be Georgia bred and born. The company was founded in 1927 in Augusta, Georgia, and, after substantial growth and acquiring billions of dollars in assets, eventually moved its headquarters to Atlanta in 1982.

Led by A.D. "Pete" Correll, Georgia-Pacific is one of the world's leading manufacturers and distributors of building products, pulp, and paper. The company employs over 50,000 people at more than 400 locations. It owns or controls over five million acres of timber and timberlands in the United States.

On the site where the architecturally distinctive Georgia-Pacific Center stands on Peachtree Street, once stood the DeGive Grand Opera House and Loew's Grand Theatre, where the 1939 world premier of *Gone With The Wind* was presented.

Since its arrival on the Atlanta skyline, Georgia-Pacific's corporate headquarters has made an indelible impression on its hometown community, employing thousands downtown. In addition to offices, the building houses the High Museum of Art—Folk Art and Photography galleries.

▶ It isn't often that those living in the deep south see snow; when it falls here, it's a special occasion. Nature's winter white takes Atlantans' breath away. Photos by Ron Sherman

ALLIED HOLDINGS, INC.

Allied Holdings, Inc. has come a long way since its humble beginnings in 1934, when Guy Rutland Sr. purchased Motor Convoy for $15,000. The company has multiplied its two trucks and trailers to become the largest carhauling company in North America. This accomplishment did not come by mere chance, but by hard work, commitment, and ground breaking developments.

Allied Holdings, Inc. is the parent company of several subsidiaries which encompass every aspect of the automotive distribution industry from hauling, logistics, and risk management services to information technology and financial, administration, communications, and human resources support functions.

But Allied Holdings, Inc. is more than a big corporation. Through it all they have maintained family business values for over 65 years. Their concern for employees' welfare, shown in the Chaplaincy Program, a nondenominational counseling service, clearly reveals dedication to these values. In a changing industry Allied Holdings, Inc. seeks to remain flexible and caring for both its customers and employees.

HEIDRICK & STRUGGLES

The ongoing recognition of Atlanta as one of the world's centers of economic, social, and international growth continues well beyond the Centennial Olympic Games, through the millennium's first Super Bowl, and forward into an uncharted time of global magnitude.

While the business environment in Atlanta is one of the best in the nation, the success of these enterprises ultimately rests with their leadership. As new companies mature and old companies evolve, the ability to attract and retain the best and brightest talent in the world to fill key management roles will have an enormous impact on long-term success.

Heidrick & Struggles, Inc., the world's leading executive search firm, is proud to be part of the burgeoning international cityscape of Atlanta. Founded in 1953, Heidrick & Struggles has been a member of the Atlanta business community since 1980.

BELLSOUTH CORPORATION

Atlanta is the headquarters city for BellSouth. The company began offering phone service in Atlanta over 115 years ago, in 1882. By the end of that same year, Southern Bell, now called BellSouth, offered phone service in eleven cities, in six states, and had 1,246 customers.

Business has picked up since then; BellSouth now has more than 24 million customers in its nine-state region and operations in 18 other countries around the world.

Today, the BellSouth network is Atlanta's primary connection to the information age and to the global economy. It is a mainstay for businesses, local and global, based in Atlanta. It's a serious responsibility few companies have to shoulder. Every year BellSouth invests more than $4 billion in its wired and wireless networks to continuously provide advanced technology and its renowned reliability. It's a $4 billion investment in the future of Atlanta, as well.

Morrison Management Specialists

Back in 1954, Candler General Hospital was struggling with food service. Seeking a reasonable solution, it turned to a popular restaurant, Morrison's Cafeteria. The arrangement worked out better than expected, and over 45 years later, Morrison is still dishing out culinary delights for Candler General and hundreds of other healthcare facilities.

Morrison Management Specialists is the largest independent company specializing in providing food, nutrition, and dining services to the healthcare and senior living industries.

Back in 1954, Candler General Hospital in Savannah, Georgia, was struggling with food service. Seeking a reasonable solution, it turned to a popular restaurant, Morrison's Cafeteria. The arrangement worked out better than expected; costs were soon under control and patient satisfaction was at an all-time high. Over 45 years later, Morrison is still dishing out culinary delights for Candler General and hundreds of other healthcare facilities.

Operated as a division of the restaurant enterprise since 1953, Morrison found such a surprising and profitable niche that, in March 1996, it became a separate corporation. Today, Morrison Management Specialists is the largest independent company specializing in providing food, nutrition, and dining services to the healthcare and senior living industries. The Atlanta-based corporation is committed to delivering innovative, retail-minded programs, high-quality services, and guaranteed low costs to clients. A publicly-held company, it trades on the New York Stock Exchange under the symbol "MHI".

Morrison now serves nearly 400 acute care hospitals, major health systems, specialty hospitals, retirement communities, and nursing homes in over 35 states, as well as five of the top ten acute care and teaching hospitals that outsource food and nutrition. Morrison Management Specialists' client roster includes some of the largest and most prominent health care systems and institutions in the country: BJC Health System in St. Louis, Missouri; LAC+USC Medical Center in Los Angeles, California; Medstar (formally Helix

Health System) in Baltimore, Maryland; University of Virginia Health Sciences Center in Charlottesville, Virginia; Northwestern Memorial Hospital and University of Chicago Hospitals, in Chicago; Jackson Memorial Hospital in Miami, Florida; the University of Tennessee Hospital in Knoxville, Tennessee; and the University Hospital at Stony Brook, New York.

Morrison's food and nutrition programs have proven so cost-effective and palate-pleasing that the longevity of client relationships is twice that of the industry average. Washington Hospital Center in Washington, D.C., reported that Morrison Management Specialists had saved the hospital over $1.5 million in food service costs in just two short years by implementing well-executed operations, an employee training program, and a profitable retail effort which bolstered its bottom line. It isn't an unusual experience for Morrison clients.

After Morrison's retail innovations at Brookwood Medical Center in Birmingham, Alabama, food court sales exceeded projections by over 40 percent. As a result, net patient food costs were reduced by seven percent.

Morrison delivered for Brookwood and other hospitals by using common sense coupled with unsurpassed service. Popular national brands like Taco Bell, Pizza Hut, and Subway were offered. Morrison signature brands like "Jupiter Grill" and "Morrison's Classic American Cooking" were added to help create the ambiance of a mall food court. Vending services were expanded and regularly rotated to provide staff more food options throughout the day.

The Morrison library of over 1,000 recipes is continuously revised to make meals more appetizing and nutritious. Retail promotions add value and improve customer satisfaction. And the Morrison catering program can serve sandwiches for five people or a five-course meal for 5,000 with equal ease. Along with this extraordinary selection of cuisine, service still counts for a lot in patient satisfaction.

Morrison's regional teams—specialists in operations, human resources, nutrition, and culinary—who assist on-site managers with day-to-day operations and problem-solving are credited as a big part of the company's uncanny success story. "The development of the regional team has made an exceptional difference," said Stephen Marino, vice president support services, Medical Center East, Birmingham, Alabama. "The quality of the individuals on that team and their constant accessibility for our manager has benefited us tremendously. They are always responsive to our needs."

A big part of the regional team's responsibilities revolve around employee training. Morrison Management Specialists' resources include a national management training center in Atlanta, a continuing education program with multimedia training, classroom sessions and on-site training modules, monthly classes that cover all aspects of food and nutrition services, and more. Beyond the details of proper nutrition and food service, the company also teaches the importance of recognizing multiple perspectives in the workplace through the "Diversity in the Morrison Workplace. . . Manager's Workshop." The supervisor training program uses videotapes, workbooks, and other resources to help participants learn about a variety of topics. Additionally, the on-the-job training program improves performance at the supervisory and unit staff level.

The results speak for themselves. According to Stephanie Dill, assistant director of food and nutrition services at Children's Hospital in St. Louis, "It's refreshing to have a company take the time and energy to provide such thorough, organized training."

Since labor accounts for over one half of food service costs, Morrison moves quickly to streamline food production. Morrison Culinary Solution is a no-nonsense approach to simplify the process. Through its centrally located Advanced Culinary Centers™, the division supplies complete meals for patients, as well as entrees, baked goods, custom sauces, and signature soups for use in retail operations.

In short, the meals are cooked from scratch, placed on trays or packaged, chilled in one central location, then delivered to the healthcare facilities. At mealtime, foods are simply brought back to serving temperature using advanced techniques that ensure all meals are consistent in quality, texture, and flavor every time.

Culinary Solutions enables Morrison to offer more programs that are real boosts to patient satisfaction. Like Breakfast a la Carte, the company's unique heated breakfast delivery system lets patients make their meal selections and be served immediately. Morrison's Chef's Special program allows patients to order and receive their meal selection the same day.

John Ray at Phoebe Putney Hospital in Albany, Georgia, says: "We were able to decrease our costs by streamlining processes such as hiring, training, vending, and reducing FTEs and waste. In the first year, we had an overall savings of $350,000, and for the second year, we saved an additional $250,000 for a total of

▲ Morrison now serves nearly 400 acute care hospitals, major health systems, specialty hospitals, retirement communities, and nursing homes in over 35 states.

◄ The company has become such an expert on nutrition, the American Dietetic Association asked Morrison to help write *Medical Nutrition Therapy Across the Continuum of Care*, a manual of protocols that have benefited the entire industry.

▲ A big part of the regional teams' responsibilities revolve around employee training. Morrison Management Specialists' resources include a national management training center in Atlanta.

► The Atlanta-based corporation is committed to delivering innovative, retail-minded programs, high-quality services, and guaranteed low costs to clients.

enhancing the way we meet the health needs of our patients, so hopefully they won't return to the hospital for surgeries or problems that could have been prevented."

Patient care through nutrition programs directly relates to reduced need for hospitalization, but such programs do not come with higher food costs for the facility. Morrison's customized solutions deliver guaranteed cost reductions, performance benchmarks, and the sharing of best practices. At Fort Sanders Regional Medical Center, Morrison reduced net operating costs by 21 percent and boosted cafeteria revenues over 15 percent.

In the hospital environment, Morrison offers everything from its Pro-health Dining program, which helps patients achieve their personal health goals through great tasting, healthy meals, to its Classic Puree Program, which offers attractive meals for people on special diets that boost mealtime consumption and reduce between-meal supplements. The company also sponsors themes and promotions to make mealtime more fun.

Patients need a little pampering now and then. Morrison's Hospitality, Plus Program includes more personal attention, prompt tray service, nutrition focus groups, and a patient advocate program. The service extras include special/late admission menus, a gourmet menu program, dessert/specialty carts, and more. The company then follows up with patient surveys to ensure that satisfaction is high and goals are being met.

Just how effective is the Morrison Management Specialists' patient satisfaction program? Consider Peninsula Regional Medical Center. In just one year, Morrison boosted its patient satisfaction

$750,000. And our patient indicator scores have been up the last three quarters."

But providing healthcare food services is more than taste, service, and cost savings. Now, more than ever, medical authorities recognize and emphasize the role of proper nutrition in healing patients and boosting employee morale.

In treating patients effectively, a broad approach to nutrition is a must. Morrison prescreens patients for malnutrition, implements special diets, and supports clients in overall health promotion. Morrison also works diligently to assist clients in disease management/prevention, compliance and cost reduction, and in educating patients, residents, staff, and the general community on nutrition issues.

The company has become such an expert on nutrition, the American Dietetic Association asked Morrison to help write *Medical Nutrition Therapy Across the Continuum of Care*, a manual of protocols that have benefited the entire industry. Jan Campbell, vice president of St. Mary's Hospital in Lubbock, Texas, says: "Medical Nutrition Therapy is an extension outside of the traditional way we provide healthcare. It's

◄ Whether serving residents in an independent living area or skilled nursing facilities, Morrison provides the services necessary to ensure that satisfaction levels stay high.

scores from a mere 15th percentile to a 91st percentile among all hospitals surveyed by Press Ganey.

A positive reputation for food has a positive impact on resident satisfaction and occupancy rates for retirement homes as well. Morrison delivers on all counts.

Morrison takes a comprehensive approach to the senior dining experience. Whether the menu calls for Roast Beef or Lobster Thermidor, Morrison Senior Dining Services, the senior living division of Morrison Management Specialists, turns every meal into a dining event that leaves residents raving. The division has a portfolio designed by a national panel of retirement specialists to provide residents with new dining themes every month, which makes both the Food Service Director and the Activity Director's job that much easier.

Serving residents in an independent living area, Morrison provides the services necessary to ensure that satisfaction levels stay high. "Morrison recognizes the vital importance of each individual resident to our community and there is a seamless effort between our organizations in exceeding our resident's expectations," says Don Houghton, President at Lathrop Community in Easthampton, Massachusetts.

Only 15 percent or so of the healthcare and senior living markets outsource their food and nutrition services. Even with the steady increases in market share that Morrison has seen over the years, there is still ample room to grow. Today's facilities are under pressure to reduce costs, and Morrison contracts can literally guarantee savings as part of its involvement—all while increasing

patient/resident satisfaction. Plus, many facilities have limited availability of capital resources, and are facing the necessity of updating kitchens. Add that to the desire to focus more on their core competencies, and one can easily see that Morrison Management Specialists has yet to reach its peak. ❧

◄ Food courts offer diners a wide selection of top-name brand fare and increase customer satisfaction as well as revenues.

Georgia Power Company

► Georgia Power helped
leverage Atlanta's hosting
of the 1996 Centennial
Olympic Games into an
economic windfall that
brought more than $5
billion in capital investments and more than
100,000 jobs into the
state.

As Georgia Power Company prepares for the twenty-first century, it can look back with pride at already having provided more than 100 years of dedicated service to the citizens of Georgia.

Meeting the needs of customers has been a trait instilled in generations of employees by the company's founder, Henry Atkinson. When the City of Atlanta sold stock to purchase an electric light plant from the Southern Light Company of New York in 1883, Atkinson, a shrewd Atlanta banker, was one of the first to invest in the new ven-ture. He quickly saw the possibilities of electricity and, by 1890, had quietly gathered enough shares of the fledgling company called Georgia Electric Light Company of Atlanta to become its majority owner.

From that auspicious beginning, and for the next four decades, Atkinson guided the company through rapid expansion and growth. Assisting him throughout these tumultuous years was a bright young lawyer, Preston Arkwright, whom Atkinson later tapped as the company's first president. Arkwright effectively held the post for 43 years.

Arkwright was the perfect person for the job. Many of his schemes to grow the business were ingenious. So, too, was the man. To win new customers, Arkwright purchased a

baseball team in 1906 called the Atlanta Crackers. He was convinced that owning a baseball team and locating its stadium near his electric streetcar line would be good for business. His intuition proved correct. Later, Arkwright formed a company band that he bussed to a town when he learned it was having trouble with its power supply. Arkwright would then march the band down to the town square, and after getting the citizens' attention, would promise them better electric service.

Again, his boldness worked, and Georgia Railway and Electric Company, as the company was then called, would add yet another city to its system. In 1926, several independent power companies merged into the modern-day Georgia Power Company and established a network to deliver dependable, economic power throughout the state.

In 1927, Arkwright, seeking to stress the importance of community service, coined the phrase "A Citizen Wherever We Serve" in an address to the National Electric Light Association in Atlantic City.

► As Georgia enters into
the next millennium,
electric vehicle usage will
become more prevalent.
Georgia Power is taking
the lead role by educat-
ing and promoting the
use of such transporta-
tion throughout the
state.

in environmental controls, is the largest contributor to environmental research at the Electric Power Research Institute, and is a major participant in the U.S. Department of Energy's Clean Coal Technology program.

The company also partners with the Georgia Department of Natural Resources to manage more than 23,000 acres of Georgia Power land. Much of that land is available for public recreation. Georgia Power is, in fact, the largest nongovernment provider of recreation facilities in the state. It operates 32 recreational areas along 60,200 acres of lakes with 1,413 miles of shoreline across the state.

Georgia Power is aggressively promoting nonpolluting electric vehicle growth within the state. The company currently is developing a public charging infrastructure in Atlanta and is buying several hundred electric vehicles for its fleet. It also is pushing a Fleet Evaluation Program, which is allowing local businesses to test electric vehicles, at no charge, in their own work environments.

Economic development is another important building block for Georgia Power. For more than 70 years, Georgia Power has understood the importance of growth and service to the communities it serves. Bringing new business to the state has been a prime goal since 1927, when the company's industrial division opened an economic development office in New York.

Economic development professionals are located strategically throughout the state, bringing a wealth of experience for assisting local communities with expansion, retention, and recruitment of jobs and investment. Well-versed in all aspects of the economic development process, they help communities marshal and direct resources needed to be successful.

The saying stuck and became emblematic of the company's desire to be not just a business but an active participant in local activities.

Today, the company continues to be guided by those words. Georgia Power employees reach into their communities and fulfill educational, environmental, economic development, and health and human service responsibilities. Whether it's getting involved in a civic organization, serving in community leadership roles, mentoring a young student, building a Habitat for Humanity home, or joining in a wide range of other activities, Georgia Power employees remain service-oriented.

Georgia Power has been instrumental in establishing 16 Georgia Youth Science and Technology Centers in the state. These nonprofit agencies work closely with school personnel to provide needed staff development services in the areas of math, science, and technology.

Georgia Power employees support some 30 schools statewide through structured partnerships or by providing services as requested. A volunteer force of some 300 company employees, retirees, and spouses statewide serves as mentors, sharing at least one hour each week with a child in need of special attention.

Few programs are as special to Georgia Power people as those impacting the environment. The company has invested $5 billion

◄ The Georgia Resource Center, located in downtown Atlanta and supported by Georgia Power, provides prospective companies with a high-tech overview of all aspects of business locations in Georgia. The center provides data on 260 communities, 500 industrial parks, and 450 available industrial buildings throughout the state.

◄ Recognizing that the state's future lies in the quality of its education, Georgia Power has undertaken numerous programs to strengthen teaching within the state, including establishing 16 Georgia Youth Science and Technology Centers.

At the state level, this group works with government and public-private partnerships to develop policies that strengthen Georgia's economic, educational, and scientific infrastructure. Ultimately, the goal is to make Georgia the state of business today and in the future.

Today, that drive to attract new business continues. During 1997, 69 new projects were brought to the state, creating 10,388 jobs and a total capital investment of more than $1 billion. Since 1985, economic development efforts in Georgia have generated more than $7.6 billion in capital investment and created more than 104,600 jobs.

For its efforts, Georgia Power has been recognized several times by *Site Selection* magazine as being one of the top industrial developers in America. Among the resources Georgia Power supports to attract development is the Georgia Resource Center, located in downtown Atlanta. The GRC uses state-of-the-art, interactive computer and multimedia technology that provides an efficient and economical process for evaluating statewide location options for manufacturing, office, and commercial facilities. More detailed visual tours of communities, buildings, and sites are accessible through interactive databases featuring extensive and current information on 260 communities, 600 industrial parks, 450 available industrial buildings throughout the state, and 2,800 available industrial, commercial, and office buildings in the metro Atlanta area.

The company operates a Technology Applications Center. The center showcases the latest developments in electrotechnologies and is available free of charge to Georgia Power's industrial customers and prospects. The center helps customers explore alternative solutions by seeing the benefits of new technologies before they have to make investments to purchase them.

Georgia Power's community development program works closely with chambers of commerce, city/county governments, and other community leaders to create a better way of life for area citizens. This public-private partnership has been in place for more than 50 years, providing both professional expertise and technical assistance.

As Georgia Power prepares to enter the new millennium, imagination and resourcefulness will continue to guide the company. As talk of electric utility deregulation continues to echo through legislative halls, and regulatory and competitive factors change the traditional way utilities do business, Georgia Power is looking forward to the challenge. The company has been competing for more than 25 years and has been winning nearly 70 percent of the large commercial and industrial accounts it seeks. Its electric rates are among the lowest in the nation and some 15 percent below the national average.

Through careful planning, attention to efficiency, and customer service, Georgia Power is strongly positioned to deal with any challenges or opportunities that may arise. And the axiom Preston Arkwright used more than 70 years ago is sure to ring true for our next 100 years as well: "A Citizen Wherever We Serve."

For more information about Georgia Power, a subsidiary of Southern Company, which is a leader in innovative energy technologies, and the largest producer of electricity in the United States, visit the Georgia Power web site at: http://www.southernco.com.

Who is Georgia Power?

Georgia Power is an investor-owned, tax paying utility serving customers in 57,000 of the state's 59,000 square miles, and its 1.8 million customers are in all but six of Georgia's 159 counties. Its net plant investment is approximately $15.6 billion and reflects sales of about 66 billion kilowatt-hours. Residential customers pay an average of 7.68 cents per kilowatt-hour, and the average annual use is 11,171 kilowatt-hours. One of the state's largest taxpayers, Georgia Power pays taxes to city, county, state, and federal agencies totaling $639 million. Nearly 40 plants across the state generate energy to power Georgia's homes and businesses. Approximately 75 percent of the company's electricity is generated from coal; nuclear sources account for 22 percent; hydro for three percent; and oil and gas for 0.7 percent. ◗

◀ Serving more than 1.8 million customers is a demanding task for the 8,300 employees of Georgia Power. The company draws on more than 150 generating units, including this one at Plant McDonough, to quench the growing thirst for electricity.

◀ (Opposite page) Preserving and protecting Georgia's natural resources remains a top priority at Georgia Power. To this end, the company operates 32 recreational areas along 60,200 acres of lakes, including the 3,000-acre Tallulah Gorge State Park, shown here, that it jointly manages with the Department of Natural Resources.

Southern Company

▲ Southern Company's operating utilities helped to electrify the South, introducing customers to new and better uses of electricity through marketing and educational programs. During the '30s, this husband-and-wife team toured Georgia with a specially equipped trailer to showcase electrical appliances for the home.

In a world of electronic wizardry and technological gadgetry, it is hard to think of electricity in terms of invention and innovation. A mundane servant, electrical current can be summoned with the simple flip of a switch or the turn of a knob. Electricity is used daily by millions of people who view it as an inexhaustible given, a certainty in an uncertain world.

Without a steady supply of electricity, we would be unacquainted with much of our modern world, and very few of our most innovative thoughts could progress beyond pen and pencil. Yet, little thought is given to how much power our dreams demand and our needs warrant.

For a commodity so valuable to exist without thought or appreciation is the ultimate testament to the efficiency and reliability of Southern Company. Providing energy across America is pervasive proof of the extraordinary power wielded by a company rarely visible to the casual eye beyond its innocuous symbol on the New York Stock Exchange.

A.W. "Bill" Dahlberg took the helm of Southern Company in 1995. In five short but remarkable years, Dahlberg proved a mastermind in competitive strategy.

Southern Company was the first United States company to buy a British utility, a move quickly copied by other energy providers. Then in 1997, the $35-billion acquisition of Consolidated Electric Power Asia positioned Southern Company as a power player in the world's fastest growing market. Southern Energy Inc., international arm of the company, has utility operations in England, Germany,

Brazil, Argentina, Chile, China, Australia, the Netherlands, the Philippines, the Bahamas, and Trinidad and Tobago and is expected to expand even further.

In the United States, the nation's energy providers are facing deregulation, initially in the northeastern United States and California, where electricity rates are the highest. In the Southeast, where rates are far below the national average, there is little motivation to hurry the process. But it is a matter of time before the electricity markets in the South open to competition. Southern Company positioned itself early in the deregulation process as a national contender. Dahlberg initiated a national branding effort in 1997 that led to the acquisition of power plants in New England, New York, Indiana, Texas, and California.

With five electric utilities in the southeastern United States—Alabama Power, Georgia Power, Gulf Power, Mississippi Power, and Savannah Electric—plus Southern Energy, Southern Company is the largest electric utility group in the United States. Each subsidiary is focused on aggressive but controlled growth strategies intricately matched to the demands of a new millennium. Other Southern Company subsidiaries include Southern Development, Southern LINC, Southern Nuclear, and Southern Company Services.

The southeastern United States remains Southern Company's core business. Economic development is still stronger in the South than in other parts of the nation and is expected to remain so into the new millennium. With that growth comes a corresponding growth in demand for power, and Southern Company's customer satisfaction rate is one of the highest in the industry.

But before there was such an illustrious present and electrifying future, there was a past built upon equal measures of foresight and tradition.

Long ago, when the backs of men and beast powered American industry, the idea of a seemingly never-ending power supply was considered little more than a fool's dream. But Thomas Edison, though a dreamer, was no fool.

Shortly after the first flicker of his incandescent light bulb, Edison and his associates generated a small flow of electricity in a

► Southern Company's international expansion includes (left to right) operations in England through its SWEB subsidiary; operations in the Philippines through its CEPA subsidiary; and operations in the Caribbean through its PowerGen and Freeport Power companies.

tiny New York City steam plant. It wasn't long before a smattering of such plants began to appear throughout the country. The trouble was that the electricity was little more than local spurts of power.

Thinking in terms of more energy, but not quite yet thinking in terms of reach, Southerners dammed rivers and sent hydroelectric power surging through the heart of towns throughout Alabama and Georgia. A young Alabama lawyer named Thomas Martin figured out that linking these power supplies together could serve more people at lower prices.

By the 1920s, a network of Southeastern power plants provided electric power through strung lines that stretched across city, county, and state boundaries. But more than line was linked pole to pole in those days. The fast-running electricity was the first step in uniting small Southern towns into an emerging industrial center. That first network became the Southeastern Power & Light Company, a forerunner of Southern Company.

Martin formed the Southeastern Power & Light Company as a holding company, a relatively new concept for the day. The holding company raised capital and cut operating expenses for individual operating companies by coordinating the power linkups. The grid covered parts of five states—Alabama, Florida, Georgia, Mississippi, and South Carolina—and was the largest interconnected power system in the nation.

In 1929, Southeastern Power & Light became part of The Commonwealth & Southern Corporation, effectively merging with a Tennessee utility and five Northern companies: Central Illinois Light Company, Consumers Power Company, Pennsylvania Power Company, Ohio Edison, and Southern Indiana Gas and Electric. The primitive network of a few short years before was now a behemoth in the world of power.

Competition, though, still existed, and it was formidable. In the late 1930s, Commonwealth & Southern teamed up with other utilities serving the South to combat the rapid territorial expansion of the Tennessee Valley Authority (TVA). The U.S. Supreme Court denied the utilities the right to sue TVA but severely limited TVA's range. The outcome cost Commonwealth & Southern the Tennessee Electric Power Company and extensive service areas in northern Alabama and Mississippi. It would not be the last properties lost in the name of the law.

The Securities and Exchange Commission mandated the dissolution of Commonwealth & Southern under the Public Utility Holding Company Act of 1935. The act required a public utility be limited to a single integrated system. With five operating companies in the north and five in the South, Commonwealth & Southern could not be contained within those limitations.

As a result, Commonwealth & Southern became several independent companies and one holding company. The holding company, chartered in 1947 and operational by 1949, was Southern Company. It had four subsidiaries: Alabama Power, Georgia Power, Gulf Power, and Mississippi Power. To meet the statutory limitation on the size of a holding company as interpreted by the SEC, Southern Company agreed to divest itself of South Carolina Power.

The end of World War II in the 1940s brought an unprecedented demand for electrical power. The South was rising into its own as a major industrialized corner of a superpower, and Southern Company was poised to light the way.

Eugene Yates, the first president of the newly formed company, brought with him the talented James Crist as his operating vice president. It was Crist's job to acquaint investors with a

◄ Southern Company CEO Bill Dahlberg made a major statement of support to the city of Atlanta when he moved the company's headquarters downtown in 1995.

▼ CEO Dahlberg has transformed Southern Company from a regional utility system to a truly international energy company.

new company with an unknown name and no track record. Charts in hand, Crist went on a national tour drumming up support and interest among investors.

Clifford B. McManus became the company's second president in 1950. He understood the potential Crist had touted to investors, and he understood that growth in the South meant growth in demand for power. McManus formed a road show to sell the South and Southern Company simultaneously to the nation, presenting a powerful picture to the country. And so it was that Southern

Company became one of the most successful economic developers in the South. To this day, Southern Company and its subsidiaries play a leading role in maintaining Georgia's economic lead over the rest of the nation.

Harllee Branch Jr. served as the third president of Southern Company during an era of frantic expansion. The Branch years were filled with technological advancements and improvements in delivery and efficiency and cheaper production and pricing.

But business travels in cycles, and the company's fourth president, Alvin W. Vogtle Jr., faced a more difficult time. The 1970s were turbulent with oil embargoes, energy crises, economic downturns, environmental impact studies, pollution controls, inflation, and regulatory overkill. For the first time in its history, rate increases became necessities. In spite of the obstacles, Vogtle returned the company to financial stability and created one of the nation's largest investor-owned electric utility groups in terms of assets, quadrupling the amount of money invested in generating facilities.

Vogtle's successor, Edward L. Addison, served from 1983 through 1994. Addison added substantially to the company's financial stability, and stockholders prospered. Addison also had the foresight to see that deregulation was bound to come and began preparing the company for competition by implementing a series of organizational changes to cut costs and improve customer satisfaction. Further, Addison created a management-development program called

◄ America's largest generator of electricity is also one of the nation's leading energy marketers, trading both natural gas and electricity on wholesale markets.

Southern Company College to prepare future leadership for greater competition.

Dahlberg has continued preparing the company for change, while also leading it into new directions with an aggressive growth strategy that has transformed the company from a regional utility system to a truly international energy company.

Beyond its business success, Southern Company is historically renowned as a strong corporate citizen in every community it serves. Certainly, Southern Company and Atlanta have a long and prosperous intertwined history of progress. These unique relationships are expected to continue unfettered. Just as Dahlberg was an original ACOG board member for the 1996 Olympics, he will be there to kick off the new century as chairman of the Atlanta 2000

Super Bowl Host Committee. He and the many people who work at Southern Company and its subsidiaries work with communities daily to meet the challenges and opportunities of a new time in a new world. ❧

Bank of America

Atlanta has a way of making and marking history. Within its ever-growing boundaries, pulses the lifeblood of the American Dream in a multitude of corporations and the vibrant financial district. These entities have each contributed to the powerful expansion of the city of Atlanta, and many have made history for themselves in the process. In the forefront of such distinguished companies stands a bank that harnesses the future and rides through history in a blaze of successes, matched by none but enjoyed by millions.

In the beginning, the bank was called C&S and retained this moniker for a little while beyond its centennial celebration in 1987. By that time, C&S had assets in the billions and 466 branches in three states—impressive numbers for a bank in that time period, and even more so when the obstacles are taken into account. For

example, the bank celebrated the grand opening of its seven-story Mitchell Street office in Atlanta at the peak of the Great Depression, when over 1,800 U.S. banks had failed.

In 1992, C&S merged with NCNB Corporation and became NationsBank, a move that made the institution one of the largest banks in the country. A mere six years later, on October 1, 1998, bank officials announced a historic-sized merger between NationsBank and BankAmerica to form the first truly nationwide bank now called Bank of America.

The following Friday, October 2, The Bank of America Foundation announced a new initiative aimed at improving life in communities the bank served across the United States. The next day, thousands of Bank of America associates celebrated by turning out in their communities coast to coast in one of the biggest grass-roots volunteer campaigns ever.

Today, it is the largest bank in the United States with over $614 billion in total assets, with full-service consumer and commercial operations in 21 states and the District of Columbia. Bank of America provides financial products and services to over 30 million households and two million businesses, as well as providing international corporate financial services for business transactions in 190 countries. Bank of America (NYSE:BAC) stock is listed on the New York, Pacific, London, and Tokyo stock exchanges.

With 5,000 banking offices and 14,000 ATMs, Bank of America is the most comprehensive financial services distribution network in the nation. One in every three U.S. households banks with Bank of America. Call centers provide around-the-clock banking convenience to more than 38 million customers each month. Every three minutes, Bank of America customers achieve their dreams of home ownership through nation-wide access and creative housing finance solutions. And 37 million checks are processed each day for customers as a matter of routine using the bank's advanced technology and accuracy standards for operations so smooth that customers rarely notice the process.

Despite the huge volume of business and multiple mergers, Atlanta customers see the same friendly tellers they have seen for years. Many of the tellers have been with the bank since the C&S days, and tellers routinely greet customers by name. It is, in effect, the best of both worlds for customers. At any Bank of America branch, customers are greeted as old friends much as would be expected at a smaller community bank; yet, collectively, customers save approximately $5 million a year in ATM

▼ In the beginning, the Bank of America was called C&S and retained this moniker for a little while beyond its centennial celebration in 1987. By that time, C&S had assets in the billions and 466 branches in three states.

fees, a feat obviously only within the means of a banking giant.

Beyond these impressive numbers and bank efforts, Bank of America has earmarked over $350 billion in community development for more new homes, more new businesses, and a level of financial opportunity for individuals in inner city and rural areas.

But equally important for the economic prosperity of individual communities and

our country at large, is the banking of immense U.S. enterprises. Two out of three large U.S. corporations use Bank of America cash management services. Global capital-raising capabilities are tailored to meet the needs of all businesses, regardless of size, based on Bank of America's network, one-stop capability of products and distribution, experience, industry knowledge, and client focus.

Bank of America is a leader in the financial industry in many ways. With its unsurpassed scope, the bank has twice the retail presence of its next largest competitor. Specifically, the bank holds eight percent of all U.S. bank deposits; leads deposit share in four of the nation's fastest growing states: California, Florida, Georgia, and Texas; is number one in households served, banking offices, ATMs, and consumer loans; and is the largest small business lender in the country. Locally, Bank of America has the largest market share of banking business in Atlanta.

In the fields of global corporate and investment banking, Bank of America is again an industry leader. The bank is the choice of 80 percent of Fortune "Global 500" companies and number one in U.S. corporate banking relationships and lending volume. It is also number one in the U.S. in loan syndications, cash management, traditional private placements, foreign exchange, and derivatives. Bank of America owns one of the world's most extensive distribution networks operating from offices in 37 nations and conducting business in 190 countries.

Principal investing and wealth management are additional areas in which the bank ranks supreme in service. Bank of America is among the leaders in U.S. private banking with more than $110 billion trust and investment assets under management and $16 billion in loans outstanding. The bank's broker-dealers are ranked among the top 20 in the country, and its mutual fund families collectively have assets in excess of $58 billion and are among the most widely distributed of bank-advised funds. As a leader in institutional investment management, the bank provides unique capabilities

and areas of focus to continuously offer new products and better services. Bank of America is also widely recognized for its worldwide capabilities in providing private equity for growth capital and other business needs.

On its way to the top, the bank has marched along the beaten path of time through two world wars, a depression, a recession, technological changes of every kind, tax and regulation changes galore, multiple mergers, and crossed borders once thought impenetrable. Along the way, the bank has overcome odds and left a mark on history, all in the name of doing business better. These achievements are noted often by historic and contemporary media alike.

On December 2, 1998, *Time* magazine named Bank of America Founder A. P. Giannini as one of *Time's* 100 Most Important People of the Twentieth Century. Giannini was the only banker among the 20 Builders and Titans honored on the magazine's list of the most influential business geniuses of the twentieth century.

His name resides permanently alongside those of a very distinguished group featured in earlier issues of *Time*, like Winston Churchill, Mohandas Gandhi, Martin Luther King, Henry Ford, Walt Disney, Akio Morita, and Bill Gates. Giannini is considered the father of modern banking. He established what is now known as Bank of America in San Francisco's North Beach in 1904. His faith in the ability of banking to help people realize their dreams inspired other banks to do the same, which made the system accessible to millions and energized America at its economic roots.

Among his many endeavors to improve the American way of life, Giannini provided the financing that made Hollywood the movie capital of the world, funding thousands of films, including *Snow White and the Seven Dwarfs* and *Gone With The Wind*. He developed new ways to finance agriculture, livestock, and dairy industries and is credited for overcoming and eradicating the old banking maxim, "Never loan money on anything that eats."

Giannini helped communities across the country fund local improvements by marketing their notes and bonds. During the height of the Great Depression, he financed the building of the Golden Gate Bridge. Filmmaker Frank Capra based Jimmy Stewart's character of George Bailey in *It's a Wonderful Life* on Giannini, because says Capra: "He was bigger than life."

Given the size and complex nature of the company and its heritage after the historic merger in 1998, Bank of America officials were

◄ In 1992, C&S merged with North Carolina National Bank and became NationsBank, a move that made the institution one of the largest banks in the country.

▲ As for its activities in the grand old city of Atlanta, the bank is both steady and prolific, providing support to organizations such as Habitat for Humanity.

Believing community health is essentially a collective measure of individual health, McColl has led Bank of America to break new ground in helping associates lead balanced, healthy lives. Through its Volunteer Time for Schools Initiative, the bank grants associates up to two hours of paid time each week to volunteer in local schools. *Working Mother* magazine honored McColl and Bank of America for the company's progressive work-and-family programs.

As for its activities in the grand old city of Atlanta specifically, the bank is both steady and prolific. United Way, The Woodruff Center, the College of Art, the Symphony, High Museum, Alliance Theatre, the Theatrical Outfit, Neighborhood Playhouse, Seven Stages, the Atlanta Shakespeare Company's Urban Literacy Project, the Atlanta Ballet (including supporting the new *Nutcracker* production with new costumes and set designs), and Young Audiences community art event, SunFest FunFest, and many other groups are all supported by Bank of America. The bank was also a sponsor of the 1996 Olympics.

The bank's In-Church Bank program is a partnership with Good Choices, a nonprofit group that promotes educational and mentoring programs for youth under the age of 18. The program reinforces both money and math skills by teaching children to make deposits, withdrawals, and other transactions at the child-sized banking centers.

Bank of America has made substantial commitments to education as well, including grants to Georgia Tech for the Sam Nunn Forum and to the Atlanta University Center Schools. Partnerships with associations like the Hispanic Chamber of Commerce and the Latin Association help local businesses and increase cultural awareness.

At the dawning of a new millennium, Bank of America is a heartening example of some of the best America has to offer to a new world and a new time. ❧

perplexed at how best to convey itself in a simple symbol. Eventually, they settled on a logo that presented the name in a new shade of blue in a clear, contemporary typeface. The accompanying art element evokes the company's breadth, scope, pride, and the unity of its people under one flag.

The word "America" was retained, despite the bank's international prowess. "While it is the name of a country, America also stands for a powerful idea to people around the world," said Chairman and Chief Executive Officer Hugh McColl. "America means freedom to pursue ideas and ideals. It means opportunity to reap the rewards of ingenuity, optimism, and hard work, and it means a pioneering spirit that can carry a people as far as they want to go."

The new look appeared on signs, stationery, and other business operations in 1999, with worldwide implementation continuing into 2000. The new logo is serendipitous with the onset of a new millennium. It isn't that the bank is tracking time; it is merely following its own destiny to a new time where banking is sure to be anything other than business as usual. But that's not a worry for a bank that routinely turns extraordinary vision into ordinary expectation.

In guiding the company to nearly 50-fold growth during his tenure, Mr. McColl has built the bank into a model for financial services. The company is a technology leader, and was one of the first banks to offer services through personal computers and the telephone.

Acting on the conviction that his company's health depends on the health of its communities (much like Giannini did before him), McColl has led Bank of America to reinvest its resources across the franchise. Beyond its community development commitment of billions, the company is also recognized as the nation's leader in expanding relationships with minority- and women-owned companies.

◄ On October 1, 1998,
bank officials announced
a historic-sized merger
between NationsBank
and BankAmerica to
form the first truly
nationwide bank now
called Bank of America.

Nortel Networks

In telecommunications today everything seems possible and nothing is predictable. In other words, it's business as usual for this leading edge industry currently in the midst of its most revolutionary changes since Alexander Graham Bell shouted into the first telephone, "Mr. Watson, come here. I want you."

▲ **In 1998, Nortel Networks completed construction of the post-modern Windward Campus, a facility that combines the marvels of science with the magic of human ingenuity.**

Nortel Networks' history began in 1895, when it made not only the first primitive telephones, but also wind-up gramophones and street call boxes for police and fire departments. In 1976, it was the first telecommunications company to offer a full line of digital communications equipment that set new industry standards.

In 1998, after more than one hundred years of experience in providing global telecommunications solutions, the company acquired Bay Networks, Inc., adding world-class, Internet protocol-based data communications capabilities that complement and expand Nortel's acknowledged strengths.

This precedent-setting union created Nortel Networks, effectively positioning the company to remove the historical boundaries between data communications and telephony, and between telecommunications leaders and the data networking innovators.

Nortel Networks understands the challenges and benefits that the convergence of voice, data, and video can bring to business. In fact, Nortel Networks built its own network—one of the world's largest global private intranets and a vast multimedia network—using its own pioneering technology. And today, 75 percent of the North American Internet travels on Nortel Networks equipment.

The world is out there waiting to be connected. Networks, as they erase distance and bind people—through copper wires, fiber optics, or wireless technology—have become the ultimate party line, bringing the world closer together. The world's citizens will be connected to a variety of electronic networks, allowing them to share information, wisdom, thoughts, and ideas.

These links to global networks are quickly becoming an essential part of living and working. Electronic "infostructure" will be counted among the most profoundly significant of civilization's discoveries. Lack of connectivity to a network will become a personal, as well as an economic, disadvantage. Nortel Networks provides the technology to ensure such worldwide connectivity becomes a reality.

The employees at Nortel Networks measure the company's success by the satisfaction and success of their customers, as well as by reactions of industry analysts and technologists. *Industry Week* called Nortel Networks "one of the world's best managed companies." The company was ranked Number 31 in *Business Week's* 1998 ranking of 500 best performers. And in 1999, Nortel Networks was listed as one of the world's top data networking powerhouses by *Network World*.

Though Nortel Networks commands a sizable workforce in Alpharetta, Georgia (14 miles north of Atlanta), there are 75,000 employees worldwide. The company has operations in more than 150 countries and territories with offices and facilities in North America, Europe, Asia/Pacific, Caribbean and Latin America, the Middle East, and Africa. This global representation encompasses more than 50 native languages and 55 national origins.

Employee satisfaction is directly related to customer loyalty, value, and satisfaction. At Nortel Networks, 89 percent of the employees say they like their work, which is a best-in-the-industry benchmark, and 84 percent say they would recommend it to others.

The company's research capabilities around the world include 42 facilities in 17 countries, numerous affiliated joint ventures, and

◀ The Information Revolution is creating a new era of human history, and Nortel Networks is at the forefront in providing the foundation of the global information industry.

other collaborations fostering innovative product development and advanced design research.

In 1998, Nortel Networks' revenue exceeded $17 billion, and its earnings topped $1 billion. While these numbers are impressive, Nortel Networks' success comes not from its size, but from a talented workforce that is dedicated to helping customers compete. Nortel Networks' employees share a passion for teaming, ingenious solutions, and customer success. Nortel's stated mission is simple: To empower people to achieve success never before possible through the effortless exchange of ideas, anywhere, anytime.

Nortel Networks' support for the environment and education has led to awards from around the world, including a United

Nations award for being the first multinational corporation in the telecommunications industry to eliminate the use of ozone-depleting CFCs from its worldwide manufacturing and research operations.

Nortel Networks established a presence in Atlanta in 1979. In 1998, the company completed construction of the postmodern Windward Campus, a facility that combines the marvels of science with the magic of human ingenuity. The campus is located in Alpharetta on Windward Parkway, called the Corridor of Influence by metro-Atlantans. Even among the prestigious group of high-tech corporations on the corridor, Nortel Networks has retained its human touch.

Customers, visitors, and workers alike enjoy the open-walled offices, bright, primary-colored appointments, and a wetland preservation area with nature trails and outdoor work pavilions

that are network accessible. Other unique amenities include micro-cellular technology between buildings and a best-in-class corporate fitness center. The campus is home to development laboratories and numerous sales and marketing teams that service such customers as BellSouth, GTE, Cox Communications, Sprint, MCI-Worldcom, and AT&T.

Many of Nortel Networks' top executives hold leadership roles in Atlanta organizations, including, but not limited to, Zoo Atlanta, Junior Achievement, SciTrek, North Fulton Chamber of Commerce, and the Metro Atlanta Chamber of Commerce Advisory Board. Beyond donating time, money, and other resources to these organizations, Nortel Networks has a long-standing commitment to strengthening the technology presence in Georgia. The company provides technology leadership for many projects and organizations, including SciTrek, Georgia Tech,

◄ Nortel Networks delivers value to customers around the world through Unified Networks solutions, spanning mission-critical telephony and Internet Protocol (IP)-optimized networks.

Technology Association of Georgia, the Business and Technology Alliance, and Women in Technology.

In addition, the company identifies 10 to 12 nonprofit or charitable local organizations each year as part of its Community Partners program. In 1998, Nortel Networks served again as a pacesetter company for the North Fulton United Way annual giving campaign and achieved record levels of giving by its employees and the company. Nortel Networks offers every employee in the Windward Campus a 32-hour/per year benefit to volunteer in the metro-Atlanta communities, one of the most generous volunteer benefits available from any company in the industry.

The Information Revolution is creating a new era of human history, and Nortel Networks is at the forefront in providing the foundation of the global information industry. John Roth, CEO of Nortel Networks, alluded to this era at the press conference announcing the acquisition and merger with Bay Networks: "Nortel Networks has prepared for the future by positioning itself as the global resource for unifying the network. Nortel Networks' competency and industry leadership in designing, building, and integrating voice, data, and video networks provides a distinctive market position and powerful competitive advantage." ✦

MARTA

"**A**t MARTA, It'sMARTA" is the phrase that gets everyone going. It gets the buses rolling and the trains moving. It epitomizes the Olympic success of the Metropolitan Atlanta Rapid Transit Authority (MARTA) and promises stellar achievements for the next millennium. Often described as "Atlanta's world-renowned public transit system," MARTA is committed to making a difference in Atlanta's quality of life by providing safe, reliable, cost-effective, and affordable public transportation. From the beginning, MARTA has made a significant impact on transportation infrastructure in metropolitan Atlanta.

As early as 1952, the Regional Planning Guide recognized the importance of mass transit to regional growth. In 1954, The Metropolitan Planning Commission noted the need for rapid transit "within a few years." In April 1962, after many proposals by the Atlanta Regional Metropolitan Planning Commission and the Atlanta Transit System, Georgia House Resolution #668-121 formed the Metropolitan Atlanta Transit Study Commission to study programs and report on the need, advisability, and economic feasibility of rapid mass transportation. Following amendments to the State Constitution and the creation of the "Rapid Transit Committee of 100," the Metropolitan Atlanta Rapid Transit Authority Act (S.E. 102) became law, having passed the Georgia Assembly in March of 1965. Subsequently, after ratification in four

counties and the City of Atlanta, MARTA was established in January 1966.

Just 30 years later, in 1996, MARTA took a bow for its outstanding performance as the Official Provider for Spectator Transportation for the Centennial Olympic Games. Atlanta brought the Olympic torch to the South, and MARTA put a spotlight on mass transit. As the first local transit agency to partner with an Olympic Committee, MARTA offered 24-hour rail service and transported 1.5 million passengers daily, totaling more than 25 million customers during the Games. The Atlanta Committee for the Olympic Games Chief, Billy Payne, said, "Atlanta could not have won the Games had it not been for

North/South and East/West lines. Whether transferring to the South Line to travel to the Airport or transferring to the West Line to visit the new Philips Arena, MARTA is accessible to many Atlanta sports venues and convention sites.

As Atlanta struggles with the issues of traffic and congestion, MARTA continues to be the most efficient and economical way to travel. MARTA has initiated several programs focused on employers, visitors, and students to encourage ridership. For example, MARTA offers the MARTA Partnership Program. This program allows employers to underwrite the cost of transit passes to employees at a discounted rate. In 1998, over 100 companies participated in the Partnership Program.

MARTA's Partnership Program offers many benefits to employers and employees alike. With fewer employees driving alone to work, the employer saves the costs of building and maintaining parking lots. With fewer employees using parking spaces, there is more space for customers and visitors. Employees benefit from a hassle-free and reliable commute, and save money on the expense of driving a car and parking fees. By participating in the program, both employers and employees are "Good Corporate Citizens" who are contributing to the improvement of the environment. Companies such as the BellSouth Corporation, the Coca-Cola Company, the Atlanta Journal-Constitution, Georgia Pacific, the Internal Revenue Service, Emory University Hospital, Georgia Power, Georgia Tech, and Turner Broadcasting are proud participants in the program.

While the Partnership Program targets commuters, the Visitor Pass offers tourists an economical way to get around Atlanta. This program offers a discounted visitor transit pass for groups of 15 or more. The pass is good for unlimited travel aboard the extensive rail and bus system for a predetermined number of days. Visitor Passes are often preordered and included in the cost of convention registration packages.

MARTA, and the Games would not have been the success they were had it not been for MARTA."

MARTA continues to play a significant transportation role in the region. With more than 700 buses covering 150 routes operating 30 million miles of bus service annually, and with 240 heavy rail cars trekking 46 miles of track between 36 stations, traveling 52 million miles a year, MARTA is the seventh-largest transit system in the nation. Operating in the City of Atlanta, DeKalb, and Fulton counties, MARTA transports more than 560,000 passengers daily. MARTA expects to carry 200 million riders by the year 2005. This increase reflects the predicted growth in the region, which will undoubtedly call for additional transportation solutions. MARTA embraces the future as an opportunity for transit expansion and service excellence.

With over 4,700 employees, MARTA is Atlanta's 21st largest employer and prides itself on its internal resources. MARTA is a successful organization because it has an experienced workforce dedicated to providing quality, customer-focused service. MARTA's busiest station, Five Points, serves more than 30,000 riders daily and is the main transfer hub between the

For students, the University Pass Program (U-Pass) is specifically designed to offer commuting assistance to universities, colleges, and vocational/technical schools within MARTA's service districts. The program allows students to purchase discounted, monthly TransCards directly through participating schools.

It is MARTA's commitment to listen and adapt to customers that has led to maintaining its high ratings in national performance measures and in customer satisfaction. In direct response to customer comments, MARTA introduced face-to-face customer service at its busiest stations in the form of Station Managers. They provide courteous, reliable, customer-focused attention to all passengers. Clearly identified with distinct apparel, the Station Managers have propelled MARTA's commitment to customer service to a new level. The customer is not just a patron but a valuable asset to the success of MARTA. Continuous commitment to improvements and renovation ensures that MARTA will remain a choice transportation mode in the future.

To accommodate MARTA's growth needs into the next millennium, the Authority recently signed its largest contract to purchase 100 new rail cars for $257 million. The additional rail cars will be needed for future ridership growth, system expansion, and improved reliability. Subsequently, to maintain these new rail cars,

MARTA recently began acquiring property in a 33-acre northeast Atlanta location for the construction of a third MARTA rail service facility. Additionally, MARTA contracted to purchase 206 new "clean fuel" buses, all of which will be powered by Compressed Natural Gas (CNG), which will make MARTA's CNG bus fleet of 324 the nation's second largest.

As Atlanta struggles with the ignominious title of "Poster City of Sprawl," these additions to MARTA's rail transit system will make a difference. It will give commuters additional transportation choices, which, in turn, lead to easing congestion and pollution. In addition to the existing service expansion, MARTA is studying four corridors for possible expansion. The North, South, East, and West Lines are being assessed to determine criteria such as ridership, cost-effectiveness, community support, and the impact on the environment. Whichever direction MARTA expands, the result will be increased ridership on MARTA's rail transit system and less congestion on area roadways.

In fact, construction is underway for two new stations on the North Line—Sandy Springs and North Springs—both scheduled to be completed by December 2000. The Sandy Springs Station will be the tenth station on the north line and will sit on a five-acre site 13.9 miles north of MARTA's central station, Five Points. The project consists of an underground station and is projected to be used by 11,000 patrons daily. The Sandy Springs Station will also have a parking deck to accommodate 1,170 cars.

The North Springs Station is designed to serve approximately 25,000 daily patrons with 3,500 persons expected to board during peak rush hours. The station is located 14.9 miles north of the Five Points Station on the North Line. The new North Springs Station is located at the intersection of Georgia 400 highway and Abernathy Road. The new station will include a multistory parking deck for approximately 2,200 cars and feature an exclusive exit/entrance to a major expressway, GA-400.

In addition to service expansion, MARTA has introduced an impressive solution to the problem of sprawl—Transit Oriented Development (TOD)—a concept that combines urban living with easy access to work, shopping, leisure, and, of course, transit. In 1998, negotiations were completed to begin a TOD project on 47 acres around the Lindbergh Center Station. Phase 1 of the project will include 200,000 square feet of office space, 250,000 square feet of retail space, 566 residential units, and a 120-unit hotel. Additionally, Atlanta-based BellSouth Corporation is committed to leasing approximately one million square feet of additional office space that will virtually guarantee the success of the development.

Other potential TOD projects include Medical Center Station (16.9 acres); Abernathy Park-and-Ride (11.4 acres); Ashby Station, where MARTA is actively working with the Atlanta Development Authority, and the City of Atlanta revealed its plans for the Westside Village; the West End Station and the Vine City Station, where MARTA is again working with the Atlanta Development Authority to help revitalize the surrounding areas and communities; and the Lakewood/Ft. McPherson Station. MARTA is always looking for opportunities to reduce sprawl and make transit more accessible.

Atlanta's growth has been a challenge, but as the new millennium approaches, MARTA is proof that the city can handle change.

MARTA continues to grow with the city and its demands. Richard J. Simonetta, General Manager/CEO of MARTA, said: "The presence of public transportation has always signified growth and cosmopolitan progress. Since its inception, MARTA has been instrumental in establishing Atlanta as a world-class city. As the greater Atlanta region continues to grow by leaps and bounds, the role of transportation becomes ever more prevalent. This is not only a testament to mass transit, but also a prelude to a new and bright future for metropolitan Atlanta." ◑

Yancey Bros. Co.

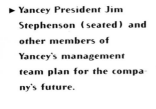

It is gloriously uplifting to read American success stories. In the tales of individuals and families who have overcome long odds and short-tempered "no's," we all find hope and a reason to persevere. But in the story of Atlanta's Yancey brothers, there is a twist: the two not only changed and conquered their own industry, but they also pushed an unrelated company into a more prosperous future using a simple photograph. Their story is a picture-perfect example of the value of striving to provide customers with better alternatives.

Founded in 1914 by two brothers, Goodloe H. Yancey Jr. and B. Earl Yancey, the Yancey Brothers Company began as the "Yancey Hardware Company," selling hardware, picks, shovels, and prison uniforms to government agencies—especially county prisons—for road construction. Considered cutting edge in their day, the brothers operated their business in downtown Atlanta on Peachtree Street and held the distinction of being the first dealer in the United States for the old Adams mule grader, a predecessor of today's motorgrader, which was pulled by eight mules.

These were relatively simple times, but the Yancey brothers were anything but simple. Seeing an opportunity to build roads throughout Georgia and across the southeastern United States, the brothers became traveling salesmen during the week, and order processors and shippers on the weekend. There were no days off, and few hours to sleep.

The long hours and hard work paid off for the Yancey brothers. In two short years, in 1916, their growth prompted moving their business offices into the old C&S National Bank Building. The company moved again in 1918, this time into a building on Marietta Street that had warehouse space in back of the office. They also opened branches in Birmingham, Alabama; Ft. Pierce, Florida; and Greenville, South Carolina.

But the world was changing. Equipment was changing. The days of the mule-powered grader were coming to an end. Savvy and flexible, the two visionary brothers took the change in stride and molded their company into the nation's first dealer of the innovative new "Caterpillar" crawler tractors manufactured by the Holt Manufacturing Company of Peoria, Illinois. This molding to match the new crawlers with Yancey Brothers' road construction business was anything but ordinary and routine. Holt Manufacturing was convinced it couldn't be done.

In 1918, Goodloe heard of a tractor made by Holt that could do the work of "40 mules, or 40 horses and countless humans." The two brothers traveled to Peoria to ask the manufacturer if they could represent the Holt line in the southeastern United States. The reception from Holt was less than warm—the company would not give the Yanceys a demo of the tractor to use.

"You're wasting your time. You can't sell these tractors for road building; we've tried," was the response of the Holt officials. They insisted that such machinery HAD to be sold direct, and that a distributor set-up would be a flop. Goodloe and Earle left Peoria after a week with only a photograph of the Holt 45 tractor and a price quote of $4,750, C.O.D., per machine. Holt then returned its attention to producing crawlers for the United States Army.

It wasn't long before the county commissioners of Troup County

In 1927 the brothers split the Georgia territory in half. Mr. Goodloe operated Yancey Bros. Co. in 83 counties in the northern half of the state, while Earle moved his operations to Albany as the Yancey Tractor Company and worked the southern half of Georgia.

As Atlanta prospered, so did Yancey Bros. Co. The company continued to grow and flourish, and still does, based on Mr. Goodloe's fundamental principle: "Always stand by your word." He delivered what he promised. He offered assistance when he could. As business grew, the need to expand across the northern half of the state also grew.

Yancey Bros. Co. has provided equipment and support for most of Atlanta's sizable construction projects since the early 1920s. When Atlanta's airport opened in 1925, the project was completed using Caterpillar equipment supplied and serviced by Yancey. The first paved road linking Atlanta and Columbus opened in 1933, and Yancey Brothers was a major player in this project. The long process of linking Atlanta to the rest of the country via the interstate highway system was achieved with the help of Yancey and Caterpillar equipment. But transportation projects aren't the only areas Yancey has provided assistance to Atlanta's growth.

The building of Atlanta-Fulton County Stadium, the Georgia World Congress Center, Centennial Olympic Park, and Turner Field were all constructed using equipment and services provided by Yancey Bros. Co. The construction of every major mall and shopping center in metro Atlanta has used Yancey-supplied equipment as well as the majority of all neighborhoods built since the 1930s. As metro Atlanta has grown, Yancey has been here all along providing the tools and services needed to build and improve metro Atlanta for the next generation of her citizens.

In 1947, Yancey Bros. Co. opened its first full-service product support branch in Augusta. Due to tremendous growth,

◄ Yancey's employees are the company's greatest strength. Chairman of the Board Goodloe H. Yancey III is pictured on the center front row.

▼ Yancey's technicians utilize the latest in modern technology and tooling in order to better serve their customers.

earned the distinction of being the first buyers of a "Caterpillar" tractor in the southeastern United States. Mr. Goodloe (as he was fondly called) traveled to LaGrange to personally drive the tractor off the railroad flatcar, and people came from miles around to see this new machine work.

Within 12 months, the Yanceys had sold all of the 45s Holt had in its inventory, using only their salesmanship and a single photograph. When Mr. Goodloe and Earle returned to the Holt factory the following year, they were hailed as conquerors, and the first jobbers contract ever given by Holt was awarded to them. Although their original agreement had been for only a five-percent commission, the Holt officials gave them a contract with a higher commission and made the deal retroactive to their first sale.

Mr. Goodloe recounted the $19,000 commission years later: "I hadn't known there was that much money in the world."

The Yancey brothers pioneered the distributor scheme of Holt, conceiving the plan and tenaciously forcing their way until accepted. They glorified their production by leading all the nation in sales of their product.

Holt merged with Best Tractor Company in 1925 to become the Caterpillar Tractor Company, now the world's largest manufacturer of earthmoving equipment. Records at Caterpillar's corporate offices in Peoria indicate that based on the original agreement date of December 19, 1918, "Yancey is the dealer with whom Caterpillar and its predecessor companies have had the longest business association." Thus, Yancey Bros. Co. is proud to claim the title of "The Nation's Oldest Caterpillar Dealer."

The partnership of Yancey Bros. Co. and Caterpillar has seen a great deal of changes and growth in the last eight decades. In 1924, the brothers established their new headquarters in downtown Atlanta at 634 Whitehall Street. When Holt Manufacturing merged with Best Manufacturing to form the Caterpillar Tractor Company in the mid-1920s, the two brothers saw their territory shrink from 4 southeastern states (Georgia, Florida, Alabama, and South Carolina with Holt) to just Georgia. This could have been an insurmountable obstacle to some, but the brothers Yancey were content to have the jewel of the southeast, Atlanta, and the rest of their home state as their sales territory.

► Yancey's Fluid Analysis Laboratory is equipped with the most modern equipment available. The lab analyzes fluids from earthmoving equipment, construction equipment, and over-the-road trucks to assure engines and other internal components are operating as expected.

In 1974, Goodloe H. Yancey III assumed the presidency of the company upon the retirement of his brother, Don. Under Goodloe III's leadership and guidance, Yancey Bros. Co. reached heights beyond the imaginations of even Mr. Goodloe. By 1980 the company opened its first full-service truck engine support branch, and in 1984 acquired the Grissom-Harrison Corporation, a mining and aggregates equipment and support distributor. By expanding into new markets, the company was positioning itself for metro Atlanta's explosive growth that was being anticipated.

the company moved its corporate headquarters to a 12-acre site at 1540 Northside Drive in Atlanta in 1951. Six years later a second full-service product support branch opened in Macon.

Don A. Yancey, a nephew of Mr. Goodloe, became president of the company in 1959. As president of the firm, he took Mr. Goodloe's vision of the company one step farther. Seeing a market for quality industrial trucks, he purchased the Cat Towmotor lift truck dealership for northern Georgia. Yancey Brothers had to grow to remain a leader.

In 1969, Don led the company in its move to the current corporate headquarters at 330 Lee Industrial Blvd. in Austell. Located at the intersection of I-20 West and Six Flags Parkway, four miles outside Atlanta's I-285 perimeter highway, Yancey's new facilities gave the company room for expansion and growth into the next century.

In 1986, the company opened a full-service product support branch in Calhoun. Another was built near Dacula in Gwinnett County in 1987 to further serve Atlanta's expanding metro area along with supporting limited-service "parts only" branches in Sandersville and Columbus.

The year 1987 also saw a new division of Yancey created. Sunbelt Power Systems was formed to provide truck engine support and primary and auxiliary electric power systems. Being the transportation center of the southeastern United States, Atlanta sees thousands of commercial trucks passing through each day. Sunbelt Power provides a full array of truck engine parts and service options for this vital part of Atlanta's economic engine. Sunbelt Power also provides equipment and engineering services for the thousands of companies that require auxiliary electric systems, both planned and in emergency situations. Combined with Caterpillar's industry-leading industrial generators, Sunbelt Power provides metro Atlanta with a valuable tool in planned energy consumption and standby power systems.

Yancey Bros. Co. announced a plan of management and ownership succession for the company in 1994 that would see the fourth generation of the Yancey family lead the company. James E. and Donna Yancey Stephenson (son-in-law and daughter of Don Yancey) would become the company's primary stockholders. A successful trial lawyer with experience in construction law, Jim Stephenson was named president of Yancey in September of 1995, thus continuing the long and proud history of the company for another generation. Stephenson completed his purchase of the company in February 1996 and assumed the responsibilities of leading "The Nation's Oldest Caterpillar Dealer" in its ninth decade of service to the northern half of Georgia.

▼ A Cat Motorgrader from Yancey's rental fleet helped prepare the baseball playing surface at Turner Field. This work was done less than a month before opening day of the inaugural season in 1997.

Under Stephenson's leadership Yancey has continued to grow along with metropolitan Atlanta. In 1998 the company rededicated its commitment to the equipment rental business by debuting "The Cat Rental Store," a chain of equipment rental outlets targeted to the needs of Atlanta's building and construction communities. The Cat Rental Store specializes in small and medium-size Caterpillar machines and associated allied equipment.

In 1999, Yancey expanded into yet another construction-related sector with the launching of a division specializing in Building Construction Products and Compact Construction Equipment. This new division provides a full menu of sales, parts, and service options related to the line of smaller Caterpillar machines not generally associated with "earthmoving" or "heavy equipment" applications. The traditional earthmoving business is still being served by Yancey Bros. Co., as well as the mining, roadbuilding, aggregates, waste disposal, and forestry industries.

Beyond the company's long-standing dedication to providing the best in products and service, Yancey has also worked hard to help Georgia and much of the southeastern United States grow and build far more than roads and infrastructure. Many civic, charity, and trade organizations have benefited from the company's time and resources. In addition to being a longtime supporter of United Way, Yancey Bros. Co. continues its tradition of funding yearly scholarships at several colleges and universities in the state. The company's matching gift program for employee contributions has steered thousands of dollars into the hands of hundreds of smaller charities and needy service organizations.

Yancey has a keen interest in providing more and better career opportunities for its employees. Financial assistance is provided to any employee that wishes to further his or her formal "classroom" education, and all Yancey employees attend classes related to customer satisfaction. For those employees involved in equipment maintenance, the company provides a minimum of two weeks classroom training each year in its in-house training center. The Yancey Training Center developed such a reputation of excellence that Caterpillar certified it as their Southeastern U.S. Regional Training Center. Now, in addition to Yancey's technicians, the Center trains technicians from Cat dealers across the country as well as technicians working for Yancey's customers.

Yancey Bros. Co. is also committed to improving the standard of living for all the citizens of Georgia. Although the phrase "environmentally responsible" has not always been a hallmark of the industries Yancey serves, the company strives every day to assure the state remains a beautiful and clean home for future generations of Georgians.

Now in its ninth decade, Yancey is not taking the time to sit back and congratulate itself. The company is constantly looking for ways to offer new services and improve on existing programs for their customers. It continues the legacy started over 85 years ago by the brothers Yancey of providing outstanding customer service to metro Atlanta and the rest of the northern half of Georgia. ❧

◀ A Caterpillar Excavator was used to repair underground utilities in Atlanta's Piedmont Park in 1994 and 1995.

▼ Yancey's technicians are the most highly skilled heavy equipment mechanics in the industry. They receive constant training both in the classroom and on the shop floor.

The Coca-Cola Company

► World of Coca-Cola Atlanta, which features the largest collection of Coca-Cola memorabilia ever assembled, has become Atlanta's most visited indoor attraction.

▼ Through its "Reaching Out" volunteer program, Coca-Cola employees contribute to community projects throughout Atlanta. Photo by Michael Pugh.

Coca-Cola is perhaps the best known brand name in the world; certainly it has served as an icon for the good life for more than a century. At the writing of this book, sales of Coca-Cola and other company products exceeded 1 billion servings a day; even so, the company is still very much in its infancy.

More than 113 years ago, John Pemberton created Coca-Cola. Later came Asa Candler, the originator of twentieth-century Coca-Cola marketing, and Robert Woodruff, who for more than 60 years was the architect of the company's success and father of The Coca-Cola Company's international expansion. After these famous visionaries came a long line of less famous but no less crucial individuals skilled in a myriad of disciplines that, combined, have led Coca-Cola to a worldwide presence admired by businesses around the globe and throughout the history of commerce.

But even with more than a billion servings per day gracing counters and tables worldwide and creating a simple moment of pleasure for people who speak more than 1,703 languages and 39,304 dialects, Coca-Cola is still only beginning to quench the world's thirst for refreshment.

In China, the world's largest market, Coca-Cola volume continues to grow. But the average resident of China drank just seven Coca-Cola products a year. Coca-Cola overtook its largest competitor in 1996 in Russia; still there is considerable untapped opportunity in that country.

And so the story goes, country by country and town by town. Coca-Cola is by far the world's leading soft drink, but it still has enormous opportunities for growth.

Company leaders see the traditional coffee break evolving into a Coke break, the widespread and ever-present water fountain accompanied by a Coca-Cola dispenser, The Real Thing replacing substitutes everywhere, and a Coke glass as standard a fixture as the wine glass in table place settings worldwide. The old adage "for all the tea in China" may someday transform to "for all the Coke in the world." When this happens, and happen it surely will given the success of Coca-Cola in tempting taste buds of every culture, a billion servings a day will be no more than a drop in the proverbial bucket.

At the cusp of a new millennium, it is difficult to determine which is the more breathtaking—the history of Coca-Cola or its future.

It all began just a few blocks down the street from the current location of The Coca-Cola Company's world headquarters in Atlanta, Georgia. On May 8, 1886, pharmacist Dr. John Stith Pemberton stirred up the fragrant caramel-colored syrup in a three-legged brass kettle and carried a jug of his formula down the street to Jacob's Pharmacy, Atlanta's largest drugstore at that time. That same day, the new product made its debut as a soda fountain drink for five cents a glass. At some point, either by accident or design, no one is sure which, carbonated water was mixed with the syrup to create what would become the world's favorite soft drink.

Thinking that "the two Cs would look well in advertising," Dr. Pemberton's partner and bookkeeper, Frank M. Robinson, suggested the name "Coca-Cola" and penned the famous trademark in his now-familiar script.

A simple oilcloth sign hung from the pharmacy's awning encouraged passersby to "Drink Coca-Cola." And on May 29, 1886, the first newspaper advertisement appeared in *The Atlanta Journal* pronouncing the drink as "Delicious and Refreshing," a theme that still echoes today. Sales in 1886 averaged nine drinks per day.

Dr. Pemberton never fully realized the potential of the beverage he had created. In poor health and in need of funds, he sold portions of his interest in the venture. In 1888, the year of Pemberton's death, Asa G. Candler began to actively purchase the outstanding shares of Coca-Cola. An Atlanta druggist and businessman, Candler recognized great potential in the beverage and acquired complete control by 1891 for a total investment of $2,300.

Asa Candler, a master marketer, expanded the advertising

strategy to include countless novelty items, which were displayed and given away at sales locations and have since become valuable collectibles. In 1894, the first outdoor painted wall on a drugstore in Cartersville, Georgia, featured Coca-Cola, the company's first "billboard."

As bottling became widespread and availability of the product skyrocketed, advertising developed too. Now-famous print ads, featuring fine illustrations by beloved artists such as Norman Rockwell, projected memorable images in leading magazines of the day. Commercial slogans like "The Pause That Refreshes," which first appeared in *The Saturday Evening Post* in 1929, began to make

a lasting impact.

In 1931 holiday advertising for Coca-Cola, artist Haddon Sundblom introduced the world to the image of Santa Claus as people know him today—the man with the flowing white beard, rosy cheeks, brilliant red suit, and portly silhouette. Until then, Santa had been depicted as everything from a pixie to an elf to a frightening gnome. Sundblom's popular Santa "portraits" continued as holiday favorites in the '50s and '60s and are still part of holiday packaging and advertising at the turn of the millennium.

Coca-Cola became one of radio's first commercial sponsors during the 1930s. And in 1950, the company's first network television advertising appeared during a live Thanksgiving special featuring Edgar Bergen and Charlie McCarthy. Throughout the century and into the future, Coca-Cola reflects the mood and the look of the time while maintaining a universal and timeless appeal.

Long before buzzwords "going global," "multinational," and "global village" flowed from the tongues of the business savvy set, Coca-Cola was living the adventure. Coca-Cola first traveled beyond U.S. borders with its introduction in Canada at the turn of the last century. About the same time, Coca-Cola crossed the Atlantic when Charles Howard Candler, the eldest son of company founder Asa Candler, made a trip to Europe to celebrate his graduation from college. Young Candler took along a gallon of syrup and introduced the new

▲ **Artist Haddon Sundblom is credited with helping to develop the modern-day image of Santa Claus in a series of oil paintings commissioned by The Coca-Cola Company from 1931 to 1964.**

◄ **The Coca-Cola Valued Youth Program provides middle and high school students who are at risk of dropping out with the opportunity to tutor younger students who are also struggling in school. In their role as tutors, students learn self-discipline, develop self-esteem, and improve their own academic performance.** Photo by Richard Cunningham.

▲ Coca-Cola has been involved with sports since the turn of the century. Today, Coca-Cola and its bottlers are involved with more than 50 different types of sports and thousands of sporting events and activities on the local, national, regional, and global levels.

▶ Bringing refreshing experiences to consumers, like the Coca-Cola Cool Zones, is part of the company's innovative marketing effort. Photo by Michael Pugh.

drink to the American owner of a London soda fountain. An order for five gallons made its way back to the United States shortly thereafter. Occasional shipments also went out to Germany, Jamaica, and Panama in the early years, and by 1906, the first overseas bottling plants had been established in Panama and Cuba.

Efforts to make Coke available around the world began in earnest when Robert Winship Woodruff took the helm of the company in 1923 as its newly elected president. In 1926, with only nine bottlers of Coca-Cola outside the United States and Canada, Woodruff established the Foreign Department. By 1930, it had been renamed The Coca-Cola Export Corporation. Woodruff's vision of worldwide availability for Coke had profoundly changed the destiny of the company. Overseas sales climbed steadily and, by 1940, Coca-Cola bottlers had set up shop in more than 45 countries.

After the United States' entry into World War II in 1941, Woodruff declared: "We will see that every man in uniform gets a bottle of Coca-Cola for five cents wherever he is and whatever it costs." In cooperation with the United States Armed Services, the company shipped and put in place 64 complete bottling plants to serve Americans in combat in Europe, Africa, and the Pacific. By the time the war ended, American servicemen and women overseas had enjoyed more than 5 billion bottles of Coke, and the soft drink had become known as the "Global High Sign." In the meantime, Coca-Cola had been integrated into local cultures and had taken up permanent residence among new friends.

By the mid-1970s, more than half the Coca-Cola served worldwide was sold outside the United States. By the mid-1990s, more than 80 percent of the company's operating income was generated outside the United States.

Indeed, one of the company's greatest strengths lies in its continuous ability to conduct business on a global scale while maintaining a local identity. While Americans proudly point to Coke as a historic achievement and the embodiment of the American Dream, people from all over the world have a common bond with Coke products and the people who make them. As a result, Coke is typically viewed as part of the local community.

Much of this unique connection with consumers springs from the bottler system and the diversity of the people working within Coca-Cola headquarters and affiliated organizations.

The company and its geographic operating units are led by a management team of seasoned business veterans from every corner of the globe. Diversity in the background and talent of its associates is a strength reflected throughout the company's global business system, from its engineers to its marketing teams to its finance division. Women and minorities serve in leadership roles on the board of directors, as company officers, as directors of business units, and in key international positions.

The company extends its daily commitments to diversity through partnerships with its suppliers. Coca-Cola operates as a local enterprise everywhere it does business. It hires and trains locally. It purchases goods and services from local businesses. In the United States, for example, the company and its bottling partners work with more than 3,000 women- and minority-owned suppliers to meet the demands of the company's growing business.

Given its global presence, it's not surprising that The Coca-Cola Company is a leading sponsor of some of the world's largest and most visible humanistic efforts. Perhaps none of these affiliations is maintained with greater pride than the Olympic Games. No other company has a relationship with the Olympic Games that is as deep or as long-lasting as The Coca-Cola Company's relationship. The company is, in many ways, more than a sponsor; it has been a true partner in the Olympic movement.

In addition to its involvement in efforts that span the globe, a vital element of The Coca-Cola Company's success in establishing a local identity in multiple markets springs from its commitment to supporting educational, cultural, and civic endeavors in every community in which it operates.

This commitment includes contributions by The Coca-Cola Foundation, the philanthropic arm of The Coca-Cola Company.

The Foundation will contribute $100 million to education worldwide by the year 2000. Coca-Cola funding supports partnerships between universities and local schools, global education programs, and "first generation" scholarships to help students become the first in their family to attend college, among other initiatives. The company believes strengthening educational opportunities for individuals represents a sound investment in those particular individuals and in our collective future. Since 1990, The Coca-Cola Foundation has awarded more than 2,500 scholarships; two-thirds of those scholarships have been awarded to minority students.

The company also supports a variety of organizations that improve the quality of life in our communities. Organizations such as The College Fund/UNCF, Hispanic Scholarship Fund, 100 Black Men, and Catalyst receive funding from The Coca-Cola Company. These organizations provide scholarships, support for mentoring programs, and funding to youth and economic development programs.

Another focus of the company's philanthropic efforts is the Native American population. A variety of Native American organizations have received support through 1999 from The Coca-Cola Company, among them The American Indian College Fund, First Nations Development Institute, Futures for Children, and the National Museum of the American Indian. Coca-Cola provides funding for innovative Native American educational programs at a number of colleges and universities around the country.

Additionally, the company supports several health organizations, including the American Cancer Society, the Sickle Cell Anemia Foundation, Juvenile Diabetes International, and the National Kidney Fund.

In Atlanta, Coke also contributes to approximately 40 organizations and endeavors in support of the arts and culture. A particularly innovative example is The Coca-Cola Foundation's partnership with The Atlanta History Center to create a program—the only one of its kind in the nation—designed to introduce minority college students to careers in the museum professions.

The Coca-Cola Company is the largest annual corporate contributor to the Woodruff Art Center with gifts that also help to support The Atlanta Symphony Orchestra, the Alliance Theatre Company, the High Museum of Art, and the Atlanta College of Art. As part of a series of grants that support the Cultural Olympiad in its goal to bring international exposure to the arts organizations in the southeastern United States, Coke contributed generously to area arts organizations. Other local arts organizations supported by the company and the Foundation include 7 Stages Theatre, Horizons Theatre Company, JOMANDI Productions, Atlanta Ballet, Inc., Academy Theatre, The Atlanta Opera, Ballethnic Dance Company, Nexus Contemporary Art Center, Arts Festival of Atlanta, Actors' Express, the Center for Puppetry Arts, and many others.

In addition, the company demonstrates its commitment to its hometown by sponsoring fund-raising events for dozens of non-profit organizations based in Atlanta. And through the company's Reaching Out program, employees donate their time to work on projects to improve their local community. Through the Coca-Cola Tutor Program, employees take time each week to tutor students in neighborhood schools.

The Coca-Cola Company's longtime leader, Robert W. Woodruff, used to say that everyone who touches Coca-Cola should benefit; the company continues to act on that principle. Today, The Coca-Cola Company satisfies consumers, creates jobs, generates economic growth, and works to improve the quality of life in nearly 200 countries around the world. ❧

◄ Each day, the 30,000 employees of The Coca-Cola system work hard to bring the company's beverages to thirsty consumers everywhere. Photo by Jeff Corwin.

◄ Each day, Coca-Cola provides a simple moment of pleasure to more than 1 billion consumers in every corner of the world. Photo by Michael Pugh.

Lockheed Martin Aeronautical Systems

When Americans think of aviation, the name Lockheed Martin comes to mind as easily as the Wright Brothers. After all, the company is one of the oldest and most respected names in the business.

Alan and Malcolm Loughead (pronounced Lockheed) successfully flew their first hand-built, three-passenger seaplane over San Francisco Bay in 1913. Three years later they founded a company in Santa Barbara, California, to manufacture a twin-engine, 10-passenger flying boat, two sea-planes for the Navy, and a small biplane.

The sky seemed the limit to the fledgling company until thousands of surplus World War I planes flooded the civilian market. The brothers sadly called it quits. Malcolm went on to develop and sell one of his inventions, the Lockheed four-wheel hydraulic braking system for automobiles. Alan, on the other hand, was hopelessly fascinated with aviation, and subsequently returned to the field in 1926, when he helped form Lockheed Aircraft Company in Hollywood.

Once again, Lockheed had a promising future, sales skyrocketed, and the company expanded and moved to Burbank. In 1929, the thriving firm was purchased by Detroit Aircraft. Shortly after the purchase, the stock market crash of 1929 forced Detroit Aircraft into receivership, but somehow, Lockheed survived for another two years. By April 1932, aircraft orders dried up and employment dropped to four people. Lockheed was finally forced into receivership, and its assets, valued at $129,961, were bought by a group of young men headed by Robert E. Gross at a cost of $40,000.

The first Model 10 Electra took off in 1934—and so did the company. For the next 15 years, civilian and military aircraft poured off the assembly lines. More than 20,000 Lockheed planes were built for World War II.

Meanwhile, at the government plant at Marietta, Georgia, Bell Aircraft turned out 668 Boeing-designed Superfortresses as part of a B-29 production pool during World War II. All contracts were canceled the day after VJ-Day in 1945, and the plant was closed within weeks.

In June 1950, the Korean War erupted, and the lines shifted once again from civilian to military. Late in 1950, the Air Force asked Lockheed to reopen the Marietta, Georgia, plant. A group of 150 employees moved from California to Air Force Plant 6 early in 1951 to begin modifying B-29 aircraft that had been in storage in Texas. In April, the newly opened company was chosen (along with Douglas) to modify and build the Boeing-designed B-47 Stratojet, and before the end of that first year, Marietta employment grew to 10,000.

While work in Marietta focused on the B-29 and B-47 programs, Lockheed won the competition to build a new medium-sized logistic and tactical military airlifter capable of operating from short, unprepared airstrips. That contract saved the Marietta workforce the fate of an earlier post-war era. This and other contracts ensured work would continue through the new millennium.

Two YC-130 prototypes were designed and built in Burbank. The manufacturing assignment was turned over to Lockheed-Georgia Company to provide production work to follow completion of the B-47 program. By the end of 1952, the plant had completed and delivered all 120 B-29s. From 1953 through 1957, 394 of the B-47s were delivered. During this same time frame, production started on what was to become one of the most functional and versatile aircraft in the world. The first C-130 Hercules production aircraft lifted off Dobbins runway on April 7, 1955.

One year later, 10 Hercules transports were delivered to the Air

Force. In 1957, 140 Hercules aircraft, along with the final nine B-47s, were delivered to the military. Australia placed a $21.7-million order for 12 aircraft that same year, marking a significant Hercules milestone as the first of foreign sales.

During all this activity, the Air Force announced in 1956 that it was in the market for a small multiengine jet utility transport to carry a crew of two and ten passengers. Two prototypes were built in Burbank, and again the production program shifted to Georgia. The first Marietta-built JetStar—and the world's first executive jet—took to the air in January 1960. While the sizable military order never materialized, the sleek jet was ordered by governments and corporations around the world. Two other small aircraft were developed during the time the JetStar was in initial production.

A brief four months prior to the JetStar's maiden flight, the first of two six-passenger single engine utility transports flew. But that is as far as the LASA-60 program got. Arrangements were later made for production of this aircraft by an associate company in Mexico.

Production was booming. The aviation industry, however, typically works on designs for the next generation of sky carriers long before production is completed on the current line. In the 1950s, focus was centered on vertical takeoff and landing (VTOL) studies. The U.S. Army contracted with Lockheed for two research aircraft, and on November 20, 1963, the first XV-4 Hummingbird took to the air. The Lockheed Hummingbird was one of the first fixed-wing VTOL aircraft to fly successfully anywhere in the world, but following a brief flight test program, the

Army decided to discontinue further development.

Instead, Lockheed-Georgia Company was awarded a billion-dollar contract to develop and manufacture the C-141, a new high-speed jet cargo and troop carrier called the StarLifter, for the Air Force. The StarLifter aircraft was Lockheed-Georgia Company's first major program to be accomplished from concept to flyaway in Marietta. The first flight of the StarLifter on December 17, 1963, occurred on the 60th anniversary of the Wright Brothers' first powered flight.

The remainder of the 1960s were filled with milestones. A new "H" model and the L-100 commercial version of the Hercules were unveiled in 1964. The largest foreign C-130 order to date was placed by the United Kingdom for 66 of the new "H" models at a cost of $99.7 million in 1965. That same year, the company was awarded a U.S. Air Force contract to build the world's largest aircraft, the C-5A, with a cargo capacity five times that of the StarLifter.

By the end of 1965, Lockheed-Georgia employed 22,344 who turned out sophisticated flying machines en masse—103 StarLifters, 58 C-130s, 22 JetStars, and nine L-100s. In August, they began to build the giant Galaxy. 1968 saw the last StarLifter delivered, the first C-5A rolled out, the 1,000th Hercules was delivered, and the first C-5A lifted off the Dobbins runway.

With the completion of the StarLifter program and the phasing down of C-5A deliveries, employment dropped from 22,364 in 1970 to 9,400 at the end of 1974. One C-5A was delivered that year, and work was contained to the remaining 46 Hercules deliveries.

But the drop in employment didn't cause employees to lose interest in their contributions to the community and nation. On June 10, 1972, Marietta plant employees donated 754 pints of

◄ Navy pilot Lieutenant Jim Flatley flew a KC-130F from the USS *Forrestal* in November 1963.

◄ The first flight of the F-22 (Raptor 4001) was made from Marietta in 1997.

blood in one day to the Red Cross. In 1975, 99.6 percent of the workforce, 9,826 employees, signed up for U.S. Savings Bonds.

The JetStar II, with its intercontinental range of 3,200 miles, entered production in 1975. The Air Force awarded the company a $24.3-million contract to "stretch" the StarLifter by extending the fuselage by 23 1/3 feet and adding an aerial fueling system. Despite the new activity and the delivery of the 1,400th Hercules, the head count continued to drop. By year-end 1977, employment was at a historic low: 8,400.

The rest of the 1970s proved to be a turn-around period for the company. In 1978, the Air Force awarded Lockheed two contracts: the first for $407 million to stretch almost the entire fleet of StarLifters and the second to build two sets of extra stronger replacement wings for the C-5A Galaxy. In 1979, production of the JetStar II was suspended and the last delivered. However, the first stretched C-141 was delivered.

The 1980s were filled with the typical highs and lows of the aerospace industry. Indonesia took delivery of the 1,600th Hercules in 1980, the Air Force issued a contract to retrofit the entire fleet of C-5As with new wings, and employment at the plant climbed to 12,800.

By 1982, production on the C-5B was under way, the final C-141B was delivered, and a world record for a non-stop Hercules flight was set by one of England's Royal Air Force C-130 crews.

In 1984, assembly of the first four C-5Bs began, 18 rewinged C-5As and 34 Hercules transports were delivered, and the company won several major contracts, including the Propfan Test Assessment program. In December that same year, employees set a state record by donating 1,409 pints of blood. A few days later, employees collected

more than 45,000 pounds of food for more than 605 underprivileged families in the area.

While employees were setting community involvement records, the C-5 set two weight-carrying records flying out of Marietta on December 17, 1984. The aircraft flew at 922,000 pounds—the greatest recorded weight at which any airplane had ever flown. The second record was set by the C-5 lifting a payload of 232,477 pounds to an altitude of 2,000 meters.

By year-end of 1985, 10 C-5B aircraft were in various stages of production, and plant employment had reached 18,700. The Hercules program established its largest sales backlog since 1976. Tunisia became the 56th nation to take delivery of a Hercules.

The company's High Technology Test Bed (HTTB) aircraft, a modified L-100 used as a flying laboratory, set three world records in 1985. In a flight from the Marietta facility, the records included Short Takeoff and Landing (STOL) time-to-climb marks to 3,000 meters, 6,000 meters, and 9,000 meters. On the record-setting flight, the HTTB lifted from the runway in less than 1,600 feet.

The emphasis toward technology continued in 1986. More than $90 million in research and development contracts were awarded to the company in areas such as artificial intelligence, metal matrix composites, thermoplastic materials, and laminar flow control. Still, the C-130 Hercules and the C-5 were the mainstays.

In 1987, Lockheed-Georgia Company, Lockheed-California Company, and Lockheed Aircraft Service Company were integrated into a single operating company—Lockheed Aeronautical Systems Company (LASC). The Marietta plant and its supporting facilities were now responsible for primary LASC production, second source production, major subcontracting, and major aircraft modification. The facility became referred to as Lockheed Aeronautical Systems Company—Georgia (LASC-Georgia).

That same year, 36 Hercules, 13 C-5Bs, and the final rewinged C-5A Galaxy were delivered. New customers for the Hercules included the People's Republic of China and France. Contracts for that year were plentiful. One was awarded to enhance the C-141B StarLifter's service life well into the twenty-first century; another was to develop a preliminary design for a modernized C-141 flight station. Additionally, more than $90 million was gained for research and development.

LASC-Georgia received numerous awards in the late 1980s, including the Collier Trophy (in conjunction with LASC-Burbank), designation as a Blue Ribbon Contractor by the Air Force, and was awarded the Outstanding Laboratory Award for advances in pollution abatement by The Georgia Water and Pollution Control Association. Work on the metal matrix composites was cited as one of the 100 most significant products worldwide. 1989 was also another year for records. The HTTB set four performance records,

◄ The C-130J, which features newer, more powerful engines, a two-crew cockpit, and other significant changes, was first flown in 1996 and customer deliveries began in 1998.

(On preceding page)
◄ (Top left) **Lockheed Martin is one of the oldest and most respected names in the business.**

◄ (Middle left) **Lockheed-Georgia Company was awarded a billion-dollar contract to develop and manufacture the C-141, a high-speed jet cargo and troop carrier called the StarLifter, for the Air Force, in the early 1960s.**

◄ (Bottom left) **U.S. Air Force F-22 Raptor 4002 flies the developmental program's 100th mission May 4, 1999, at Edwards Air Force Base in California.**

and at the Air Force Airlift Rodeo, a C-5 set a world record by airdropping four Sheridan tanks and 767,673 paratroops on one flight.

With the end of the C-5B program, LASC-Georgia began a transition from prime contractor to major subcontractor. To better compete in the changing aerospace environment, the Burbank facility was closed in 1990, and two operating companies were formed.

Lockheed Aeronautical Systems Company (LASC) was consolidated with headquarters in Marietta, while Lockheed Advanced Development Company, known as Skunk Works, was formed with headquarters in Palmdale, California.

In 1991, LASC, along with General Dynamics and Boeing, was chosen to develop the F-22, the Air Force's new air superiority fighter. The F-22, with its stealth, integrated avionics, advanced technology, and ability to supercruise, is expected to dominate

the air battlefield well into the twenty-first century. The F-22 was first flown in 1997 and is now in flight test. It is expected to be operational starting in 2005.

The early 1990s were a time of major change in the aerospace industry. Lockheed acquired General Dynamics in 1993, and then merged with Martin Marietta to form Lockheed Martin Corporation in 1995. In keeping with the new corporate name, the Marietta operation was renamed Lockheed Martin Aeronautical Systems.

The C-130J, which features newer, more powerful engines, a two-crew cockpit, and other significant changes, was first flown in 1996 and customer deliveries began in 1998. The C-130J looks like the venerable Hercules, but is almost a completely different aircraft. C-130J sales are expected to be the company's bread and butter well into the early part of the next millennium. ✈

The Esthetic Dental Practice of Goldstein, Garber, Salama & Gribble

▶ **The tastefully decorated reception room makes you feel as if you are sitting in a friend's comfortable living room with fresh flowers, unique art pieces, and live birds.** Photo by Bill Lisenby.

▼ **(front row, left to right) Dr. David Garber, Dr. Ronald Goldstein. (back row, left to right) Dr. Angela Gribble Hedlund, Dr. Henry Salama, Dr. Maurice Salama, and Dr. Cathy Goldstein Schwartz.** Photo by Bill Lisenby.

The dental practice of Goldstein, Garber, Salama & Gribble is often referred to as "the most technologically advanced" dental practice or "the dentists to celebrities." Indeed, the practice has been creating million-dollar smiles for models, film actors and actresses, television personalities, and a slew of the rich and famous for decades.

People travel to the Buckhead area of Atlanta from Hollywood, Paris, Sidney, South America, Asia, and Europe for the privilege of a master's touch. Nearly half of their patients come from outside Georgia, and about a fifth come from foreign lands. Most are not "celebrities" but come from all walks of life—teachers, nurses, homemakers, and factory workers.

All have one thing in common: the desire for a beautiful smile. Some have wanted an attractive smile for many years but have been unable to find someone to really listen to them, make an accurate diagnosis, and have the expertise and technology to bring forth a successful result. Many are dazzled by the esthetic value alone, but having the best in dentistry also means having the best oral health.

"Good dentistry is not expensive," says Dr. Ronald Goldstein. "Lack of treatment always is." He should know. Goldstein is a prolific author, an industry leader, a dental researcher and designer, and a practitioner second to none. From his accumulation of knowledge, experience, and perfected techniques, Goldstein has literally written the book on esthetic dentistry. His *Esthetics In Dentistry* was a groundbreaking text and is still used today in universities and dental schools around the world. His *Change Your Smile* book— written for the dental consumer—has been translated into six different languages and has been read by over a million consumers.

Esthetic dentistry, known simply as cosmetic dentistry to most lay people, is the science that deals with improving the smile. But it is also an art. Coloration of natural teeth, in order to be both beautiful and natural, for example, must be dealt with as deftly as a master artist would apply color to a painting. But before that stage is reached, the dentist must determine precisely what the patient is trying to achieve, even when the patient is not entirely sure.

Changing the shape and alignment of teeth, adjusting the color and brightness of teeth, moving gum tissue, contouring or enhancing the length or width of teeth—each of these options, plus hundreds more, are only a hint of what this team deals with once the patient says, "Give me a beautiful smile."

World-Class Dental Team

Although Dr. Goldstein is regarded as the "chief architect of esthetic dental care" worldwide, the rest of the team are also experts renowned for their special abilities in achieving what many in the dental field would have earlier thought impossible.

What is unique here is the assembly of a cohesive team consisting of 3 dual-degree specialists. The team includes general dentists, periodontists, prosthodontists, an orthodontist, and an implantologist. No detail of the total picture is overlooked. Together, the team develops harmony and balance between a patient's facial shape, lip form, the amount of gum showing, and even hair and skin color. Consulting with an oral surgeon, plastic surgeons, and other specialists

also makes up the extended family of specialists.

Partner Dr. David Garber, periodontist and prosthodontist, is a vital member of the team. He is renowned for his research, teaching credentials in both specialties, and personable manner with patients. His expertise enables him to alter gum tissue, as well as teeth, to create a total smile, not just pretty white teeth. His clinical work is considered some of the most amazing ever done in the field.

Dr. Garber has practiced in South Africa, London, and Philadelphia and teaches at the Medical College of Georgia School of Dentistry. He has authored and coauthored numerous articles and books, many of which have been translated into French, German, Italian, Spanish, and Japanese.

Dr. Maurice Salama served as the dental expert on WAGA TV's *Good Day, Atlanta!* and is a frequent television guest. Dr. Salama is an orthodontist and a periodontist who also completed a fellowship in implants. The dual nature of his specialty training makes him a frequent author on adult orthodontics and implantology. A sought-after dental lecturer nationally, he has spoken at dental meetings throughout the world on contemporary orthodontics and periodontal treatment.

Dr. Henry Salama's specialties include periodontics, prosthodontics, and implant surgical techniques. He is director of the practice's state-of-the-art Implant Center and currently holds a Clinical Assistant Professorship at the University of Pennsylvania. He has pioneered the research in the area of "immediate implants" or "teeth in a day." Dr. Henry Salama is the author of numerous scholarly publications and is a renowned speaker on the global circuit.

Dr. Angela Gribble Hedlund is a general dentist who treats a vast array of restorative and esthetic needs. She is a member of the American Academy of Cosmetic Dentistry and has written articles for the *Journal of Esthetic Dentistry* and the *Journal of the American Dental Association.* Her patients often comment how sensitive and gentle she is and that her injections are "the best I've ever been given."

Dr. Cathy Goldstein Schwartz joined the practice in 1986. Dr. Schwartz has a special interest in helping patients keep

▲ Esthetics permeate the office, especially in the spacious hallways in which various forms of art are displayed. Photo by Bill Lisenby.

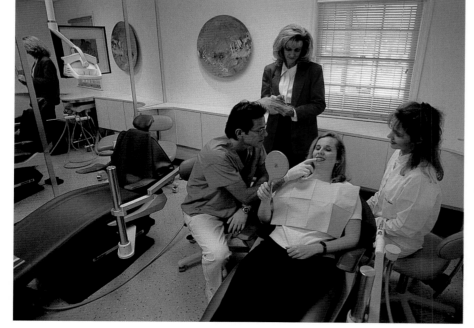

◀ Orthodontist-periodontist Dr. Maurice Salama examines patient Lynn Cheshire as the dental assistant and treatment coordinator discuss the next step of treatment. Photo by Bill Lisenby.

their natural teeth strong and healthy all their lives. Dr. Brian Beaudreau, a general dentist, rounds out the team with his expertise in fixed and removable bridges, as well as all phases of general dentistry.

In-House Dental Lab

Another unique feature of this dental practice is the presence of an in-house, state-of-the-art dental laboratory. Ceramists Pinhas Adar and Frank Loegel often work side-by-side with the doctors to create beautiful, one-of-a-kind restorations that are not distinguishable from natural teeth.

Their expertise and techniques produce results unimaginable in the standard dental lab. Everything from the materials them-selves to the molding, shaping, blending, coloring, light reflections, and depth contours are custom-designed by these ceramists. The teeth they create are so lifelike that they cannot be distinguished from natural teeth except by a dental professional. Over the years ceramists from Japan, France, Italy, Israel, Switzerland, and Russia have come to Atlanta for the opportunity to work with the doctors of GGS&G. Also working "behind the scenes" are laboratory technicians Mark Hamilton, Jeremy Temple, and Stanley Nayshtut.

Visualize The Final Result Before Treatment Begins

With all the advantages technology now offers, patients can even see results of the treatment plan before the work is begun. For example, a patient may come in requesting that a gap be filled between the front two teeth. Ordinarily, a dentist would merely comply. At Goldstein, Garber, Salama & Gribble, an imaging computer would first create the look the patient is asking for.

With the imaging system the dentists can show how closing the spaces between four teeth, instead of two, lend the effect the patient really wants. They can also show other options the patient may not have considered. With this technology, patients are more in control of the results, the costs, the timing, and inevitably happier with their smiles when all is said and done.

But imaging is only the beginning. Exacting technology is used in every phase of treatment, allowing maximum flexibility, efficiency, and predictability. The GGS&G team is able to make even the most minute adjustments easily and control the outcome. It's also far more efficient, an advantage appreciated by anyone who has better things to do than spend hours in the dentist's office.

Recently featured by a leading dental magazine as "The Dental Office of The Future," the practice of Goldstein, Garber, Salama & Gribble offers an abundance of technology few can only dream about:

• **Laser** surgery is a high-tech favorite among patients, as it reduces postoperative discomfort and causes no bleeding at all. This practice is the first in the Southeast to have the Millennium Laser System—which is the world's first laser that can sculpt hard or soft tissue.

• **Air-Abrasive Technology,** a drill-less, spray-away-decay device, is available to treat shallow tiny pits of decay and external staining. This instrument often eliminates the need for anesthetic or the drill.

• **The Wand,** which addresses most patients' top concern, is a new computerized anesthesia system. Most patients do not feel any discomfort with The Wand.

• **RadioVisioGraphy** is a low radiation method of x-raying that is instantly projected onto a monitor and reduces patient radiation exposure by 9 percent.

• **ShadeEye-EX,** an amazing computerized shade-matching tech-nology, ensures exact matching of tooth color.

• **Cerec CAD-CAM** uses the computer to duplicate a new crown to the identical size and shape of the natural tooth.

• **Voice-Activated Charting** gives the patient an instant color printout showing precisely the condition of a patient's gum tissue. The doctor and patient together can view which areas are healthy and which may show evidence of gum disease. This is a sterile procedure unsurpassed by anything on the market.

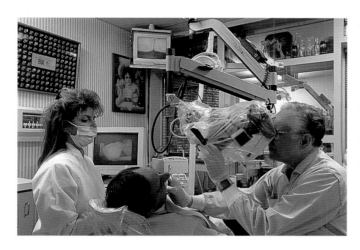

dental care is just the beginning of a patient relationship. The patient's desires, hopes, and dreams are never discounted, ignored, or depersonalized.

The doctors at GGS&G believe that the smile is key to each person's unique look and contributes greatly to a person's self-image and ability to interact with the world. So each person and each smile is treated as though this dental practice exists solely for him or her. ✪

◄ Dr. Ronald Goldstein uses special video photography and microscopic close-ups to obtain precision esthetic results. The state-of-the-art technology in this dental practice sets the pattern for dentistry worldwide. Photo by Bill Lisenby.

One of the Country's Oldest Dental Practices Continues To Improve

In 1999, the office celebrated its 70th anniversary as an ongoing comprehensive dental practice. Though the practice has always been dedicated to superb dentistry, the technology it now uses is, of course, very new. An old commitment coupled with new technology means patients get the best of both worlds: experience and new knowledge. It's a winning combination that can't be overestimated.

Founded by Dr. Irving Goldstein, who philosophically was well ahead of his time, the practice has always understood that superior

◄ Dr. David Garber, periodontist-prosthodontist, treats this patient in one of two state-of-the-art surgical suites. Photo by Bill Lisenby.

AT&T

Perhaps the reason AT&T is such a common household name is simply that the company is so uncommonly good at what it does.

The world's largest and most sophisticated communications network is a postmodern paradox of sorts. Although AT&T is a high-tech company, consumers using the company's services find it is a comfortable and familiar means of staying in touch for business and personal needs. And while AT&T serves more than 80 million customers in the U.S. alone with 270 million voice, data, and video calls on an average business day, consumers feel their individual calls are handled in what has come to be known as the quality "AT&T" tradition.

The numbers and technology involved in the giant communication company's daily business are mind-boggling. AT&T completes more than 99.99 percent of all U.S. calls on the first attempt.

The company uses 144 4ESS switches to route calls on the mainland over more than 51,000 miles of fiber-optic cable in the United States alone, and transmits all switched traffic in 100 percent digital format.

Within its complex workings, AT&T uses a Real Time Network Routing (RTNR) system to automatically complete U.S. calls on any of 134 possible routes. It uses the FASTAR® and FASTAR II® system to automatically reroute circuits following a failure on the core network. FASTAR II uses SONET ring technology to reroute traffic within 60 milliseconds of a network failure, while the original FASTAR system generally reroutes 95 percent of circuits within two to three minutes of a network failure.

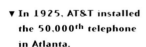

Network operations is just one of the broad range of AT&T businesses located in metropolitan Atlanta. As one of Georgia's largest employers, with more than 10,000 employees, there are major AT&T offices in midtown, downtown, and northeast Atlanta; Alpharetta; Marietta; Conyers; and Augusta. These locations are responsible for business and consumer customer care, wireless services, and numerous sales, administration, finance, and other staff functions.

Beyond its tremendous market coverage in Atlanta and other parts of the U.S., AT&T has more than 70 years of experience providing communications services to countries around the world. To be exact, AT&T service is available in 250 countries and territories and direct-dial is offered in more than 240.

AT&T gives travelers access to AT&T's

network from more than 150 countries and offers AT&T Direct Service to the United States from all of them. The AT&T Global Calling Card and AT&T Global Corporate Calling Card make it easy for residential and business customers to call from more than 90 countries to more than 200.

As a founding member of the WorldPartners alliance, AT&T offers one-stop shopping for seamless services to multinational companies in 33 countries, including more than 450 of the 1,500 largest firms in the world. AT&T's reach will extend even further with the Global Venture planned between AT&T and British Telecommunications plc (BT). This new business plans to combine the trans-border assets and operations of AT&T and BT, including their international networks, traffic, products for business customers, and multinational accounts in selected industry sectors. The global venture's public network will reach 237 countries and territories, and its managed networks will have 6,000 nodes in 52 countries.

In short, the company spans into even remote corners of the globe, and still AT&T is adding more technology, more connections, and more customers. In 1999, AT&T had already planned to invest more than $8 billion to add as much capacity as the entire long-distance network had just six years ago, to expand its wireless network, and to introduce a multitude of new services.

One of those new services is broadband cable. Between 1998 and 1999, AT&T made over $100 billion in cable acquisitions to bring the next communications revolution into homes and businesses throughout America. This change will combine voice, data, and video services and the devices—television, telephone, and PC—that have traditionally transported these services to households and places of work. Internet access is now "always on" and 100 times faster than 28kbps modems with no dial-up needed. Constant and immediate, cable also offers multiple phone lines at lower prices and with fewer wires running to homes and buildings.

AT&T Wireless's national footprint covers more than 130 million people, making AT&T the largest digital wireless service in North America. The company introduced the industry's first national one rate wireless service plan with AT&T Digital One Rate. This plan provides customers a single, all-inclusive rate (with no long-distance or roaming charges) for incoming or outgoing calls made throughout the 50 United States.

Growth and change, however, are nothing new to the telecommunications giant. AT&T has a history of conquering man's most stubborn communication obstacles in either the actual or virtual realities, in high-tech or personal modes, and in foreign and domestic territories.

AT&T Corp. was formerly American Telephone and Telegraph Company, which was incorporated on March 3, 1885, to manage and expand the burgeoning long-distance business of American Bell Telephone Company and its licensees.

It continued as the "long-distance company" until December 30, 1899, when it assumed the business and property of American Bell and became the parent company of the Bell System. It remained the Bell System parent, providing the bulk of telecommunications services in the United States, until January 1, 1984, when it divested itself of the Bell operating companies that provided local exchange services.

On September 20, 1995, AT&T announced that it would be splitting into three companies: a "new" AT&T to provide communications services; Lucent Technologies, to provide communications systems and technologies; and NCR Corp., to concentrate on transaction-intensive computing. The strategic restructuring was completed on December 31, 1996.

From the company's start-up to present day, AT&T has left many historically significant marks on the legacy of the nation and the emerging telecommunications industry. In 1927, AT&T was the first company to achieve commercial trans-Atlantic telephone service and the first to employ an electrical digital computer 10 years later. In 1947, it was the first to have a transistor and, that same year, became the first to develop cellular wireless communications technology. In 1957, AT&T was the first to employ a computer modem. Though modems and cellular phones are a common sight in the 1990s and later, it is remarkable that AT&T developed these products and services some 40 to 50 years earlier.

Other firsts for the company include the first use of laser in communications in 1958, the Telstar satellite in 1962, the first commercial lightwave system in 1977, the first Karmarkar linear programming algorithm in 1987, the first commercial ISDN long-distance network service in 1988, and the first optical digital processor in 1990.

And AT&T leads in other areas as well. In 1994, AT&T formally launched the program AT&T CARES, which provides cash grants ranging from $250 to $5,000 to nonprofit institutions where AT&T

employees volunteer their time. Two years later, the company began providing one paid workday for employees to use each year in volunteer work at the community organization of their choice. In Atlanta, AT&T employees have given volunteer hours in support of a number of local projects and initiatives, including school clean-up and painting, student tutoring, food sorting at the Atlanta Community Food Bank, and Job Shadow Day in partnership with Junior Achievement. Though AT&T is a high-tech company, it values people.

AT&T WorldNet® hosts some 8,000 business web sites but recognizes that the value of technology goes beyond business as usual. In 1995, AT&T created the AT&T Learning Network, an award-winning education program designed to help families, schools, and communities use technology to enhance teaching and learning. The program offers on-line resources and professional development for teachers, a Web tour on education-related uses of the World Wide Web, and AskLN, an exclusive mentoring program for teachers by teachers. In recognition of the AT&T Learning Network's impact on education through technology, the program was chosen by a panel of national experts to receive the 1997 EdNet HERO Award, recognizing private industry's support of education.

Though AT&T is often thought of as a huge global corporation, and, of course, it is, the impact of the company is oftentimes very personal and direct—especially in terms of educational support. In the metro Atlanta area, AT&T is a major supporter in many communities. The AT&T Mini-Grant Program awards grants to secondary and postsecondary teachers for their creative integration of technology in the curriculum. AT&T is a member and supporter of the TECH CORPS™ Georgia Task Force, a nonprofit group that organizes businesses and education leaders to work to enhance technology in all schools. And AT&T has awarded grants to the following local organizations: Foundations for the Future Forum, Talent Growth Initiative at Clayton College and State University, and the Southern Region Education Board.

For the quality of its many achievements, the company was awarded the Malcolm Baldrige National Quality Award three times, another first—twice in 1992 and once in 1994. AT&T is the recipient of many prestigious awards and citations, but perhaps the most meaningful comes from the companies and individuals who use AT&T products and services every day. It is their continual use of the company over the years that has proved mutually beneficial and brought about extraordinary advancements that many world-wide now enjoy. ❦

▲ AT&T CARES volunteers enjoy giving back to the community. More than 50 AT&T employees volunteered for a group project at the Atlanta Community Food Bank, sorting and boxing food for distribution to local nonprofit organizations.

◄ AT&T CARES volunteers proudly show off a newly planted tree at Adamsville Elementary School. A total of 300 AT&T employees joined in to refurbish and land-scape Adamsville Elementary and six other elementary schools in the City of Atlanta.

Georgia State University

Much of postmodern-day criticism of higher learning circulates around the perceived chasm between the learned halls of theory and the world of hard knocks. But a well-honed university can lead, rather than lag, the real world in everything from exploratory to definitive work. As the state's second-largest university, Georgia State University (GSU) keeps reinventing itself in its quest for excellence in both theoretical education and real world application. One of the long-lasting effects of this quest has been a research arm that reaches out and embraces the real world in infinite and intimate degrees. The city of Atlanta and other urban centers may never be the same again.

Founded in 1913, Georgia State University underwent a series of metamorphoses that led to the emergence of an urban powerhouse destined to perform preeminent works that would change the scope and nature of a world in flux. From the School of Policy Studies to research on viral studies, Georgia State University has found a niche in research, especially as it applies to urban application, unfilled by other universities, even those of the ivy persuasion.

A close study of the world at large and Atlanta in particular accentuated the city's need for a high-profile center in policy studies—to rival the likes of Harvard's Kennedy School of Government and the LBJ School of Public Affairs at the University of Texas. Georgia State officials began several years ago studying how to fill a void that the University of Georgia, Georgia Tech, and Emory University were not moving to occupy. The final plan was to consolidate three powerful engines—the departments of economics, public administration, and urban studies—into the efficient, energized vehicle that Georgia State's School of Policy Studies (SPS) has quickly shown itself to be.

Experts from SPS don't yet regularly appear on network television news, but that day is not far off, given the results the university has consistently generated. Since its formation in 1996, the school has steadily worked to become one of America's great policy think tanks, leaving interesting impressions in the futures and histories of more than 30 different countries and around the nation. SPS specialists have already affected change in Russia, Asia, Africa, Latin America, and the Middle East through research and advice on issues ranging from taxation to terrorism.

As though deciphering new world trends and unraveling old world secrets were not sufficient fortes for a premier research institution, Georgia State simultaneously chased elusive answers to new urban problems in both real and virtual modes.

Georgia State research scientists in the university's Center for Biotechnology and Drug Design are at the forefront of new discoveries that benefit humanity as a whole and give Atlanta's economy a decided push. The scientists study diseases and develop treatments for problems from fungal infections to pneumonia. The center is also fostering growth in the local biotechnology industry through the university's "business incubator" program. Fledgling biotech companies receive a helping hand via lab space on campus and assistance from Georgia State researchers to aid in their launch and advancements.

The combined thrusts of scientific discovery, coupled with collaboration on commercial efforts, make the Atlanta region more attractive to the biotechnology industry. The university's high-tech laboratories also provide an excellent training ground to produce highly skilled employees to work in the field.

Microbial contamination problems are also being studied and solved at Georgia State, where faculty from a dozen disciplines work under the umbrella of the Environmental Research Center (ERC). Their work on a plethora of projects has already discovered much about how bacteria and fungi cause illness by growing on everyday surfaces like contact lenses, ceiling tiles, carpets, cars, catheters, and hot tubs.

Manufacturers want the answers to prevention and destruction of the microbes and biofilms, and they want them now, even if they're not exactly raising a national alarm about the problem. So it is that ERC constantly strikes a delicate balance, attracting funding from both government and industry, to educate scientists while producing basic research with countless commercial applications.

Disease studies at Georgia State are not, however, limited to the microbe. GSU's Memory Assessment Clinic and Alzheimer's Disease Program has been instrumental in developing a statewide consortium of university-based programs to study memory disorders. An estimated 4 million Americans have Alzheimer's disease, and Georgia State is in steady search of a cure and preventative measures to offset the predicted climb to 9 million afflicted Americans by the year 2030.

While these are intriguing problems to the questioning minds of some of America's best brainpower, disease and deterioration are

not the only questions under study at Georgia State. Other postmodern plagues, like the common tribulations faced by many metro Atlantans, who, largely because of drugs, alcohol, or violence, have found themselves parents again to their grandchildren and great-grandchildren, are also under scrutiny. Project Healthy Grandparents, founded in 1996 in the College of Health Sciences, seeks to better the situation for both the older adults and the young children living in these situations through real world solutions.

Technology also raises issues on the postmodern horizon that often perplex even the most adept in cyberworld. The university's Center for Digital Commerce is on a mission to educate students, reach out to Georgia corporations working or evolving on-line, and do relevant, yet practical, research in this new field.

The minds behind the center hope that Georgia State will do for electronic commerce what Stanford University did for the high-tech field of Silicon Valley—i.e., provide the brain power, applied imagination, and support to make the industry soar. It is a goal even the Atlanta Chamber of Commerce extols: to make Atlanta, already the center of business transactions, the center of electronic trading of every kind.

Physically, Georgia State University anchors downtown Atlanta with its influx of bright minds, an extremely diverse student body, and housing that renders the streets a more sophisticated and savvier flair day and night. Its research furthers the understanding and the betterment of man's condition, particularly in urban settings. It is a living, breathing institution interwoven into the city itself, and spreading outward. It is the conductor of American dreams and the lifeline of metro Atlanta's aspirations. ❧

◄ The Georgia State University Village opened in fall of 1996 after serving as part of the Olympic Village during the Summer Games. With the addition of the Village, which houses 2,000 students, Georgia State's student body has changed dramatically. In fall of 1999, more than 90 percent of the freshman class were under 19 years old. Photo by Adam Taylor.

◄ At Georgia State University, more than 24,000 students get real-world experience in the learning laboratory of the city.

United Parcel Service

First there was ground delivery service, then air, and now electronic delivery. Through it all, UPS has been the first, the best, and the biggest in the industry. With 1998 revenues in excess of $24.8 billion, the world's oldest and most respected name in the business is expected to get even larger as the emerging global economy increases the demand for goods and information.

More than 330,000 dedicated UPS employees worldwide, combined with one of the largest transportation fleets make all of these services possible. The UPS transportation fleet consists of more than 157,000 package cars, vans, and trucks to handle the massive daily volume of packages delivered. The UPS air fleet, begun in 1929 as the nation's first air cargo service, is one of the 10 largest in the world with 216 company-owned jet cargo planes and 302 chartered aircraft making more than 1,500 flights each day to 610 airports on every continent.

UPS made Atlanta its home when it moved its headquarters to this international city in 1991. Since that time, the UPS Logistics Group and the UPS Capital Corporation, two UPS subsidiaries, have also made Atlanta their home.

UPS chose Atlanta because it was truly a global city and it had an exceptional quality of life. UPS helped preserve the quality of life through its environmentally friendly construction of a new headquarters. The result is a 623,000 square foot campus-like facility surrounded by trees; some just 15 feet from the building. In fact, UPS added 900 trees–Dogwood, Magnolia, and Oak–throughout the building site.

As a global city, Atlanta is the perfect location for UPS, the largest express carrier and package delivery company in the world. UPS serves more than 200 countries and territories around the globe and has been rated the world's most admired mail, package, and freight delivery company by *Fortune* magazine in 1997 and 1998, and has been named as America's most admired transportation company for 16 consecutive years (1983 through 1999). Not a bad entrance to the new millennium for a company that began on $100 borrowed capital.

It all began in 1907, when a 19-year-old entrepreneur, Jim Casey, borrowed $100 from a friend to found American Messenger Company in Seattle, Washington. By 1915, the company had expanded its service to California and changed its name to United Parcel Service. Today the company operates a high-tech system that in 1999 delivers more than 3.4 billion packages annually through a global system with the capacity to reach more than 4 billion of the Earth's 6 billion people. This well designed and managed system serves the company's ground deliveries and Next Day Air® deliveries.

Today, UPS has expanded the reach of its transportation network with the creation of the UPS Logistics Group, also headquartered in Atlanta. The UPS Logistics Group provides comprehensive supply chain management solutions—a sophisticated process that entails the movement, warehousing, and fulfillment of physical goods, as well as information and funds. Logistics Group customers range from manufacturers of sophisticated computer hard disk drives, to guitars to pizza.

UPS's "transportation" network covers both the physical and the virtual worlds. UPS was the first transportation company to market in June 1998 with a digital document delivery service–UPS Document Exchange SM. UPS Document Exchange is a highly secure, customizable Internet delivery service that enables users to immediately ship anything over the Internet that can be contained in a digital file, including documents, images, and software.

UPS Document Exchange is one of the most innovative examples of hi-tech solutions at UPS. Technology is in the fiber of everything UPS does, from the very moment a package enters the UPS system to the time a customer signs for it on the familiar hand-held computers carried by UPS drivers. To maintain its technological leadership, the company spends more than $1 billion on information technology each year, far more than it spends annually on vehicles and nearly as much as it spends on airplanes.

A global telecommunications network has been instrumental in UPS's success, linking over 250,000 users in 70 international locations, and making UPS the largest user of cellular technology in the world. UPS uses the industry's most advanced electronic and satellite information, giving its customers unparalleled capability in tracking and distribution of intelligence as convenient as the nearest computer screen. Customers can access this information at www.ups.com, the award-winning UPS web site.

And how does UPS manage the global flow of all this information? Through its state-of-the-art data center located in Atlanta. The UPS Windward Data Center is the central nervous system of UPS's global technological empire. It has been recognized as one of the largest and most advanced private information centers in the world. Among other things, the Center serves as a fortress to the world's largest private database–even larger than that of the U.S. Census Bureau. Day in and day out, the Center works in tandem with the company's mirror facility in Mahwah, New Jersey to keep vigilant watch over the inner workings of UPS's global information systems and telecommunications network.

Behind the bits and bytes of UPS lies another equally well-known dimension of the company. UPS knows that its success ultimately depends on the well-being of its employees and customers and the communities in which they live. Therefore UPS engages in socially responsible programs all over the world with contributions in time, money and resources.

In Atlanta, UPS invests heavily in scholarship programs as well as mentoring and tutoring programs at local schools. In 1998, the company won a Daily Points of Light Award from the national Points of Light Foundation for its work at Thurgood Marshall Middle School, where UPS volunteers have organized a Saturday tutorial program for students and a "Teacher of the Month" recognition ceremony. In addition, through its Community Service Scholarship Program, The UPS Foundation funds 40 scholarships each year at four historically black colleges and universities in Atlanta. The scholarship program provides $5,000 scholarships to the students and requires that they spend at least 150 hours each semester as mentors and tutors at local elementary schools. UPS's community web site, www.community.ups.com, details the company's involvement in communities across the world.

On a global scale, UPS is one of only 11 worldwide Olympic partners. In 1997, the company launched the most far-reaching, sponsor-driven philanthropic endeavor in Olympic history with the announcement of the UPS Olympic Sports Legacy Program, which has provided more than half a million pieces of new sports equipment to underprivileged children in youth recreation organizations in seven countries. The Boys & Girls Clubs of Metro Atlanta has been a beneficiary of the Olympic Sports Legacy Program.

While the familiar brown trucks with the customary UPS logo will still be comfortable and reliable sights throughout the next century, UPS will forever be revving the engine of global commerce. Whether in the real or virtual worlds, it's a comfort to many to move forward in the company of an old friend. ❧

▲ UPS is one of only 11 worldwide Olympic partners. UPS was a sponsor of the 1996 Games in Atlanta, the 1998 Winter Olympic Games in Nagano, Japan, and the 2000 Summer Games held in Sydney, Australia.

◄ The UPS air fleet, begun in 1929 as the nation's first air cargo service, is one of the 10 largest in the world with 216 company-owned jet cargo planes and 302 chartered aircraft making more than 1,500 flights each day to 610 airports on every continent.

Federal Home Loan Bank of Atlanta

▲ **The Federal Home Loan Bank of Atlanta serves over 1,000 financial institution members and their communities throughout the Southeast by providing low-cost wholesale credit, correspondent services, and assistance with CRA initiatives.**

reminders to all generations that followed. Substantial legislation was enacted during the Depression years to increase consumer access to credit, and to support lenders' efforts to continue lending to their communities. Though many received more attention, one piece of legislation, The Federal Home Loan Bank Act, was specifically aimed at supporting that most basic element of America's economic well being: home ownership.

The new law created the Federal Home Loan Bank System, which consisted of 12 district banks, each serving a specific region of the country. In the words of President Herbert Hoover, the system would become "not a government, but a cooperative institution between the building and loan associations, the savings banks, and other home loan agencies."

In the 1930s home lending was almost entirely the domain of the thrift industry. Savings and Loan Associations, chartered for the specific purpose of making home mortgages in their local communities, were hit hard by the Depression and needed a mechanism to safely provide mortgage credit. The creation of the 12-bank Federal Loan Bank System provided thrifts in each district a much needed source of liquidity. Though similar legislation had been introduced by 1919, the economic boom of the 1920s had decreased the emphasis placed on creating such a system. When Congress passed the Federal Home Loan Bank Bill, and President Hoover signed it in 1932, the United States was at the low point of the Depression, and many depositors— who were the source of funding for home mortgages— were pulling funds out of financial institutions.

The ability to draw funds from their district Federal Home Loan Bank allowed the local thrifts to extend longer-term mortgages, in good and bad times, without depending entirely on local deposits. This innovation facilitated the creation of the 30-year fixed-rate mortgage, which remains the most popular among homeowners today. Long-term funding not only allowed a thrift to be less vulnerable to downturns in local market conditions, but it also allowed the homeowner to spread out payments over several years and avoid the treacherous short-term renewal notes of earlier years.

The Fourth District Federal Home Loan Bank was established to serve member institutions in Alabama, Florida, Georgia, North and South Carolina, Maryland, Virginia, and the District of Columbia. Nearly from the beginning, the Fourth District Bank—now known as the Federal Home Loan Bank of Atlanta—

The Federal Home Loan Bank of Atlanta, a $50-billion wholesale credit bank, serves over 1,000 financial institution members and their communities throughout the Southeast by providing low-cost wholesale credit, correspondent services, and assistance with CRA initiatives. Its history, like that of all successful American enterprises, is one of growth, service, and evolution to meet the challenges presented by an ever changing industry.

The rigors of the Great Depression are deeply embedded in the memories of those who lived through it, and serve as cautious

In addition to the remarkable growth of recent years, and its success in adapting to a broader financial industry base, the Federal Home Loan Bank of Atlanta has consistently proven true to its original mission—that of serving the needs of communities through community banks. Primarily through home loan funding, where the original goal was to make home loans available to citizens throughout the Southeast, the Bank has enabled community institutions to make loans and engage in economic development in ways they could not otherwise undertake. The focus on this mission continues into the future. As the bank's role in the financial services industry has grown, so has its vision grown, to include new initiatives in loan consortia, rural and urban development lending, and other innovative programs.

Throughout its 67-year history, the Federal Home Loan Bank of Atlanta has helped its members provide credit to their communities in many forms. It has enhanced the profitability of many institutions, and for others, provided services they might not otherwise have been able to offer. In the future, the bank's mission may evolve, but its commitment to providing credit to communities will remain. Through new programs and initiatives, the bank will seek new opportunities. Above all, it will remain committed to helping its member institutions meet their own objectives, in their own communities. ✿

◄ Primarily through home loan funding, the Bank has enabled community institutions to make loans and engage in economic development in ways they could not otherwise undertake.

established itself as a leader in the system. In fact, the bank became the first of the 12 regional banks to show profit, in its first full year of operation. Originally located in Winston-Salem, North Carolina, the bank moved its headquarters twice before relocating to Atlanta in 1971. Though Atlanta was further from the geographic center of the District, it was thriving and had become a major financial and transportation hub. The bank, with assets then reaching $1 billion, moved into its first Atlanta headquarters on Peachtree Street in downtown, and has thereafter been referred to as the Federal Home Loan Bank of Atlanta. In 1986, the bank moved to its current location at 1475 Peachtree Street in midtown.

The 1980s were a time of incredible change for the financial services industry. The role of the Federal Home Loan Banks changed as well. The enactment of the Financial Institutions Reform Recovery and Enforcement Act (FIRREA) in 1989 opened up Federal Home Loan Bank membership to commercial banks and credit unions. The trend toward bank-financed mortgage lending made commercial bank membership in the system a logical step, and a number of market trends created an urgent need for a stable funding source for all community-based financial institutions, specifically the Federal Home Loan Banks.

PricewaterhouseCoopers LLP

▶ **Anthony Chan, Alumnus.** Photo by Sam Jones.

When PricewaterhouseCoopers (PwC) announced its merger, this marked a new beginning and a turning point in the world of business. Two of the largest and most enterprising names in professional services, Coopers & Lybrand LLP and Price Waterhouse LLP, united for the sake of serving customers with greater sophistication and ingenuity. The merger doubled the Firm's collective knowledge and gained cultural and professional diversity that promised potential beyond anything imaginable. By Day One, the new entity was ready to break with the past and show the world a new way of doing business, based on the belief that there are no limits to what PwC can achieve. The Firm performs services, cultivates relationships, and creates solutions that neither legacy organization could have done alone. The synergy created by the integration of so many top consulting minds fuels a dynamic environment, one in which our services, talent, and human capital generate an unparalleled fusion of experience. The result is the boundless knowledge that flows in the organization and between the professionals and their clients.

PwC is now the largest professional services organization, one of the largest recruiters of people, and one of the biggest investors in technology. But it knows that there needs to be more to a company than just physical size in a marketplace that no longer finds size that impressive. In launching PwC, the Firm has achieved something that others have failed to do. Its boldness, passion, and inspiration have created not just a partnership between two entities, but an integration of people, knowledge, and worlds.

PwC is now uniquely positioned to generate endless possibilities in the new millennium. By bringing together such a rich intersection of experience, expertise, and knowledge, the Firm has set a goal to synthesize this diversity and deliver its unparalleled value to its clients. Companies today need strategic counsel that will guide their decisions to help achieve the highest possible return on their investments, assets, and vision. The Firm recognizes that knowledge is a source of power and is greatest when shared. It grows by circulating among those who need it. What is known in PwC must be knowable across all worlds, wherever knowledge is needed. And it must be accessible at the precise point in time that it is needed, regardless of geographical boundaries. This is what underpins PwC's growth. PwC is peerless in its ability to access the precise expertise and knowledge and make it available to its clients exactly when needed.

▼ **Renee Long, Executive Receptionist.** Photo by Sam Jones.

As a company that leverages its global resources without diminishing its local market responsiveness, PwC fuses its resources to help clients solve problems and present them with new ideas and approaches. To create something that unique, PwC offers a broad array of services to ensure that each client can meet future challenges effectively. Rather than offering set products to solve problems, PwC draws from those services to weave a unique strategic plan developed exclusively for each client. It discovers the issues and challenges of each client situation and then adapts its teams to address client-specific needs. These services include Assurance Business Advisory Services (ABAS), Financial Advisory Services (FAS), Global Business Process Outsourcing, Global Human Resource Solutions (GHRS), Management Consulting Services (MCS), Tax and Legal Services (TLS) and Middle Market Advisory Services (MMAS). The industries PwC advises include the Services Industry, the Financial Services Industry, the Global Energy and Mining Industry, Consumer and Industrial Products (CIP), and Technology, Info/Comm and Entertainment (TICE).

All 155,000 people in the Firm's offices worldwide have been selected to work in these areas based on their knowledge, experience, and commitment to the organization. However, it is the Firm's shared vision that enables it to service the world's top-tier clients. PwC's offices in Europe, the Middle East, and Africa house nearly 66,000 employees, a figure just shy of the Americas' theater headcount of 67,000. For a technological company or industrial distributor, that kind of international presence demonstrates the Firm's ability to command resources and information by simply picking up the phone and contacting a neighboring office. PwC prides itself on its

making a profit but by considering how the Firm views the community and how PwC can contribute to its health and continued growth. Time and again, its professionals have assisted local organizations, agencies, and schools. Since 1990, PwC has maintained a partnership with Sutton Middle School, encouraging its professionals to participate in tutoring and mentoring programs designed for these students. In 1998, the Firm earned the City's "A+ Award," given by the Atlanta Partners for Education in cooperation with the Atlanta Chamber of Commerce. In the spring of 1998, several PwC professionals collaborated with the Firm's Marketing team to assist local Russian residents with their income tax forms. Another Atlanta partner in the fall of 1998 assembled employees from four offices to support the United Way. In the same year, another partner devoted his expertise to the city's arts by serving as president of the Atlanta Arts Festival. And then there was an Atlanta professional who initiated a Women's Forum to raise awareness for women's issues in the workplace, at home, and in their day-to-day lives.

Globalization, market demands, employment patterns, capital flows, and technology are dramatically reshaping our worlds. Given PwC's ability to harness these changes for the benefit of its clients, it is no wonder that the name PricewaterhouseCoopers has headlined so many publications. For the Firm, every engagement marks another opportunity to view the world of business from a different angle. Perhaps it has been the Firm's ability to wear so many different hats that has enabled it to set the stage for continued market expansion and leadership. It's the Firm's unwavering pursuit of achievement and the relationships that it cultivates with its customers that create value. ✿

◀ **Michael Flaharty, Partner Management Consulting Services.** Photo by Hannes Schmid.

critical mass of expertise, along with the ability to deploy that expertise quickly. And, on numerous occasions, many of its professionals have relocated to the region where the client resides, learning about the area and cultivating relationships with local community groups. This focus on knowledge sharing between PwC people and the many interconnected worlds of our knowledge economy positions the Firm to deliver value to its clients.

The merger gives the Firm unprecedented opportunities—the ability to harness the union of people, knowledge, and worlds. The Middle Market Advisory Services practice is staffed with dynamic people, many of whom were once private business owners and entrepreneurs before joining the Firm. One Atlanta partner, who primarily assists the Firm's Dutch and German clients, participates in different international organizations such as the American-Japanese Chamber of Commerce and the Finnish Chamber of Commerce. Out of the Atlanta office comes one of the nation's experts on the utilities industry. PwC's manufacturing practice has sought out some of the country's top names to serve the automotive, pharmaceutical, retail, industrial, and consumer products industries.

While all of PwC's practices have driven up shareholder value and created breakaway opportunities, it is the Firm's vision that enables it to create value for each customer. Through "best in class" service, value-based management, and resource synergy, clients discover a business world without boundaries or limits, where advancement and growth evolve out of the Firm's ability to generate progress in novel ways.

Sometimes that progress stems not from closing a deal or

▼ **Francesco Nagari, Manager Assurance and Business Advisory Services.** Photo by Michael O'Neill.

Kaiser Permanente

A partnership for quality, service, and affordability.

That's Kaiser Permanente's approach to health care in Metropolitan Atlanta, and it's been the health care company's legacy for more than 50 years nationally.

With some 8.6 million members, Kaiser Permanente has long been one of America's most successful and unique health plans. It has earned a similar reputation in Metropolitan Atlanta, where it began operating in 1985.

In less than 15 years, more than a quarter of a million people in the metro area have joined Kaiser Permanente. It counts among its diverse membership employees in major corporations, education, the service professions, government, health care, and small businesses. It also covers retirees, Medicare recipients, and individuals without group insurance. The one bond they share is a health plan that offers comprehensive benefits, convenience, and doctor-directed care.

To meet the needs of its members, Kaiser Permanente's goal is to provide high quality care and excellent service at an affordable price. Quality begins with the physicians. The Southeast Permanente Medical Group, Inc. (TSPMG) provides or arranges care for members in the 20-county service area. In addition, the medical group has developed relationships with a select number of doctors in the community who also see Kaiser Permanente members. All physicians are reviewed carefully and must meet high standards. The medical group places a premium on board certification and continuing education and improvement. More than 94

percent of TSPMG physicians are board certified. They graduated from or participated in residency programs at Emory University, the Medical College of Georgia, and a variety of other leading institutions.

Kaiser Permanente takes part in external quality reviews such as HEDIS measurements and the National Committee for Quality Assurance (NCQA) accreditation process. But the toughest quality reviewers are internal. The Medical Directors' Quality Review Committee examines all Kaiser Permanente medical groups and health plans annually using standards more stringent than those used by external agencies. These surveys support mutual problem solving and quality improvement. In addition, TSPMG physicians can share information, research results, and best practices with more than 9,000 Permanente physicians across the country.

In Atlanta, most care is provided in nine conveniently located medical centers where TSPMG physicians practice. Not only do these centers offer a pleasant, member-friendly atmosphere, but they also provide the convenience of "one-stop" shopping. Physicians' offices, lab, radiology, and pharmacy are all under one roof. And Kaiser Permanente's services aren't just nine to five. Members can also call a 24-hour nurse advice line and visit designated centers that provide nonemergency after-hours care. For emergency services and inpatient care, members have access to leading hospitals in the metro area. As for health plan coverage, Kaiser Permanente was a pioneer in offering comprehensive benefits ranging from preventive care, such as well-baby checkups and immunizations, to surgical and hospital care.

To keep the focus on service, Kaiser Permanente surveys patients about their care experience. Results factor into doctors' annual evaluations and into incentives for other staff as well. Members also get a service guarantee. If an individual is not pleased with service at a Kaiser Permanente medical center, the co-pay is refunded.

The Atlanta plan's laser-like focus on quality and service has been recognized in a number of national surveys and publications, and it consistently ranks first among health plans in Georgia.

▲ **With some 8.6 million members, Kaiser Permanente has long been one of America's most successful and unique health plans. It has earned a similar reputation in Metropolitan Atlanta, where it began operating in 1985.**

► **In Atlanta, most care is provided in nine conveniently located medical centers where TSPMG physicians practice. Not only do these centers offer a pleasant, member-friendly atmosphere, but they also provide the convenience of "one-stop" shopping.**

► **To meet the needs of its members, Kaiser Permanente's goal is to provide high quality care and excellent service at an affordable price. Quality begins with the physicians.**

This concept captured the imagination of industrialist Henry J. Kaiser, who had built the dam that fed the aqueduct. And in it, he saw an inventive way to keep his own workers healthy. When World War II broke out, Kaiser set out to build warships in the shipyard near San Francisco and asked Dr. Garfield to provide health care. The system worked so well that when the war was over, 10,000 people stayed on the plan, and Kaiser Permanente was born.

From its inception, Kaiser Permanente's goal was not only to treat sickness, but also to promote health. Dr. Garfield envisioned an affordable nonprofit health plan that focused on caring for its members. But like many start-ups, the visions of the founders soon clashed. The doctors, trained to take responsibility for patients, battled with Kaiser over who would make organizational decisions. The two sides came to a resolution that created a unique partnership. Physicians remained in charge of medical care, and businessmen would oversee health plan administration.

That legacy of partnership continues to guide the organization's work today with Kaiser as the health plan part of the equation and Permanente as the doctor side. It's a partnership that works for members because it's a partnership built on the principles of quality, service, and affordability in health care. ☙

The impressive story of Kaiser Permanente Georgia started in California, where the country's largest not-for-profit health plan was born. It began with Sidney Garfield, M.D., a doctor who practiced medicine in remote construction sites where there were no other sources of medical care. In the California desert, he built a small hospital to administer health care to over 5,000 aqueduct workers. And since he knew they might be reluctant to spend their hard-earned dollars on health care, he created one of the first modern prepaid health plans. For a dime a day workers got coverage for their health care needs.

▲ **In less than 15 years, more than a quarter of a million people in the metro area have joined Kaiser Permanente.**

◄ **The Atlanta plan's laser-like focus on quality and service has been recognized in a number of national surveys and publications, and it consistently ranks first among health plans in Georgia.**

◄ **From its inception, Kaiser Permanente's goal was not only to treat sickness, but also to promote health.**

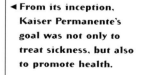

Alston & Bird LLP

A century ago, lawyers at the firm now known as Alston & Bird were using their legal expertise to help reorganize railroads and charter national banks. At the time, the firm was at the cutting edge of legal practice. Today, the firm is still at the cutting edge, forming global joint ventures and alliances, protecting the security of electronic commerce, handling the most important health care transactions in the country, negotiating licensing and advance pricing agreements, and facilitating the financing of manufacturing facilities in growing markets from Europe to Latin America to Asia.

The firm's 100 year-plus experience at the forefront

of business and technology has positioned it to provide its clients with the most technologically advanced and sophisticated legal capability possible. While Alston & Bird has been serving its clients and facilitating the growth of the Southeastern economy, the firm and its lawyers have committed themselves to enhancing the quality of life in the communities it serves.

A Broad Range of Legal Services

With more than 450 lawyers, Alston & Bird provides high quality, broad-based legal services that are recognized nationally. Thirty practice groups are closely coordinated to provide clients with a breadth and depth of legal expertise unequaled by other law firms. In the words of Ambassador Philip H. Alston Jr., "Commitment to our clients' best interests; insistence on a quality performance; thoroughness of preparation in all matters; unerring adherence to the highest ethical standards—all are qualities which we claim as cornerstones for the Firm."

Clients range from many of the largest corporations in the country to individuals starting their own businesses. The firm is committed to maintaining and expanding this diversified base of clients. Alston & Bird's capabilities allow it to respond to legal needs that are increasingly complex and require wide-ranging legal experience. And the firm's national reputation has helped it to attract and retain lawyers who are among the most talented and partners who are recognized as leaders in their practice areas.

Alston & Bird's practice groups are coordinated into four larger divisions. The Transactional Group includes Capital Markets,

Finance, Financial Services, Health Care-Corporate, Health Care-Regulatory, International, Public Finance, Real Estate, Technology, and Utilities. The Adversarial Group includes Antitrust and Investigations, Bankruptcy, Construction, Environmental and Land Use, Labor and Employment, Medical Products and Services, Securities Litigation, and Trial and Appellate Practice. The Intellectual Property Group includes IP Litigation, Patent Solicitation (including Biotechnology, Chemical, Electronics and Computer Technology, and Mechanical), Trademark and Copyright, and Transactional. The Tax Group includes ERISA Litigation, Estate Planning and Fiduciary, Employee Benefits and Executive Compensation, Exempt Organizations, Federal Income Tax, International Tax, and State and Local Tax. This focused grouping of practices provides seamless delivery of legal services to the client.

While remaining firmly rooted in its historical commitment to the Atlanta area, Alston & Bird has grown from a strong regional firm to a national and international firm. With offices in Atlanta, Washington, D.C., Charlotte, and the Research Triangle in Raleigh, North Carolina, it is uniquely positioned to take advantage of the area's strong appeal to global investors.

The geographical area served by the firm leads the country in the creation of high-technology jobs. Alston & Bird's recent

merger with the Southeast's premier intellectual property law firm of Bell Seltzer Park & Gibson has provided the firm with more Intellectual Property capacity than any law firm based in the Southeast and more patent capacity than any general practice firm based in the eastern United States.

▲ With more than 450 lawyers, Alston & Bird provides high quality, broad-based legal services that are recognized nationally.

▶ While Alston & Bird has been serving its clients and facilitating the growth of the Southeastern economy, the firm and its lawyers have committed themselves to enhancing the quality of life in the communities it serves.

Technology as the Currency of the Future

With the boom in new technology, Alston & Bird's Intellectual Property Group has become the largest in the Southeast and continues to grow. Clients include developers and suppliers of computer software, hardware, and services; Internet, cellular, paging, and personal communications providers; cable and broadcast companies; biotechnology enterprises; venture capitalists; and clients engaged in acquisitions or outsourcing of technology systems and services.

The high-technology focus is not limited to Alston & Bird's areas of practice or clients. "Alston & Bird views technology and information as the currency of the future," says Managing Partner

Ben F. Johnson III. "In line with this thinking, we have committed significant resources to the continuing development of our technological and information-processing capabilities to enhance the proficiency of our own operations and our ability to serve and interact with clients."

This marriage of technology and the practice of law has provided the firm's clients with more comprehensive, efficient, and customized representation. Alston & Bird's use of technology not only sets it apart from competitors, but also places it firmly in the lead. Indeed, *The American Lawyer's AmLaw Tech* ranked Alston & Bird tops among America's 100 largest law firms in terms of its "technological prowess." As it has for the last 100 years, the firm looks for opportunities to utilize cutting-edge technologies and applications to benefit and serve its clients.

Service to the Community

Alston & Bird, as a law firm, is committed to serving its profession and community and believes that lawyers have a role in creating a just society. Many lawyers and employees of the firm and their families help with significant contributions of time and leadership in serving the needs of important professional and community

activities. Of course, as with all relationships of this type, the benefit is mutual. By enriching and helping others, those who give are rewarded in ways that transcend material success.

The firm's lawyers have served as members of the Brown, Duke, Emory, Princeton, and Vanderbilt University Boards of Trustees; as Chairman of the American Symphony Orchestra League, Chairman of the Trust for Public Land, and President of The Association of American Rhodes Scholars; as Chairman of the Atlanta Symphony Orchestra, Alliance Theatre, and High Museum of Art Boards; and on the Board of the Metropolitan Opera of New York. Others serve as Little League coaches and volunteers helping to house and feed the homeless.

While the firm's commitment to serve arts, educational, and civic organizations is strong, none can be more illustrative than Alston & Bird's association with the Truancy Intervention Project (TIP), which the firm co-founded. TIP is a nationally recognized program that has represented more than 1,000 truant, at-risk young people in Juvenile Court, with better than a 70 percent success rate in returning these children to school without further Juvenile Court referrals. TIP was specifically mentioned as the reason why Alston & Bird recently was named as the only Atlanta-based law firm on *The American Lawyer's* Honor Roll of leading pro bono firms over the past five years.

Just as its commitment to helping the local economy has led to international engagements, the firm's commitment to community service has spread beyond national borders. Members of the firm have taken on voluntary advisory projects for the governments of Russia, the Ukraine, Croatia, and Moldova.

From Century to Century

In 1893, just before the dawn of the twentieth century, Judge Augustus Holmes Alston wrote to his son Robert C. Alston: "I know of no one who has a brighter future before them than you have. The world is open to you, and you can be anything that an honorable ambition may aspire to." That son went on to found the firm that is now Alston & Bird. With the twenty-first century now unfolding, those prophetic words are still a guiding principle for the future of the firm. ❧

▲ This marriage of technology and the practice of law has provided the firm's clients with more comprehensive, efficient, and customized representation. Alston & Bird's use of technology not only sets it apart from competitors, but also places it firmly in the lead.

◀ Alston & Bird is at the cutting edge, forming global joint ventures and alliances, protecting the security of electronic commerce, handling the most important health care transactions in the country, negotiating licensing and advance pricing agreements, and facilitating the financing of manufacturing facilities in growing markets from Europe to Latin America to Asia.

Akzo Nobel

Akzo Nobel, headquartered in Arnhem, The Netherlands, is a market-driven and technology-based company, serving customers throughout the world with health care products, coating chemicals, and fibers. The company employs 87,500 people and has activities in more than 60 countries. Consolidated sales for 1998 exceeded $12 billion.

Eka Chemicals

Eka Chemicals established its offices in Atlanta in 1983 and is the Pulp and Paper Chemicals Business Unit of Akzo Nobel. Eka Chemicals' North American headquarters are located in Marietta, Georgia. The main customer focus is in serving the pulp and paper industry, and other industries, with sodium chlorate (chlorine dioxide), hydrogen peroxide, and paper chemicals such as retention and sizing chemicals.

Eka Chemicals' leadership in pulp bleaching and paper chemicals technology is due to the innovative approaches the company has introduced to customers. The focus has been directed toward improving and minimizing the environmental impact of the pulp and paper mills, improving productivity, reducing manufacturing costs, and upgrading product quality in the pulp, paper, and board production. The acceptance of the technology-driven approaches by Eka Chemicals has made the company the largest supplier of sodium chlorate and hydrogen peroxide for pulp bleaching and the second largest supplier of performance paper chemicals worldwide.

Eka Chemicals invests almost 5 percent of revenues in Research and Development. This significant commitment to the future has resulted in many major breakthroughs over the

years. In the pulp bleaching area, Eka Chemicals has significantly contributed to new and better environmental technologies for both mechanical and chemical pulp. These technologies allow mills to replace chlorine gas with the combination of chlorine dioxide and hydrogen peroxide. Eka-patented technologies for generating chlorine dioxide from sodium chlorate have helped mills expand their capacity in a cost competitive and environmentally improved manner.

The company's patented Compozil™ technology allowed papermakers to increase productivity levels while enhancing the aesthetic appearance of the paper and improving production economics. The system enables the papermaker to maximize the substitution of virgin fiber with mineral fillers. One of the most recent breakthroughs has been the introduction of both odor and solvent free alkylketenedimer sizing agent (AKD). This technology complements the existing range of synthetic sizing agents, providing water resistance and enhanced printability. Eka Chemicals has also pioneered the development of a wet strength agent free of chlorinated by-products.

As further evidence of the company's commitment to the environment, incorporated within the business is the Recycled Fiber Chemicals division, which enables papermakers to recover fiber for reuse and send less paper to landfills.

Eka Chemicals' bleaching chemicals, sodium chlorate and hydrogen peroxide, require large investments in building world-class production facilities. Eka is the largest producer of sodium chlorate in North America with plants located in Columbus, Mississippi, and Moses Lake, Washington, in the United States, and Magog and Valleyfield in Quebec, Canada. It produces hydrogen peroxide at the Columbus, Mississippi, site. Eka Chemicals' paper chemicals manufacturing facilities are located in Toronto, Canada; Moses Lake, Washington; Augusta, Georgia; and South Gate, California.

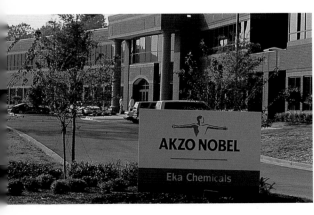

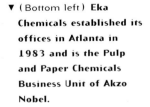

These are just a few of the significant contributions Eka Chemicals has made to the pulp and paper industry, allowing papermakers to supply quality products for a variety of uses at affordable prices in an environmentally friendly way. The company continues to work on more innovative and exciting projects within the pulp and paper area.

Based on the company's position on sodium chlorate and hydrogen peroxide, Eka Chemicals has developed additional usages for sodium chlorate, chlorine dioxide, hydrogen peroxide, and colloidal silica products outside the pulp and paper industry. This has allowed the company to get involved, contribute, and improve processes in the areas of electronic industry, water treatment, agricultural uses, textile bleaching, the food industry, and many others.

North American Car Refinishes

North American Car Refinishes' business unit, headquartered in Atlanta, manufactures and markets Sikkens-brand paint refinishing systems to high-quality collision repair shops throughout the United States, Canada, Mexico, and Central America.

These products include Colorbuild™ primer/surfacer primer/sealer, Autocryl® acrylic urethane, Autobase® basecoat, Autoclear® II clearcoat, and a low single VOC product offering that includes stage Autocoat® LV and Autoclear® Ultra LV.

For more than 200 years the Sikkens brand has helped body shops turn out one high-gloss, durable finish after another. Since Akzo Nobel brought the industry's first urethane technology to North America in 1983, Sikkens has been recognized as the collision repair industry's premium refinishing system.

Akzo Nobel's mission is to "be the best at enabling body shop profitability," and it's this dedication that allows the company to leverage its knowledge and add value beyond the basic paint product.

That's because today, the more business people know, the greater their chances of success. And nowhere is this more apparent than in the collision repair industry. Shop owners know it's not enough to be the best at repairing vehicles. They've got to be top-notch business people too.

Shop owners need well-trained, professional employees, an efficient and organized shop, clear-cut business and marketing plans, and extensive resources to back them up.

This is where Akzo Nobel comes in, because nobody knows more about enabling body shop profitability than Akzo Nobel. And when shop owners choose Sikkens-brand paint, they know every can comes backed with the know-how that only a company like Akzo Nobel can deliver.

In shop after shop, it has shown how the powerful combination of technically proficient sales representatives, technologically advanced Sikkens products, and Akzo Nobel's real-world training and support can help shop owners increase the number of cars they can repair each month, reduce errors, and decrease materials cost and usage.

From Sikkens-brand refinishing systems to Consultive Service such as the internationally acclaimed Acoat® selected business development program and its Facility Planning and Design Service, Akzo Nobel has helped shop owners increase the number of cars they can repair by as much as 30 percent.

And all Sikkens finishes deliver the kind of good looks and durability that has made the company the exclusive choice of NASCAR's premier racing teams.

What's more, the Sikkens Refinish Assurance Plan includes lifetime coverage that is valid from the date the repair is completed for as long as the customer owns the vehicle.

One of the unique benefits of the Sikkens Refinish Assurance Plan is that even if a customer has moved more than 100 miles away from the shop that originally handled the repair, the customer can still visit an approved Akzo Nobel collision repair center and have the lifetime warranty honored.

Akzo Nobel realizes that, on average, consumers are keeping their cars for five to seven years. This, combined with today's more mobile society, means there is a likelihood that a customer may be transferred to a new city for work, or be relocated after a repair is completed.

The Sikkens lifetime warranty will give consumers the peace of mind of knowing their vehicle is protected, no matter where they live. ❧

◀ **North American Car Refinishes' business unit, headquartered in Atlanta, manufactures and markets Sikkens-brand paint refinishing systems to high-quality collision repair shops throughout the United States, Canada, Mexico, and Central America.**

◀ **Antique pigment boxes.**

Trammell Crow

When Trammell Crow started out in the real estate business in 1948, he couldn't have imagined how far his dream would go. In those early days, Crow focused primarily on warehouse and office properties in the Dallas area. By the 1960s, he had expanded his efforts to include hotels and merchandise marts. In fact, he founded both the Dallas Market Center and the Wyndham Hotel chain.

Atlanta Roots

Crow first began working in the Atlanta market in 1968. His first Atlanta project was a warehouse for Mueller Brass, which he worked on together with Frank Carter. Together with Ewell Pope, they soon formed Crow, Pope & Carter, a partnership which quickly grew in Atlanta and throughout the Southeast.

With his timely entry into the Atlanta market, Crow found himself on the cusp of one of the greatest real estate booms of the twentieth century. To take advantage of these opportunities, Crow split his partnership with Carter and Pope. The two new companies were Crow, Carter and Associates, and Crow, Pope and Land, which included another well-known Atlanta real estate developer, A. J. Land.

In 1976, Trammell Crow Company was formalized and its Atlanta operation was established under the leadership of Don Childress. By this time, Trammell Crow had become the largest developer of commercial real estate in the entire country with an ownership interest in its developed properties.

Bracing for More Change

The biggest changes for Trammell Crow Company were still yet to come, though. In 1991, the company underwent a major transition—from a property owner/developer to a full-service real estate firm.

From 1991 through 1997 Trammell Crow Company grew its initial $18-million investment to a market valuation of more than $500 million.

In 1997, the company completed its initial public offering and was listed on the New York Stock Exchange (NYSE: TCC). The company's evolution then became fueled by an aggressive acquisition program that has enhanced the diversity of its development and management portfolio. In July of 1998, Trammell Crow Company acquired the assets of Faison & Associates Inc., a Charlotte, North Carolina-based commercial real estate firm specializing in the

development, leasing, and managing of office, industrial, and retail properties, for $39.1 million. The acquisition brought together a team of experts of outstanding ability in every area of commercial real estate. It significantly enhanced Trammell Crow Company's operations in Atlanta, increasing its portfolio from 12 million to over 26 million.

"The coming together of our two fine organizations here in Atlanta was a powerful combination," noted Pat Henry, Trammell Crow Company-Atlanta managing director. "It helped advance Trammell Crow's business plan to grow to the number one or number two service provider in each of our five core lines of business and to be the premier real estate services firm in each of the top U.S. markets. We came a long way toward achieving those goals by significantly adding to our leasing and property management business, dramatically expanding the size and scope of our retail business, and providing a deal pipeline and a new capital program for our development services business."

Added Trammell Crow Company-Atlanta Managing Director Morris Ewing: "We were also able to add a significant number of real estate owners as new customers and expand several key relationships in our third party management and leasing portfolio. The Atlanta office of Trammell Crow Company has set a new standard in terms of a service platform for our customers. The depth and experience of our Trammell Crow Company-Atlanta team is unsurpassed in this market."

Significant development projects in Atlanta with roots that touch preceding companies include Concourse, a mixed-use complex consisting of three mid-rise and two high-rise office buildings; the Westin Atlanta North Hotel; Concourse Athletic Club; KinderCare; and numerous other business-supportive amenities. Promenade, located in Midtown, was developed in 1991 for AT&T Southeast Regional Headquarters. The property consists of 786,840 square feet on 38 floors. Other projects include The Atlanta Galleria, the city's first suburban mixed-use development, with 1.9 million square feet of office space in five buildings; Stouffer's Waverly Hotel; and the Galleria specialty mall.

Today, the Trammell Crow Company is one of the largest providers of diversified commercial real estate services in the United States and Canada, managing more than 437 million square feet of property. Through its

150 offices, the company delivers a comprehensive range of services within its five core lines of business: property management and leasing, brokerage, infrastructure management, development and construction, and retail.

The relationships that the Trammell Crow Company has forged throughout its 50-plus-year history are extensive and include more than 550 investor/owner clients and 16,200 tenants nationwide. The longevity of many of these relationships has proved the company's ability to provide important competitive advantages, such as client focus, geographic scope balanced with local market knowledge and execution, applied technologies, and strong, committed personnel.

Trammell Crow Company is the largest commercial property manager in the United States and has held that position since 1989, based on National Real Estate Investors' 1998 Top Property Managers Survey. This same publication just named Trammell Crow Company the Best Office Management Company in the United States for 1998. The objective of the company's property management business is to enhance its owners' investment values by maintaining high occupancy levels and to lower operating costs by offering a wide range of management services.

The company has historically provided project leasing services for real estate owned by clients and managed by the company. In 1993 the company expanded its brokerage services to include tenant representation, investment sales, listings, and land sales. During the five years to 1998, the company's revenues from Brokerage Services increased by more than 93 percent and in 1997 reached $91.1 million, or 29 percent of the company's total revenue. Additionally, the company facilitated more than 6,000 sales and lease transactions in 1997 alone.

The company is also a leading provider of infrastructure management services to major corporations in the United States and Canada. It has maintained many long-term relationships with its corporate clients, often providing on-site personnel and integrating its accounting and management information systems with those of the client.

Since 1991, Trammell Crow Company has focused its efforts in the commercial real estate development business on providing development and construction services to third party build-to-suit customers and investors in office, industrial, and retail projects. While the company has decreased its economic exposure related to the cyclic nature of the real estate investment markets by shifting to a service-oriented approach, it has retained the capability to implement active and sizable development programs, not only on behalf of its clients, but also for its own account.

The Trammell Crow Company Retail Services business provides comprehensive real estate services to major retailers and retail real estate owners. In 1996 the company formed a subsidiary, Trammell Crow Retail Services, Inc. (TCRS), to consolidate the focus of the company's retail services management group and to take better advantage of market growth opportunities. By providing a full array of services through TCRS, the company is able to better serve its national retail customers, who demand specialized property and market knowledge.

Trammell Crow Company was founded on the belief that the highest priority is to serve the needs of the customer-owners, tenants, corporations, investors, and the communities in which they do business. Trammell Crow Company personnel identify with an owner's goals; they are conditioned to think from an owner's perspective. The company understands that real estate is more than a series of transactions; it is a business, and as such, shares many of the same day-to-day operational functions and challenges faced by clients. The carefully measured results of this approach clearly prove its effectiveness. Since 1948, the company has continued to build its reputation on that conviction.

Trammell Crow Company's formula for success is based on strong local market knowledge, a long-term commitment to deliver the highest standard of customer service, and the combined experience of its seasoned professionals. The formula has manifested itself in long-term profitable client relationships and industry awards. ◐

◄ John Whitaker is a managing director with Trammell Crow Company.

◄ A significant Trammell Crow Company development in Atlanta is Concourse, a mixed-use complex consisting of three mid-rise and two high-rise office buildings.

WORLDSPAN®

If the world seems smaller today, it's partly because of WORLDSPAN. As a leading travel technology developer and provider, WORLDSPAN helps millions of people travel the world every day.

WORLDSPAN is an electronic commerce company that provides high quality, efficient travel information services. For a multitude of customers, the company provides immediate and reliable access to all types of global travel services, including airlines, hotels, car rentals, rail and tour operators, entertainment, and more. Today, WORLDSPAN takes great pride in being one of the most customer-friendly, flexible, and responsive companies in the travel marketplace.

With its world headquarters in Atlanta and international headquarters in London, WORLDSPAN also has offices or representation in more than 60 countries. WORLDSPAN employs more than 3,100 people around the globe, with about 1,800 located in Atlanta. That makes WORLDSPAN Atlanta's third-largest computer service company and among the area's top 25 high-tech employers. WORLDSPAN is also one of Atlanta's top 20 privately held companies.

While enjoying a leadership position in the travel industry, WORLDSPAN is committed to enhancing the communities in which it operates. Charitable activities include the implementation of employee-sponsored mentoring and reading programs for local schools. Other projects in which WORLDSPAN and its employees are actively involved include Habitat for Humanity, the Susan G. Komen Race for the Cure, and the AIDS Walk, as well as Toys for Tots and Food Harvester campaigns. In addition, company-wide activities center on fund-raising for the March of Dimes and the United Way.

Backed by more than 200 years of combined travel experience, WORLDSPAN is owned by Atlanta-based Delta Air Lines, Northwest Airlines, and Trans World Airlines. In addition to providing services to its three airline owners, WORLDSPAN supplies a number of other airlines with various technology services, such as mainframe hosting, reservations and airport processing, and voice/data network communications.

Innovative Technological Solutions

WORLDSPAN goes well beyond the services offered by traditional travel technology providers. In the realm of travel automation, WORLDSPAN develops creative technological solutions to meet customer needs, provides superior customer service, and proactively anticipates change by providing its customers with the tools they need to stay ahead. Customers can plan their travel more easily with WORLDSPAN's fast and dependable access to the world of travel information. In addition, WORLDSPAN is responding to the rapidly changing travel marketplace and is at the forefront of leveraging Internet technology.

WORLDSPAN offers a broad array of Internet-based solutions, including products that meet the unique needs of travel agencies, corporate travel departments, and consumers. Also, WORLDSPAN is one of the top 10 electronic commerce development companies on the Internet. The company's strategy is to provide the right mix of tools to enable customers to thrive, while delivering broader ranges of support, increasing consultancy services, and providing Internet options.

The Value of Superior Processing

At the heart of the WORLDSPAN system is the state-of-the-art data processing center in Atlanta, which is about the size of two football fields. The mainframe computers have available disk storage of more than 3,000 gigabytes, all of which is essential to allowing the center to manage the massive amounts of information stored and processed daily.

For example, the data center handles an average of 2,100 messages per second and processes well over two billion messages each month. In the airline and travel industry, where rates, fares, and schedules change constantly, WORLDSPAN typically stores as many as 600 million U.S. and international air fares in its database. On an average day, the system handles more than 135,000 fare changes for the numerous airlines participating in the system.

The data center also contains travel records of more than 17 million individual passengers worldwide. But perhaps the most telling statistic about the WORLDSPAN data processing center is its unparalleled reliability and dependability. In spite of the massive amounts of information handled by the system, especially during peak periods, WORLDSPAN maintains virtually 100 percent availability, 24 hours a day, seven days a week.

Products and Services for Tomorrow's Needs

WORLDSPAN continues to evolve to be ready with the products customers demand. By working to understand its customers' needs, WORLDSPAN has taken the lead in providing a variety of sophisticated business management travel solutions. One example is WORLDSPAN TRIP MANAGER℠, an Internet-based, self-booking tool. TRIP MANAGER allows travelers to take travel planning into their own hands, while giving travel agencies and travel managers the means to administer and enforce corporate travel policy and to realize significant cost savings.

WORLDSPAN GO!℠ is another unique travel management tool. GO! facilitates comprehensive travel planning in one integrated system and enables travel agents to easily utilize information available on the Internet to check out a variety of topics of customer interest, such as local weather and traffic conditions, state department warnings, and maps. With WORLDSPAN GO!, travel agencies can better serve their customers without learning or managing new technology.

WORLDSPAN offers a wide assortment of customized training programs to help familiarize customers with products and to address particular needs and issues. The company is also developing highly advanced types of training technology, including distance learning programs.

WORLDSPAN recognizes the changing nature of its marketplace and is committed to continuing its leadership role in electronic commerce, delivering solutions for every travel challenge. Whether providing transaction processing for millions of travelers worldwide or data processing and network communications for some of the world's largest airlines, WORLDSPAN is the travel industry's preferred automation partner. For more information, visit the WORLDSPAN web site at www.worldspan.com. ❂

▲ WORLDSPAN was one of the first companies to leverage Internet technology and is now a leading processor of Internet travel bookings. The company web site is located at: www.worldspan.com. Design by Point of Vision.

◀ Through employee-driven programs, WORLDSPAN is actively involved in the communities in which it does business. Photo by Point of Vision.

AGL Resources Inc.

To help symbolize the company's devotion to its home city, Atlanta Gas Light Company and WSB Radio cosponsor the Shining Light Award. Joining Georgia Governor Zell Miller (second from right) at the dedication ceremony are (left to right) Walter M. Higgins, president and CEO of AGL Resources; Paula G. Rosput, president and COO of Atlanta Gas Light Company; and Scott Slade, morning anchor of WSB Radio. Photo by Warren Bond.

Walter M. Higgins is president and CEO of AGL Resources. Photo by Gittings.

Gas utilities are a given in postmodern life—gas is simply an expected service and a reliable servant. Though AGL Resources, an Atlanta-based, New York Stock Exchange-listed utility holding company, has recorded revenues in excess of $1.3 billion and total assets of over $2.1 billion, there was a day in Atlanta when the flicker of gas light wasn't much more than a spark of hope.

In the early 1850s, Atlanta was a frontier town of about 3,000 people. The typical home was primitive by comparison to today's residential standard. It had no central heat, no phone, no lights, no indoor plumbing, no refrigeration—not even an icebox. There were no water heaters and few tubs. Not that many minded the lack of tubs and heated water; bathing was largely considered unhealthy at the time, and it was even banned or restricted in many other U.S. cities.

Savannah was the hub of civilization in Georgia then, and Atlanta was largely the end of the line—the railroad line, that is. In its earliest days, the city was a mere spot in the Georgia clay called Terminus, as it was quite literally the southern terminal of the new Western & Atlantic Railroad. In 1843, a town was shaped there and renamed Marthasville. As the town grew, it gradually became known as Atlanta—a shortening of the railroad's name, and incorporated in December 1847.

City council and citizens struggled with the issues of the time; they solved some, gave up on others, and tabled more than a few. Among the issues set aside for another day was the lack of street lighting. Moving about Atlanta after dark was a hazardous affair; muggings and accidents were frequent nighttime scares.

An 1852 editorial from the *Atlanta Intelligencer* described the treacherous nightscape as being peppered with pits, some as large as 15 by 18 feet, some larger, which were most suitable for ruining evening attire, trapping as many as five persons at a time, and even killing a man who broke his neck in a fall. Occasionally pits were covered over, usually after a particularly tragic mishap, but most of the holes would then reappear shortly thereafter. There were a few

streetlights, fueled by oil at the expense of shopkeepers, but they were too few, too dim, and largely useless in illuminating the pitfalls in Atlanta's streets.

Atlanta city councilmen were aware of gas lighting and gasworks, but their interest was cautious and measured. Even though Athens, Augusta, Macon, and Savannah had gas service in place already, Atlanta had neither the capital nor the knowledge to follow suit. The matter became a frequent subject of small talk but of little consequence in the day-to-day city planning. Until one day in 1855, when William Helme of Philadelphia, and the builder of Augusta's gas plant, approached the council with plans to build another in Atlanta.

Helme's proposal was accepted after a council committee studied the details and inquired of citizens their interest in the new-fangled convenience. The deal was that Helme, within 10 short months, would erect a coal-gas plant and lay at least three miles of pipe; the city would contract to erect and use at least 50 streetlights and pay $30 a year for the gas to light them; the cost of the system would be $50,000; and the city would become a stockholder to the extent of $20,000. Additionally, Helme and the council agreed to work together to get the new company incorporated, and the council further agreed to give the gas company the exclusive privilege of lighting the city for 50 years.

The Atlanta Gas Light Company was duly incorporated on February 16, 1856, making the company the oldest corporation in Atlanta and in the state.

As the work on the new gas plant and lamp installation neared completion, someone suggested an unveiling of sorts on Christmas. Plans were made accordingly, and on December 25, 1855, city folks gathered around to see Atlanta's first gas light turned on. Since the unveiling occurred seven weeks before the incorporation became official, the company essentially celebrates two birthdays: December 25, 1855, and February 16, 1856. The remaining streetlights were functional and in use within the first months of 1856.

Even with the excitement surrounding such a modern event, city council began to doubt the value of its gas company stock and decided to sell one-half of it to liquidate outstanding city debts. But by August of the same year, a resolution was passed rescinding the sale. By keeping the faith, the city received a total return of $2,280 the first year, a net gain of $821 after the cost for the streetlamps. Shortly thereafter, the city ordered the installation of 25 more gas lamps.

Atlanta Gas Light Company (AGLC) is a subsidiary of AGL Resources and has grown to serve nearly 1.5 million residential, commercial, and industrial customers in 243 communities

throughout Georgia and southeastern Tennessee. AGLC is the eighth largest natural gas distribution utility in the United States, and the largest in the Southeast with a historically higher growth rate than the industry average.

At the cusp of the new millennium, AGL Resources has interests in nonregulated businesses in retail and wholesale natural gas, electricity and propane marketing, energy-related consumer products and services, and gas supply services. Deregulation of gas utilities, while posing one of the more challenging scenarios for the 143-plus-year-old company, also poses interesting possibilities for a company that from its very beginning lit the way for a brighter and more prosperous Atlanta. ◐

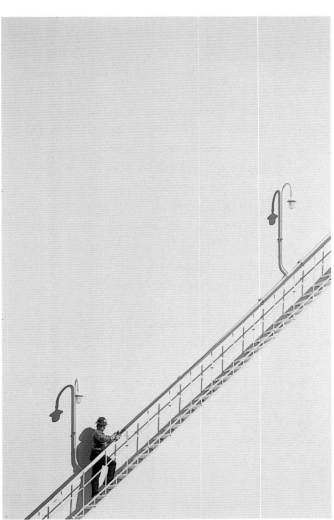

▲ Atlanta Gas Light Company is the fastest growing natural gas distribution company in the country outside California. Rolls of plastic pipe are needed to bring natural gas to more than 30,000 new customers each year. Photo by Warren Bond.

◄ Atlanta Gas Light Company's four liquefied natural gas plants, including this one in Riverdale, Georgia, provide the gas storage capability to ensure service to 1.5 million customers even on the coldest days of the year. Photo by Warren Bond.

Troutman Sanders LLP

Troutman Sanders is one of Atlanta's oldest and largest law firms. Tracing its origin to 1897, the firm touts a long and fruitful history in case resolutions, client relationships, and civic involvements. Its diverse clientele runs the gamut from Fortune 500 companies, small businesses, nonprofits, and multinational corporations to federal and state agencies and foreign governments.

Troutman Sanders is a full-service law firm engaged in virtually every aspect of civil and commercial law. Its reputation and stability are evidenced by long-standing relationships with many major business organizations. The firm's clients are active in a broad range of industries, such as telecommunications, banking and financial services, computer hardware and software, energy services, transportation, food services, health care, entertainment and sports, lodging, and real estate. Its lawyers have represented clients in transactions around the world, and the firm's practice reflects the broad reach and complex concerns of businesses operating in a global economy.

Names like AGCO Corporation, Associates First Capital Corporation, AT&T, Bank of America, Bank of Tokyo, Chick-fil-A, CNN, Columbia/HCA Hospitals, Cousins Properties, Deuteron GmbH, First Union, Georgia-Pacific, Holiday Inn, Johnson & Johnson, McDonalds, Siemens Corporation, Southern Company, The Sumitomo Bank, Time Warner, UPS, The Zale Corporation, and dozens of others rely on Troutman Sanders for legal services. The firm's mission is to provide all its clients with state-of-the-art services that are responsive to the clients' legal needs and rendered in an efficient, cost-effective, and timely manner.

Troutman Sanders has formed more than 25 interdisciplinary practice groups to better serve its clients. With offices in Atlanta, Washington, D.C., and Hong Kong, the firm offers clients a unique perspective on the legal and policy processes affecting almost every aspect of business.

► **Bank of America Plaza, Atlanta, Georgia.**

One of the more notable aspects of Troutman Sanders is the Media and Entertainment Practice Group. The firm has over 30 years of experience in representing sports, media, and entertainment clients, and is uniquely positioned to assist individuals and businesses in this field because of the depth and breadth of its expertise. From copyright and trademark to antitrust, and from stadium development issues to the First Amendment, Troutman Sanders provides a full range of legal services. Representative clients of the group include Time Warner, Paramount Pictures, Turner Broadcasting, World Championship Wrestling, PGA Tour, Goodwill Games, Sony Music Entertainment, Twentieth Century Fox, Atlanta Hawks, Carmike Cinemas, CNN, and the Atlanta National League Baseball Club.

Intellectual Property is another interesting practice group of the firm. In today's increasingly service-oriented, high-tech society, products are coming more frequently from human minds than human hands. Intellectual properties appear in forms as varied as inventions, web sites, manuscripts, blueprints, mailing lists, films, advertisements, slogans, computer programs, music, art, designs of every kind, and even manufacturing techniques. All of these are ideas in a commercial form. With each comes a new set of obstacles and opportunities and an increasing need to protect and sell or license at the same time. Often intellectual property is more valuable in a corporate transaction than the physical plant. With the coming of a new millennium, intellectual property is expected to increase in value, and intellectual capital to become the most sought-after in the world.

Troutman Sanders represents many clients, both large and small, in intellectual property rights and trade. A representative client list includes AT&T, Chateau Elan, Chick-fil-A, Dun & Bradstreet Software, Fuji Development, Georgia Governor's Commission on Privatization, Gulfstream Aerospace Corporation, IBM, Rheem Manufacturing, Science Applications International Corporation, Southern Company, and dozens of others.

A distinguishing aspect of Troutman Sanders is the strength and global nature of its Project Development and Finance practice. Troutman Sanders has represented clients in the electric power industry since the 1920s and has been actively involved in the independent power industry since the early 1980s. During this time, Troutman Sanders has assisted clients in acquisitions and development of power plants and electric utility systems in the United States and in over 30 foreign countries, including Argentina, The Bahamas, Brazil, Chile, Mexico, Nicaragua, Puerto Rico, Trinidad and Tobago, Venezuela, Australia, Bangladesh, China, Indonesia, Pakistan, Philippines, South Korea, Taiwan, South Africa, Austria, Croatia, Czech Republic, Hungary, Israel, Italy, Netherlands, Spain, Turkey, and the United Kingdom. Troutman Sanders' experience in the electric power industry enables it to provide practical and creative advice to clients engaged in independent power project development, electricity privatization, mergers and acquisitions, and project and corporate financing.

The firm is well versed in cyberspace and virtual reality issues and practices. The Electronic Commerce practice has already broken new and important ground and is hard at work helping establish protocols and protection for emerging electronic commerce from e-cash to e-malls. In fact, Troutman Sanders helped clients break new ground from the beginning—from the world's first satellite superstation, to its first continuous television news network, to its first Internet business park, to its first consumer-driven infomediary business, to its first coalition to promote good public policy for e-commerce.

Other areas of the firm's practice that are equally vital to the livelihood of businesses worldwide include the Complex Litigation Practice Group, the Health Care Practice Group, the Corporate and Banking Practice Group, the Federal Regulatory Practice Group, the International Practice Group, the Labor and Employment Practice Group, the Environmental Practice Group, the Mergers, Acquisitions, and Corporate Finance Practice Group, the Torts and Products Liability Practice Group, and the Real Estate Leasing and Development Practice Group. Though organized practice groups

represent specialty practitioners, the reality of business today demands a blend of these experts to effectively deal with the issues. Gone forever are the days of the general practice lawyer; these are the days of legal teams whose strength comes from the specialty expertise provided by each member. Troutman Sanders' legal teams are customized to precisely fit each client's particular situation.

Troutman Sanders is not only known for its dedication to clients, but also for its commitment to the communities in which the firm's staff and attorneys live and work. Members of the firm are active in civic, charitable, religious, educational, professional, international, governmental, and arts-related organizations.

Troutman Sanders is a firm truly defined by its progressive approach to understanding its clients' business and legal challenges, and its proactive focus on developing successful solutions. It is an approach that has earned the firm long-standing client relationships and the respect of its peers. ❦

▲ Two Exchange Square, Hong Kong.

◄ Franklin Square, Washington, D.C.

Jones, Day, Reavis & Pogue

Tracing its origins to 1893, Jones, Day, Reavis & Pogue has long been one of the world's largest and most prestigious law firms, with more than 1,200 lawyers resident in 22 locations in major centers of business and finance around the globe. As one of the most geographically diverse legal providers in the world, it is not surprising that Jones Day has a major presence in the city of Atlanta, the undisputed center for international business and finance in the southeastern United States.

Jones Day's Atlanta office was opened in 1989 through a merger with the 100-year-old Atlanta law firm of Hansell & Post, then one of the leading law firms of the region. Jones Day's Atlanta office now includes approximately 100 lawyers, supported by a highly qualified staff and state-of-the-art communication and computer systems. As an integral part of an international law firm that spans four continents and has locations in 10 major U.S. cities, Jones Day's Atlanta office offers valuable experience in local and regional legal matters, as well as issues of national and international scope. The Firm's fully integrated structure and management focus allow the experience of the entire Firm to bear on matters originating in any office, facilitate the exchange of information on new developments in the law, and allow for the efficient coordination of work within each practice area on a cost-effective basis.

The Atlanta office has substantial practice capability in each of the Firm's primary practice groups, including banking and finance,

corporate, environmental, general litigation, health care, intellectual property, international, labor and employment, product liability and regulation, real estate, securities, taxation, and technology. It is proud to offer broad coverage and sophisticated counsel to Atlanta's corporate leaders of today—and tomorrow.

Although the Firm's perspective is international, the Atlanta office takes seriously its civic responsibility and commitment to the metro Atlanta area. The Atlanta office encourages all of its lawyers to engage actively in a broad array of activities essential to the continued development of Atlanta, not only as a truly international city, but also as a highly desirable place for new businesses to locate and for their personnel to live and raise their families.

Jones Day is particularly proud of its long-standing role as general counsel to the Woodruff Arts Center, the primary Atlanta umbrella arts organization, which includes the Atlanta Symphony Orchestra, the High Museum, the Alliance Theatre Company, and the Atlanta College of Art. Jones Day attorneys are also involved at significant leadership levels in many other important Atlanta charitable, educational, and civic organizations, as diverse as the Atlanta Botanical Gardens, the Atlanta History Center, the Atlanta International School, SciTrek Museum, Central Atlanta Progress, Boy Scouts of America, Girl Scouts of America, the Metro Atlanta Chamber of Commerce, the Salvation Army, and the World Trade Club.

In the United States, in addition to the Atlanta office, Jones

▼ Jones Day's Atlanta office now includes approximately 100 lawyers, supported by a highly qualified staff and state-of-the-art communication and computer systems.

Day maintains offices in Chicago, Cleveland, Columbus, Dallas, Irvine, Los Angeles, New York, Pittsburgh, and Washington, D.C. The Firm acts as principal outside counsel to, or provides significant legal representation for, approximately one half of the *Fortune* 500 companies, as well as to a wide variety of other entities, including privately held companies, financial institutions, investment firms, health care providers, retail chains, foundations, educational institutions, and individuals. Independent surveys repeatedly identify Jones Day as one of the law firms most frequently engaged by U.S. corporations, and many of the Firm's lawyers have achieved national recognition in their disciplines.

The Firm's international practice is significant and growing. In addition to representing a large number of its United States-based clients in international matters, Jones Day represents many major companies based in Eastern and Western Europe, the Middle East, Asia, and Latin America. Jones Day maintains a significant presence in the principal legal and regulatory capitals of the world. In Europe, more than 100 lawyers are based in Brussels, Frankfurt, Geneva, London, and Paris. In Asia, more than 50 lawyers are resident in Hong Kong, New Delhi (through Pathak & Associates, an associated firm), Shanghai, Sydney, Taipei, and Tokyo. The Firm's Middle East office is in Riyadh. The Jones Day Latin America practice team is composed of approximately 20 lawyers based in the New York Office and in other significant financial centers, including Atlanta.

The Firm's international practice focuses primarily on mergers and acquisitions, joint ventures, and other investment transactions; securities and financial matters; tax, labor, environmental, competition, and other significant regulatory matters; and international litigation and arbitration. The Firm's international practice balances U.S. lawyers posted outside the United States and foreign lawyers experienced in representing U.S.-based clients. Jones Day attorneys are licensed in most significant jurisdictions in Europe and Asia, and many are fluent in virtually all principal languages relevant to international business.

Jones Day is an integrated partnership that operates as one firm worldwide. All Jones Day locations are fully integrated into the Firm's practice structure, which facilitates client access to the experience and skills of the Firm's lawyers resident throughout the world. All personnel, locations, and practice groups are linked by state-of-the-art communications systems, shared databases, and word processing systems. The Jones Day computer network is one of the largest law firm automation systems. All locations are supported by local area networks, many of which use high-speed optical cabling. The local area networks are linked together in a global wide area network, which offers instantaneous communications and creates a worldwide legal resource. The Firm's commitment to high-tech advantages for its clients has been nationally recognized, including by *PC Week* magazine, which ranked Jones Day 14th—and the only law firm in the top 50—in its first-ever "Fast-Track 500," an exclusive list of trend-setting companies that are the first to adopt the newest technologies. The Firm's continuous investment in technology reflects its determination to build and maintain a global legal resource offering the highest quality legal service, ensuring the security of private information, and matching clients' most sophisticated needs and capabilities.

As a worldwide organization, Jones Day faces the same economic and political realities that its clients face: the globalization of the world's capital markets and industries and the consolidation of mature business—in centers of business and finance throughout the world.

As Atlanta progresses in the new millennium, Jones Day looks forward to continuing to play a significant role in the future of Atlanta and Atlanta's business and commerce, consistent with the Atlanta office's motto: "At home in Atlanta and around the world." ❧

◄ **The Atlanta office offers broad coverage and sophisticated counsel to Atlanta's corporate leaders of today—and tomorrow.**

◄ **As an integral part of an international law firm that spans four continents and has locations in 10 major U.S. cities, Jones Day's Atlanta office offers valuable experience in local and regional legal matters, as well as issues of national and international scope.**

Georgia-Pacific Corporation

▲ Company headquarters moved to Atlanta in 1982. The architecturally distinctive Georgia-Pacific Center at 133 Peachtree Street has become a modern-day landmark in Atlanta.

▶ Georgia-Pacific's separate operating group, The Timber Company, owns and manages more than 5 million acres of timberland in the United States, making it the third-largest private landowner in the United States.

Twenty-four-year-old Owen Cheatham was a salesman and a dreamer. As the world marveled at Lindbergh's triumphant transatlantic flight and Babe Ruth's 60 home runs, Owen believed anything was possible. He promptly borrowed $6,000 to add to the $6,000 he had, and placed his bet on a future in trees. He began with a simple lumberyard in Augusta, Georgia. The year was 1927.

Cheatham's enterprise back then was called the Georgia Hardwood Lumber Company; now it is the Georgia-Pacific Corporation. It began as a lumber wholesaler, but today is one of the world's largest forest products companies, producing and distributing building products, pulp, paper, packaging, and chemicals.

The company's products are among the leaders in their categories and touch millions of people every day.

For example, Georgia-Pacific is the United States' largest manufacturer of structural wood panels—chiefly plywood and oriented strand board used in home construction. The company also is renowned for its production and quality in other building products such as lumber and wood-based products like particleboard, hardboard, and medium-density fiberboard, used in a variety of applications by ready-to-assemble furniture makers, the manufactured housing industry, and even Georgia-Pacific's own decorative paneling plants.

The company dramatically expanded its gypsum products manufacturing in the mid-1990s, and has become the country's second-largest producer of gypsum products, such as gypsum wallboard, joint compound, and industrial plaster.

Georgia-Pacific's separate operating group, The Timber Company, owns and manages more than 5 million acres of timberland in North America, making it the third-largest private landowner in the United States.

The company's chemical division is the leading supplier of resins and adhesives used in wood products manufacturing, as well as chemicals used in papermaking.

The company's distribution division is among the leading wholesale building materials distribution systems in the United States. More than 100,000 different items, only some of which are produced by the company, are delivered every day to Georgia-Pacific customers: lumber dealers, home improvement centers, commercial contractors, and industrial manufacturers.

If it is in a box, chances are good that Georgia-Pacific products are involved. Besides being the second-largest producer of containerboard in the United States, the company is one of the top makers of kraft paper, bleached paperboard, and corrugated containers and packaging. The company's packaging plants produce standard corrugated containers, boxes, and bulk bins, as well as water-resistant packaging, high-finish and preprinted packaging for displays, and other specialty packaged products.

As the second-largest producer of communication papers in the United States, the company makes printing, office, premium text, cover, and writing papers distributed throughout the world. Commercial printers use Georgia-Pacific printing papers in a variety of colors, textures, and weights.

Georgia-Pacific is also one of the nation's major suppliers of consumer paper products—paper towels, napkins, and bath tissue—under the brand names Angel Soft, Sparkle, Coronet, and MD. But the company also produces these types of paper products for the industrial, food service, office, hotel, and hospital markets.

All papermaking, however, starts with pulp, and Georgia-Pacific is a worldwide seller of this product, too. The company manufactures a variety of pulps used in a multitude of paper grades and types, and even in disposable diapers and sanitary products.

In 1999, Georgia-Pacific acquired Unisource Worldwide, one of North America's largest marketers and distributors of printing and imaging paper and supply systems.

All told, the company employs more than 50,000 people and operates more than 500 plants, mills, distribution centers, and facilities throughout the nation.

After its founding in Augusta, Georgia, company headquarters moved to Olympia, Washington, in 1953 and then to Portland, Oregon, in 1954, and finally to Atlanta in 1982. The architecturally distinctive Georgia-Pacific Center at 133 Peachtree Street has become a modern-day landmark in Atlanta. At the time the company moved into its new headquarters, its sales were about $5 billion, and Atlanta had a population of around two million people. Since then, the company's annual sales have climbed above $20 billion and Atlanta's census to nearly three million.

The company chose Atlanta because of the city's excellent quality of life, reliable transportation network, its probusiness environment, the South's abundant and available timber supply, and the quality of the available workforce.

Georgia-Pacific, often called "the growth company," has continued to grow since its headquarters relocated to Atlanta. In 1990, the company acquired the assets of Great Northern Nekoosa Corp., officially making Georgia-Pacific one of the world's largest pulp

and paper manufacturers. Led by current Chairman and Chief Executive Officer A.D. "Pete" Correll, the employees at Georgia-Pacific are guided by a burning desire to be the best at everything the manufacturing giant does. Being the best, according to their vision, means being the low-cost producer of the highest quality forest products available, without compromising employee safety, environmental protection, or resource conservation.

The more than 4,500 people employed by Georgia-Pacific in metro Atlanta alone are excellent examples of the company's collective and individual commitment to helping communities across the nation. In fact, local community involvement and contributions are a hallmark of Georgia-Pacific. The company actively encourages employees to participate and often contributes goods, services, and money to many worthy causes.

Since 1954, the Georgia-Pacific Foundation has awarded more than $10 million in college scholarships nationally; Atlanta students often qualify. The firm's matching gift program lends financial support to educational and medical institutions, cultural organizations, and public television and radio. In addition to being one of Atlanta's leading United Way supporters and top annual contributors, the company and its employees have a history of providing paper and building products and assistance to those in need in the wake of natural disasters. Atlanta's cultural community also benefits from the company's presence in Atlanta—corporate headquarters is the site of the High Museum of Folk Art and Photography.

The company has donated money, as well as thousands of trees, to support green spaces in and around metro Atlanta, including Centennial Olympic Park, Emory University's Hahn Woods, and the U.S. Forest Services Urban Treehouse. Employees and the company are dedicated to these and other ongoing, long-term projects in the city.

Since its arrival in the city, Georgia-Pacific has dedicated itself to adding more than just another beautiful structure to the downtown skyline. From its many efforts, the company has created an indelible impression on Atlanta, as the city has also made upon the company. Georgia-Pacific is committed to continuing a strong and beneficial relationship with its headquarters community. ❧

◄ Georgia-Pacific Corporation began as a lumber wholesaler, but today is one of the world's largest forest products companies, producing and distributing building products, pulp, paper, packaging, and related chemicals.

◄ Georgia-Pacific is the United States' largest manufacturer of structural wood panels—chiefly plywood and oriented strand board used in home construction.

125

Equifax

► (Left to right) **Lee A. Kennedy, Equifax President and Chief Operating Officer, and Thomas F. Chapman, Equifax Chairman and Chief Executive Officer.**

Equifax is a worldwide leader in shaping global commerce, providing information management, transaction processing, and knowledge-based services that bring buyers and sellers together around the globe. For over 100 years, Equifax has facilitated commerce, expanding locally, then nationally, and now to an international corporation operating in 17 countries and partnering with customers in almost 50.

The company provides knowledge-based information and solutions to such industries as finance, banking, retail, credit and debit card, healthcare, telecommunications, utilities, and automotive—and to the government. Equifax facilitates the transaction process for its customers by providing services and systems that help grant credit, authorize and process credit card and check transactions, manage receivables, predict consumer behavior, market products, manage risk, authenticate identity, and enhance the privacy and security of transactions over the Internet and other networks.

Equifax is a leader in the consumer financial information sector in the U.S. and a leading provider of commercial and consumer information in Canada, Europe, and Latin America. The company also leads in full-service card processing for independent banks and credit unions in the U.S., and further extends its global reach with

► **Global data transmission is monitored around the clock in the Equifax Technology Command Center.**

card processing operations in Brazil, the U.K., and India. Equifax also has leading check verification services in North America, Europe, Australia, and New Zealand. Through innovative, effective product and service offerings that include risk management, modeling, software, analytics, and consulting, Equifax brings buyers and sellers around the world together in millions of transactions that span the globe.

The company that is Equifax today began as an idea shared by brothers Cator and Guy Woolford in Atlanta over 100 years ago. As innovative, young businessmen in a city rebuilding itself with unparalleled energy, they knew the retail marketplace was rapidly expanding beyond the boundaries of local, "done-on-a-handshake" transactions. There was a real demand for accurate information on the paying habits of retail store customers, and the brothers determined to fill that demand. They persevered through a slow first year, and their efforts paid off as the business began to grow. Theirs was a business on the move.

Equifax has been on the move ever since. Publicly owned since 1965, the company is listed on the New York Stock Exchange and is a member of the S&P 500 Index; it has paid cash dividends for more than 85 consecutive years. Equifax is, and always has been, focused on creating shareholder value through superior financial performance. Since 1992, the company has relied on a performance measurement system of economic value added. This tool has served as a financial discipline for Equifax's strategic planning process and acquisition and investment analysis, enabling the company to focus on three key goals: profitable revenue growth, margin improvement, and efficient use of capital. Additionally, a company-wide program to increase employee stock ownership has

enhanced this singular focus on creating shareholder value. The result is a dedicated team of professionals who behave as if they owned the company—because they do.

Equifax operates on another key philosophy: that a company is only as strong as its people and the communities it serves. This philosophy is borne out by the company's Youth Enlightenment Series (YES®) program, a unique, credit education program for U.S. teenagers, and by Equifax's extensive involvement in community service projects wherever the company operates around the world.

Poised to begin another century, Equifax is once again pioneering in a new kind of business: the world of electronic commerce. As business shifts to cyberspace, Equifax will be there with innovative solutions, state-of-the-art technology, and a reputation built on a century of trust—bringing buyers and sellers together in the marketplace of the future. The company has changed the shape of global commerce for 100 years, and stands ready to do so in the next century and beyond. ◐

◄ The Gateway to Midtown: Equifax's new corporate headquarters in Atlanta.

◄ Equifax's J.V. White Technology Center near Atlanta.

BellSouth Corporation

▲ **BellSouth's corporate headquarters is located in midtown Atlanta.**

▶ **More than five million customers subscribe to BellSouth's wireless services, making it one of the nation's largest providers.**

A Fortune 100 company, BellSouth is a $24-billion international communications company, headquartered in Atlanta, that provides telecommunications, wireless communications, cable and digital TV, directory advertising and publishing, and Internet and data services to nearly 34 million customers in 19 countries worldwide.

With more than $39 billion in assets, BellSouth companies operate throughout the United States and in a number of countries in Latin America, Europe, and Asia/Pacific. With 94,000 employees, the company has more than 24 million local telephone service customers in the Southeast U.S., more than 5 million domestic wireless customers, and nearly 5 million international wireless customers. In fact, BellSouth serves the most wireless-intensive region in the U.S., according to a study released in 1998 by Scarborough Research. Based on the percentage of adults in households with wireless phones, 10 of the top 20 wireless markets are in BellSouth's primary service territory.

Technology continues to change the way people live, work, and communicate. As one of the largest telecommunications providers in the world, BellSouth is at the heart of this communications revolution. The company has built a world-class network that includes more than 2.6 million miles of optical fiber and 10,000 high-speed, advanced fiber-optic rings (SONET) throughout its region.

BellSouth's largest subsidiary, BellSouth Telecommunications, serves local, residential, and business customers in nine Southern states, including Alabama, Florida, Georgia, Kentucky, Louisiana, Mississippi, North Carolina, South Carolina, and Tennessee. Besides local telephone service, other business services include high-speed voice and data connections, networking, and Managed Network Solutions. Residential products include local telephone service as well as MemoryCall voice messaging service, CallerID,

BusyConnect, and other calling features.

BellSouth's domestic wireless business now includes nearly 60 million POPs (potential customers), and the company's state-of-the-art networks provide the highest quality service with a wide array of advanced products and services. BellSouth now offers digital service to substantially all of its wireless markets. In addition, BellSouth's Wireless Data subsidiary delivers interactive paging and other two-way data communications to more than 93 percent of the urban business population in 266 U.S. metropolitan areas.

In international markets, BellSouth has a footprint that covers more than 231 million POPs with a $2-billion revenue stream in 1998. Last year, BellSouth International, the leading provider of wireless services in Latin America, grew its international customer base by more than 82 percent.

In addition, BellSouth operates one of the world's leading directory advertising and publishing companies that publishes more than 1,000 directories and also offers The <u>REAL</u> Yellow Pages ONLINE and the At Hand Network Yellow Pages on the Internet.

The company continues to grow in other communications areas as well. BellSouth Entertainment, another subsidiary based in Atlanta, is now offering wired and wireless analog and digital TV services in 11 markets throughout the Southeast. BellSouth.net is one of the fastest growing Internet service providers in the country and will have more than 800,000 customers in the U.S. alone by the year 2000.

The company's strong commitment to customer service is widely recognized. For the fourth year in a row, JD Power and Associates named BellSouth the top local communications company. And BellSouth.net earned multiple A+ ratings from April through July 1999 by Inverse Network Technology, a leading independent firm that measures the performance and reliability of large Internet providers nationwide.

Given the success of the company's operations, it is no surprise that BellSouth has delivered superior financial returns as well. Since

BellSouth enjoys a rich tradition of community service. In its 15 years of service, the company and its employees have contributed more than $2 billion to charitable and other organizations in its communities. The investment includes nearly $2 billion in volunteer time (based on the Points of Light Foundation valuation formula); $300 million in monetary contributions from the company, its subsidiaries, matching employee gifts, and the BellSouth Pioneers; and $35 million made in education grants through the BellSouth Foundation.

BellSouth strives to help improve the communities where it operates. It further demonstrated its commitment to Atlanta earlier this year with the announcement of its decision to consolidate most of its local operations into three business centers located near rapid transit stations (MARTA). The company is consolidating more than 70 offices into the new office complexes, each

◄ BellSouth is offering new services like digital wireless TV in Atlanta and other markets in the South.

the company's first day of trading on November 21, 1983, BellSouth shareholders have enjoyed a more than 1,800 percent return on their investment. The company's stock has also become one of the five most widely held in the country.

In addition to its strong stock price appreciation, BellSouth has had a major impact on the economy of the Southeast. A study in 1998 conducted by the research firm DRI valued BellSouth's nine-state economic impact at nearly $200 billion over the past 15 years.

The study also found that BellSouth has employed an average of 94,000 people each year since 1984 and generated another 100,000 additional jobs that are directly or indirectly linked to the company. BellSouth has paid more than $74 billion (inflation adjusted) in wages and pensions over the past 15 years, which has resulted in a personal income impact of more than $180 billion. Finally, the company has paid more than $17 billion (inflation adjusted) in taxes to help Atlanta and communities throughout the Southeast become the productive centers of commerce they are today.

within walking distance of a MARTA station. More than 13,000 of the company's 18,000 local employees will work in the new centers, which will help reduce employee commute time and traffic congestion in the city. ◐

◄ BellSouth is the leading provider of cellular service in Latin America, including Brazil, where the company now has more than one million customers.

Heidrick & Struggles, Inc.

Headhunters. Not the kind who shrink human remains, but the extraordinary kind. Heidrick & Struggles is an extraordinary executive search firm that has redefined the term and the industry.

Heidrick & Struggles doesn't just make a change; they make a difference. The firm doesn't just hunt for executive talent; it searches for solutions. With offices in major business centers on six continents, Heidrick & Struggles specializes in identifying chief executives, Boards of Directors, and senior-level managers for many of the world's leading *Fortune* 500 companies, family-

owned businesses, hospitals, universities, not-for-profit institutions, and many other types of organizations, including high growth venture-backed enterprises.

In 1980, Heidrick & Struggles established itself as an integral member of Atlanta's business community. Since then, Heidrick & Struggles has been an active and high profile organization with a strong emphasis on being an important resource for creating strategic management teams for the area while also being a responsible corporate citizen in the community. Heidrick & Struggles Atlanta is led by Managing Partner A. Wayne Luke, who firmly believes that business success is driven by ardent attention to clients' needs and by being a good neighbor. He attributes this philosophy and attitude to the office's pre-eminence.

In response to rapid growth and diversification of the marketplace, Heidrick & Struggles pioneered the development of industry-specific specialty practices in the field of executive search. Today, Heidrick & Struggles serves most major industries though its network of practices.

Heidrick & Struggles' practices include cover placements for boards of directors, chief financial officer, consumer, family-owned business, financial services, health care, higher education/not-for-profit, industrial, international technology, and professional services sector.

Each of the practices is represented by one or more consultants in the firm's Atlanta office, directly benefiting Atlanta's economic mix. Heidrick & Struggles' diversity of skillsets and experience ensure that, like the industries in Atlanta, no one specialty practice dominates another, yet each plays its own important role.

Heidrick & Struggles' consultants are experienced executive search professionals who generally have prior operating experience in the industries they now serve. Some of the previous positions the consultants in the Atlanta office held were that of president of Northside Hospital, assistant to the President of the United States and Director of Presidential Personnel, and founder of two high-tech companies in the Silicon Valley. As a result of their individual histories and connections, each consultant has uncommon access to senior management, continually stays abreast of trends and changes within their particular sector, and has a keen understanding of the industry's inherent dynamics and demands on leadership.

Heidrick & Struggles' greatest advantage is the ability to leverage the diverse and vast knowledge and industry experience of its global network of consultants to meet the leadership needs of the clients. Heidrick's executive search professionals also capitalize on the firm's highly advanced technology and sophisticated methods of analysis. Indeed, Heidrick & Struggles' business practices have fundamentally raised the standard for executive search worldwide.

It is particularly interesting to note that Heidrick & Struggles has two important footprints in Atlanta—the regional executive search office and the firm's Office of the Chief Executive Officer. The

The Heidrick & Struggles offices are a global network of professionals who exchange expertise and experience in a collaborative effort across geographic borders. This network is facilitated and enhanced by the firm's Intranet system, which provides Heidrick & Struggles professionals immediate and proprietary client, candidate, and industry information. At the same time, each office is an integral part of its local business community and serves as the expert on its region's economic needs and culture. Heidrick & Struggles' global network consists of offices in principal business centers on six continents, which include more than 65 offices and over 300 consultants worldwide. Heidrick & Struggles has the global access and influence to reach and build key strategic management teams not only around the world, but also right here at home in Atlanta. ◐

◀ Heidrick & Struggles' consultants are experienced executive search professionals with operating experience in the industries they serve. Photo by Ron Sherman.

executive search office is the largest of its kind in Atlanta finding executive talent for the area's businesses and organizations. While Heidrick & Struggles' corporate headquarters are located in Chicago, the international executive search firm is actually run by Patrick S. Pittard, president and CEO, from his office in Atlanta. This structure strongly supports Atlanta as a growing hub of international business.

In addition to the extraordinary talent of its search professionals, an underlying theme for Heidrick & Struggles' success is the firm's partnership structure supported by a single, fully integrated profit center. This unique structure ensures that every client has access to the best resources, regardless of location of each assignment.

The firm's spirit of partnership is also extended to the Atlanta community. In addition to the firm's high profile search assignments for local businesses and organizations, Heidrick & Struggles Atlanta is also known as being a good neighbor. The firm supports the community through sponsorships and direct involvement with a variety of cultural organizations. Examples include Hands On Atlanta, local universities, an annual Corporate Challenge event, and the Atlanta and Georgia Chambers of Commerce. The firm is a cosponsor of Georgia's Most Respected CEO Award.

Heidrick & Struggles and its Atlanta office consultants work very closely with clients to understand their organizational styles, cultures, personalities, and dynamics. The firm assesses client needs to determine the ideal skills and experience a candidate should possess. After identifying the organization's needs, consultants recruit candidates who will perform well in the environment as well as enhance the organization. Once the client company selects a candidate, they typically assist in structuring a compensation package and then help the newly hired executive assimilate into the organization. The leadership teams built by Heidrick & Struggles have had a profound and continuing positive effect on the companies' growth, profitability, and shareholder value.

◀ A. Wayne Luke is managing partner of the Atlanta office and Patrick S. Pittard is president and CEO of Heidrick & Struggles International. Photo by Ron Sherman.

Allied Holdings, Inc.

As the parent company of several subsidiaries engaged in the automotive distribution business, Allied Holdings' vision is to be the leading global provider of automotive distribution, logistics, and transportation services. Its subsidiary, Allied Automotive Group, is the largest motor carrier in North America specializing in the delivery of automobiles and light trucks and operates more than 5,200 modern tractor-trailers out of 121 terminal locations that crisscross the United States and Canada. AAG partners with all major manufacturers, domestic and import, to deliver over 11 million vehicles a year. This includes transporting vehicles to dealers from plants, rail ramps, ports, and auctions, and providing railcar loading and unloading services.

The Allied Automotive Group moves more vehicles by truck than any company in the world; in fact, the company delivers most of the shiny new cars seen on the showroom floors. Throughout the United States and Canada, the AAG rig is the recognized symbol of innovation and efficiency in vehicle distribution.

It all began in 1934, when Guy Rutland Sr. purchased Motor Convoy for $15,000. With that investment came two trucks and trailers which could haul three cars each on their flatbeds. The first customer was Ford Motor Company, still a primary customer. Guy Rutland Jr., a Georgia Tech graduate, soon joined the firm and put his engineering skills to work developing a rig with two decks that could haul four cars at a time. Once the new equipment was introduced, Motor Convoy expanded its fleet to 55 rigs.

Motor Convoy relocated its company headquarters in 1947 to an office adjacent to the Ford plant in Hapeville, Georgia. During the 1950s, rig capacity was reengineered to five vehicles, General Motors and American Motor Company (later acquired by Chrysler) became customers, and the company hauled its first import: Volkswagen Beetles.

During the 1960s, the company installed its first computer system to manage its 11 terminals, while the fleet expanded to approximately 200 rigs.

With the deregulation of the industry in 1980, Motor Convoy began an aggressive expansion plan—extending its geographic reach with key acquisitions like Dealers Transport and Associated Transports. A company's success is based largely on its management philosophy, and in 1984 Motor Convoy implemented programs that focused on productivity, damage prevention, efficiency, and safety.

Motor Convoy merged with Auto Convoy in 1988 to form Allied Systems, and a program was launched to enlarge most rigs to 75 feet. In 1993 Allied Holdings, Inc., (AHI) was formed as the parent company for Allied Systems and other subsidiaries, and became a publicly traded company on the NASDAQ stock market. It has since moved to trade on the New York Stock Exchange.

Allied Holdings, Inc. and its subsidiaries expanded significantly, acquiring Auto Haulaway (later renamed Allied Systems [Canada] Company) and with it, 90 percent of the automotive distribution market in Canada. The Allied Automotive Group (AAG) was formed as a wholly owned subsidiary of Allied Holdings, and is the parent company of Allied Systems, Ltd. in the U.S. and Allied Systems (Canada) Company in Canada.

In 1997, AHI acquired the Ryder Automotive Group (Ryder Automotive Carrier Services and RC Management Corp) for approximately $114.5 million. With this acquisition, AAG became the largest carhauling company in North America, with approximately 5,200 specialized tractor trailers and 121 locations in every state and Canada. The number of employees increased from 3,300 to more than 8,500, the share of North American market rose from 25 percent to 65 percent, and annual revenues surged from $393 million to more than $1 billion.

That same year, Robert J. Rutland, chairman of the board and CEO, was awarded the 1997 Executive of the Year by the Georgia Securities Association, and Toyota presented Allied Automotive Group with the President's Award for Logistical Excellence. Then in 1998, AAG was awarded the ISO-9002 certification by American Quality Assessors by meeting strict quality guidelines. This certification is required by all manufacturers of the companies which do business with them.

▲ Allied Holdings began in 1934, when Guy Rutland Sr. purchased Motor Convoy for $15,000. With that investment came two trucks and trailers which could haul three cars each on their flatbeds.

► Allied Automotive Group is the largest motor carrier in North America specializing in the delivery of automobiles and light trucks and operates more than 5,200 modern tractor-trailers out of 121 terminal locations that crisscross the United States and Canada.

"One of the key strategies of Allied Holdings has been to prosper by growing, to do more of what we do best. As a result, we extended our vehicle transportation business. We also answered new opportunities with new ventures that are a natural extension of that business, one of which was forming the Axis Group," says A. Mitchell Poole Jr., president, Allied Holdings, Inc.

Axis Group, Inc. is the logistics services subsidiary of AHI. Axis provides logistics solutions and services to the automotive industry, with a primary emphasis on automotive distribution and related activities. The company serves vehicle manufacturers and marketers, vehicle dealers, and the pruned vehicle market. Services provided by Axis include vehicle processing and accessorization, equipment and services for containerized vehicle shipment, transport carrier management, and logistics design and professional services. As the global logistics management arm of AHI, Axis Group currently has operations in the United States, Canada, Mexico, Brazil, South Africa, and the United Kingdom.

Allied Industries is the subsidiary that provides financial, administrative, communications, and human resources support functions for all AHI subsidiaries, freeing them to concentrate on their core businesses.

The subsidiary *Link Information Systems*, AHI's information technology group, is absolutely critical to doing business in the automotive industry. Link provides access to immediate, accurate data—from back office coordination to vehicle tracking. Utilizing many of the leading technologies, Link supports its sister companies, as well as other parties in the automotive distribution market.

Haul Risk Management, AHI's risk management and claims handling subsidiary, offers a full range of "peace of mind" services to companies that operate large private fleets. Their services include consulting for the purchase of insurance, liability and workers' compensation claims handling, environmental audits and reviews, catastrophic claims, and the utilization of AHI's "shared" captive insurance company.

One of the company's unique commitments is the Chaplaincy Program, a nondenominational counseling service which helps employees with personal issues. Each AAG terminal is assigned a chaplain who visits on a weekly basis and is also on call whenever and wherever needed to help employees function, both on and off the job. The Director of Chaplaincy is located in the corporate office and selects the chaplains for the AAG terminals. The less than 10 percent turnover of the Allied employees, compared to the traditional industry standard of 100 percent or more, has been attributed to the caring atmosphere of management, of which the Chaplaincy program is an extension.

Several members of the founding family are still very much a part of AHI today—Guy W. Rutland III, chairman emeritus; Robert J. Rutland, chairman of the board of directors and CEO; Guy Rutland IV, executive vice president of U.S. Operations for Allied Automotive Group; and Dawn Rutland Trygg, marketing director for Haul Risk Management.

Allied Holdings' future direction is one of quality service built around lasting relationships, steady growth, maximized technology, equipment superiority, and the maintenance of a caring culture, where performance is measured by positive reinforcement. Allied Holdings is clearly positioned—in terms of its rich heritage, proven management style, and steady momentum—to continue advancing along the road to the future.

"The automotive industry is a changing business, and Allied has remained flexible for its customers. Allied has experienced growth through the changes to rail, deregulation, and now logistics, or outsourcing, while holding to the core values," said Bob Rutland, Chairman and CEO. "A caring atmosphere coming from the 'family business' has been difficult to maintain, but not impossible. And we are committed for the culture of Christian values to be constant while change continues," stated Mr. Rutland. ❧

◀ AHI's information technology group is absolutely critical to doing business in the automotive industry. It provides access to immediate, accurate data—from back office coordination to vehicle tracking.

◀ (Left to right) A. Mitchell Poole Jr., president and COO, and Robert J. Rutland, chairman and CEO. Allied Holdings' reputation is one of quality service built around lasting relationships, steady growth, maximized technology, equipment superiority, and the maintenance of a caring culture.

CHAPTER TWO
1830s-1900

ⓐ

The story of Atlanta begins along the banks of the Chattahoochee River at an Indian village called Standing Peachtree.

Photo by Ron Sherman

In the early 1800s the Chattahoochee marked the boundary between the Creek Indians to the south and the Cherokees to the north. Anyone traveling the river probably stopped to trade at Standing Peachtree, and the village was also the entry point for white traders who had permission to enter Creek land.

Where the name Standing Peachtree came from isn't known exactly. One story tells of a large peach tree crowning an Indian mound. Another says it was a pine tree that provided rosin—or "pitch"—to villagers, the name of which was gradually corrupted into "pitch-tree."

Regardless, the name was so entrenched that during the War of 1812 when two forts were built in the area—one where Peachtree Creek joins the Chattahoochee and the other in Gwinnett County— the 30-mile trail connecting them was immediately dubbed Peachtree Road.

► Atlanta has had a "Peachtree Street" from its earliest days. Where the name comes from isn't known exactly, but one theory holds that a large tree crowning an Indian mound was a pine tree that provided rosin— or "pitch"—to villagers, the name of which was gradually corrupted into "**pitch-tree.**" Photos courtesy of Georgia Department of Archives and History

The state of Georgia gained ownership of Standing Peachtree in 1821 by way of a land concession signed by the Creeks. After the concession, the land was opened to any and all white settlers. By 1825 there was enough need to commission a U.S. Post Office, which was promptly named Standing Peachtree. The second post office in the area—in Decatur—came along eighteen months later.

A decade later, the state authorized a ferry crossing of the Chattahoochee at Standing Peachtree. Named Montgomery's Ferry, it eclipsed the name Standing Peachtree for good, except for the dozens of street names that would incorporate Peachtree over the next 150 years.

The movement of white settlers during the early 1800s was primarily westward from Savannah and the coast. One of the earliest towns to emerge in the area was Decatur, which quickly became the county seat of DeKalb County and by 1825 was home to twenty-five hundred settlers.

As the inland population grew, issues of trade became important. To the east and south, there were a number of privately owned railroads. It became apparent to railroad boosters that these lines should push north and connect the more established towns of central Georgia to northern markets like Chattanooga. In 1836 the state authorized the chartering of a new railroad company, the Western & Atlantic Railroad. Surveyors determined that a route south from Chattanooga should naturally end near the Chattahoochee.

After a false start, the chief engineer, Colonel Stephen Long, located the terminus of the Chattanooga line near what had been Standing Peachtree. Fearing the dirt and disruption, many Decatur residents were openly relieved the site was several miles to the east of them.

While most predictions were that the terminus would be home at best to a couple of minor stores, Alexander Stephens, later to become governor of Georgia, visited the site in 1839 and prophesied that "a great inland city will at no distant date arise here."

At the time of Stephen's prediction, there were just a handful of settlers in the area. Hardy Ivy and his family had come west from Decatur to establish a farm where Peachtree Center sits now. Another farmer, Charner Humphries, built a two-story frame building that housed a tavern and store just south of what is now Five Points.

For lack of a better term, the area was inelegantly known as Terminus until 1843, when the town residents got permission to form a government. The name was then changed to Marthasville, in honor of the daughter of former Governor Wilson Lumpkin, a fervent railroad booster.

At about the same time, the Western & Atlantic moved the terminus point a few thousand feet farther east—to a point adjacent to

▲ Before finally getting the name "Atlanta"—in honor of the Western & Atlantic railroad—the city was known simply as Terminus, as the end of the rail line, and then as Marthasville, in honor of the daughter of former Governor Wilson Lumpkin, a fervent railroad booster. Photo by Ron Sherman

today's Underground Atlanta—and built a small, wooden depot. At the end of 1842, the railroad brought in a locomotive from Madison, to the east, to make a demonstration run from Terminus to Marietta, twenty-two miles to the north. It was a festive occasion for the town, but regular train service was still years off in the future.

Even so, the intersecting rail lines were attracting ambitious merchants. James Loyd and James Collins opened a general store along what became Marietta Street. Jonathan Norcross opened first a horse-powered sawmill, and then a general store. Within a year, commercial land lots near the tracks were being sold. The lot Norcross bought for his general store, for instance, cost him two hundred dollars. It sat at the point where four rustic roads— Whitehall, Peachtree, Marietta, and Decatur—converged. The intersection later became known as Five Points, and Norcross' general store eventually became the site of the First National Bank.

While Marthasville was perhaps an improvement over Terminus, it too lasted only a couple of years before another name emerged. The occasion was the day the Georgia Railroad brought its first locomotive to Marthasville from Augusta by way of Decatur. The line's chief engineer suggested Atlanta—in honor of the Western & Atlantic line—and began using the name in its timetables. The state ratified the new name by the end of the year.

Regular train service to points north, south, and east kicked off Atlanta's first boom. Lawyers, doctors, teachers, schools, churches, homes, and hotels all sprang up around the intersection of road and rail. In 1847 Atlanta boasted twenty-five hundred residents and the city was incorporated.

For a time, Atlanta was a rough, frontier town. The first municipal election was marred by dozens of street brawls among

▲ Dozens of streets throughout Atlanta now bear the name of "Peachtree." Photo by Ron Sherman

◄ Atlanta's growth convinced the state to create a new county—named Fulton after the inventor of the steamboat, most believe— and to name Atlanta as the county seat. Photo by Ron Sherman

► Around 1843, the
Western & Atlantic
moved the terminus
point to an area adjacent
to today's Underground
Atlanta and built a
small, wooden depot.
Photo courtesy of the
Atlanta History Center

► So vital was the railroad
to the growth of Atlanta,
the city's name was born
from its Western &
Atlantic line, and regular
train service to points
north, south, and east
kicked off Atlanta's first
boom. Historic image
courtesy of the Atlanta
History Center. New photos
by Ron Sherman.

In 1856, the state legislature chartered the Atlanta Gas Light Company, making the company the city's oldest continuing corporate citizen. More businesses and factories arrived, including the manufacture of freight cars, iron foundries, tanneries, and cotton warehouses.

At the beginning of the Civil War, the city population was nearly eight thousand. While the men of the city organized dozens of militia units, Atlanta's contribution to the war effort was primarily one of supply. So important were the city's factories that the town was put under marital law in 1862. Guns, uniforms, and steel plate were manufactured in the city, and the railroads were critical to efforts to supply the Southern armies. Later, Atlanta became a giant convalescent ward, with thousands of Confederate soldiers recuperating from their wounds.

When Vicksburg fell to the Union in 1863, the war took on a new urgency. Work began on a series of well-designed fortifications that nearly ringed the city. As the Union Army advanced south to Chattanooga, refugees clogged the streets and prices for just about anything soared.

over-exuberant voters. The city was split between the Moral Party and the Free and Rowdy Party. After some Rowdies fired a cannon at Jonathan Norcross' store, the citizenry organized a volunteer police force and expelled many of the town's bad apples.

Civic ambition was on display right from the start. One of the first items of city business was to petition the state to move the capital from Milledgeville in central Georgia to Atlanta. The proposal was hooted down, but the city fathers promised to keep trying. They did manage to persuade the state to create a new county—named Fulton after the inventor of the steamboat, most believe—and to name Atlanta as the county seat.

The Western & Atlantic line finally reached Chattanooga and replaced its wooden depot with a new brick one in 1854. The first banks began to pop up: Atlanta Bank in 1852 and Bank of Fulton in 1853. The first closed quickly, but the latter survived for ten years. Fire insurance firms prospered; most downtown buildings were wood, and fire was a constant threat.

Atlanta got its first hospital and first society of doctors—formed as Atlanta Medical College—in 1855. Dr. Crawford Long, credited with being the first doctor to use ether as an anesthetic during surgery, spent a year practicing medicine in Atlanta in 1850 before moving east to Athens.

In the spring of 1864, General William Tecumseh Sherman was given orders to break the back of the Confederacy by capturing Atlanta. Confederate General Joseph E. Johnston was appointed to counter Sherman. Johnston commanded an inferior force but fought a skillful retreating campaign through northwest Georgia. By the time Johnston withdrew into the now-fortified city, though, the citizenry had had enough of retreat. They demanded action and Johnston was replaced by General John Bell Hood. Hood immediately attacked Sherman and fought several bloody engagements on the outskirts of the city. Despite the bravery, the city and its civilian population was nearly encircled.

Sherman had large siege guns shipped in and commenced bombardment of the city. Although relatively few civilians were killed by the shelling, the siege completed the city's descent into near-anarchy, particularly when Hood evacuated his army to save it from complete destruction. The next day, what was left of the city's government surrendered the city to Sherman. Sherman ordered civilians to evacuate the city and sent troops to plunder supplies from the nearby countryside in preparation for his next campaign.

Sherman's orders were to destroy the city's usefulness to the Confederacy. On November 14, 1864, ready to commence his

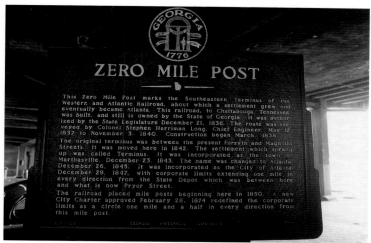

ZERO MILE POST

This Zero Mile Post marks the Southeastern Terminus of the Western and Atlantic Railroad, about which a settlement grew and eventually became Atlanta. This railroad, to Chattanooga, Tennessee, was built, and still is owned by the State of Georgia. It was authorized by the State Legislature December 21, 1836. The route was surveyed by Colonel Stephen Harriman Long, Chief Engineer, May 12, 1837 to November 3, 1840. Construction began March, 1838.

The original terminus was between the present Forsyth and Magnolia Streets. It was moved here in 1842. The settlement which sprang up was called Terminus. It was incorporated as the town of Marthasville, December 23, 1843. The name was changed to Atlanta, December 26, 1845. It was incorporated as the City of Atlanta, December 29, 1847, with corporate limits extending one mile in every direction from the State Depot which was between here and what is now Pryor Street.

The railroad placed mile posts beginning here in 1850. A new City Charter approved February 28, 1874 redefined the corporate limits as a circle one mile and a half in every direction from this mile post.

▶ In the spring of 1864, General William Tecumseh Sherman was given orders to break the back of the Confederacy by capturing Atlanta. On November 14, 1864, his army began to destroy the railroad depots, and factories were set ablaze, and fires spread to the homes. Photo courtesy Georgia Department of Archives and History.

▶ Sumter Light Guards, Company "K", 4th Regiment, Georgia Volunteer Infantry, Confederate Army, April 1861. Photo courtesy Georgia Department of Archives and History.

▶ After Sherman's invasion, only about 100 families were left in Atlanta. One of the few homes to survive the fires was Hull House, owned by Alexander Stephens. Photo courtesy Georgia Department of Archives and History

march east to the sea, his army began to destroy the railroad depots, tracks, and roundhouse. Factories were set afire or blown up, and the fires spread to the homes. When it was over, dead animals and rubble littered the streets, and the housing stock of the city was devastated. At best, only 100 families were left in Atlanta.

Yet within a week, people began to trickle back. Newspapers began to publish, merchants restocked their stores. The city treasury contained but $1.64, but the rebuilding process was underway.

Less than a year later, two banks opened. One, Atlanta National Bank, prospered and, as First National Bank, eventually occupied the Five Points corner once owned by Jonathan Norcross. Although Reconstructionists in Washington, D.C., sent federal troops to the city in 1867—they stayed for the next ten years—Atlanta won its fight to grab the state capital in 1868, an amazing achievement for a city still largely in ruins.

The prodigious commercial energy unleashed after the war produced some notable entrepreneurs. Hannibal Kimball built an opera house and lavish hotel, in large part with state funds. Morris Rich, a Hungarian emigrant, arrived in the city with some experience in the dry goods business. He opened a small store downtown called Rich's, and as it prospered he brought his brothers to Atlanta to help run it. The city's businessmen revived the pre-war Board of Trade but soon changed the name of the group to the

Atlanta Chamber of Commerce. In 1868, *The Atlanta Constitution* newspaper began publishing. The famed editor, Henry Grady, joined the paper eight years later.

The intense pace of business in the rebuilding city was cited by some observers as socially positive, leaving the men of Atlanta little time to loaf or get drunk. "Our people are emphatically a business people, who come here to work..." wrote one. By 1870 city population stood at twenty-one thousand, and would rise to thirty-seven thousand in 1880. In 1890 there were nearly ninety thousand citizens. The bustling atmosphere attracted the attention of northern journalists. "Atlanta is a new, vigorous, awkwardly alert city in which there is little that is distinctly Southern," wrote one.

The new vision of Atlanta was most clearly articulated by editor Henry Grady, who was a tireless champion of the city. He counseled the development of more homegrown industry, spurred on local entrepreneurs, and established himself as a spokesman for the "New South." He dabbled in politics while editor of the *Constitution*, even managing a successful gubernatorial campaign in 1886. Unfortunately, Grady caught cold during a trip and died prematurely in 1889 at age 39.

Grady's call for more home-grown exploitation of the area's natural resources was partially answered by the establishment of a new school devoted to training engineers. The Georgia Institute of Technology admitted its first class—129 students—in 1888, establishing a campus on the northern fringes of downtown by erecting an administration building still in use today.

During these years Atlanta spread its New South gospel through a series of large expositions. Atlanta sponsored fairs in 1870 (agriculture), 1881 (cotton), 1887 (the Piedmont Exposition, held on land later converted into Piedmont Park), and 1891. All were successful, but the greatest of them all was the International Cotton States Exposition of 1896. Held at Piedmont Park, now owned by the city, it cost three million dollars and filled the 180 acres of the park with specially erected buildings that showcased artists, industrial innovations like electricity, entertainment like Buffalo Bill and his Wild West Show, and a newfangled invention called the motion picture. It drew eight hundred thousand visitors in less than four months.

All the elements of city government were now in place. A public school system was established in 1870, but the number of children in the fast-growing city quickly outstripped the classroom space available and temporary school facilities had to be built. Municipal service like garbage pickup and a water system—pumped from a reservoir at Lakewood, south of downtown—began. The first telephones were installed downtown in 1877. In 1882, Ivy Street Hospital boasted the first emergency room in the city. It was replaced ten years later by Grady Hospital, built with 100 beds for charity and ten for paying customers. The city established its first uniformed police department in 1873 and a paid fire department in 1882.

Several clubs that mixed business and social activities—Capital City Club, Piedmont Driving Club, and Atlanta Athletic Club—were established during the late 1800s. A number of important businesses came into being, such as Southern Railway, St. Joseph's Hospital, Davison's department store, *The Atlanta Journal*, The Coca-Cola Company, Haverty's, The Robinson-Humphery Co., Trust Company Bank, Georgia Power Co., Citizen's and Southern National Bank, King & Spalding law firm, and Southern Bell.

In 1889 the state dedicated a handsome new state capitol just south and east of Five Points that featured a dome covered in gold leaf. The cost: just under one million dollars. ❦

◄ Atlanta's contribution to the Civil War effort was primarily one of supply. Later, Atlanta became a giant convalescent ward, with thousands of Confederate soldiers recuperating from their wounds. Despite the heavy damage inflicted by Sherman's invasion, within a week families began trickling back. Businesses grew strong and the city flourished.
Photos by Ron Sherman

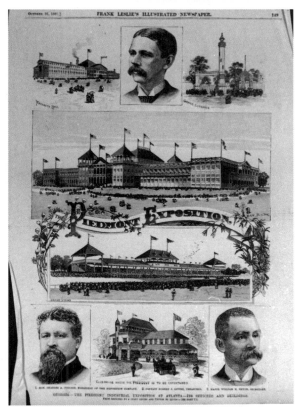

◄ **Atlanta spread its New South gospel through a series of expositions, including fairs in 1870 (agriculture), 1881 (cotton), and 1887 (the Piedmont Exposition), and 1896 (the International Cotton States Exposition). The Piedmont Exposition was held on land later converted into Piedmont Park, still a favorite oasis of city residents.** Historic photos courtesy of Georgia Department of Archives and History. New photo by Ron Sherman

► The Georgia Institute of Technology admitted its first class—129 students— in 1888, establishing a campus on the northern fringes of downtown by erecting an administration building still in use today.
Historic photos courtesy Georgia Department of Archives and History. New photo by Ron Sherman

GRATEFUL MEMORY
TECH MEN WHO GAVE THEIR LIVES
IN THE CAUSE OF LIBERTY IN THE WORLD WAR
THIS MEMORIAL IS DEDICATED
BY THE CLASS OF 1923

◄ The new vision of Atlanta was most clearly articulated by Henry Grady, editor of *The Atlanta Constitution*. He established himself as a spokesman for the "New South" and prompted the establishment of the Georgia Institute of Technology with his call for more home-grown exploitation of the area's natural resources. Although managing a successful gubernatorial campaign in 1886, Grady died prematurely in 1889 at the age of 39. In 1892, Grady Hospital was named for him. Historic photo of Grady Hospital (pictured below) courtesy Georgia Department of Archives and History; historic images of The Atlanta Constitution building (pictured opposite) and Henry Grady portrait courtesy of the Atlanta History Center. New photo by Ron Sherman.

◄ **Atlanta established its first uniformed police department in 1873 and a paid fire department in 1882.** Historic photo courtesy Georgia Department of Archives and History. New photos by Ron Sherman

▲ In 1889 the state dedi-
cated a handsome new
state capitol just south
and east of Five Points
that featured a dome
covered in gold leaf. The
cost: just under one mil-
lion dollars. Historic
photo courtesy Georgia
Department of Archives
and History. New photo by
Ron Sherman

Metro Atlanta Chamber of Commerce

Sam A. Williams serves as president of the Metro Atlanta Chamber of Commerce. Photo by Teryl Jackson.

Long before official word came from the U.S. Environmental Protection Agency, the Metro Atlanta Chamber of Commerce recognized that air quality would threaten Atlanta businesses' ability to operate and get employees to work. The Metro Atlanta Chamber went to work, studied the problem, formed a powerful think tank of the region's business leaders, and proposed a bold solution: the creation of a regional transportation authority. When changing EPA regulations suddenly raised the stakes for Atlanta business interests, a solution was ready.

As one of his first orders of business as Georgia's governor, Roy Barnes established a new state authority with broad new power to administer transportation plans on a regional scale.

The story is just one of many successes produced by a chamber of commerce establishing itself as one of the most forward-thinking in the nation.

The Metro Atlanta Chamber of Commerce is adapting to the shifting conditions and challenges of business in the postmodern world. It has focused its agenda on attracting quality jobs, improving quality of life, promoting balanced growth across the region, and providing valuable service to its 8,600 members from across metro Atlanta.

In another example of its progressive leadership, the Metro Atlanta Chamber has put itself on the leading edge of economic development for the new millennium with an initiative dubbed "Industries of the Mind."

Though metro Atlanta has long been acknowledged as one of the most progressive cities in the United States, that progress demands an ever larger, skilled workforce. So the Chamber is implementing innovative marketing programs to stock the local supply by aggressively attracting high-tech employees to the region.

"In the past, Chambers have always targeted companies," says Sam A. Williams, president of the Chamber. "We are the first to also target talent."

To further stoke metro Atlanta's economic engine, the Chamber has a plan to attract high-tech industry to the region. These high-tech Industries of the Mind produce services and products that will give way to fortunes and power in the next century.

High-tech corridors and geographic clusters of high-tech enterprises already exist in the metro area. The emphasis now is on expanding those existing corridors, rapidly establishing new corridors and links, and marketing Atlanta's strengths.

Because of Atlanta's global recognition, broad-based marketing is no longer the priority. Targeted growth that provides the region with quality jobs is the next sensible step. The Chamber will consistently work to reinforce the Atlanta "brand," but more importantly, it will focus on growing Industries of the Mind. But it will do so not solely for the sake of having those industries.

The Chamber's targeted Industries of the Mind are telecommunications, computer-related services and software, high-tech manufacturing, and biotech/biomedical. They do not exist in a vacuum. They affect every existing business. Their presence lends innumerable benefits to every industry and business in metro Atlanta and the State of Georgia.

Beyond identifying new advantages, markets, and industry development, the Metro Atlanta Chamber will not shy away from any issue important to metro Atlanta businesses.

The Chamber's early recognition and leadership on the sensitive issue of air quality is one example. So is Hartsfield Atlanta International

Businesses come to metro Atlanta because of the prestige of an Atlanta address and to rub shoulders with some of the top names in virtually every industry and discipline. Photo ©Robb Helfrick/Aristock/ 800-261-6150.

Airport, already the world's busiest airport, and under close study by the Chamber.

The Chamber believes Hartsfield can produce even more business for the Atlanta region. Once again, the Metro Atlanta Chamber studied the possibilities, derived a plan, and drove home new profits in the form of more jobs and companies.

The world's leading corporations and organizations are those that make the bold moves, take the risks, and aggressively seek new answers. They don't do so just to get to the top—they do it to stay on top.

Metro Atlanta is unmistakably on top. Nowhere on the globe have people not heard of Atlanta. Businesses come to metro Atlanta because of the prestige of an Atlanta address and to rub shoulders with some of the top names in virtually every industry and discipline. It is therefore both logical and expected that the Metro Atlanta Chamber would perform with that same boldness and foresight to bring Atlanta to its current world status.

As a result, metro Atlanta continues to lead the nation in job creation and a host of other key economic indicators. Experts from around the world have declared the region successful by every conventional measure. Atlanta consistently ranks high in surveys conducted by the world's leading magazines, newspapers, and polling firms. *Entrepreneur* magazine ranked Atlanta "the Number One U.S. City to Own a Business." *World Trade* magazine named Atlanta the "Best U.S. City for Global Companies." *FORTUNE* magazine ranked Atlanta number four, behind only Hong Kong, New York, and London, in its "World's Best Cities For Business" survey. Atlanta has also appeared in *FORTUNE'S* "Best Cities" top 10 list more times than any other city.

This is the top—and the Metro Atlanta Chamber of Commerce played a key role in getting there, as it also plays a key role in keeping metro Atlanta on top. ❧

◄ In an example of its progressive leadership, the Metro Atlanta Chamber has put itself on the leading edge of economic development for the new millennium with an initiative dubbed "Industries of the Mind." Photo ©Robb Helfrick/Aristock/800-261-6150.

King & Spalding

The law firm of King & Spalding has been at the forefront of providing excellent legal services to its clients for over a century. Since its establishment in 1885, the firm has had a tradition of attracting and developing many of this country's finest attorneys.

Today, from its offices in Atlanta, Washington, D.C., New York, and Houston, King & Spalding continues to provide the highest caliber legal counsel to its clients from the United States and abroad. According to a 1998 *American Lawyer* survey, King & Spalding ranked among the top 50 law firms in the world as measured by gross revenue.

King & Spalding's Clients

The clients served by the firm are its proudest achievement and perhaps most convincing credential. King & Spalding's diverse client base encompasses both U.S. and foreign corporations and individuals, businesses, industry associations, nonprofit organizations, and coalitions of clients with parallel interests. The firm currently represents more than 250 public companies, including nearly half of the Fortune 100 companies. King & Spalding also represents hundreds of clients with new ventures and midsized companies in emerging industries.

Long-standing client relationships are one of the surest barometers of a law firm's success. King & Spalding prides itself on developing continuing relationships that are productive, professional, and collegial. A few examples include:

The Coca-Cola Company has been a client of the firm since the 1920s. Four former King & Spalding partners have served as general counsel to The Coca-Cola Company, including the current general counsel, Joe Gladden.

King & Spalding assisted SunTrust Banks, Inc., a longtime firm client, in the acquisition of Crestar Financial Corporation. The $9.5-billion transaction created the country's 10th largest banking company.

The firm acts as principal outside transactional counsel for Sprint Corporation. Transactions handled by the firm, including the formation of Global One, a joint venture among Sprint, France Telecom, and Deutsche Telekom, are enabling Sprint to accomplish its goal of becoming a global telecommunications company.

The Firm and its Members

As the firm looks toward the new millennium and its 115th anniversary, it is mindful of its legacy of professional excellence. With approximately 500 attorneys in 24 practice areas, King & Spalding's attorneys maintain their reputation for excellence by earning it through favorable results and valuable client services.

Recognized legal and political leaders with decades of unparalleled experience fill the firm's attorney roster.

Griffin Bell served as the U.S. Attorney General during President Carter's administration. Before becoming Attorney General, President Kennedy appointed him to the Fifth Circuit Court of Appeals bench, where he served for 15 years.

Sam Nunn, who as U.S. Senator earned a reputation as one of the nation's leading experts on computer security issues, is a key advisor to the President's Commission on Critical Infrastructure Protection.

Former Georgia Governor George Busbee is a retired partner. President Carter paid tribute to Governor Busbee's extensive experience in international trade by appointing him to the President's Export Council, a position to which he was reappointed by President Reagan.

Both Griffin Bell and Frank Jones served as president of the American College of Trial Lawyers (ACTL). King & Spalding is one of only two firms to have two presidents chosen from its ranks. As of 1999, ten of the firm's senior trial lawyers are fellows of the ACTL.

Larry Thompson, Stephen Cowen, and Kent Alexander each served as the U.S. Attorney for the Northern District of Georgia. In that role, Mr. Thompson directed the Southeastern Organized Crime Drug Enforcement Task Force and served on the Attorney General's Economic Crime Council. Mr. Alexander successfully prosecuted the infamous Legion of Doom case, one of the first federal cases of complex computer fraud, and chaired the Attorney General's Computer Working Group.

Litigation matters encompass a substantial portion of King & Spalding's practice. The firm's litigation group has extensive experience in trying major jury trials in various courts nationwide and has represented clients before the United States Supreme

▲ (Left to right) **Sam Nunn, former U.S. Senator and partner in King & Spalding's International Practice; Walter W. Driver Jr., chairman of King & Spalding's Policy Committee and partner in the Banking & Finance Practice; Chilton D. Varner, member of the Policy Committee and partner in the Product Liability Practice; and Ralph B. Levy, King & Spalding's managing partner and member of the Policy Committee.**

Court and the U.S. Courts of Appeals. For example, as defense counsel for Texaco Inc. and Texaco Pipeline Inc., King & Spalding won a toxic tort case involving more than 17,000 individual plaintiffs. *The National Law Journal* highlighted this case as one of the major defense victories of 1997.

A glance at the firm's representations reveals a mastery of the subtleties and complexities of a changing world. King & Spalding serves a wide spectrum of clients ranging from health care, to telecommunications, consumer and industrial products, real estate, and computer security providers.

As one of the leading firms in corporate law, the firm's track record proves its expertise in virtually all types of corporate and financial matters. King & Spalding consistently ranks first among Georgia's bond counsel and 25th among bond counsel nationally. It is the only law firm to have had three of its attorneys serve as president of the National Association of Bond Counsel, including 1998 President Floyd Newton. Also in 1998, King & Spalding partner Glen Reed assumed the presidency of the newly formed American Health Lawyers Association.

Institutional Values

King & Spalding's high degree of collegiality is the hallmark of its professional partnership and serves as a testament to the firm's internal culture and stability. The firm's commitment to the professional and personal development of its attorneys is the backbone of this culture. Three examples of this pledge include K&S University, the firm's continuing legal education program; its in-house courtroom used for training and trial preparation; and the Link Program, an internal attorney mentor program. The firm's Internet web site, www.kslaw.com, contains more information on all of these programs.

Commitment to Community

Throughout its history, the firm has supported a wide variety of local and national charitable and community services. King & Spalding's efforts to promote the city of Atlanta were rewarded when the International Olympic Committee selected Atlanta to host the 1996 Summer Olympic Games. Three of the firm's partners were members of the "Atlanta Nine," the committee responsible for bringing the Olympic Games to Atlanta. The firm also served as general counsel to the Atlanta Committee for the Olympic Games.

King & Spalding's commitment to community service was particularly evident in 1998, when the firm built its third home for Habitat for Humanity in Atlanta and was the leading United Way law firm sponsor in Georgia, raising over $370,000.

The Next 100 Years

After more than 100 years of service to its clients, King & Spalding continues to prosper by building on the firm's fundamental roots and values. The firm's mission statement confirms its commitment to three core objectives: premier quality legal work, client service, and community stewardship. These basic tenets ensure that the firm will continue to thrive and succeed into the next 100 years of the firm's existence. ❧

▲ (Left to right) **Judge Griffin Bell, former U.S. Attorney General, and former U.S. Attorneys for the Northern District of Georgia, Larry D. Thompson and Kent B. Alexander. These three partners practice in King & Spalding's Special Matters/Government Investigators Practice Group.**

The Atlanta Journal-Constitution

For all its glory now, nothing came to be in the South without tremendous struggle. Perhaps there are no better illustrations of the indomitable Southern spirit, and the effect of that spirit on a nation, than the stories of the city of Atlanta and *The Atlanta Journal-Constitution.*

When the *Atlanta Constitution* began on June 16, 1868, it was just three years after the end of the Civil War, and Atlanta was writhing in the throes of Reconstruction. Much of its former assets liquidated by fire, Atlanta's government could barely provide the most basic of municipal services. The northern occupation added insult to injury.

The Intelligencer, the town's leading newspaper of the day, offered only a feeble protest to military rule. Incensed by *The Intelligencer's* lack of backbone, Confederate veteran Colonel Carey W. Styles and business partners James H. Anderson and William A. Hemphill purchased a small local paper and thus began the *Atlanta Constitution.* Named after its mission "to reestablish constitutional guarantees and constitutional liberty in all the states of the Union," the *Constitution* debuted with a lively four-page edition of protest.

Many a newspaper was founded on strong passion, but few remained beyond the initial goal of its beginnings. The *Atlanta Constitution* was one of only two papers, in a field of over a hundred, to last for more than a century. The *Atlanta Journal* arrived on the scene 15 years after the *Atlanta Constitution,* in 1883, and it, too, survived and flourished for more than a century. For years, the two papers were bitter competitors, but from their competitiveness rose aggressive news reporting surpassed by none in the nation.

From the same paper that spoke loudly and colorfully against northern oppression, came a man who did more to reconcile the North and the South than any other. His name was Henry W. Grady, editor of the *Constitution* from 1880-89. Between 1876 and 1880, Grady had worked as a correspondent for various American newspapers; he excelled at reporting conditions in the South to northern papers, like the *New York Herald,* and the positions of the North to southern papers, like the *Constitution.* Gradually understanding was built on both sides, largely from Grady's efforts. In 1880, only four years after working for the *Constitution,* he borrowed $20,000 and purchased a one-quarter interest in the *Atlanta Constitution* and shortly became the managing editor. In December 1886, Grady's "New South" speech to the New England Society of New York City brought him national fame overnight. His words humbled a torn nation and seeded the political grounds for unification. Shortly thereafter, Grady was suggested as a presidential possibility by many northern newspapers and mentioned as a running mate for President Grover Cleveland. He declined all in favor of pursuing the rebuilding of Atlanta.

Grady Memorial Hospital, Grady High School, the Grady School of Journalism in Athens, Grady County, and a public housing project in Atlanta are all named after Grady in recognition of his work. But Grady was not the only hero, sung or unsung, to rise from the womb of Atlanta's best newspapers.

Both William Hemphill and Evan Howell served as mayor of Atlanta during their years as *Constitution* executives. Howell also served as a Democratic National Committeeman for 32 years; two terms in the state legislature, one as Speaker of the House; and in the state senate as President of the Senate. He served on three presidential commissions, as well, and was named a chevalier of the Legion of Honor by the French government.

In June of 1887, Atlanta lawyer Hoke Smith purchased the *Atlanta Journal.* By 1893, President Cleveland appointed Smith to the cabinet as secretary of the interior in recognition of the paper's great talent for pioneering news coverage. The appointment gave the *Journal* national prestige.

The impressive impact of the two papers on local and national politics and social developments was exceeded only by the literary talent found within the bowels of the respective newsrooms. Working behind news desks at the *Journal* were the likes of

Margaret Mitchell, author of *Gone With The Wind;* Harold Ross, founder in 1925 of *The New Yorker* magazine; golfing great Bobby Jones; humorist Will Rogers; Ward Greene, who was later head of King Features (which supplied articles to papers across the country); and novelists Edison Marshall, Erskine Caldwell, Corra Harris, Catherine Marshall, Frank Slaughter, and Medora Field. The tradition of writing excellence continues to contemporary times with the likes of Colin Campbell (a descendant of Grady), Cynthia Tucker, and Rheta Grimsley Johnson.

By 1939, James Middleton Cox, former school teacher, reporter, state congressman, and governor of Ohio, bought the *Journal* and its radio station, WSB, to augment his holdings of newspapers and radio stations in Ohio and Florida. In 1950, Cox added the *Atlanta Constitution* to its ranks. Today, the two Atlanta papers are the largest of 17 dailies published by Cox Newspapers, a division of Cox Enterprises, Inc. Headquartered in Atlanta, Cox Enterprises is the second largest privately held company in Georgia. Cox is also the 12th largest media company, and the 39th largest privately held company in America.

Much has changed since the beginnings of *The Atlanta Journal-Constitution,* but the basic mission of the papers has not. Relevance is still the burning passion; where once it was defiance of northern military rule followed by a smoldering desire for peace and unification, now it is an insatiable appetite for balance and depth on topics as diverse as the city's population. As the world becomes smaller, Atlanta becomes larger—the domain of a people united by locale, but divided by interests.

In response, *The Atlanta Journal-Constitution* delivers integrity and relevance in daily dosages by focusing on issues in its 16-county coverage area with equal intensity. Multiple sections, special features, community focus inserts, and other efforts ensure dispatch of news that can be used. This focus is unlikely to change, though delivery vehicles have. Once committed solely to newsprint, the postmodern *Atlanta Journal-Constitution* can be accessed via the Internet.

The web site allows access to the extensive archives, recent past issues, stories of the day, and other matters of relevance to readers and interested parties worldwide. However it arrives, in paper or electronically, *The Atlanta Journal-Constitution* will always be there every day to inform, educate, evaluate, and lead a changing people through destiny. ❧

◄ (Far left) **Founder James Cox had a progressive vision for the paper that continues today.** *The Atlanta Journal-Constitution* **is the largest of the Cox newspapers.**

◄ **Popular columnist Celestine Sibley brought her insightful personality to the pages of** *The Atlanta Journal-Constitution* **for decades. Just before her death in 1999, she received the National Society of Newspaper Columnists' Lifetime Achievement Award.**

▼ **A rich history has transformed** *The Atlanta Journal-Constitution* **into a fixture in Atlanta. The paper is prepared to be a key player in the technology-filled future.**

The Atlanta Journal-Constitution

www.ajc.com

Agnes Scott College

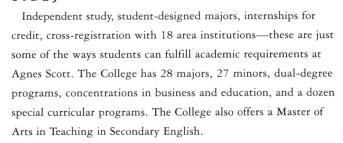

For more than a century, Agnes Scott College has been educating and cultivating leaders—Rhodes and Fulbright scholars, state Supreme Court justices, physicians, educators, scientists, artists, and corporate leaders. And it's been called "one of the best small liberal arts colleges to be found anywhere."

Why is it "one of the best"? It's because of a commitment to superior women's education, as well as an unusually challenging academic environment, and the proximity to Atlanta, one of the fastest growing major cities in America, not to mention a wealth of career, social, cultural, and educational resources.

Why do students select Agnes Scott? Students select Agnes Scott because they enjoy the advantages of award-winning professors and programs, an enviable student-faculty ratio of nine to one, an extraordinarily diverse student body, a century-old honor system that allows students to take self-scheduled, unproctored exams, and a spectacular campus listed on the National Register of Historic Places.

Once at Agnes Scott, students discover course work that stretches their minds, opinions, and beliefs. They make friends who inspire and motivate them. They develop a fun and memory-making social life to balance academics. And they realize all the opportunities to make a difference in the community and establish footholds for a fulfilling career after graduation.

Learn from the Best

One-hundred percent of Agnes Scott's regular, full-time faculty hold the highest degree in their field. Agnes Scott's professors are experts and scholars. They've earned degrees from such institutions as Harvard, Stanford, Cal-Berkeley, Yale, and Duke. And they stay current in their disciplines by researching, networking with colleagues, and publishing in leading academic journals. Students work side by side with them on original research projects; they gain firsthand experience and knowledge in their major; and they even present their findings at national conferences. At larger schools, only masters or doctoral candidates do this kind of collaborative work.

Unlimited Options for Study

Independent study, student-designed majors, internships for credit, cross-registration with 18 area institutions—these are just some of the ways students can fulfill academic requirements at Agnes Scott. The College has 28 majors, 27 minors, dual-degree programs, concentrations in business and education, and a dozen special curricular programs. The College also offers a Master of Arts in Teaching in Secondary English.

International education is an integral part of this academic experience. The curriculum, the study opportunities abroad, the presence of international students and scholars on campus, and collaborations with partner institutions and organizations around the world contribute to the education of globally competent citizens. Agnes Scott students can develop a better understanding of themselves and the world in which they live through study abroad. To encourage students to study abroad, the College annually sponsors two faculty-led study tour programs—Global Awareness and Global Connections—as well as exchange and affiliate programs at more than 130 institutions located in over 40 countries.

Just Six Miles from Downtown Atlanta

Downtown Atlanta lies just six miles from campus. By car, bus, or rapid transit, it's easy to reach the cultural, sports, business, shopping, and social centers that pepper this exciting city, dubbed "Capital of the New South."

Agnes Scott's proximity to Atlanta allows students to try on countless career hats and gain valuable experience and contacts in their discipline. The College's Career Planning office provides more than 250 internship opportunities in Atlanta and other cities in finance, the sciences, the arts, journalism, and many other fields.

And there's always Agnes Scott's very own, unique program—The Atlanta Semester—which focuses on women, leadership, and social change and invites students from all over the world to join the campus community for a semester. In addition to classes, students in the The Atlanta Semester attend speakers' forums, network with Atlanta leaders, and intern in the community.

Leadership Opportunities Abound

Most Agnes Scott students round out their studies with membership in several campus and volunteer organizations. After more than a century, this campus has plenty of them to offer—dozens, in fact—so students can try new activities and pursue long-standing interests.

Or they can choose from NCAA Division III sports teams, volunteer opportunities with organizations like Habitat for Humanity, Honor Court and Student Government Association, *The Profile*, a student-run campus newspaper, Agnes Scott's Blackfriars, the oldest theater group in Atlanta, and many more. The point is, whether a student-athlete, an actor in the making, a published poet, or "simply" a woman bent on improving the world, there's a leadership role for all students who want that experience at Agnes Scott.

A Springboard for Success

Look at the graduates. They're the true measure of an Agnes Scott education. The College boasts Georgia's first female Rhodes scholar, five Fulbright scholars in five consecutive years, two Goldwater scholars, television newscasters, a NASA engineer, a Pulitzer Prize-winning author and Tony Award-winning playwright, a former governor of the Federal Reserve Board, countless CEOs, writers, politicians, educators, community activists, and more—even presidents. Agnes Scott's President Mary Brown Bullock, an Asia scholar, is one of the College's many successful alumnae. Agnes Scott women share a drive to succeed, a limitless curiosity, and a propensity for leadership.

Students are Challenged

At Agnes Scott, students meet a bright, diverse group of women from all over the United States and around the world. Approximately half have graduated in the top 10 percent of their high school senior class. And the mid-50 percent of S.A.T. scores range from 1100 to 1310. They're academically successful, active in extracurricular activities, and passionate about succeeding in college, community, and life. ☙

Agnes Scott in 30 Seconds

Profile: Independent, national liberal arts and sciences college for women. Founded in 1889. Affiliated with the Presbyterian Church (U.S.A.). Ranked a "Best Value" by *U.S. News & World Report* (2000) and consistently rated one of the best women's colleges in the country. Students from diverse religions and backgrounds welcome.

Location: In the heart of metropolitan Atlanta, approximately 100 acres in a national historic district and residential neighborhood in Decatur, Georgia. $100 million expansion and renovation underway over the next five years.

Enrollment: Nearly 900 students, from 35 states and 25 countries (fall 1998).

Degrees: Bachelor of Arts in 28 majors. Master of Arts in Teaching Secondary English.

Campus: Over 100 acres; six residence halls and an apartment complex that house approximately 90 percent of the student body; 24 buildings.

Technology: Computer network with one port per student in residence hall rooms, automated library, interactive learning center, multimedia classroom, Macintosh lab, Internet access for each student.

Athletics: NCAA Division III intercollegiate sports teams. Eight-lane 25-meter pool, basketball court, weight and training rooms, dance studio, tennis courts, and a 40-meter track.

Endowment: $429.1 million (6/30/99). Ranks eighth nationally among all colleges and universities in endowment per student and second among national liberal arts colleges (NACUBO, 1999).

◀ Agnes Scott students can develop a better understanding of themselves and the world in which they live through study abroad.

◀ Agnes Scott students participate in NCAA Division III sports.

NCR

every portion of a retailer's business enterprise, as well as solutions that keep all parts of the business enterprise connected, including business and technology consulting, software development, and services; data warehousing processes, driven by powerful computing systems and accompanied by database management software, which together help retailers manage their information; self-service checkout solutions and Web kiosks with touch-screen customer information displays, which allow consumers to conveniently obtain information, or purchase products and services electronically; electronic shelf label systems, which ensure consistent pricing of products—from the shelf to the checkout; a wide variety of point-of-sale terminals and bar code scanners; and user-centered design and human factors expertise which result in "smart" systems that are easier for people to operate.

NCR Corporation is joining forces with the world's best retailers to improve the way the world makes purchases—helping retailers get the right products in the right place at the right time. NCR also shapes how consumers shop, whether it's on-line or in-store, or both. Duluth, Georgia, is corporate headquarters for NCR's retail business, whose customers include five of the world's six largest retailers.

NCR's retail vision is "Neighborhood Retailing," referring to the days of the corner store, when neighborhood retailing was a way of life. Shopkeepers knew their customers by name. They shared a neighborhood, and offered the merchandise they knew their customers would want. In those days, every transaction was part of an ongoing relationship, based on personal knowledge and trust. Today, NCR is in the business of doing exactly this—helping retailers transform transactions into relationships. This more personalized way of doing business is making a big comeback with retailers who rely on NCR—to help them manage each store as if it were the only store, each product as if it were the only product, and each customer as the only customer.

NCR's mission is to be the best at providing "technology-enabled business solutions." By this, NCR means an innovative combination of industry expertise, services, software, and hardware. NCR solutions help retailers respond to labor costs and availability, increase gross margins, better serve and retain customers, and develop effective channels to market. NCR offers solutions for

At a time when retail companies around the world are challenged by exploding technology and expanding consumer choice, NCR is the single company with the expertise and experience to provide virtually any retail business solution. The solution may include consulting, support services, software, or hardware. And NCR can provide these anywhere in the world, wherever they are needed.

But whatever the specific business or technology need, NCR knows that enduring success depends on how well retailers develop relationships with their customers—relationships of trust as well as value. And that applies in every retail neighborhood—whether that neighborhood is five city blocks, or five continents. For this important reason, NCR is known as the company that "transforms transactions into relationships." ☻

◄ With the intuitive NCR Web Kiosk, consumers can find valuable product and store information during their shopping experience—at the touch of a screen.

▼ The NCR Electronic Shelf Label Solution ensures accurate pricing at the shelf and the checkout.

Rich's

The story of Rich's began in Atlanta with a young immigrant whose vigor and optimism matched the city's own.

In 1867, 20-year-old Morris Rich saw an opportunity to help the devastated city rise from the ashes of the Civil War. He borrowed $500 from his brother William and opened a small retail dry goods store with five employees on Whitehall Street. The first year's sales volume was $5,000 and delivery was by a mule and wagon. But even then, Atlanta was the fastest growing city in the New South, and M. Rich and Brothers grew right along with it. By 1924, the store, expanded to 75 departments and 800 employees, moved to Broad Street.

From the very beginning Morris Rich believed that his department store was more than a collection of merchandise. Rich's philosophy was to put the people, both customers and employees, first. This became apparent in 1917, when a terrible fire raced through 73 blocks of Atlanta, wiping out 1,553 homes.

Rich's employees helped to fight the fire and then the store offered clothing and household goods to the families who'd lost everything in the blaze. The bottom dropped out of the state's cash crop of cotton in the 1920s. Rich's

stepped in and bought 5,000 bales at above market value. Farmers survived, and their families became loyal customers that never forgot the store that stood by them.

During the Depression, Atlanta teachers were going unpaid until the city issued scrip that Walter Rich personally guaranteed. Rich's would cash the scrip at full value, with no obligation to spend it in the store. Rich's believed in Atlanta, and the city kept faith in the store.

Over the years Rich's made Atlanta history by turning events into traditions. Generations of Atlanta children celebrated the holidays with the Lighting of Rich's Great Tree and a ride on Rich's Pink Pig, a pint-sized train with porcine appeal that chugged around the rooftop of Rich's downtown store.

The first celebration of the Lighting of the Rich's Great Tree took place in 1948 on top of the "crystal bridge," the downtown store's four-story glass-enclosed bridge. Families gathered in the streets of downtown Atlanta, faces upturned, babes in arms and grandmothers alike, watching as the choirs sang and the tree sprang to life, blazing with lights and shining ornaments. Today, the tradition continues with Rich's Great Tree located atop Underground Atlanta.

A memorable milestone occurred in 1959 when Rich's opened its Lenox Square store, the first major suburban mall built in Atlanta. Rich's now operates 13 stores in metro Atlanta, as well stores in Augusta, Savannah, Athens, and Macon, Georgia. Rich's also has three stores in Birmingham, Alabama, as well as stores in Columbia and Greenville, South Carolina.

A new era began when Federated Department Stores acquired Rich's in 1976. Prized for its strong ties to the community and history of service to citizens and the city, Rich's retained its Southern identity, while gaining the support and resources of one of the nation's strongest, most influential merchandising organizations.

▲ From the very beginning Morris Rich believed that his department store was more than a collection of merchandise. Rich's philosophy was to put the people, both customers and employees, first.

▶ Rich's is at the heart of Atlanta, a trusted resource that generations of customers have relied on.

Federated Department Stores, Inc. is the nation's largest operator of department stores, with 403 department stores located in 33 states. In 1995, Federated selected Rich's for the corporate headquarters of its Rich's/Lazarus/Goldsmith's division (RLG). From the Atlanta headquarters, the RLG division operates more than 75 stores in 9 states.

The RLG division manages Rich's stores in three southeastern states. The division is guided under the direction of Chairman Arnold Orlick and President Edwin J. Holman.

Rich's has continued to be part of, and partners with, the city that supported it from the start. A community leader in the United Way, Rich's has also raised hundreds of thousands of dollars for nonprofit organizations through fashion shows and events. In 1998, Rich's and Piedmont Hospital joined together to open a mammography center at Rich's Perimeter.

Rich's has helped to build a magnet program in the Atlanta public schools, supported a wide range of arts organizations, contributed the Panda exhibit at Zoo Atlanta, and supported numerous AIDS causes. The store is proud to be one of the largest teams in the Atlanta AIDS Walk and the number one business contributor to the Atlanta Community Food Bank during the 1998 holidays, with over 41,000 pounds of food donated.

Rich's associates volunteer 36,000 hours annually in company-sponsored projects. Rich's Partners in Time, an employee volunteer force started in 1989, allows employees and their families and friends to share their time and talents in community-wide volunteer projects. The White House recognized Partners in Time with its Volunteer Action Award in 1991 and Rich's received the IMPACT Award from General Colin Powell (Ret.) in 1998.

The store continues to make a difference in the lives of young and old in other ways, too. Rich's organized its annual backpack event for students, distributing backpacks to over 900 disadvantaged kids last fall, to give them a good back-to-school start. Also, every year crafts, cookies, and cards are hand-delivered by Rich's employees to 2,000 seniors at parties Rich's hosts at seven Atlanta-area nursing homes.

Rich's is at the heart of Atlanta, a trusted resource that generations of customers have relied on. It's not hard to find shoppers with their own family stories of promises kept, services rendered, and satisfactions enjoyed from Rich's over the years. Whether native or newcomer, Rich's is the store that knows how to celebrate Southern style. ✿

▲ **The first celebration of the Lighting of Rich's Great Tree took place in 1948 at the downtown store's four-story glass-enclosed bridge. Today, the tradition continues with Rich's Great Tree located atop Underground Atlanta.**

◄ **Rich's is the store that knows how to celebrate Southern style.**

Wachovia Corporation

Corporations are becoming mega-sized and multicontinental. Consumers are knowledgeable and discerning. Advancing technology is raising the bar continually in terms of capabilities and expectations.

So how does today's bank—or, more accurately, today's provider of financial services—distinguish itself, compete for business, and make its mark as a provider of choice?

Wachovia Corporation stands as proof that it can be done—and that size alone is not the key. An interstate bank holding company with dual headquarters in Atlanta and Winston-Salem, North Carolina, Wachovia has operated for more than a century as a respected financial institution known for its emphasis on long-term customer relationships. Today, it serves regional, national, and international markets and has a customer base that includes individuals, companies of all sizes, governmental agencies, and charitable institutions.

▲ **Walter Leonard.** Photo by Leviton-Atlanta. Inc.

▶ (Top right)
G. Joseph Prendergast

▶ (Bottom right)
D. Gary Thompson

Wachovia Corporation is parent to Wachovia Bank, N.A., Wachovia Corporate Services Inc., and Wachovia Capital Markets Inc.

Approximately 10,000 large corporations and midsize companies in locations around the world look to Wachovia for help in achieving their financial goals. Corporate customers include 86 percent of the Fortune 100 companies, excluding banks.

Wachovia also serves more than 200,000 small businesses with annual sales up to $2 million and more than 24,000 companies with sales between $2 million and $25 million. Small business bankers and Wachovia On Call Business Support assist small businesses with their specialized banking needs.

Wachovia serves consumers through more than 700 offices and some 1,300 ATMs strategically located throughout Georgia, North Carolina, South Carolina, Virginia, and Florida. Other Wachovia locations include corporate offices and representatives in Chicago, New York, London, Hong Kong, and Tokyo. Banco Wachovia is located in Sao Paulo, Brazil.

Wachovia is one of the leading financial institutions in Georgia. In Atlanta alone, Wachovia customers perform more than 47,000 teller and ATM transactions in an average day.

To serve the escalating needs of this key Southern city, Wachovia has placed an emphasis on customer convenience. In-store banking centers—introduced in Atlanta-area Harris Teeter grocery stores in 1997—feature ATMs, telephone suites for connections to Wachovia customer service centers, and interactive kiosks that enable customers to obtain product information, perform calculations for education and retirement savings needs, and explore

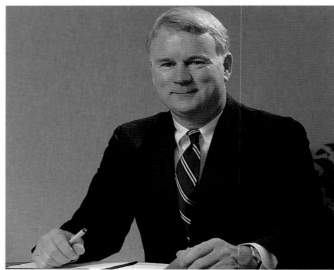

options for loans and investments. Wachovia's Internet site—www.wachovia.com—offers Internet trading, on-line banking, and a host of other interactive financial services.

With an eye to the future, acquisitions and partnerships are being implemented to extend Wachovia's home territory, further expand product offerings, and provide greater accessibility to customers. Areas of emphasis include providing corporate customers with efficient access to capital, connecting customers to the global economy, providing cost-reducing, technology-based processing services, and delivering solutions-oriented advisory services.

While priorities may shift with the times and changing customer needs, Wachovia's overriding focus on service and integrity has remained a constant in the organization's growth and success over the years. ❧

SunTrust Bank

From modest beginnings in the 1980s, SunTrust Bank, Atlanta is today the cornerstone of 28 banks owned and operated by SunTrust Banks, Inc. With assets in excess of $90 billion, the parent company has become the 10th largest banking business in the nation and the largest based in Atlanta and Georgia.

Back when this burgeoning railroad center was recovering from the Civil War, the records offer no clues as to why anyone thought Atlanta needed another bank. The city's population of 75,000 already had a choice of 21 relatively small institutions. Nevertheless, on September 21, 1891, the Georgia General Assembly granted a charter for the Commercial Traveler's Savings Bank.

With a second-hand iron safe, the little bank opened for business in the Gate City Building at the corner of old Pryor and Alabama Streets, now the heart of Underground Atlanta. An 1892 financial statement reported assets of $36,048.17. The next year, Joel Hurt, one of the founders and an early president, led the move to change the name to Trust Company of Georgia, which he felt would be more indicative of the great institution he envisioned. The bank also moved into the new eight-story building at the corner of Pryor Street and Edgewood Avenue, hailed as the South's first "skyscraper" complete with steam-powered elevators.

In its early years, Trust Company concentrated on investment banking and fiduciary services, developing long-standing relationships with many of Atlanta's most successful businesses and leading citizens. A notable event occurred in 1919 when Trust

Company played a key role in the $25-million purchase of the Coca-Cola Company from the Candler family by a group headed by Ernest Woodruff, then president of the bank. With what is now Morgan Guaranty Trust Company of New York and Chase Securities, Trust Company underwrote the first ever public sale of Coca-Cola stock. For its efforts, Trust Company acquired Coca-Cola stock then valued at $110,000. This has proved to be a valuable investment. Through stock splits and dividends, each original 1919 share has multiplied 4,608 times, giving SunTrust 48.3 million shares. The only written copy of the formula for Coca-Cola resides in a safe deposit box at the bank's main office.

It bears noting that Messrs. Hurt and Woodruff were brothers-in-law. Ernest was the father of Robert W. Woodruff, the legendary genius whose leadership propelled Coca-Cola to the heights of American business enterprises. Robert and his brother George maintained an avid interest in the affairs of Trust Company throughout their lives.

The first super-regional banking company established under southeastern reciprocal interstate banking laws, SunTrust Banks, Inc., was created in 1985 through the combination of Trust Company of Georgia and Sun Banks of Florida. The following year, Third National Corporation, based in Nashville, was acquired. In the interests of consistency, banks in the group adopted the name of "SunTrust" in 1995. At the end of 1998, Crestar Financial Corporation in Richmond was added to the organization.

Financial services are provided through more than 1,000 locations in Georgia, Florida, Tennessee, Alabama, Virginia, Maryland, and the District of Columbia.

The old Trust Company building at Pryor and Edgewood was replaced in 1969 with a 26-story tower and adjoining low-rise structure faced with Georgia marble across from Woodruff Park in the heart of downtown. The Atlanta bank's executive offices remain at the location. Headquarters of the holding company occupy the 60-story SunTrust Plaza at the corner of Peachtree and Baker Streets. Operations are centered at a facility in Henry County, south of the city. ❧

Oglethorpe University

Founded in 1835, and listed on the National Register of Historic Places, Oglethorpe University is dedicated to delivering personalized education through a coherent under-graduate curriculum in the arts and sciences, business administration, and teacher education. The Gothic exterior of Oglethorpe University houses Georgia's only coeducational Baccalaureate 1 institution, The Carnegie Foundation for the Advancement of Teaching's highest classification for a liberal arts college.

Oglethorpe's faculty members are recognized nationally for their teaching excellence and scholarly research. The student-to-faculty ratio is 13 to 1, and the average class size of all programs is 16. Oglethorpe students come from more than 35 states and 40 countries. They represent the best of their graduating classes with an average GPA about 3.6, an average SAT above 1,200, and an average ACT about 26. The newest freshman class includes student government and class presidents, valedictorians and salutatorians, yearbook and newspaper editors, nationally recognized Latin scholars, National Merit Award winners, and an award-winning horticulturist.

Graduate and professional programs at universities like Johns Hopkins, Cambridge, Georgetown, Duke, and Princeton welcome Oglethorpe graduates. In addition to having an interactive classroom experience, students are invited to extend their learning beyond the classroom into Atlanta.

Oglethorpe has long encouraged students to pursue internship experiences under the tutelage of individual faculty members at sites such as the Centers for Disease Control and Prevention, CNN, the Carter Center, Coca-Cola, King and Spalding, and numerous others. Oglethorpe offers a special certificate program in Urban Leadership, which invites students to investigate the various roles and perspectives of the leaders of Atlanta, while at the same time furnishing for the students the opportunity through courses, internships, and seminars with community leaders and local alumni to work on actual local problems and matters of community concern.

Oglethorpe offers exciting theatrical and musical productions, art exhibits, and literary events to Atlanta. The year 2000 marks the 14th season of Shakespeare on campus, presented by the Georgia Shakespeare Festival. Oglethorpe University Museum exhibited "The Grand Tour: Landscape and Veduta Paintings—Venice and Rome in the 18th Century" and "The Mystical Arts of Tibet Featuring Personal Sacred Objects of the Dalai Lama," who visited the exhibit in May of 1998. A Hermann Hesse exhibition opened in the spring of 1999, its first showing in a U.S. museum.

Since 1988, Oglethorpe has added or renovated space equivalent to more than two-thirds of the campus's existing buildings. New facilities include a performing arts center, a sports and recreation center, a 71-bed residence hall, six houses for fraternities and sororities, and a $1.1-million campus computer network. Renovations include an addition that tripled the size of the library and an expansion of the Museum.

Larry D. Large became Oglethorpe's 15th president on April 1, 1999, and looks forward to leading the way into a new century. As Oglethorpe University continues to grow, academically and materially, it is ever mindful of its distinguished heritage and will still remain, in the affectionate words of poet and alumnus Sidney Lanier, "a college of the heart." ❧

▲ **Oglethorpe students come from more than 35 states and 40 countries. They represent the best of their graduating classes with an average GPA about 3.6, an average SAT above 1,200, and an average ACT about 26.**

▶ **Founded in 1835, and listed on the National Register of Historic Places, Oglethorpe University is dedicated to delivering personalized education through a coherent undergraduate curriculum in the arts and sciences, business administration, and teacher education.**

Grady Health System

In the 1800s, Atlanta's poor had no place to turn when they were sick or injured. Henry W. Grady, editor of *The Atlanta Constitution* championed the cause of health care for all Atlanta citizens, regardless of their race or income. Thanks to his vision, the Grady Health System®, one of the South's largest public hospital systems, got its start. The City Council of Atlanta approved plans and partial funding, and Grady Memorial Hospital opened in 1892, with 100 charity beds and 10 paying patient beds.

Initially, Grady was run by the City of Atlanta as a municipal hospital, but in 1946 The Fulton-DeKalb Hospital Authority assumed management of the hospital, serving as its governing and policy-making body. The Authority built additional hospital facilities in the 1950s, including a new Grady Memorial Hospital building and Hughes Spalding Pavilion, the first hospital to treat private-paying African-American patients.

During the 1960s, The Hospital Authority led the way in desegregating medical facilities, and served as a catalyst for others to do the same. In the 1970s, The Hospital Authority also pioneered managed care by establishing community health centers that offered medical services to those living outside the downtown area. An outdated building and the pressing need for additional space prompted a $300-million renovation and expansion project completed in 1995.

Grady Health System® today consists of Grady Memorial Hospital, Hughes Spalding Children's Hospital, Crestview Health & Rehabilitaion Center, the Infectious Disease Center, Edward C. Loughlin, Jr. Radiation Oncology Center, Manuel J. Manloof Imaging Center, 10 community primary care centers, a Regional Perinatal Center, Burn Center, Diabetes Detection and Control Center, Rape Crisis Center, Georgia Comprehensive Sickle Cell Center, and a regional Level One Trauma Center.

Grady Health System® touches many lives. In 1998, the Grady Health System® provided care to 32,892 inpatients, delivered 4,341 babies, and treated 731,156 clinical outpatient visits, of which 127,818 were emergency room visits. Grady has the busiest Level One Trauma Center east of the Mississippi River. Grady Emergency Medical Services (EMS) responded to 61,313 calls in 1998.

Grady Health System® has strong affiliations with the Emory University School of Medicine and Morehouse School of Medicine to provide state-of-the-art patient care, teaching, and medical research. It is estimated that more than 25 percent of all physicians practicing in Georgia received training at Grady. Grady also operates three professional training programs in medical technology, radiation oncology, and radiation therapy. Student nurses, technologists, pharmacists, social workers, and doctors all receive clinical experience at Grady.

Grady has been recognized over the years for its outstanding programs and is the recipient of numerous awards. As recent examples, the National Association of Public Hospitals bestowed a first place Safety Net Award to Grady in 1996, 1997, and 1999 for its Breast Health, Diabetes, and Teen Services programs, respectively. The American Hospital Association (AHA) has also recognized Grady. In 1999, the AHA named the Grady Social Services Department the recipient of the Eleanor Clark Award for Innovative Programs in Patient Care for its housing and treatment program for homeless patients with tuberculosis.

For more than 100 years, Grady has maintained its historic commitment to the health care needs of all Atlanta residents, offering medical care in a compassionate, respectful, and dignified manner. Grady Health System® is the cornerstone of Atlanta's medical community and with vision is continually reinventing itself to remain a leading health system for the new millennium. ❂

▲ For more than 100 years, Grady has maintained its historic commitment to the health care needs of the disadvantaged, offering medical care in a compassionate, respectful, and dignified manner.

◀ Grady Health System® is the cornerstone of Atlanta's medical community and with vision is continually reinventing itself to remain a leading health system for the new millennium.

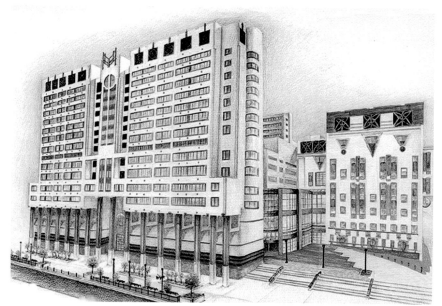

The Atlanta Cyclorama

There is a time machine in Atlanta. It is housed in a stately building located in Historic Grant Park. For over 100 years The Cyclorama has taken millions of visitors back to 1864, back to the "Battle of Atlanta," back to the days when brother fought brother.

The centerpiece of the time machine is a massive cylindrical painting-in-the-round, hence, the name Cyclorama. First developed in the late 1700s, cycloramas became hugely popular following the American Civil War and the Franco-Prussian War, when the triumphant parties commissioned stirring portrayals of climactic battles. Of the 1,000 originally painted, the "Battle of Atlanta" is one of the best of the 20 remaining cycloramas. The painting is 42 feet high and 358 feet in circumference. It weighs over 9,000 pounds and covers an area of 16,000 square feet. It is the largest painting in the world and has been a major attraction in Atlanta since 1893.

The "Battle of Atlanta" is a mesmerizing work of art that captures the imagination of visitors and thrusts them into the heat of battle.

The foreground of the painting, the diorama, contains 128 figures, cannons, trees, and railroad tracks. The diorama blends perfectly with the painting to create a three-dimensional effect. Complete with hills, ravines, and shell-blasted stumps, it is topped with wagons and fighting men. Included is a figure of Clark Gable, who viewed the painting during the 1939 Atlanta premiere of *Gone With the Wind*. It is said he remarked to Mayor Hartsfield, "The only thing missing to make the Cyclorama complete is Rhett Butler." The Mayor had him added.

The painting was completed in 1886 by a group of German, Austrian, and Polish artists. It was painted from actual accounts given by veterans in a series of interviews.

Once completed, the painting spent several years as a touring exhibit. It was brought to Atlanta in 1892 and purchased by George V. Gress 1893. In 1898 Gress donated the painting to the City of Atlanta, who began the show that continues today. With over 100 years of presentations, the "Battle of Atlanta" is one of the longest running shows in the country.

Even though this magnificent time machine transports thousands of visitors to yesteryear, it features many modern-day comforts. In earlier days, a guide illuminated points of interest with a flashlight as visitors walked around the scene. Today, the revolving platform of stadium seating enables visitors to view the painting in air-conditioned comfort. As spotlights highlight scenes in pace with narration, sound effects, and music, travelers take their place in history. With narration in English, French, German, Japanese, and Spanish, international guests are able to experience our history.

Included in the museum is a unique collection of Civil War memorabilia. The centerpiece is the locomotive "TEXAS" of *The Great Locomotive Chase*. Other relics include photographs, uniforms, weapons, and equipment displays. Videos, computer databases, historic maps, and special displays provide historic details of events occurring throughout the war. There is an excellent bookstore and gift shop that carries books, videos, CDs, and momentos for collectors, historians, and tourists alike.

Great care has been taken to preserve the Atlanta Cyclorama as a brilliant and historic depiction of a turbulent era in our nation's history. Visitors, students, historians, and Civil War buffs find this masterpiece an unforgettable and moving experience. The Cyclorama is a must-see for anyone coming to Atlanta.

◄ Photo by Ron Sherman.

CHAPTER THREE
3
1900-1929

❧

During the first three decades of the twentieth century, Atlanta's municipal charms and economic opportunity began drawing new citizens from the surrounding farms and rural areas of Georgia.

Photo by Ron Sherman

CHAPTER THREE
1900-1929

❦

During the first three decades of the twentieth century, Atlanta's municipal charms and economic opportunity began drawing new citizens from the surrounding farms and rural areas of Georgia.

Photo by Ron Sherman

The city's population increased to 154,000 in 1910 and

rose to nearly 200,000 in 1920. Ever since then, Atlanta

has represented the biggest concentration of people in Georgia.

To accommodate the influx, the city began to expand in nearly every direction. The arrival of electricity in the 1880s had given rise to electric streetcars and an entrepreneur named Joel Hurt. A civil engineer by training, Hurt formed his first streetcar company in 1885. His idea was to pair transportation and real estate development.

Hurt built a streetcar line to an area east of downtown, where he owned several hundred acres of land. He named the area Inman Park and built large Victorian homes arranged around a series of small parks. He then marketed the homes to buyers looking for an easy way to get to work downtown.

Other entrepreneurs created their own streetcar lines to undeveloped parts of the city, and a lively competition was underway. Hurt aggressively bought and consolidated competing streetcar lines, as did the company that would later become Georgia Power Company. Hurt would later serve as president of Trust Co. Bank.

Residential growth also began moving north along Peachtree Street. The major obstacle was six hundred acres of undeveloped forested land—known as the Northside Dam—owned by George Washington Collier. Collier's death in 1903 finally broke the dam. The property was quickly developed into residential neighborhoods like Ansley Park, home for many years to the Governor's Mansion and, later, Sherwood Forest.

Not long after the electric streetcar came another mode of transportation that would alter Atlanta in significant ways—the automobile. William Alexander, a bicycle dealer, is given credit for bringing the first cars—steam-driven models—to Atlanta in 1901. This new form of transport was quickly adopted by an adventurous citizenry and by 1904 the city had registered its first fatal auto accident. Auto dealerships sprang up, as did a taxi company. Horse-drawn cabs quickly died out; automobiles were cheaper.

Ford Motor Company came south in 1915 and built a factory on Ponce De Leon Avenue to make Model Ts. There was even a local car manufacturer—the Hanson Six cost one thousand dollars in 1917— although it folded in 1925.

Atlanta even had its own automobile speedway: the two-mile Candler Field oval. Complete with grandstand for spectators, it was built south of the city in 1909 by Asa Candler and his son. Several decades later, Candler Field would become the site of Hartsfield Airport.

More cars meant the need for more and better-paved streets, which in turn forced the city government to float a bond issue.

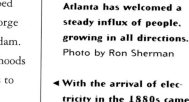

◄ Since the early 1900s, Atlanta has welcomed a steady influx of people, growing in all directions. Photo by Ron Sherman

◄ With the arrival of electricity in the 1880s came the electric streetcar line. One of the earliest was established by civil engineer and entrepreneur Joel Hurt. The electric streetcars are visible in this view of Marietta Street, c.1904. The monument in the middle may be one erected to Henry W. Grady. Photo courtesy of Georgia Department of Archives and History

The new mobility also meant the freedom to live farther away from the job. The grand mansions that fronted on Peachtree Street only two or three blocks north of the downtown train tracks quickly disappeared in favor of new office and commercial buildings like the Davison's (later Macy's) department store. Today only the Capital City Club building suggests that Peachtree Street north of Five Points has ever been anything other than a commercial and business district.

The invention of the electric elevator made larger, multi-story office buildings possible. The 1906 Candler Building, for instance, towered seventeen stories above city streets. A new downtown post office and federal court building arrived in 1911. The Healey Building, another grand office structure, was finished a couple years later. New downtown hotels followed right behind. The Piedmont (1903) was known as the luxurious "New York" hotel. The Georgian Terrace opened in Midtown in 1911 and the Winecoff in 1913.

One of the most innovative structures of the time was the Peachtree Arcade, built in 1917 for $500,000. The arcade was an indoor shopping center with two levels of storefronts fronting along a central walkway and a skylit roof. Fifty years later, the concept would return to Atlanta as the mall.

In 1914 President Woodrow Wilson, who had briefly practiced law in Atlanta during the 1880s, awarded the city a Federal Reserve Bank. Four years later it moved into a new headquarters building on Marietta Street.

The early 1900s also marked the emergence of the company that came to be most closely identified with Atlanta: Coca-Cola.

The Coca-Cola story had begun in the mid-1880s, when John Pemberton, a pharmacist, had mixed up a new syrup intended for sale as headache reliever. It was modestly successful, but the real innovation came in 1887 when a counterman at Jacobs Drugstore downtown experimented mixing the syrup with carbonated water.

Pemberton was neither healthy enough nor wealthy enough to fully exploit his creation, and he sold a half-interest in the drink in return for more capital. The ownership of the formula was finally wholly acquired by Asa Candler in 1891 for approximately $2,300.

▶ As more people flowed into Atlanta, residential neighborhoods were established. Joel Hurt paired his ideas for transportation with a knack for real estate development to create Inman Park, made up of large Victorian homes arranged around a series of small parks. Photos by Ron Sherman

▶ The home of Joel Hurt was built at 85 Elizabeth Street in Inman Park. He developed Inman park and built the Hurt Building at Edgewood, Ivy, and Exchange Place. Photo courtesy Georgia Department of Archives and History

▲ **Soldiers filled Fort McPherson in 1917, on their way to the battles of World War I.** Photo courtesy Georgia Department of Archives and History

Candler was a good businessman and an astute marketer. By the turn of the century he was franchising the rights to produce and sell Coca-Cola to businessmen in other southern cities, thus indirectly founding a number of enduring family fortunes in the region. By 1916, the now-wealthy Candler resigned in order to serve as mayor of Atlanta and, in 1919, the family sold Coca-Cola to Trust Co. Bank for $25 million. The bank quickly converted it into a publicly traded company and sold the stock to investors. Robert Woodruff, the son of Trust Co. President Ernest Woodruff, was so intrigued by the company that he quit his job to join up in 1923. Robert W. Woodruff would go on to run The Coca-Cola Company for nearly sixty years. Under his shrewd direction, it would become perhaps the greatest multi-national business in history.

It was Asa Candler who first linked civic generosity and Coca-Cola. Candler's brother was head of a small Methodist college east of

Atlanta and in 1914 Asa decided to bring the school to Atlanta. He found a site in Druid Hills, a residential area he was masterminding, and the Chamber of Commerce pitched in $500,000 to finance the move. Candler himself pledged one million dollars for the school's endowment and in 1919 Emory University came to Atlanta.

Another private university came to Atlanta in a similar way. Oglethorpe University was founded in Milledgeville but closed after the Civil War. In 1912 the Atlanta business community raised $500,000 to reincarnate the school in Atlanta.

Economic growth and education weren't just limited to white Atlantans during these years, although segregated facilities like libraries, movie theaters, and public pools were the rule.

The pioneer of black education in Atlanta was Reverend Frederick Ayer. In 1867 he and others obtained a charter for a school for blacks that would become Atlanta University. Two years

◄ **Two young men sit and talk in Piedmont Park, c. 1904.** Photo courtesy Georgia Department of Archives and History

◄ **The White Star Automobile Company's first two models. White Star was the first southern automobile factory.** Photo courtesy Georgia Department of Archives and History

Ernest Duke + Friend

like the *Atlanta Daily World*, which still publishes today.

As early as the 1880s, blacks were distinguishing themselves as entrepreneurs. Alonzo Herndon was a former slave who opened a string of barbershops—the most lavish boasted twenty-five chairs and elegant fixtures—that catered to whites and blacks. In 1905 he came to the rescue of several ailing insurance companies. By the 1920s he had consolidated them into one agency, Atlanta Life Insurance, that survives to this day.

Another black businessman, Herman Perry, parlayed a rudimentary education into a career in several insurance companies, banks, and professional service firms in the early 1920s. Business reversals eventually devastated his empire but one of his creations, Citizen's Trust Bank, is still one of the largest black-owned banks in the country.

The railroads were still important to Atlanta. A new Spanish-styled Terminal Station was built in 1904. In 1919 one of Atlanta's Fortune 500 companies, National Service Industries, opened as Atlanta Linen Supply. A steel hoop company founded in 1901 grew to become Atlantic Steel Company by 1913. New banks, like Fulton National (later to become Bank of the South) and Atlanta Savings & Loan (which became National Bank of Georgia) opened.

later, another black school was chartered; it would become Clark University. In 1879, another black school, this one in Augusta, moved to Atlanta. It would become Morehouse College, a school for black males. Morris Brown College was organized in 1881 and in that same year a seminary school for black females appealed successfully to John D. Rockefeller for financial help. To thank him, the school's name was changed to Spelman in honor of Rockefeller's mother. By 1929, the schools had agreed to a compact that would draw them together on a campus complex southwest of downtown, forming the Atlanta University Complex.

The center of black business and church life in Atlanta was Auburn Avenue. "Sweet Auburn," as it was dubbed, evolved into one of the largest concentrations of black wealth in America. By the 1920s the street was full of black doctors, lawyers, engineers, and other professionals. To keep up, they read black-owned newspapers

During these years it was sometimes hard to tell where city government ended and the Chamber of Commerce began, in part because the two organizations were crammed into a single building. Robert Maddox, a banker, served as head of the Chamber and later was drafted by the business community to serve a successful stint as mayor. Under his urging, the city floated a bond issue to upgrade its infrastructure, and constructed an auditorium in 1906. In 1912 the Chamber of Commerce formed the Atlanta Convention Bureau.

Many of today's leading hospitals emerged in the early 1900s. Asa Candler and his family were the primary benefactors of Wesley Memorial Hospital in the early 1900s. Later it was moved to the

▲ One of the most innovative structures of the time was the Peachtree Arcade, built in 1917 for $500,000. The arcade was an indoor shopping center with two levels of storefronts along a central walkway and a skylit roof. Fifty years later, the concept would return to Atlanta as the mall. Photo courtesy Georgia State University Special Collections

new Emory University complex and in 1925 the title was given to the school, which promptly renamed it Emory University Hospital.

Another hospital, Amster Sanatorium, was founded downtown in 1905 but was quickly reorganized as Piedmont Hospital and moved to a Peachtree Road site that had been the suburban estate of one of the founders of King & Spalding.

Thomas Egleston, a local insurance executive, left money in his 1916 will for the creation of a fifty-bed hospital for children. The hospital, named after his wife, Henrietta, opened twelve years later and today sits on the Emory University campus.

New social and business clubs kept coming, particularly as residential areas pushed out away from the city center. In 1904, the East Lake Golf Club was formed, which later became the home club of the great amateur golfer Bobby Jones. Jewish Atlantans organized the Standard Club in 1905. The Piedmont Driving Club, which had sold a large chunk of its property to the city for the great expositions of the late 1800s, was destroyed by fire in 1906 but regrouped and reopened the next year. The Brookhaven Country Club opened well north of the city in 1911. Two years later it affiliated with the Capital City Club, which had opened its

own new building downtown on Peachtree Street in 1911. The Ansley Park Club began in 1912 as a public golf course before going private. The Druid Hills Golf Club opened in 1912 as well. All these clubs became important intersections of Atlanta's growing social and business elite.

Although Atlanta had seen its shares of fires in the last century, the city's greatest blaze took place in 1917. It started downtown and raced north with the wind. It was finally stopped just before it reached Piedmont Park, in part because desperate firemen began dynamiting housing blocks to create a firebreak. Many of the nearly two thousand buildings destroyed housed black families, and nearly ten thousand were left homeless. Fortunately, there was only one fatality. ☙

◄ The early 1900s marked the emergence of the company that came to be most closely identified with Atlanta—Coca-Cola. The Coca-Cola story had begun in the mid-1880s, when pharmacist John Pemberton mixed up a new syrup intended for sale as a headache reliever. In 1887, a counterman at Jacobs Drugstore downtown experimented mixing the syrup with carbonated water, and the famous drink was born. In 1891, Asa Candler acquired the formula. In 1923, Robert Woodruff joined the fledgling company. He would go on to run The Coca-Cola Co. for nearly sixty years, guiding it to status as perhaps the greatest multinational business in history. Historic photo courtesy of the Atlanta History Center. New photos by Ron Sherman

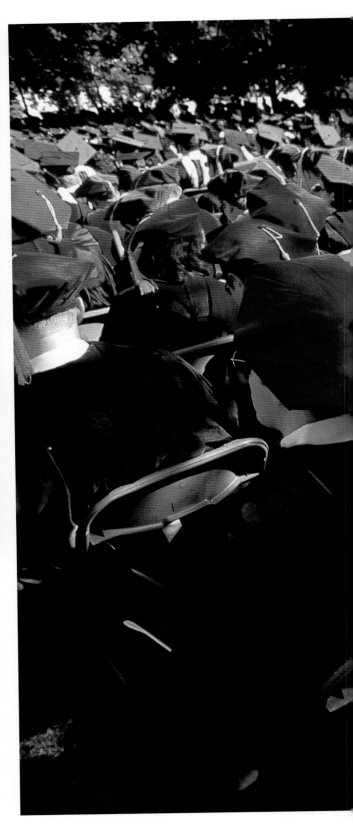

▶ It was Asa Candler who first linked civic generosity and Coca-Cola. Candler's brother was head of a small Methodist college east of Atlanta and in 1914 Asa decided to bring the school to Atlanta. He found a site in Druid Hills, a residential area he was developing, and the Chamber of Commerce pitched in $500,000 to finance the move. Candler himself pledged one million dollars for the school's endowment, and in 1919 Emory University came to Atlanta.

Photos by Ron Sherman

◀ **The pioneer of black education in Atlanta was Rev. Frederick Ayer. In 1867 he and others obtained a charter for a school for blacks that would become Atlanta University. Two years later, another black school was chartered; it would become Clark University. In 1879, another black school, this one in Augusta, moved to Atlanta. It would become Morehouse College. In 1881, Morris Brown College and Spelman, a seminary school for black females, were founded. In 1929, the schools agreed to a compact that would draw them together on a campus complex, forming the Atlanta University Complex.** Photos by Ron Sherman

▲ The center of black business and church life in Atlanta was Auburn Avenue. "Sweet Auburn," as it was dubbed, was home to black doctors, lawyers, engineers, and other professionals. Today, Auburn Avenue is still a thriving part of Atlanta, hosting an annual arts festival and home to much Atlanta history. Historic photo courtesy of Georgia State University Special Collections. New photo by Ron Sherman

◄ The *Atlanta Daily World* newspaper was started in the 1920s as the source of news by, for, and about the black population in Atlanta. The newspaper still publishes today. Photo by Ron Sherman

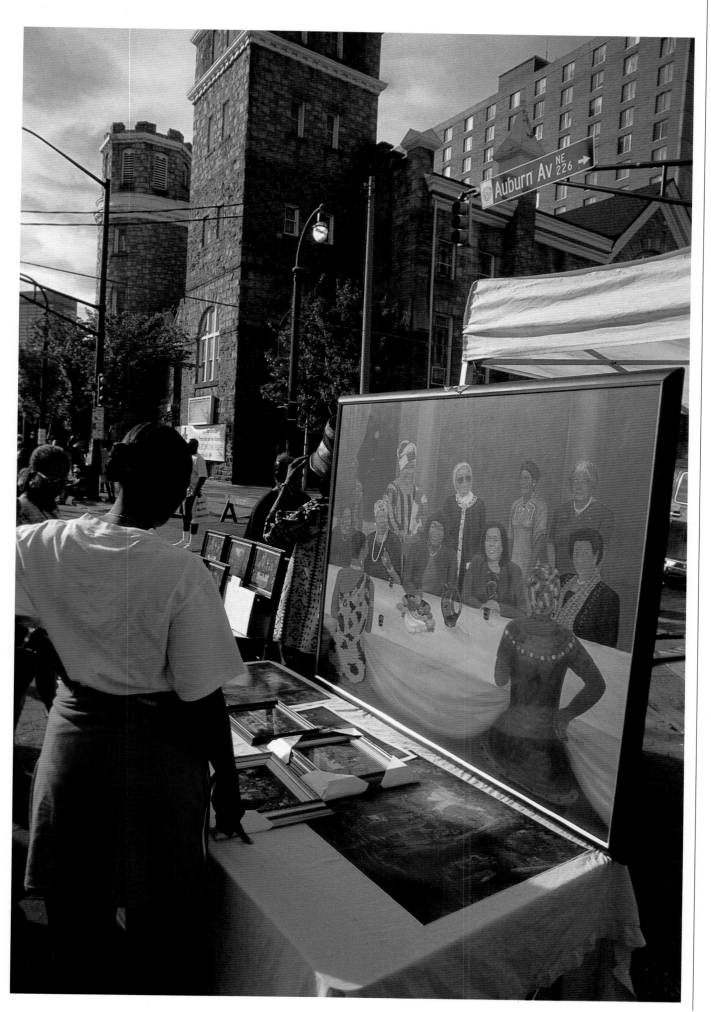

▲ **Atlanta's greatest blaze occurred May 21, 1917.
Called the Great Northside conflagration, the fire
started in a stack of mattresses in a structure on
Fort Street near Decatur Street that was being used
by Grady Hospital as a storage warehouse. The fire
spread rapidly and burned an area of more than
three hundred acres and destroyed 1,938 structures.
Property loss amounted to $5,000,000 and 10,000
people were left homeless.** Photo courtesy Georgia
Department of Archives and History

▶ **In 1904, the East Lake Golf Club was formed, which
later became the home of the great amateur golfer
Bobby Jones.** Historic photo courtesy of Georgia
Department of Archives and History. New photo by
Ron Sherman

Carithers Wallace Courtenay (CWC)

▶ **The CWC showroom presents over 38,000 square feet of the finest contract furnishings in the office furniture marketplace.** Photo by Rion Rizzo.

CWC first opened in 1929 in a tiny showroom in the heart of downtown Atlanta with a few dollars' worth of inventory and a pound of hope. James Wallace was president, John B. Courtenay was vice president, and Harold G. Carithers was secretary and treasurer. They built the business with a staff of three on the premise of trust and a gentleman's handshake.

Over the course of 40 years, CWC's space and inventory grew in controlled stages. The team concentrated on providing quality products and real customer service. As the business grew, so did the company's reputation.

In 1969, CWC moved into a new building with 39,000 feet of warehouse, showroom, and office space. Spacious and modern, the facility seemed the epitome of success for a homegrown enterprise. Inventory was readily available for customers, but the favored styles of the time were mostly along traditional lines.

By 1987, the 39,000 feet that were so spacious in 1969 now cramped the company's growth as Atlanta businesses regularly sought out CWC for goods and design services. In February 1988, CWC moved again. This time to 178,000 square feet, including 148,000 feet of warehouse space and 30,000 feet of showroom and office space. But this move took CWC from downtown north to the perimeter, an area which then President George Brandon felt would eventually become the heart of Atlanta.

By 1999 the postmodern facility was still the company's headquarters and housed a staff of 135 full-time employees. Today, the showroom presents over 30,000 square feet of the finest contract furnishings in the office furniture marketplace. Beautifully accessorized vignettes, representing over 250 different furniture manufacturers, are displayed for ease of viewing by the discerning eyes of decorators and corporate heads from Fortune 500 companies and other business notables.

Herman Miller and Kimball, two of the leading manufacturers of furniture and furniture systems, are represented heavily throughout CWC's extraordinary inventory of office furniture ranging from the traditional to transitional and contemporary. Through Herman Miller, the original innovators of the panel system, CWC offers products with the highest residual value in the furniture industry. These products grow and evolve as technology changes and are easy to install and reconfigure.

Beyond excellent furniture, CWC offers complete service

capability, including design, project management, delivery and installation, customer storage, warranty repairs, electrostatic painting, reupholstery and refurbishing, refinishing and touch-up, and rental and leasing programs.

CWC is also a technology-driven company. Salespeople often travel to a client's office with laptop in hand. Using Z-Axis laptop technology, the salesperson can lay out a floor plan in color 3-D to allow clients to see options in their completed state before purchases are made. Product selections can then be automatically ordered via computer and delivery made in as few as 10 days. The technology gives CWC customers quick response times, guaranteed accuracy, and exceptional service, not to mention the cost savings and stress relief from correcting errors that can be detected prior to order.

In addition to the furniture division, CWC has both an office supply and a coffee division. The supply division stocks over 5,000 quality office supplies with next-day delivery available on most items. The Coffee Butler, the coffee and vending division, offers personalized service for all in-house vending needs. Fresh products and weekly service provide customers with the very best of in-house coffee and vending products.

CWC has achieved its long-lived success through a dedicated focus on core competencies, the highest quality processes, customer attention and commitment, and maintaining a staff that is technically skilled and service oriented.

CWC is a company that emphasizes timely responses to customers' needs. The company is committed to "wowing" customers by providing excellent customer service throughout the entire buying process, from the salespeople, to customer service, to the installation crews.

As CWC has done in the past, the company will continue to grow and embrace new technology and new product offerings, always maintaining the highest regard for customers and continuing to "WOW" them throughout the course of the relationship. ❧

◄ The CWC team concentrates on providing quality products and real customer service. Photo by Rion Rizzo.

Mercer University
Cecil B. Day Campus—Atlanta

Over the past 165 years, Mercer University has established itself among the largest Baptist-affiliated institutions in the world, and the only university of its size in the nation to offer programs in liberal arts, business, education, engineering, medicine, pharmacy, law, and theology. In addition to Mercer's main campus in Macon, the University operates the Cecil B. Day Campus in Atlanta and four centers throughout Georgia.

Serving nearly 7,000 graduate and undergraduate students, Mercer University prides itself on exceptional teaching, a commitment to public service, and a growing involvement in research. It is a caring community of learning that integrates rigorous academic expectations with a persistent concern for the personal and spiritual

▲ For 10 consecutive years, U.S. News & World Report has ranked Mercer University among the top 15 regional colleges and universities in the South.

▶ Mercer's Cecil B. Day Campus in Atlanta is home to the James and Carolyn McAfee School of Theology.

growth of its students. Mercer's commitment to the education of the whole person has earned the University a rank among the top 15 regional colleges and universities in the South by *U.S. News & World Report* for 10 consecutive years.

Mercer's Cecil B. Day Campus in Atlanta is home to the University's Graduate and Professional Center, as well as its newest academic unit, the James and Carolyn McAfee School of Theology. Established in 1972 when Mercer merged with Atlanta Baptist College, the Atlanta campus currently serves graduate and professional students from all over the Southeast.

Because most Mercer University Atlanta campus students are working professionals, classes are routinely offered during late afternoons, evenings, and on Saturdays. Many programs may be completed through programs that meet once a week for about five months, or the length of a semester.

The Eugene W. Stetson School of Business and Economics combines business theory with practical application. Students graduate with the necessary skills to address competitive business pressures, global expansions, and the accelerating role of technology in today's business environment. Faculty members are active professionally and highly attuned to the changing scope of business

needs. Students are encouraged to expand their experiences beyond the classroom early in the course of their education. Leadership seminars and the Executive Forum, one of Georgia's longest-running business enrichment programs, enables students to hear from some of the country's most sought-after speakers on topics of business, politics, and current events.

Mercer's Center for Business Research and Development, an organization designed to provide economic development programs for Georgia communities and local governments, enables students to gain practical marketing research experience. As part of the course requirement, students enrolled in the Executive Master of Business Administration program travel abroad for two weeks to study different business practices in foreign lands such as England, Russia, and Hong Kong. Students graduate from the Eugene W. Stetson School of Business and Economics upon course completion with a master's in one of four degree programs: Business Administration, Health Care Management, Technology Management, or Executive Master of Business Administration.

Mercer's School of Education is dedicated to preparing outstanding educators for the twenty-first century. The School offers a

Master of Education and Education Specialist degree with either an early childhood or middle grades emphasis. Students can also obtain a postbaccalaureate certificate with an emphasis in early childhood, middle grades, or secondary education.

As one of only two comprehensive engineering programs in the state of Georgia, Mercer's Macon-based School of Engineering began offering graduate degrees and certification programs on the Atlanta campus in 1992. The programs enable working engineers to further their academic and technical expertise through once-a-week classes while maintaining their careers. The curriculum includes both theoretical and practical courses taught by graduate faculty members who all hold doctorates in appropriate disciplines. Programs of study include a Master of Science in Engineering with an emphasis in either electrical engineering or engineering management, a Master of Science in Technical Communication

◄ Beyond the University's many recognitions, Mercer prides itself on exceptional teaching, a commitment to public service, and a growing involvement in research.

Management, and graduate level certificates in technical communication management or object-oriented software development.

A nationally recognized leader in pharmacy education, Mercer's Southern School of Pharmacy was the first pharmacy school in the Southeast and the fifth in the nation to offer the Doctor of Pharmacy degree as its sole professional degree. The School of Pharmacy also awards the Doctor of Philosophy degree in pharmaceutical sciences, the highest graduate degree offered by the University. Five times in the last 10 years, Mercer's chapter of the Academy of Students of Pharmacy received national recognition as the most outstanding chapter in the nation. This is the highest award presented by the American Pharmaceutical Association.

The James and Carolyn McAfee School of Theology opened its doors in August 1996 with 44 students. Enrollment increased to nearly 150 students by fall 1999, representing 14 states and Brazil, Japan, Liberia, and Bulgaria. The first class graduated in the spring of 1999. Faculty, staff, and students are housed in the new 32,000-square-foot School of Theology building on Mercer's Cecil B. Day Campus. Led by a generous gift from James and Carolyn McAfee of Atlanta, nearly 6,000 individuals and organizations have pledged their financial support to the School.

In response to Atlanta's growing international population, the English Language Institute was established on Mercer's Atlanta campus to serve the needs of non-native English speakers. Distinguished as a leader in innovative curriculum design, the English Language Institute's courses are academic in focus and are offered at all levels of proficiency. Courses of study include full-time and part-time academic programs, a professional English skills program, private tutoring, and individually designed courses on an as-needed basis.

Beyond the obvious benefits to society in general and students in particular, a significant number of Mercer's staff and faculty engage in research activities, including scholarly and service-oriented efforts. The Schools of Pharmacy, Engineering, and Medicine are major research contributors within the university community.

A University Research Office was established in 1994 to help faculty and staff secure funding for research efforts. In addition, the

◄ Because most Mercer University Atlanta campus students are working professionals, classes are routinely offered during late afternoons, evenings, and on Saturdays.

Office tracks grant funding and assists the Institutional Research Committees in the review process. Research funding comes from a variety of sources, including the state and federal governments, corporations, foundations, non-profit agencies, individuals, and the University. ❦

Citizens Trust Bank

► Citizens Trust Company, which became one of the largest black owned and operated community banks in the country, was founded in 1919 by five prominent Atlantans. Its first office is shown here circa 1921.

Citizens Trust Bank of Atlanta is the largest African-American-owned bank in the Southeast with $200 million in assets, 11 branch offices, and over 140 employees.

Citizens Trust has been a partner in the community since 1921, creating new homeowners, new business owners, and new community growth throughout metro Atlanta for nearly eight decades. Citizens Trust Company, which became one of the largest black owned and operated community banks in the country, was founded in 1919 by five prominent Atlantans. These five foresighted men envisioned a bank which would primarily serve the black citizens of Atlanta. These "fervent five," led by businessman Heman E. Perry, pooled their time, money, and resources to develop a bank which would offer its customers improved financial security.

Perry had founded the Standard Life Insurance Company in 1909. By 1921 it had grown to become the largest black insurance company in America. Seeing the need to expand the scope of his insurance company into other fields of business for minorities, Perry began organizing subsidiaries of Standard Life. The first was a holding company, the Service Company, organized in 1917. Some of the new enterprises originated by his holding company were the Service Pharmacies, the Service Laundries, Service Printing Company, and the Service Realty and Development Company.

Citizens Trust opened its doors on Auburn Avenue in 1921, in the heart of downtown Atlanta's historic Sweet Auburn Avenue. The goal of the bank was threefold: to promote the financial stability and business development, to stress the principle of thrift, and to make home ownership possible for more people.

As a new bank, Citizens Trust had to overcome many obstacles

► L. D. Milton became president during 1926, and under his leadership Citizens Trust Company survived the 1929 stock market crash.

inherent in serving a low-income, economically disadvantaged community. Within 18 months, despite the nation's grave financial crisis, the bank's resources grew to over $1 million. Mr. L. D. Milton became president during 1926. Under his leadership Citizens Trust Company survived the 1929 stock market crash. The bank also financed the Morris Brown subdivision and homes in the Mozley Park, Bankhead, and Hightower Road communities. The construction of the 12-story Citizens Trust Bank Building was completed under his tenure. Citizens Trust made home ownership possible for thousands of African-American Atlantans, while serving as a financial agent for individuals and corporations. In 1971, Citizens Trust Company became Citizens Bancshares Corporation (a holding company), parent of Citizens Trust Bank, an organizational change spearheaded by the bank's new president and CEO, Charles McKinley Reynolds. By 1972 the bank had assets of over $34 million and agreed to the purchase of Atlanta Mortgage Brokerage and Servicing Company, which allowed the bank to become more competitive in the mortgage origination and servicing business.

Over time, Citizens Trust became a proven partner in the economic growth of Atlanta, encouraging young entrepreneurs applying for a first-time loan as well as serving the financial needs of established corporate clients. In 1975, I. Owen Funderburg became the bank's fourth president. Under his leadership, the bank opened in-store branches, installed ATMs, and brought the technology of the bank into a new era. Funderburg doubled operations from approximately $60 million to over $120 million. During the Funderburg administration, Citizens Trust was named as 1985 Bank of the Year by *Black Enterprise Magazine*.

The legacy and success of Citizens Trust encouraged 17 Atlantans to come together to organize the First Southern Bank of Lithonia in 1987, the first new bank founded by minorities in the state of Georgia in 60 years.

Located in southern Dekalb County, the bank served small- and medium-sized businesses as well as individuals and professionals, offering a full range of banking services, including a variety of consumer and commercial checking accounts, as well as commercial real estate and installment loans. In 1993 James E. Young joined the bank as the new president and CEO. Under his successful leadership, First Southern Bank flourished as a vital presence in the South Dekalb community. In 1996, First Southern purchased American Financial Mortgage, a mortgage brokerage company. The name of the company is now Citizens Trust Bank Mortgage Services, Inc. and offers nearly 100 different mortgage products.

In 1998 Citizens Trust and First Southern Bank of Lithonia

Citizens Trust has shown its commitment to the community it serves over many decades by underwriting the construction and expansion costs of many black churches, co-sponsoring the Harper Center for Financial Services, which provides training to students interested in finance-related careers, and by supporting such respected organizations as the Atlanta Business League, United Way, Atlanta Metropolitan Boys Club, YMCA, YWCA, and the United Negro College Fund. In 1998, Citizens Trust Bank pulled together three other minority-owned banks and loaned the historic Ebenezer Baptist Church, the church home of Dr. Martin Luther King, Jr., $5.5 million to finance the construction of a new sanctuary for its 2,000 members.

Today, after several decades of meeting a variety of banking needs, Citizens Trust Bank is a proven partner in the economic growth of the community. The bank's customer base extends well beyond individuals and small business persons to include major corporations and nonprofit organizations. Whether the customer is a young entrepreneur applying for a first-time loan, or a large corporate client looking to expand its banking relationships, Citizens Trust stands ready to give sound financial advice within a professional, yet personal, atmosphere. Under the continued leadership of James E. Young, CTB will continue to be a vital and respected financial institution in the new millennium. ❧

◀ Citizens Trust is a proven partner in the economic growth of Atlanta, encouraging young entrepreneurs applying for a first-time loan as well as serving the financial needs of established corporate clients.

merged to create Citizens Trust Bank of Atlanta, and Mr. Young became CTB's sixth president and CEO. The merger created challenges that ranged from managing the consolidation of two workforces, two data systems, and two boards of directors, while at the same time operating the company efficiently enough to generate a profit and strengthen shareholder value.

In 1999, the company recently announced that its common stock was made available in the public market. Citizens Bancshares Corporation entered into an agreement with J.C. Bradford and Co. that provides for Bradford to act as Principal Market Maker and in turn increased the liquidity of the company's stock. The publicly traded stock is now identified by the ticker symbol CZBS.

Citizens Trust Bank weathered those challenges and made substantial progress on a number of fronts. Citizens Trust Bank achieved total revenues of $22.7 million—which compared very favorably to the $21.1 million reported for fiscal 1997. More importantly, the net earnings achieved for 1998 in the amount of $1.8 million was more than five times the $317,000 earned in 1997, a record unsurpassed since the bank's doors opened in 1921. The Board of Directors authorized a 15 cents per share cash dividend for shareholders, the highest ever dividend payment.

During 1998, Citizens Trust Bank invested heavily in technology to prepare for potential Y2K problems and to further advance its technology for the new millennium. In fact, while the nation celebrated Reverend Martin Luther King Jr.'s 70th birthday, the King Center prepared itself to approach year 2000 with help from Citizens Trust. CTB donated the services of Comp USA to help the King Center approach the new millennium with updated technology.

◀ In 1993 James E. Young joined the bank as the new president and CEO. Under his successful leadership, the bank has flourished as a vital presence in the community.

Beers Construction Company

Begun as a dream built by the sweat of an Atlanta native, Harold W. Beers Sr., and now a subsidiary of a Swedish holding company, Beers Construction Company is one of the oldest construction firms in the southern region. Its list of accomplishments and awards spans almost 100 years.

Beers was founded in 1905 as an engineering construction firm that offered high-strength concrete building frames as an alternative to steel frame construction. The benefits of better fire protection, lower cost, and flexibility in foundation and frame design caught on quickly, and Beers entered a period where it built

virtually all of the major concrete buildings in Atlanta in the 1920s and 1930s. It opened an office in Florida in the 1930s and built the first Federal Courthouse in Tallahassee, Florida, and several other major public buildings as well as federal Works Project Administration projects throughout Georgia and Florida.

In 1965, then President Lawrence Gellerstedt Jr. led a friendly employee buy-out of the company from the Beers family. By June 1994, the successful company was acquired by Skanska USA, a diversified construction services group that has operated in the United States for over 23 years. Skanska USA is a subsidiary of Skanska AB, Danderyd, Sweden, an international construction and industrial group with offices in 33 countries. As of 1999, the parent company had an audited net worth exceeding $3 billion, giving it considerable leeway in financing long-term growth strategies with its operating units.

Beers' spirit of innovation and commitment carries forward to the present day. The innovations are not so much in building techniques these days, as they are in management systems and creative project delivery mechanisms to continuously improve cost, schedule, and building performance. The construction of the $175-million Georgia Dome in just 29 months, the $207-million

▲ Emory's Robert W. Woodruff Library is a fine example of the quality work performed by Beers Construction Company.

► On October 30, 1936, Beers Construction broke ground on an addition to the Florida State Capitol.

Olympic Stadium and its conversion to the new Atlanta Braves Stadium, and increasingly cost-effective office buildings, hospitals, and municipal/government projects reflect this attitude. Beers has completed many other notable projects in Atlanta, including The High Museum, The Carter Library, UPS Corporate Offices, Home Depot Store Support Center, and the headquarters buildings for Coca-Cola and Southern Bell. Its works, however, are not limited to the metro area, as Beers builds throughout the South. Its works are not dominated by large, high-profile projects. Specialized groups ensure clients focus regardless of size.

The company provides construction services for a wide range of clients. The Beers Education Group is one of the largest builders of schools and universities in the South, and is the largest school construction manager in Georgia. Also one of the largest builders of office space in the South, another division, Beers Healthcare Group, is the largest builder of health care and hospital facilities in Georgia and is the seventh largest in the nation.

Other major project types include government sector construction, laboratories, and high-tech industrial construction, and a heavy/civil unit that builds infrastructure, wastewater, and related projects.

The Beers organization and affiliates have worked in 25 states on projects ranging from $1 million to hundreds of millions. Its work has led to the company's consistent ranking among the top 10 firms in *Engineering News Record's* listing of the Top General Building Contractors in the United States. ❧

Sutherland Asbill & Brennan LLP

Sutherland Asbill & Brennan LLP has long been known as one of the nation's leading tax law firms. To this day, some 75 years later, many of the nation's largest corporations and thousands of smaller corporations, plus cooperatives, partnerships, joint ventures, tax-exempt organizations, trusts, estates, and individuals deliberately seek legal help from the firm to resolve their most perplexing tax problems. Despite this notoriety for unparalleled results in the tax field, and the tremendous success such a reputation delivers, Sutherland Asbill & Brennan shunned the temptation to restrict its vision to the world of tax strategy and litigation.

Shortly after World War II, the partners decided to expand the practice to include the general legal needs of businesses caught up in a growing economy and changing times. The addition of greatly expanded corporate and financial services and the increase of specialized attorneys brought about increased opportunity. However, the firm never lost sight of its famed dedication to integrity and ethics, or its love of the law. From the depths of this dedication came many wins for clients in landmark cases—some of which were highly unpopular at the time. As Sutherland Asbill & Brennan pursued the spirit of the law with an enthusiasm built on faith in constitution and country, it impacted society in ways few firms have ever accomplished. For example, during the 1950s, when the country was in the grips of tremendous social and legal turbulence, Sutherland Asbill & Brennan was the only firm of note, of any stature and size, to take on civil rights cases in the Southeast.

From the beginning, in 1924, the firm's attorneys have practiced and affected law in this country in many ways. Founders Bill Sutherland, who once served as a law clerk to Justice Brandeis, and Elbert Tuttle, who became a judge on the United States Court of Appeals and was later awarded the Presidential Medal of Honor, were only the first of a long line of Sutherland Asbill & Brennan attorneys to deliver exemplary performance. Though recognition for noteworthy performance is difficult to achieve in a field where high ethics, perfectionism, and duty are merely expected, and seldom praised, it becomes all the more impressive considering the firm's multinational practice.

Today, Sutherland Asbill & Brennan represents clients nationally and internationally from their offices in Atlanta; Washington, D.C.; New York; Austin, Texas; and Tallahassee, Florida. At last count, the firm had over 300 lawyers handling matters in every part of the world. Like twins, the Atlanta and Washington, D.C. offices grew together from the early years. The other offices were added because of high demand from major clients in the last two decades. Additional locations are planned after the turn of the millennium. However, with Sutherland Asbill & Brennan's current presence on the legal scene, little in the way of law is beyond their reach. On any given day, lawyers within the firm's international practice are embroiled in cross-border transactions and the settlement of multinational disputes.

On the home front, the firm's litigators have appeared in federal or state courts in 47 states in the last five years alone. The firm's success rate in achieving cost-effective outcomes has attracted several Fortune 100 companies, who now regularly retain the firm for regional and national litigation services.

For over 75 years the firm of Sutherland Asbill & Brennan has built on the high standards of its founders with a commitment to integrity and the highest quality of service for its clients. ❧

◀ As Atlanta has grown into a business center of the Southeast, Sutherland Asbill & Brennan's practice areas have broadened and diversified. Photo by Brian Robbins Photography.

◀ Sutherland Asbill & Brennan is an active participant in Atlanta's civic community. It recently partnered with a client to build a house for Habitat for Humanity.

Coca-Cola Enterprises

In 1899, a customer would have to be sitting at a drugstore soda fountain to enjoy a Coca-Cola. One hundred years later it's available worldwide, not by accident but through the hard work of Coca-Cola Enterprises and other Coca-Cola bottlers.

It all begins with the concentrate made by The Coca-Cola Company, sold to bottlers, and shipped to production facilities. Suppliers deliver sweetener to the bottling facilities, which blend sweetener, concentrate, and purified water (essential to make products that taste exactly the same no matter where they are produced) together to make a simple syrup. Carbon dioxide is added for that tingly, tongue-pleasing carbonation.

Suppliers deliver empty aluminum cans that are rinsed and sent to the fillers, which can produce up to 2,000 cans a minute. Cans are closed with a seamer that attaches the metal lid, and a code date is printed on each can.

Finished beverages are packaged in another container for distribution and spend a brief time in a warehouse until a truck delivers them to be stocked in one of Coca-Cola's distinctive vending cases, or on the grocer's shelf. The can feels right, curved to fit the hand. A pop of the cap releases a quick fizz of carbonation, a few tickling, ice-cold bubbles rise, and it's brought to the lips for that first refreshing swallow.

When Coca-Cola was first invented by pharmacist John Pemberton in 1886, Atlanta's most famous drink was only available at soda fountains. Then two Chattanooga lawyers, Benjamin

Thomas and James F. Johnston (grandfather of the current chairman of Coca-Cola Enterprises, Summerfield K. Johnston, Jr.), opened a bottling plant in Tennessee in 1899 and began granting franchise rights in other locations.

Atlanta soon boasted the flagship bottling plant, which opened on Edgewood Avenue in April of 1900. That first year 2,815 gallons of syrup were bottled, and the most distant distribution point was determined by how far a mule team could travel in one day. By 1903 syrup gallonage jumped to more than 18,000, and it's been growing ever since.

Today, The Atlanta Coca-Cola Bottling Company serves millions of consumers through 12 distribution centers, a vending services facility, and 2 production plants. In full production, one production facility can produce 5,500 bottles and cans a minute, 330,000 an hour, and 2,640,000 in an eight-hour day.

Coca-Cola Enterprises is the world's largest marketer, producer, and distributor of bottle and can liquid, nonalcoholic refreshment, distributing some 3.8 billion equivalent unit cases of product in 1998. The company distributes more than 74 percent of The Coca-Cola Company's North American bottle and can volume and is the sole licensed bottler for products of The Coca-Cola Company in Belgium, Great Britain, Luxembourg, France, and the Netherlands. Coca-Cola Enterprises' product line includes carbonated and noncarbonated soft drinks, as well as still and sparkling waters, juices, isotonics, and teas. ❡

The Varsity

"What'll ya have? What'll ya have? Next! What'll ya have?"

In what appears to be utter mayhem, cooks, counter workers, and curb service personnel at The Varsity work together like a precision machine to satisfy the appetites of 10,000 hungry Atlantans daily.

Recognized as the world's largest drive-in restaurant, The Varsity sells two miles of hot dogs, a ton of onions, a ton and a half of potatoes, 300 gallons of chili, and 5,000 fried pies daily. The Varsity has long held the distinction of selling more fountain Coca-Cola than any single outlet in the world.

Frank Gordy founded this bustling hot dog heaven in 1928. He is quoted as saying, "The Varsity is my life and I love it." That love has continued through the years and shows in the quality of the food and the loyalty of the many generations of Varsity fans who regard it as their favorite eatery.

Gordy was born in 1904 in Thomaston, Georgia. He attended high school at what is now Reinhardt College in Waleska, Georgia. After attending Georgia Tech and Oglethorpe University, he went to Florida to try his luck in the real estate boom. Returning to Atlanta at 21 with a nest egg of $1,200, Gordy used his entrepreneurial skills and crowd-pleasing good taste to start a fast-food business that has become legendary.

Gordy called his original store the Yellow Jacket to attract the students from Georgia Tech. It was located at the intersection of North Avenue and Luckie Street. It was an immediate hit. Shortly thereafter, he moved to the present location and named his restaurant The Varsity.

Frank Gordy always insisted that all of the food be of the highest quality with only the best ingredients and freshest produce used. He was fond of saying, "The only thing frozen here is the ice cream." That tradition continues today—the potatoes and onions

are fresh; they are fried in canola oil. The meat for the hot dogs and hamburgers is custom blended from secret recipes developed with the help of Gordy's "million-dollar taste buds."

A visit to The Varsity is a tradition for thousands of Atlanta families who make dining out at the "V" an event. The menu features hot dogs, chili dogs, hamburgers, chiliburgers, fried onion rings, and French fries. To satisfy lighter appetites, grilled chicken, sandwiches, and salads are available.

When Frank Gordy died in 1983, he left his legacy of free enterprise to his family, which remains dedicated to maintaining the same high standards he set. During the 1996 Olympics, The Varsity was a major center of activity, serving record crowds daily. A huge pin trading tent was set up in the parking lot. Athletes and visitors from all over the world came to trade pins and make new friends. The Varsity "Onion Ring" pin became the hottest item around, selling for as much as $1,200.

The Varsity family looks forward to the new millennium. With locations in Athens, northeast Atlanta, Gwinnett County, and Cobb County, in addition to the "Big V" in downtown Atlanta, the tradition is growing. The Varsity is committed to doing what they do best—say "What'll ya have?"—and keep the hot dogs rolling at the "fun place to eat." ❧

▲ Recognized as the world's largest drive-in restaurant, The Varsity sells two miles of hot dogs, a ton of onions, a ton and a half of potatoes, 300 gallons of chili, and 5,000 fried pies daily.

◄ "Meet me at The Varsity" . . . parking for 600 1950s wheels as curb men sang and danced their way to fame.

The Flagler Company

▶ Stone Mountain Park's Memorial Hall was built in 1996.

The Flagler Company has been an intrinsic part of Atlanta from the days when mules were used in site grading and rivets were heated in a blacksmith's forge, right up to present day's powerful earth-moving machinery and computerized architectural plans.

In continuous operation for 88 years, the oldest Atlanta-based construction firm has been a cornerstone of civic growth and, in a very literal way, helped to build the "brave and beautiful" city of Atlanta. Thomas Thorne Flagler, a founding member of the Associated General Contractors of America guild and a national president of that organization, created The Flagler Company in 1911. Upon the death of Mr. Flagler in 1949, his son Thomas Thorne Flagler Jr. assumed leadership until his son, T. Thorne Flagler III, continued the family tradition by becoming president in 1984.

One of President Emeritus Thomas Thorne Flagler Jr.'s most memorable jobs was working on what is now Fort Stewart, an entire facility built virtually overnight. "I learned more in that six months than I did in four years at Georgia Tech," recalls Flagler.

▶ The Atlanta Athletic Club was built in 1927 by The Flagler Company.

From the graceful stone and brick of old Atlanta's Phinizy Calhoun residence, to the soaring glass and steel of the Georgia Federal Bank Building, to the exacting renovation of the stately Henry County Courthouse, The Flagler Company turns architectural ideas into reality. The company's expertise and abilities see each job through, whether they are renovating the ballroom of the Capital City Country Club, or constructing new operating rooms at Crawford Long Hospital.

Recipient of a number of awards, the company counts among its honors the Build America Award for the Simmons Mattress Company's corporate headquarters, and two Build Georgia Awards, one for the 1988 Democratic National Convention and another for rebuilding the Margaret Mitchell House in 1998. Experts in historical renovation, The Flagler Company is currently

involved in the restoration of Rhodes Hall and the Fox Theater and has completed numerous renovations to Georgia's State Capitol, Atlanta's premier landmarks.

The Flagler Company was the first in the world to build a double ramp parking deck, which would allow parking from both the entrance and exit ramps. Garages during the 1950s were built with one ramp up and a continuous circular exit ramp. This Parking Garage is located at Peachtree and Decatur Streets, having been masterminded by Roy Livingston.

The Flagler family is active in the Atlanta philanthropic community and presently supports the Union Mission and GlenCastle Constructors, as well as other charities through Flagler's Foundation.

Today, The Flagler Company is able to mix personal attention with large-scale construction, a rare skill among today's large, impersonal construction firms. Flagler has strong ties to its subcontractors and suppliers, which it feels is a reflection of fair business practices and organized procedures. The results—top-notch construction, quality buildings, and satisfied clients.

The Flagler Company owes much of its success to the superb team of men and women in its employ. In a highly competitive market, skilled and experienced workers would be invaluable to any contractor, yet they remain loyal to Flagler. "One of the things I like most about this business is working with our field people, who do an honest day's work for an honest day's pay and take pride in what they do," says Thorne Flagler.

"Build for Endurance" is the company's motto—a promise three generations have kept to the city of Atlanta, and one The Flagler Company can be depended upon to keep in the new millennium.

"It is very gratifying to drive by one of our projects decades later and see the quality still there," says Thorne Flagler. "In addition to that, I have had the rare opportunity to renovate a structure built by my father 47 years ago."

The family business atmosphere that emphasizes moral values and community involvement has resulted in a legacy of lasting achievement. ❧

State University of West Georgia

Formal education has become more complex as the world continuously changes. Today more than ever, picking the right institution is important, as much so as choosing a career. Now and throughout the new millennium, students must be able to assimilate and use knowledge in applications that once existed only in dreams.

But students are not the only ones who pin goals to education—businesses also look to the State University of West Georgia to produce the caliber of thinkers and doers their very futures depend upon. Intellectual capital is the most desired and valued asset in America today, and West Georgia is continuously refining and developing programs that make businesses work in the highly fluid global marketplace.

The State University of West Georgia is an institution dedicated to teaching students the latest data available—and how to use it. The low student-to-teacher ratio fosters personal development in innumerable ways.

Located in Carrollton, Georgia, minutes outside of Atlanta proper, the beautiful wooded grounds lend a feeling of calm serenity that encourages undisturbed focus. The buildings range from historic structures to a new 110,000-square-foot, $19.4-million technology-enhanced Learning Center. A $26-million, 166,000-square-foot Health, Wellness, and Lifelong Learning Center will soon be constructed, allowing West Georgia to usher in the twenty-first century with facilities worthy of the new millennium.

Within these walls, major milestones for the state and nation are routinely achieved. West Georgia is home of the only Honors College among Georgia's public or private colleges and universities. The first certification program for distance learning in the state of Georgia was developed at West Georgia. One of only six known programs in the United States, the Distance Learning Certification Program provides a curriculum for instructors, administrators, managers, and trainers involved in distance learning or preparing for leadership roles in this area.

The College of Education will soon offer a doctoral program in school improvement providing advanced learning for current and aspiring school leaders in the use of research, technology, and leadership and collaborative skills to improve student success. The College of Education also houses one of the state's newest Educational Technology Training Centers. A collaborative project with the Georgia Department of Education, the center offers hands-on training to enhance teachers' knowledge of instructional technology.

There are numerous examples of West Georgia's impact on the national level as well. West Georgia is one of only five U.S. schools—including Harvard—that have qualified for 27 consecutive years for the National Debate Tournament. Students and graduates are routinely recognized by prestigious entities for outstanding

work and leadership ranging from the National Collegiate Honors Council Conference in Chicago, where seven West Georgia students presented undergraduate research papers and projects (more than any other institution in the nation), to West Georgia's ranking of seventh in the nation for colleges producing completers of programs leading to advanced licensure in education.

Internationally, West Georgia is repeatedly singled out for special projects and outstanding service. The Office of International Programs coordinates study-abroad programs to China, Paris, Cuernavaca, and London. The Richards College of Business ranks in the top 130 universities in the world in accounting programs, and recently celebrated its 10th anniversary of the International Banking and Finance Program in London.

The Office of Student Development is piloting a tracking program for the Immigration and Naturalization Service designed to test the use of bar-coded entry forms, a new student/exchange visitor card, and the electronic submission of events which affect student/exchange visitor's status. The campus is even international itself, with a student base representing 51 foreign countries.

West Georgia's president, Dr. Beheruz N. Sethna, says: "At the State University of West Georgia, both undergraduate and graduate students receive a world-class education, second to none, in an environment where faculty members not only know your name, but they also know your dreams." ❧

▲ At the State University of West Georgia, the 25-to-1 student-to-faculty ratio keeps classes small and dynamic. Students have easy access to their professors and to advanced technology, as well as research opportunities not usually available to undergraduates.

◀ Reaching out to grasp a college diploma is reaching out for the future. Fulfilling its mission of providing "Educational Excellence in a Personal Environment," the State University of West Georgia is preparing Georgians of tomorrow for the twenty-first century.

CHAPTER FOUR
1930-1949

❧

Atlanta had grown so much during the previous three decades that no one could be faulted for not anticipating the coming lean years. Certainly the city's business leadership was busy laying the groundwork for continued growth.

Margaret Mitchell House.
Photo by Ron Sherman

In the promotional spirit of the great industrial expositions of the late 1800s, the Chamber of Commerce launched the Forward Atlanta campaign in 1926. The idea was simple: advertise and market the city by buying ads in national media extolling the advantages of Atlanta as a place for business.

The campaign—which would be widely copied by other cities in the future—lasted three years and cost some $800,000. Ivan Allen Sr., the head of a local office supply company, served as chairman. Reports afterward credited the campaign with drawing 762 new businesses and 20,000 new jobs to Atlanta.

The campaign effectively established Atlanta as the leading city in the South. National corporations entering the South began to choose Atlanta for branch offices. Sears Roebuck built a mammoth store next to the Ford factory on Ponce De Leon Avenue, where a spring had once provided a shady picnic spot for city dwellers. General Motors brought a factory to Atlanta in 1928.

Atlanta's first commercial radio station, WSB, began transmitting in 1922. The station's motto—WSB, it was often said, stood for "Welcome South, Brother"—also contributed to the image of a city with a permanent welcome mat out.

The rapid pace of business development kept construction booming. At twenty-one stories, the Rhodes-Haverty Building was now the largest structure downtown. A luxe hotel, the six-million-dollar Biltmore opened in Midtown, while the Henry Grady Hotel went up on Peachtree Street and became the unofficial headquarters for the annual session of the state's General Assembly. Another northern firm, R.H. Macy, built a grand building on Peachtree Street for its Davison's department store.

There was an inevitable collision between the railroads and the automobiles now beginning to clog downtown streets. The noise and dirt of the freight and passenger trains was increasingly noxious to downtown office workers, but it was the obstacles the tracks posed for automobiles traveling through downtown that proved the last straw.

The first viaduct—which elevated the street above the level of the tracks—was built along

► In 1926, the Chamber of Commerce launched the Forward Atlanta campaign, under the leadership of Ivan Allen, Sr. The campaign advertised and marketed the city through a national media promotion, and it drew 762 new businesses and 20,000 new jobs to Atlanta. The campaign effectively established Atlanta as the leading city in the South. Historic image courtesy Georgia Department of Archives and History. New photo by Ron Sherman

▲ Among the first national corporations to choose Atlanta as home for a branch office was Sears Roebuck. The company built a mammoth store on Ponce De Leon Avenue. Photo courtesy of Georgia State University Special Collections

▶ The Atlanta Biltmore Hotel was constructed on Peachtree Street in 1923. Photo courtesy Georgia Department of Archives and History

Spring Street in 1923. It was so successful that the city raised a bond issue in 1929 to build more. In many instances, businesses along the new viaducts had to build new entrances and some of the oldest parts of Atlanta—the streetscape directly alongside the railroad tracks—disappeared from view for nearly forty years.

If the railroads and the automobile were fighting for local supremacy, a third mode of transportation—the airplane—was coming up quickly on the outside.

One of Atlanta's early automobile dealers, Lindsay Hopkins, was also a flying enthusiast. Along with a partner, Hopkins made the first air mail delivery in 1911. Since then, aviation in Atlanta had become centered at Candler Field, the automobile racing track south of the city. In 1925, Asa Candler offered the city the opportunity to lease the nearly three hundred acres.

The job of evaluating the proposal went to a newly elected city councilman named William B. Hartsfield. Hartsfield was an enthusiastic booster of flying and took the job seriously. After an aerial survey of every possible airport site in the area, Hartsfield recommended the city go ahead and make a deal with Candler.

Not long after, Hartsfield spotted an opportunity to put Atlanta on the aviation map. A new federal law authorized the creation of an airmail route between New York and Miami. Hartsfield identified the bureaucrat who would be drawing the map, invited him to Atlanta and put on a lavish welcome and briefing session. Soon after, Atlanta was designated a way-station, beating out Birmingham, Alabama, among others.

By 1930, the city had purchased Candler Field for $94,500, again at Hartsfield's urging. The primary traffic was air mail and a few passenger flights, but the runways had been improved and there was a new hangar/terminal, built by a company that would soon become Eastern Airlines.

That same year, a gleaming terra cotta-clad City Hall opened. At one million dollars, it was the pride of city government, but in Midtown, across from the Georgia Terrace Hotel, was an

▲ The grand mansions that fronted on Peachtree Street only two or three blocks north of the downtown train tracks quickly disappeared in favor of new office and commercial buildings like the Davison's department store. Photo courtesy of Georgia State University Special Collections

Eastern Air Transport
Greensboro N.C.
1933.

LINCOLN BEACHEY   CONSTANCE KNOWLES   JOE BROWN CONNALLY
(MRS. JESSE DRAPER)

ATLANTA JOURNAL MEET FALL 1910 — CANDLER FIELD

even grander structure. The Middle Eastern-themed Fox Theater cost approximately three million dollars, could seat five thousand for movies, and was equipped with a giant organ for sing-alongs. As magnificent as the building was, its timing was awful. It opened on Christmas Day, 1929, two months after the stock market crash. Within two years, the theater operator was bankrupt and the building was shuttered for several years.

Prior to the New Deal, there was no government-sponsored safety net. Jobs melted away in the early years of the Depression and the Chamber of Commerce even briefly promoted a "back to the farm" program to city residents. Most observers agree it could have been worse, though. The local banks stayed in business during the 1930s and new President Franklin Roosevelt, who traveled often to Warm Springs, Georgia, for medical treatment, made Atlanta a regional headquarters for federal government operations, giving rise to the nickname "Little Washington" and helping stabilize the local economy. In 1940, the city population stood at just over 300,000, a healthy 12 percent increase during the 1930s.

Aviation continued to grow at Candler Field. The city built a terminal of its own in 1932 and added an air control tower half-a-dozen years later. Flying wasn't for the faint of heart, though. A flight from

While railroads and the automobile were fighting for local supremacy, a third mode of transportation—the airplane—was coming up quickly on the outside.

◄ Pictured is an early Eastern Air Transport, c. 1933. Amy Mollison, foreground, is said to have been the first woman to solo westbound across the Atlantic Ocean. One of the men is Dick Merrill, said to have been the original airmail pilot working out of Atlanta.

◄ Aviation in Atlanta was centered at Candler Field, the auto racing track south of the city. In 1925, Asa Candler offered the city the opportunity to lease the nearly three hundred acres. The job of evaluating the proposal went to a newly elected city councilman named William B. Hartsfield. By 1930, the city purchased Candler Field at Hartsfield's urging. The primary traffic was air mail and a few passenger flights, but the runways had been improved and there was a new hangar/terminal, built by a company that would soon become Eastern Airlines. Photo of Eastern Air Transport courtesy of Georgia Department of Archives and History. Early Candler Field and Atlanta Airport photos courtesy of the Atlanta History Center.

▲ **President Franklin Roosevelt, who traveled often to Warm Springs, Georgia, for medical treatment, made Atlanta a regional headquarters for federal government operations, giving rise to the nickname "Little Washington."** Photo courtesy of Georgia State University Special Collections

Atlanta to New York on Eastern Airlines, for instance, was an all-day, low-altitude affair, in large part because the route called for nine stops along the way.

Hartsfield was elected mayor in 1936 and quickly went about putting the city's financial house in order. Two nearby counties—Milton and Campbell—weren't so lucky, however. They went bankrupt and merged with Fulton County in 1932.

Though America was battered by the Depression, many took solace in sports. Some of Atlanta's most revered sports figures enjoyed their greatest glory in the 1930s. Bobby Jones, who was a lawyer by trade, won the Grand Slam in 1930, winning the U.S. and British Opens and the U.S. and British Amateur titles. The city gave him a ticker tape parade down Peachtree Street. The last of the great amateur golfers, Jones went on to organize the Augusta National golf club and the Masters Tournament, one of the modern Grand Slam events. Charles Yates was another well-known amateur golfer from Atlanta and Bryan "Bitsy" Grant put Atlanta on the map in the tennis world during these years.

College football was well-entrenched in Atlanta by then. The first game played in the city, Georgia versus Auburn, took place in 1892 in Piedmont Park. Georgia and Georgia Tech began playing annually the next year. Georgia Tech was a national powerhouse during these years. Coached by William Alexander, the 1928 team beat California in the Rose Bowl and routinely played to massive crowds on the Tech campus.

During the 1930s, there was another event that left a permanent stamp on Atlanta: the publication of *Gone With The Wind*.

Margaret "Peggy" Mitchell was a local newspaper reporter of accomplishment but had never tried writing fiction. While she was laid up with a sprained ankle, though, she wrote a long novel set in Atlanta during and after the Civil War. She put it away in a drawer for several years before an agent heard about it from one of Mitchell's friends. In 1936, he persuaded her to let him read it and he immediately bought it.

Retitled *Gone With The Wind* (one early title: "Tomorrow is Another Day"), the novel was a sensation, winning the Pulitzer Prize in 1937. More than a million copies were printed in just the first six months and it was eventually translated into more than two dozen languages.

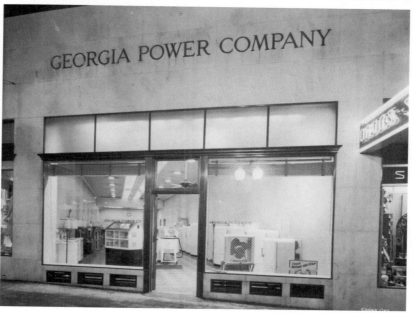

◄ In 1940, the city population stood at just over 300,000, a healthy 12 percent increase during the 1930s. Consumers in 1941 could choose from these shiny new Pontiacs on the showroom floor. In 1950, Georgia Power Company offered the latest modern marvels in household appliances. Photos courtesy Georgia Department of Archives and History

Hollywood producer David O. Selznick immediately purchased the film rights and launched a highly publicized nationwide talent search for the lead role of Scarlett. The long and complicated filming of the movie only whipped up greater expectations and the invitation-only premiere of the film—December 15, 1939—was one of the greatest single events in the city's history. Much of Peachtree Street from the Georgian Terrace Hotel in Midtown, where the cast members stayed, to the Loew's Grand Theater downtown, was closed and crowds four and five rows deep lined up to watch the stars arrive. The theater was given a plantation-house facade for the occasion and there was a grand ball afterward. The film went on to win ten Academy Awards, including Best Picture.

Mitchell was troubled by her sudden celebrity and never really came to terms with it. She never wrote another book and was killed by a taxi while crossing Peachtree Street in 1949.

produce high-quality manufactured goods and although it closed down after the war it would be reopened in the 1950s. Because of its transportation links, Atlanta was a major processing center for new recruits, many of whom were exposed to Atlanta for the first time and returned after the war.

In late 1946, the Winecoff Hotel on Peachtree Street downtown caught fire. Although reputed to be of fireproof construction, it lacked sprinklers and the hotel furnishings burned brightly. Guests on the upper floors had no recourse but to jump or make bedsheet ropes because there were no ladders long enough to reach them. Dozens died in view of crowds gathered on the streets. In all, the fire killed 119, including more than 30 high school students visiting Atlanta for a conference and Christmas shopping. It still ranks among the most deadly hotel fires in U.S. history.

The end of World War II released the commercial energies that had been held in check, first by the Depression and then by the war. Airplanes were shrinking travel times and the U.S. was emerging as a unified market. National firms needed strong regional outposts—the city was home to twelve hundred regional offices by 1954—and Atlanta quickly resumed exploiting its budding name recognition, transportation network, central location, and previously acquired status as the leading city of the South.

That same year, James Cox, a former governor of Ohio, purchased the afternoon *Atlanta Journal* newspaper and WSB radio. Cox then bought two other afternoon papers and shut them down. After the war, Cox obtained a license for WSB-TV, the first television station in the south, and eventually acquired the morning *Atlanta Constitution* newspaper as well. Cox moved to Atlanta and these four properties provided him the cornerstone for building a major media company.

As it was during the Civil War, Atlanta was an important manufacturing center and transit point during World War II. The largest war factory in the area was the Bell Aircraft plant in Marietta. The massive facility built B-29 bombers and at its peak employed thirty thousand workers, many of them women. The Bell plant proved to skeptics that Southerners could indeed

Ford (1947 in Hapeville) and GM (1948 in Doraville) both built large new assembly facilities to augment or replace older factories; and the housing shortages of the war years fueled a residential construction boom that would soon put real estate back in its place as one of Atlanta's leading industries. ❧

▲ Some of Atlanta's most revered sports figures enjoyed their greatest glory in the 1930s. Perhaps at the top of that list was golfer Bobby Jones, a lawyer by trade, who won the Grand Slam in 1930, taking the U.S. and British Opens, and the U.S. and British Amateur titles. The city gave him a ticker tape parade down Peachtree Street. Today, Atlantans are just as enthusiastic for great golf, with crowds lining the greens to see the famed Tiger Woods in a locally hosted tourney. Parade photo courtesy Georgia Department of Archives and History. Historic image courtesy of Georgia State University Special Collections. New photo by Ron Sherman

◄ College football was
well-entrenched in
Atlanta by the mid-1930s.
The first game in the city,
Georgia versus Auburn,
took place in 1892 in
Piedmont Park. Georgia
and Georgia Tech began
playing annually the next
year. Georgia Tech was a
national powerhouse,
winning the Rose Bowl
in 1928 and 1946.
Historic photo courtesy of
the Atlanta History Center.
New photos by Ron
Sherman

◄ The Middle Eastern-themed Fox Theater cost approximately three million dollars, could seat five thousand for movies, and was equipped with a giant organ for sing-alongs. It opened on Christmas Day, 1929, just two months after the stock market crash. Within two years, the theater operator was bankrupt and the building was shuttered for several years. In the 1970s, the theater, which couldn't compete as a movie house anymore, was in danger of demolition. A grassroots preservation effort saved the building, which was renovated and now hosts Broadway-style theater performances, concerts, and other arts events. Historic images courtesy of the Atlanta History Center. New photos by Ron Sherman

◄ Local newspaper reporter Margaret "Peggy" Mitchell, while laid up with a sprained ankle, penned a novel set in Atlanta during the Civil War. The novel was published in 1936, retitled *Gone With The Wind* (an early title: *Tomorrow Is Another Day*) and won a Pulitzer Prize in 1937. Hollywood producer David O. Selznick purchased the film rights, and Gone With The Wind made its premiere in Atlanta at the Loew's Grand Theater downtown on December 15, 1939. Crowds lined up four and five rows deep to watch the stars arrive. Historic images courtesy of Georgia State University Special Collections.

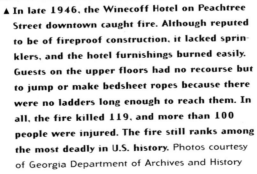

▲ In late 1946, the Winecoff Hotel on Peachtree Street downtown caught fire. Although reputed to be of fireproof construction, it lacked sprinklers, and the hotel furnishings burned easily. Guests on the upper floors had no recourse but to jump or make bedsheet ropes because there were no ladders long enough to reach them. In all, the fire killed 119, and more than 100 people were injured. The fire still ranks among the most deadly in U.S. history. Photos courtesy of Georgia Department of Archives and History

▲ When America went to war, women went to work. While men shipped out overseas to fight World War II, women entered the factories and the services to lend a hand in the war effort, and in the process changed the role of the American woman in society forever.
Photo courtesy of the Atlanta History Center

Blue Cross and Blue Shield of Georgia

Since 1937, Georgians have depended upon Blue Cross and Blue Shield of Georgia (BCBSGA) to meet their health insurance needs. By 1998, more than 1.7 million Georgians depended on BCBSGA, making it the state's largest health benefits insurer. The tremendous growth in the number insured and the products and services offered by BCBSGA are a reflection of the changing times; the mission of the company, however, remains the same: "To provide access to quality, affordable health care coverage to as many Georgians as possible."

Blue Cross and Blue Shield of Georgia has been in existence almost as long as the national Blue Cross and Blue Shield Association itself. In 1929, Baylor University Hospital in Dallas, Texas, implemented a 50-cents-a-month health insurance plan for teachers proposed by Justin F. Kimball, a local public schools administrator. It was the first program of its kind in the U.S., and the Blues concept spread quickly throughout the nation. The Blues Plans evolved as not-for-profit organizations that could process and pay members' claims. In 1937, the concept became a reality in Atlanta.

The Atlanta Blue Cross Plan began as the United Hospitals Service Association of Atlanta, created by an act of the state legislature and funded by five local hospitals. The company had one product: a single-member hospitalization insurance plan that cost 90 cents per month. Seventeen years later, in 1954, the Atlanta Blue Shield Plan was formed to cover physicians' costs.

Meanwhile, in other parts of the state, the Blues Plan concept took root in the Savannah Blue Cross Plan in 1939 and the Columbus Blue Cross Plan in 1946. The two merged in 1966 to form Blue Cross and Blue Shield of Georgia/Columbus. In 1985, the Columbus and Atlanta Plans merged to form Blue Cross and Blue Shield of Georgia.

The company operated as a not-for-profit throughout most of its existence. In order to continue to provide the quality of service expected by its members, BCBSGA converted to for-profit status in 1996 through an act of the General Assembly and approval by the state Insurance Commissioner.

Cerulean Companies, Inc. was created as the holding company for Blue Cross and Blue Shield of Georgia and affiliate companies, including HMO Georgia, Inc., Greater Georgia Life Insurance Co., and Group Benefits of Georgia, Inc. In 1998, BCBSGA also announced the formation of a Georgia-based nonprofit charitable

▲ Dick Shirk serves as president and CEO of Blue Cross and Blue Shield of Georgia.

▶ In 1998, more than 1.7 million Georgians depended on "Georgia Blue," making BCBSGA the state's largest health benefits insurer. Photo by Lauren Schiller.

This program offers members direct access to network chiropractors for the medically necessary treatment of acute spinal conditions for an additional fee. Blue Cross and Blue Shield of Georgia is headquartered in Atlanta; its operations center is in Columbus. More than 2,400 employees staff these two locations and regional sales and customer service centers in Albany, Athens, Atlanta, Augusta, Brunswick, Cartersville, Columbus, Dalton, Gainesville, Macon, Savannah, and Valdosta.

Blue Cross and Blue Shield of Georgia and Greater Georgia Life offer a variety of coverage options for employers, groups, and individuals. The companies' products include BlueChoice PPO; Traditional Indemnity; FLEXPLUS; 65 Plus; Disability Income Insurance; Hospital Income Plus; and Group Term Life Insurance and Accidental Death and Dismemberment Insurance for Employees. HMO Georgia offers BlueChoice Healthcare Plan, BlueChoice Option, and BlueChoice Platinum.

As the new millennium brings about advancements and challenges to the health and welfare of Georgians, Blue Cross and Blue Shield of Georgia will be there to make the passage both safe and affordable. ❡

health foundation whose mission was "to improve the delivery of health services to medically underserved Georgians." Blue Cross and Blue Shield of Georgia is actively involved in contributing to the health and wellness of the people in Georgia's communities. For example, the Georgia Caring Program for Children, funded by BCBSGA and generous corporate and private donors, has coordinated health care for children of families whose parents are employed, but unable to afford health care services. Thousands of children have received medical care thanks to the efforts of the Caring Program.

Blue Cross and Blue Shield of Georgia's many community activities also include the Playground Olympics program, which donated playground equipment to public recreation areas around the state, along with wellness educational materials distributed in state schools; the SAFE! program, a collaboration between BCBS-GA and the Georgia Coalition on Family Violence, which raises awareness of domestic violence issues through an educational program in the workplace; and the Partners in Education program, where BCBSGA and employees help support elementary and secondary public schools in Atlanta and Columbus.

As part of the ongoing commitment to deliver quality coverage and respond to the needs of a changing market, BCBSGA became the first insurer in Georgia to offer a complementary alternative medicine program. This program offers BCBSGA members savings on wellness items and a broad range of complementary medicine services, including acupuncture, herbal therapy, massage therapy, mind-body techniques, neurofeedback, nutritional therapy, and traditional Chinese medicine. To continue to respond to the market's growing interest in complementary or "alternative" medicine services, BCBSGA also introduced a program that offers chiropractic care through a stringently credentialed network of chiropractors.

Arnall Golden & Gregory, LLP

Founding partners of the firm are Ellis G. Arnall, Sol I. Golden, and Cleburne E. Gregory Jr.

At Arnall Golden & Gregory, LLP, one of Atlanta's largest law firms, the attorneys share a commitment to help clients meet their business goals while preparing for the challenges of the new millennium. The varied experience of the attorneys provides the legal and business diversity to help clients solve problems and make smart decisions. Because of the broad scope of its practice, built on more than a half century of tradition, the firm has attracted a client base ranging from large, publicly held companies to smaller, private companies and individuals.

History

In 1949, as the population of Atlanta crossed the half-million mark, Ellis Arnall, Sol Golden, and Cleburne E. Gregory Jr. formed the law firm of Arnall Golden & Gregory. As individuals, each had already gained significant recognition. Ellis Arnall, who served as Georgia's Governor from 1943 to 1947, spearheaded reforms including ending unequal freight rates favoring northern industrial states—a move which opened the way for the postwar economic boom throughout the South. Sol Golden had developed a

A statue of Governor Ellis Arnall graces the lawn of Georgia's State Capitol Building.

reputation as a skilled corporate attorney who initiated a number of innovative corporate financing techniques in Georgia. Cleburne Gregory had been Assistant Attorney General in the state of Georgia and worked with Governor Arnall in the early 1940s before serving in World War II.

Throughout the past half century, Arnall Golden & Gregory's attorneys have kept pace with the city of Atlanta's aspirations, marking each decade with growth in both the number of attorneys practicing within the firm and the types of legal services offered. Looking back at the past decades illustrates how the firm has grown to be among Atlanta's top ten largest law firms.

In the 1950s, Atlanta experienced stunning growth, particularly in its transportation and communications systems. This laid the groundwork for the development of the firm's national client base. The firm counts among its clients major national manufacturing companies, retailers, and distributors who are headquartered in the South.

In the 1960s, the firm expanded its representation of national and regional trade associations and cooperatives, particularly in the food and medical device industries. Arnall Golden & Gregory celebrated its 15th anniversary by moving to the then new Fulton Federal Building at Five Points in downtown Atlanta.

The firm continued to expand in the 1970s. Contributing to the firm's growth was the evolving technological revolution, which brought forth new types of businesses and expanding practice areas; the shopping center "boom," which furthered the development of the firm's commercial real estate practice; and representation of a healthcare association, which created the firm's healthcare practice.

The 1980s were marked by the rapid growth of the firm from partners joining laterally from other firms. Also significant was the activity of the firm's corporate practice, dealing with the acquisition, mergers, and financing of businesses and the development and growth of its environmental law and venture capital practices. Many of the firm's clients shared the entrepreneurial spirit of its attorneys, as is still the case today. In 1985, the firm expanded beyond Atlanta, by merging with a Macon law firm with a strong practice in bankruptcy litigation.

The 1990s have seen the firm continue to grow in unprecedented ways, which will continue into the next millennium. The firm, which has grown from the original three partners to more than 125 lawyers, is now located in midtown Atlanta. Ever sensitive to the needs of its clients, the firm's practice is now organized around specially focused practice groups, which has enabled the firm to enhance its understanding of clients' businesses and to foster the exchange of professional ideas and the delivery of effective, integrated legal services. The essence of this approach is to listen closely to clients and ensure that the accumulated wisdom, experience, and knowledge of the firm is used creatively and efficiently to meet the needs and problems of each client.

Although the practice of law today does not resemble the practice at the firm's founding, what has remained stable is the strong sense of camaraderie felt among the firm's attorneys and the emphasis placed on the importance of personal relationships between lawyer and client, as well as the emphasis on operating in a client-focused manner.

According to William H. Kitchens, chairman of the firm's Management Committee, "We had the ability to grow fast and still hold on to the unique atmosphere of our firm, the sense that our work is a team effort. We're with people we respect, doing intellectually challenging work we like, for clients we value."

AG&G Today

The ability to adapt to the changing marketplace has contributed to the development of a practice mix responsive to clients' needs. Today, the firm's practice includes traditional areas of law and some which were unheard of and, in some instances, unimagined previously, such as biotechnology, tissue and genetic engineering, Internet, telecommunications, governmental deregulation, Y2K, alternative dispute resolution, and privatization of government services. Building on knowledge gained historically, the firm continues its well-established practices in areas such as sophisticated corporate transactions, mergers and acquisitions, securities, tax, commercial real estate, leasing, financial institutions, commercial litigation, healthcare, food and drug law, environmental, estate

planning and administration, international and immigration, patents, trademarks and copyrights, employment law and employee benefits, professional liability,

bankruptcy and creditors' rights, and public sector. The key to success in many of these practices is the ability to listen to clients' needs and help them avoid problems before they arise. The firm has accomplished this with a number of service initiatives such as the Client Service Review program, the Employment Law Compliance Review, and the frequent development of general and customized client educational programs and materials.

According to Managing Partner Jonathan Golden, son of founder Sol Golden, "Atlanta has uniquely been a city where entrepreneurs have prospered. It's always been a transportation center. Railroads then, airplanes now. It's not a city that's been dominated by a single industry like coal or steel. And distribution centers attract entrepreneurs. Almost all of the really big companies we represent started with us when they were small. We've grown with them. That's carried us up. We made the investment to grow with them."

As the firm has grown, so has its impact on Atlanta. The firm is committed to giving back to the community of which it has been such an integral part for the past five decades. It supports a wide range of pro bono programs and activities such as a pilot program of the Atlanta Volunteer Lawyers Foundation to reduce domestic violence, contributes to various community service organizations, and sponsors the annual Ellis Arnall Lecture at the Atlanta History Center.

Having celebrated its 50th anniversary in 1999, the firm is looking forward to the next century by listening closely to its clients and continuing the tradition of being responsive to a constantly changing and challenging world. ❧

The Centers for Disease Control and Prevention (CDC) and the CDC Foundation

► (Left to right) James M. Hughes, M.D., Director of the National Center for Infectious Diseases, CDC, and Sherif R. Zaki, M.D., Ph.D., Chief of Infectious Disease Pathology Activity for the National Center for Infectious Diseases, CDC, look at an autoradiograph (X-ray film) to identify the presence of an infectious agent in a clinical sample. An electron microscope is in the background.

► A Smoking Machine at the National Center for Environmental Health, CDC, collects smoke using a standardized puffing technique and enables CDC scientists to measure cancer-causing agents, additives, tar, nicotine, and other toxic substances in tobacco.

For more than a half century, the Centers for Disease Control and Prevention (CDC) has been on the front lines protecting America's health and safety. But while safeguarding people is the role for which CDC is best known, the agency performs two other functions vital to the health and well-being of people—namely, providing information that guides health decisions and promoting good health through strong partnerships in communities across the United States.

Most people know CDC from the media. Movies such as *Outbreak* and books such as *The Hot Zone* depict the brilliance and bravery of CDC's scientists, and news reports cover the agency's scientific findings every day.

It's true that CDC has played a major role in battling infectious diseases. The agency was a key player in eradicating smallpox from the world in 1977, and CDC's famed "disease detectives" travel the globe at a moment's notice to investigate disease outbreaks. In fact, CDC teams were on the scene for many recent outbreaks, including hantavirus and *E. coli* in the United States, Ebola in Africa, and Avian flu in Hong Kong.

But fighting infectious disease is just one aspect of what CDC does. CDC's responsibilities

as "the nation's prevention agency" have evolved to address prevention of contemporary threats to health—injuries, environmental threats, occupational hazards, behavioral risks, and chronic diseases such as cardiovascular disease, cancer, and diabetes.

A Storied Past

CDC's roots trace back to 1942, when the agency's mission was simple and singular—that is, keep malaria out of armed forces bases and war-industrial establishments in the southern United States. The agency's name, the Office of Malaria Control in War Areas, reflected this narrow mission. Because the South is the area with conditions most hospitable to malaria, the agency was based in Atlanta instead of Washington, D.C.

At the end of World War II, the Office of Malaria Control took on the broader role of guarding the public's health and was renamed the Communicable Disease Center. As this role expanded over the years, the name evolved into the Center for

Disease Control. In recognition of the importance of prevention, the name was changed in 1992 to Centers for Disease Control and Prevention. Today, CDC employs more than 7,000 professionals who are stationed in all 50 states and in over 20 countries worldwide.

A Partner and Friend in Communities

Many people aren't aware that CDC is a unique federal agency because of its strong connections to communities throughout the U.S. More than 75 percent of CDC's budget supports prevention and public health programs provided by state and community partners. The philosophy is that for public health to be effective, it must be close to the public. As a result, CDC works closely with state and local health departments, volunteer organizations, educational institutions, businesses, and a wide array of community-based organizations.

In connecting CDC with the people, the agency has a strong ally and friend in the CDC Foundation. The CDC Foundation is

the fund-raising and grant-making enterprise that responds to health threats by connecting the public to the scientists of CDC, building partnerships to champion CDC initiatives, and leveraging resources and talent to do more, faster.

The CDC Foundation is a relatively young enterprise–it opened its doors in February 1995–but in that short time it has launched more than 70 innovative programs. Each effort addresses a serious health concern, and each involves the CDC. The issues addressed range from training health officials from other nations to prevent the spread of disease to gaining new insights into teen smoking, from studying and preventing violence on a global scale to fighting antibiotic resistance.

Many individuals, foundations, companies, and organizations have recognized the potential of making an impact on a health concern by working with the CDC Foundation. While most of the Foundation's programs are born from the initiative of CDC scientists, many represent the ingenuity–as well as generosity–of people outside CDC. In its 1998-99 year, the CDC Foundation raised more than $8.5 million for its programs.

Together, CDC and the CDC Foundation are a powerful team, working to realize a vision of "healthy people in a healthy world, through prevention." ◐

◄ CDC's Visiting Scientist Program allows health professionals from around the world to come to CDC to learn new public health skills–which they then utilize to improve public health in their home countries. Pictured (left to right) are Visiting Scientists Janna Vuopio-Varika of Finland, Moises Hernandez of Peru, Heba Rashed of Egypt, and Rachanee Cheinsong of Thailand. CDC Director Jeffrey P. Koplan, M.D., M.P.H. is seated.

◄ The Annual Epidemic Intelligence Service (EIS) Prediction Run at Lullwater Park is a two-mile "fun walk/run." The winner most closely predicts the time it will take him or her to complete the run. The walkers and runners predict their time at the beginning of the race, are not allowed to wear watches, and are given their time when they cross the finish line. Photo by Marilyn Suriani.

Crawford & Company

Just prior to the outbreak of World War II, America was at peace, and the streets, even in the larger cities, were tranquil and sleepy. It was a simpler time, when life's little rituals had their rightful time and place, when people knew their neighbors, and when milk was delivered door-to-door.

It was in the quiet hours before dawn one summer's morning that Jim Crawford leaned in the doorway of his Atlanta home and gazed thoughtfully on his still slumbering surroundings. Crawford was an energetic, restless, and driven man. He was equally blessed and cursed with the ability to see what escaped others, to mentally connect ideas that seemed invisible to the common man, and cursed because his visions allowed him no rest.

On this particular morning, he watched as three milk trucks made their delivery routes on his street, one-by-one. Each stopped at addresses unattended by the others. The process seemed redundant and inefficient to Crawford's logical mind. In an instant, he visualized a better way for the dairies to deliver their goods, and an opportunity for himself. That morning he decided to approach the dairies with his idea; if all went well, he would soon be adding to his strictly limited income as a Liberty Mutual claims adjuster.

The dairy companies in Atlanta were either unable or unwilling to grasp the benefits of consolidated, independent service delivery. However, the nation's insurance companies were, and as a result, the remarkable story of a visionary and the unique company he created began on the basis of a single, really good idea.

On May 27, 1941, Jim Crawford bought a secondhand desk and typewriter, rented a small office in the Murrah Building in Columbus, Georgia, and thus founded Crawford & Company. Today, the company is based in Atlanta, Georgia, and provides strategic solutions for managing risks and controlling risk-related costs. Crawford provides loss adjusting, claims management, and health care management services worldwide. This powerful organization now represents the world's largest risk and claims management enterprise—serving a global client base of insurance companies, self-insured corporations, and public entities. The company meets its clients' diverse needs with sound, reliable service, benchmarked by stringent professional standards.

Throughout its global network, Crawford & Company professionals work to understand each client's local market needs and customize service accordingly. Crawford employs more than 10,000 professionals in more than 700 cities and 65 countries. The NYSE trading symbols are CRDA and CRDB.

Services range from managed care, liability claims administration, and property claims services to catastrophe services and information management and analysis. The idea of providing network solutions to the industry for claims administration has proven both historically sound and futuristically alluring. The year 1998 was the 28th consecutive year in which Crawford has increased its cash dividends to shareholders—a record matched by few publicly owned companies. ◐

Selig Enterprises, Inc.

One of the oldest and most respected names in the history of modern Atlanta is Selig Enterprises. The company has played such a significant part in the metropolitan emergence of the city and its evolution to international status that the founder, Ben J. Massell, is often referred to as "the father of Atlanta's skyline." The late Atlanta Mayor William B. Hartsfield called Massell a "one-man boom." During his lifetime, Massell oversaw the construction of more than 1,000 buildings—from a one-story single-tenant structure to the Merchandise Mart on Peachtree Street.

A commercial real estate firm still privately owned and operated by the Selig family, the company began in 1918 as Massell Properties. In 1942 CMS Realty Company was formed, named after its major stockholder, Caroline Massell Selig. After Ben Massell's death in 1962, son-in-law Simon S. Selig Jr. divided his time between the Massell Companies and Selig Chemical Industries. After selling Selig Chemical Industries in 1965, Simon Selig focused on CMS Realty and guided the company through astute acquisitions and new developments. In 1968, CMS Realty transformed into Selig Enterprises, Inc. as Simon Selig and his son S. Stephen Selig III managed the company's operations. Continuous family ownership has been the key to the firm's stability and its rich tradition of leadership in business, civic, and cultural endeavors that has added significantly to the Atlanta experience for over eight decades.

Selig Enterprises has become a constellation of office buildings, office parks, industrial complexes, and shopping centers throughout the Southeast. The properties total in excess of 10 million square feet and are divided equally among retail, industrial, and office sites. The company provides leasing, development, acquisition, space design, construction,

legal, property management, brokerage, and accounting services for more than 250 properties. The company also owns and operates AAA Parking, which manages over 100 parking facilities located primarily in the metropolitan Atlanta area.

Founded in 1956, AAA is the oldest locally owned and operated parking management company in the Southeast. Operating in excess of 50,000 parking spaces, AAA's diverse operations include hospitals, medical professional buildings, prominent office buildings, colleges, surface lots, and valet services at prestigious hotels.

Now under the direction of Massell's grandson, S. Stephen Selig III, Selig Enterprises is one of the largest privately held real estate companies in the Southeast. The company's stability and integrity have fostered steady growth and financial strength, enhancing its reputation as an industry leader.

Long-term ownership is one of the company's basic strengths. An equally important factor in Selig's exceptional reputation and growth is its relationship with tenants, from small start-up businesses and local merchants to Fortune 500 corporations and national retailers. A history of responsive, efficient service is the foundation for ongoing relationships and decades of repeat business.

From etching Atlanta's shape against the sky to designing its future, Selig Enterprises is a major player in Atlanta's business and real estate evolution. Therefore, it is both natural and fitting to begin any exploration of Atlanta's addresses with Selig Enterprises. ❦

◄ **From etching Atlanta's shape against the sky to designing its future, Selig Enterprises is a major player in Atlanta's business and real estate evolution.**

◄ **Selig Enterprises has become a constellation of office buildings, office parks, industrial complexes, and shopping centers throughout the Southeast. The properties total in excess of 10 million square feet and are divided equally among retail, industrial, and office sites.**

Delta Air Lines

Delta Air Lines, the air traveler's choice from Atlanta for 70 years, is proud to call Atlanta home.

Started in 1929 with 14 employees and a handful of simple aircraft, today Delta employs more than 70,000 people, with 30,000 based in Atlanta, making Delta the largest private employer in the state of Georgia. It is also Hartsfield's most frequent flier, with additional hubs at Cincinnati, Dallas/Fort Worth, Salt Lake City, and international gateways at New York's JFK and Portland,

▲ Today, Delta employs more than 70,000 people, with 30,000 based in Atlanta, making Delta the largest private employer in the state of Georgia.

► When Delta Air Lines relocated its corporate office to Atlanta from Monroe, Louisiana, in March 1941, the entire complex consisted of one office building with an attached aircraft hangar. Fifty years later, the original building still forms a part of the Delta office complex adjacent to Hartsfield International Airport, but it is joined by 13 other training, administrative, and operations buildings and three mammoth aircraft hangars.

Oregon. And Delta is Atlanta's gateway to the world, with a global route system that provides efficient nonstop and connection services to most U.S. cities and 56 countries throughout the world.

It all began in 1925, when Delta's founder, C. E. Woolman, an agricultural extension agent in Louisiana, joined Huff Daland's crop-dusting division to help eradicate a devastating plague of boll weevils. When Daland put the company up for sale in 1928, Woolman purchased the business and founded Delta Air Service. The following year, Delta Air Service inaugurated passenger service with a fleet of three, five-passenger, 90-mph Travel Air monoplanes. When the U.S. Postal Service put all airmail runs up for bid in 1934, Delta won the route from Fort Worth, Texas, to Charleston, South Carolina, via Atlanta.

Delta's general offices and overhaul base were moved to Atlanta in 1941 to what was then Atlanta Municipal Airport. The $14-billion

company operates today on virtually the same site.

Delta prospered and grew, expanding its service through four mergers and acquisitions, including Chicago and Southern Airlines in 1953, Northeast Airlines in 1972, and Western Airlines in 1987. Finally, Delta acquired the transatlantic and European operations of Pan American World Airways in 1991, which expanded its presence in Europe and beyond, and introduced New York's JFK airport as a new transatlantic gateway for Delta.

Today, Delta's Worldport at Hartsfield Atlanta International Airport, the world's busiest passenger airport, is the single largest airline operation in the world—and is the only airline ever to have flown more than 100 million passengers in a single year. Delta Air Lines, Delta Express, the Delta Shuttle, the Delta Connection carriers, and Delta's 15 worldwide airline partners now operate more than 5,200 flights each day to 353 cities in 56 countries.

Atlanta and Delta have grown together as virtual partners since Atlanta became the company's headquarters in 1941. The presence of an airline committed to building a hub and providing domestic and international service helped to accelerate the expansion, commerce, and progress of the entire Atlanta metropolitan region. The civic vitality and spirit that have contributed to Atlanta's success are also part of Delta's success.

Delta's employees have taken an active part in the well-being of metropolitan Atlanta's communities, donating thousands of hours of time and financial support. The Delta Foundation encourages this spirit of giving, concentrating on families with young children, community building, and cultural understanding.

Through the 70 years since the founding of Delta Air Lines, the company has been focused on one purpose—the safe transportation of people. ❀

◄ Photo by Ron Sherman.

CHAPTER FIVE
1950-1960

❦

While Atlanta had never really stopped

growing, the Depression and World War II

kept a lid on the city. When the war

ended, Atlantans were more than ready

to go back to business.

Photo by Ron Sherman

The central figure in Atlanta during these years was Mayor

William B. Hartsfield. Elected first in 1936, Hartsfield was

voted out of office in 1940, losing to prominent businessman Roy

LeCraw. Shortly thereafter LeCraw resigned to join the military

and Hartsfield was back in for good, serving as mayor until 1960.

Although Hartsfield's legal practice and other business ventures were never as successful, he was a superb mayor. His political instincts were shrewd and he was totally devoted to ensuring that Atlanta reached its fullest potential.

For instance, he was no great fan of *Gone With The Wind*. A sixth-generation Atlantan, Hartsfield had no illusions about the Civil War and the antebellum South. But when Scarlett O'Hara caught the world's imagination, Hartsfield saw an opportunity to put Atlanta once more into the national spotlight. He moved heaven and earth to make sure the movie premiere was in Atlanta. If some northern industrialist put a factory in Atlanta because his wife wanted to see Tara, that was just fine by Hartsfield.

He was also willing to do anything within reason to accommodate business. His police chief cracked down on street crime but was relaxed about enforcing the blue laws. Businessmen got the message that Atlanta wasn't a Bible-thumping town, which explained in part why branch offices came to Atlanta and not other Southern cities.

◄ **During World War II, planners were already at work trying to figure out how to better accommodate downtown and the automobile. The centerpiece was an expressway that would run north and south, connecting both ends of the downtown district—the Downtown Connector. It would be another seven years before the federal interstate highway construction program would begin, but Atlanta was moving forward. Today, an elaborate traffic management system works to keep the city's traffic flowing smoothly.** Photo by Ron Sherman

▼ **The central figure in Atlanta was Mayor William B. Hartsfield (third from left). He was an excellent mayor, with shrewd political instincts and a total devotion to ensuring Atlanta reached its fullest potential. He actively promoted the city to businesses, motivated his police force to crack down on street crime, strongly backed aviation as a stronghold for the future, and continually pushed the city's boundaries outward.** Photo courtesy of the Atlanta History Center

number of private automobiles, downtown streets were chaotic. In 1948, the city finally banned most downtown street parking. In 1950 Georgia Power sold the transit system to a group of businessmen.

Hartsfield was also fixated on continuing to push the city's boundaries outward, particularly north to Buckhead.

Buckhead was nearly as old as Atlanta itself. In 1840 a settler named Henry Irby built a general store—featuring a stuffed deer head over the door—near what is now the intersection of Peachtree Street and West Paces Ferry Road. For decades Buckhead was a mere outpost along the Peachtree trail. Gradually, though, it began to develop as a hamlet of its own, near the city but not of it. As development began to move northwards up Peachtree Street at the turn of the century, Buckhead began to be seen as a bucolic bedroom community for wealthy Atlantans. Magnificent estates and homes, many designed by Atlanta architects like Philip Shutze, sprouted on wooded acreage. But once the automobile arrived, Buckhead began losing its physical separateness from the city.

Hartsfield realized the importance of the railroads to early Atlanta and he was determined to keep Atlanta in the forefront of anything new that came along. He was "airminded" from the beginning and grasped the magnitude of the change that automobiles would bring to the city.

During World War II, planners were already at work trying to figure out how to better accommodate downtown and the automobile. The centerpiece was an expressway that would run north and south connecting both ends of the downtown district. At war's end, the city passed a bond issue providing sixteen million dollars to begin acquiring right-of-way for what is still known today as the Downtown Connector.

After securing more state and federal financial help, construction began three years later. It would be another seven years before the federal interstate highway construction program—which incorporated the Connector and crossed it with Interstate 20, a major east-west route—would begin, but Atlanta was moving forward again.

The streetcar lines that Joel Hurt and others worked to build in the early part of the century had been in decline for decades. They were gradually replaced with trackless trolleys—rubber-tired buses connected to overhead power lines—but even the trolleys were now considered old-fashioned. Between the trolleys and the increasing

Hartsfield tried to annex Buckhead and Cascade Heights in 1947 but failed. Hartsfield didn't give up and finally got his way in 1952. The annexation tripled the land area of the city and added another 100,000 citizens.

Many of these new Atlantans were black. Relations between white and black Atlanta were as distant as ever. Segregation was as entrenched as it was prior to the Depression. But there were unmistakable signs that the status quo was increasingly untenable.

Above all a practical politician, Hartsfield had challenged black leaders to show their political muscle. Their big chance came in 1944 in an unusual congressional election. Blacks were still barred from voting in Democratic Party primaries, but this election featured no primary. After a vigorous get-out-the-vote effort, black votes carried the day decisively. Hartsfield was impressed, particularly after an additional eighteen thousand blacks registered to vote not long after the election. Two years later, eight carefully chosen black policeman went on duty, the first in Atlanta.

By 1953 Dr. Rufus Clement, the president of Atlanta University, had won election to the Board of Education, the first black to win a citywide election since Reconstruction.

◄ Streetcar lines were gradually replaced with trackless trolleys—rubber-tired buses connected to overhead power lines. Between the trolleys and the increasing number of private automobiles, downtown streets were chaotic. Photo courtesy of Georgia State University Special Collections

◄ As early as the 1940s, traffic was a concern for the busy, bustling city of Atlanta. Photo courtesy of the Atlanta History Center

◄In the 1950s, Atlanta's boundaries were pushed out to Buckhead, an area nearly as old as Atlanta itself. Around the turn of the century, the area was seen as a bucolic bedroom community for wealthy Atlantans. Once the automobile arrived, Buckhead began losing its physical separateness from the city. Mayor William B. Hartsfield succeeded in annexing the area into the city in 1952, tripling the land area of Atlanta and adding 100,000 citizens to its population total. Today, the area is a mecca of fine dining, upscale shopping, exciting nightlife, business headquarters, and upscale living. Photos by Ron Sherman

When the Supreme Court outlawed segregated public schools in 1954, there was much talk of organized resistance around the state. In Atlanta, though, Hartsfield was working to loosen the chains of segregation, but always in a low-profile way. For instance, the city's golf courses were one of the first public facilities desegregated, accomplished on Christmas Eve 1955.

Black leaders like A.T. Walden, Clarence Bacote, Grace Hamilton, and John Wesley Dobbs kept the pressure on. Atlanta was also exporting leadership talent around the region, epitomized by Martin Luther King, Jr. His father, Martin Luther King, Sr., was the influential pastor of Ebenezer Baptist Church on Auburn Avenue. King, Jr. had graduated from Morehouse and Boston University and had taken the pastor's job at a church in Montgomery, Alabama, in 1955.

Almost immediately, King played a major role in the celebrated Montgomery bus boycott sparked by Rosa Parks. King quickly gained a national reputation and moved back to Atlanta. He agreed to co-pastor with his father at Ebenezer Baptist but his primary activity was building the Southern Christian Leadership Conference.

The Atlanta business community was unleashed by the war, too. The post-war housing boom returned real estate to the ranks of leading industries. Home builders pushed out from the city into adjacent DeKalb County, building thousands of brick ranch homes

in the northern reaches of the county in the first great wave of suburban growth.

To the northwest, the reopening of the Bell Bomber plant by Lockheed in 1951—the first product was the C-130 cargo plane—gave suburban Cobb County and Marietta an important economic anchor.

In many ways, Coca-Cola had greatly benefited from the war. Robert Woodruff had vowed to provide Coca-Cola to American soldiers anywhere in the world and, with the help of the military, he set up portable bottling plants in every war theater. Those plants stayed behind after the war and were the platform for Coca-Cola to become one of the earliest multi-national corporations.

Prodded by Hartsfield, the city built its first passenger terminal at the airport in 1948. Constructed primarily out of surplus war materials, it resembled an overgrown quonset hut. It was inexpensive, but it kept Atlanta's airport among the busiest air fields in the country. Eastern Airlines was well-established and Delta Air Lines—a former crop dusting company from Louisiana that had moved to Atlanta in the 1940s and switched to hauling passengers—was growing under the leadership of C.E. Woolman.

In addition to his interest in highways, railroads, and air transportation, Hartsfield dreamed of improving the Chattahoochee River enough to carry barge traffic from Atlanta to the Gulf of Mexico. That grandiose goal never materialized but in 1956 the

Corps of Engineers finished building a dam at Buford well north of the city. The dam created Lake Lanier, which quickly became a favored recreation spot for Atlantans and also served as a reservoir for the city.

Grady Memorial Hospital built a massive new building in 1958. The mission to serve emergency and indigent patients stayed the same.

The 1950s was also the heyday of the one of the Atlanta's most unique and beloved institutions: The Varsity. The Varsity began as a quick lunch spot for Georgia Tech students in 1929. It relocated to North Avenue and became a popular place for students and Tech football fans because it was close to Grant Field. Proprietor Frank Gordy made onion rings, hamburgers, and chili dogs family fare for generations of Atlantans. He pioneered curb service by fast-talking car hops and expanded The Varsity into the largest drive-in restaurant in the country, capable of accommodating hundreds of automobiles in his sprawling lots.

Newspaper publisher James Cox, the owner of the dominant afternoon *Atlanta Journal*, acquired the morning newspaper, *The Atlanta Constitution*, in 1950. The editor of the *Constitution* during

▼ **With the annexation of Buckhead and Cascade Heights, many new Atlantans were black, but relations between white and black Atlanta were as distant as ever. Segregation was still entrenched. But there were unmistakable signs that the status quo was increasingly untenable. Hartsfield had challenged black politicians to show their political muscle. Their big chance came in 1944 in an unusual congressional election. Blacks were still barred from voting in Democratic Party primaries, but this election had no primary. After a vigorous get-out-the-vote effort black votes carried the day decisively. An additional eighteen thousand blacks registered to vote not long after the election.** Photos courtesy of Georgia State University Special Collections

REGISTER HERE
COLORED ONLY

the 1950s, Ralph McGill, wrote a front-page column several times a week. Although by nature conservative on the subject of race relations, McGill gradually realized the danger that racial hatred posed to the South generally and Atlanta in particular.

In 1958 the city was shocked awake by a powerful bomb blast at The Temple on Peachtree Street, home to a Jewish congregation led by a rabbi who was a prominent desegregationist. Although the alleged bombers were tried but never convicted, the bombing convinced city and business leaders that they could not afford to be neutral about desegregation. On the day of the bombing McGill wrote that the city was reaping "the harvest" of resistance to desegregation, a column that helped win him the Pulitzer Prize.

The bombing was a sobering end to the 1950s. While the metropolitan population reached one million in 1959—the "M Day" celebration was a recognition that Atlanta was becoming something more than just what was inside the city limits—there was much uneasiness about whether the city and its economy could survive desegregation unscathed. ❧

◄ Black leaders like A.T. Walden, Clarence Bacote, Grace Hamilton, and John Wesley Dobbs kept the pressure on in Atlanta for Civil Rights. Atlanta also was the home of black leaders who went on to lead the movement throughout the region. The most famous of these is Martin Luther King, Jr. His father, Martin Luther King, Sr., was the influential pastor of Ebenezer Baptist Church on Auburn Avenue. King, Jr. had graduated from Morehouse and Boston University and had taken the pastor's job at a baptist church in Montgomery, Alabama, in 1955. After playing a major role in the Montgomery bus boycott, sparked by Rosa Parks, a black seamstress who refused to yield her seat on a city bus to a white man, King, Jr., returned to Atlanta to co-pastor with his father at Ebenezer Baptist and to build the Southern Leadership Conference. His message of peaceful protest was a strong theme in the battle for Civil Rights. Historic photo of King, Jr. at his home courtesy of the Atlanta History Center. New photos by Ron Sherman

▲ In many ways, Coca-Cola had greatly benefited from World War II. CEO Robert Woodruff had vowed to provide Coca-Cola to American soldiers anywhere in the world and, with the help of the military, he set up portable bottling plants in every war theater. Those plants stayed behind after the war and were the platform for Coca-Cola to become one of the earliest multi-national corporations. Today, the Coca-Cola Company is perhaps the company most linked to Atlanta, and its headquarters is in the heart of downtown. Additionally, the company built the Coca-Cola Museum downtown, which features memorabilia and interactive exhibits about Coke throughout the years. Historic image courtesy of Georgia State University Special Collections. New photos by Ron Sherman

▲ The 1950s was the heyday for one of Atlanta's unique and
most beloved institutions, The Varsity, begun as a quick lunch
spot for Georgia Tech students in 1929. It relocated to North
Avenue and became a popular place for students and Tech football fans because it was close to Grant Field. Proprietor Frank
Gordy made onion rings, hamburgers, and chili dogs family
fare for generations of Atlantans, and pioneered curb service
by fast-talking car hops and expanded The Varsity into the
largest drive-in restaurant in the country, capable of accommodating hundreds of automobiles in his sprawling lots. Today,
The Varsity, located on Spring Street, is still a favorite. Historic
photo courtesy of Georgia State University Special Collections.
New photos by Ron Sherman

◄ Prodded by Mayor William B. Hartsfield, Atlanta built its first passenger terminal at the airport in 1948. The airport continued to grow throughout the 1950s, and as his last hurrah before leaving office in 1960, he cut the ribbon at the new airport terminal, and $18 million, 11-story tower. Significantly, the new terminal no longer carried the word "municipal."
Historic photos courtesy of the Atlanta History Center.
New photo by Ron Sherman

▶ In 1956 the Corps of Engineers finished building a dam at Buford well north of the city, creating Lake Lanier, which quickly became a favored recreation spot for Atlantans and also served as reservoir for the city. Photo by Ron Sherman

◄ **Atlanta was beginning to recognize itself as a metropolitan area, with homes, business, and shopping drawing people for work and family life.** Historic photos courtesy of Georgia State University Special Collections. New photo by Ron Sherman

Portman Holdings

Serving clients throughout the world from its headquarters in Atlanta, the Portman organization brings creativity and vision to the design and development of successful real estate. Portman Holdings is the international real estate development arm that was established in 1995 to bring together the experience of 40 years in real estate development, management, and finance under one umbrella. John Portman & Associates is the award-winning architectural firm that created much of Atlanta's distinctive skyline.

Since 1953, the companies have played an active role in shaping downtown Atlanta. Specializing in hospitality/mixed-use development, Portman set the stage for Atlanta's thriving convention industry. Peachtree Center started with a downtown trade mart and grew into a 13-block complex. It includes three of the city's landmark hotels, the Hyatt Regency Atlanta, Westin Peachtree Plaza, and the Marriott Marquis; seven high-rise office towers, plus the new SunTrust Plaza Tower and Garden Offices', Peachtree Center Mall, and AmericasMart, a 7.7-million-square-foot trade mart. The Peachtree Center neighborhood is a signature of the firm's founder, John C. Portman, Jr. Pedestrian-friendly bridges link the buildings, landscaped plazas and parks punctuate the high-rise

structures, and artwork abounds at the street level. The hotels reflect dramatic use of the interior space that continues to attract guests and win the praise of those who visit.

With a strong commitment to the central city, the Portman design and development teams worked together to create Peachtree Center and have developed projects in San Francisco, New York, Los Angeles, and cities overseas. Portman has numerous projects in Asia, such as Shanghai Centre and Marina Square in Singapore. Currently, teams are working on hotel/mixed-use developments in Charlotte, Philadelphia, India, and Poland.

John Portman & Associates also works directly for other owners and developers. In Atlanta, key buildings on the campuses of Emory University, Georgia Tech, Southern Polytech, and Agnes Scott were designed by Portman, as well as schools, shopping centers, and suburban office buildings.

With Atlanta's expansive growth, Portman will continue to create urban design and development solutions to make Atlanta a better place to live in the century ahead. More plans lie ahead for the downtown environs. New projects are on the boards for other cities in the U.S., and major development is planned abroad. ◗

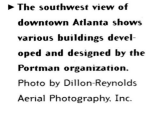

▶ **The southwest view of downtown Atlanta shows various buildings developed and designed by the Portman organization.** Photo by Dillon-Reynolds Aerial Photography. Inc.

A M E R I C A S M A R T · A T L A N T A

AMERICASMART·ATLANTA is the world's largest and most comprehensive wholesale marketplace. In essence, AMERICASMART·ATLANTA is a shopping mall for retailers.

The who's who of retailers worldwide come to AMERICAS-MART·ATLANTA to shop its 3.9 million square feet of new and innovative merchandise to stock their own stores. The product selection under one roof is unequaled, and admission to AMERICASMART·ATLANTA is highly coveted and available only to qualified buyers. Everything from the exotic and one-of-a-kinds to lifestyle product essentials is among the merchandise, and buyers come from all 50 U.S. states and 72 countries to buy the gift, home furnishings, area rug, and apparel industries' hottest products.

AMERICASMART·ATLANTA is owned by AMC, Inc., a dominant player in the worldwide multibillion-dollar wholesale trade and retail industry. The world's largest trade mart and trade show company, AMC's principal business unit and flagship is AMERICASMART·ATLANTA. Led by founder and chairman John C. Portman Jr., AMERICASMART·ATLANTA traces its origins to 1962. It is the nation's number one gift, home furnishings, and area rug marketplace and the preferred market for a growing number of apparel retailers to do business.

Located in the heart of downtown Atlanta, AMERICASMART·ATLANTA is comprised of three buildings, the Gift Mart, Merchandise Mart, and Apparel Mart. The facility is open to qualified buyers throughout the year. AMERICAS-MART·ATLANTA hosts six gift and home furnishings markets, two area rug markets, and nine apparel markets annually. The convergent markets include both permanent and temporary product offerings. Showrooms are open weekdays only, from 10:00 A.M. to 4:00 P.M.

Among the specialty product centers to be found at AMERICASMART·ATLANTA are gift; home accents and furnishings; home accents and fine linens; garden; holiday and floral; area rugs; fashion accessories and fine jewelry; resort and souvenir gift; and apparel. Product also is available at markets in temporary booths presented in as many as 27 distinctive merchandise categories.

Through the years, AMERICASMART·ATLANTA has been cited by market retailers from every U.S. state and 72 countries worldwide as the most important market to their business, as compared with all domestic and international markets. But AMERICASMART is just as essential to Atlanta's convention business and has become both a downtown anchor and a landmark.

From its early days through the new millennium, AMERICASMART·ATLANTA is a mainstay on the wholesale front. As an international cornerstone in a multibillion-dollar industry, AMERICASMART·ATLANTA is a unique addition to the international city. As the brainchild of a local businessman/developer, it is representative of the dreams and accomplishments of the city's own people and their impact on the world. ◑

◀ Led by founder and chairman John C. Portman Jr., AMERICAS-MART·ATLANTA traces its origins to 1962.

Hines Interests Limited Partnership

Hines Interests Limited Partnership manages a large portfolio of 530 properties, with 70 million square feet of office retail and residential space under management and 24 million square feet of office retail and residential space under development. A privately owned firm, founded in 1957 and headquartered in Houston, Hines has main offices in New York, Chicago, Aspen, San Francisco, and London, as well as additional offices in 47 other U.S. cities and nine foreign countries—not surprising for a firm that is one of the largest real estate organizations in the world, with assets in excess of $8 billion. Hines opened a major regional office in Atlanta in 1981.

A developer of landmark buildings, Hines is perhaps best known in Atlanta for the Ravinia and One Ninety One Peachtree Towers properties. Ravinia, the largest building outside of downtown Atlanta, offers over 1.6 million rentable square feet, and is served by the 500-room Crowne Plaza Ravinia. The development was completed in stages—Ravinia One in 1985, Ravinia Two in 1987, and Ravinia Three in 1991—and is home to MCI and the national headquarters of Holiday Inn.

Ravinia is acclaimed for its setting and has won a national award for landscaping design. "We preserved a 10-acre forest in the middle of dense office development," says Senior Vice President Robert Voyles. "We nestled everything into the existing forest and topography." Ravinia was not only carefully set in the heart of a beautifully wooded site, but Ravinia Three also contains one of the Southeast's largest privately owned botanical conservatories. The late Ann Crammond, former executive director of the Atlanta Botanical Garden, consulted in the design of the conservatory, which features tropical waterfalls and Norfolk Island pines. Hines continues its relationship with the ABG through sponsorship of summer interns, and has been a major supporter of The Garden of Eden Ball fund-raiser.

Wachovia and the law firm King and Spalding are among the distinguished firms headquartered at One Ninety One Peachtree Tower. "We have some major corporate citizens in our buildings," Voyles says. Fifty stories high, One Ninety One Peachtree Towers

connects via a seventh-story atrium to the Ritz Carlton. The multi-level parking facility elevators open directly into the main lobby and serve 1.3 million square feet of office space.

Real estate management of choice for the world's leading corporations, from low-rise buildings to urban towers, Hines is the recipient of numerous industry awards, including the 1999 International Building of the Year, awarded by the Building Owners and Managers Association for One Ninety One Peachtree Tower. "Our firm has received three Building of the Year awards from the Urban Land Institute, the premier organization for the real estate sector," says Voyles. "No other developer has received more than one."

Hines is attracted to Atlanta for many reasons. "It's a very pro-business community, with a good quality workforce," says Voyles. "We first came here at a time when Atlanta was booming, and I think that the things that were good about Atlanta then, are still good about it now."

Voyles mentions Atlanta's pleasant suburban lifestyle, excellent schools, and good climate as among her best assets. "Despite the sprawl people complain about, the Fortune 500 companies that send people here have a hard time pulling them out," Voyles says. Hosting the Centennial Olympic Games is another Atlanta achievement that made a difference. "We do a lot of business with European investors, and the Olympics helped validate Atlanta on the international scene, in terms of foreign investment," Voyles explains.

He predicts Atlanta will continue to experience tremendous economic growth. "Atlanta's regional transportation network—interstate, rail, and Hartsfield Airport—makes it unique among southern cities."

Hines offers a wide range of services to corporate and institutional owners of real estate, including asset management, property management, marketing and leasing, development and redevelopment, acquisition and disposition, finance and accounting, and engineering. Hines develops as well as rehabilitates existing projects through site selection, rezoning, architectural design, construction bidding and coordination, purchasing operations, and financing.

Known for the personal commitment and attentions to detail it brings to each project, Hines' properties consistently enjoy highest occupancy rates, lowest operating costs, and greatest financial return to investors. "We offer all the benefits of a large firm, but we combine them with a locally oriented team," explains Voyles.

Hines has owned many of its properties for more than three decades. Average tenure of the firm's senior management is 20 years, and turnover among the firm's employees is low. This longevity creates a strong corporate culture of seasoned professionals, knowledgeable in all facets of real estate management and development. "Most of the people in our office have been here in Atlanta all their working career," Voyles says. "At the end of the day, all real estate is a local business."

Hines currently has four large projects in development in the Atlanta area, and has already broken ground for 3003 Perimeter Summit (located on Ashford Dunwoody, inside 285), a 400,000-square-foot building scheduled to be completed by the third quarter of 2000. 3003 Summit is part of a mixed-use development that will eventually include 750 units of residential, 2.6 million square feet of office, hotels, and retail, all in a pedestrian-friendly, light-rail served environment. Also underway is Deerfield Commons One (located at Windward Parkway and Georgia 400), a 120,000-square-foot building scheduled to be completed by May of 2000.

Another new project Hines has under way in the Atlanta area is Overton Park, a mixed-use development that overlooks the Chattahoochee National Park, with a million square feet of office development, 400 units of residential, and 700

hotel rooms planned. "It's a twenty-first century workplace, designed in keeping with Hines' determination to be on the cutting edge of office technology," says Voyles. Hines is recognized in the industry for pioneering many building design systems that improve building efficiency and maximize tenant comfort and safety.

A third venture, Deerfield, is a 550-acre multiuse project located in North Fulton's Georgia 400 corridor. "We do a lot of corporate headquarters. GTE Wireless and Alltel have already located in this project, as well as the Marriott Courtyard and a major Home Depot retail store," says Voyles.

Hines is also in the process of negotiating another major downtown site in the heart of the city. "We feel quite positive about Atlanta and the future health of the city," says Voyles. ◐

◀ Ravinia, a 1.6-million-square-foot mixed-use office development in suburban Atlanta, was designed by Kevin Roche.

◀ A 3-million-square-foot mixed-use development, Perimeter Summit is located in the Central Perimeter market.

U.S. Army Forces Command

▶ U.S. Army Forces Command (FORSCOM) is the largest major command in the Department of the Army. FORSCOM supervises the training of more than 741,000 active and reserve component soldiers to provide a strategic, power-projection ground force capable of responding rapidly and successfully to crises worldwide.

One of Atlanta's worldwide corporate headquarters is close to downtown and yet a world away. Although it has a budget in the billions, it isn't a Fortune 500 company. What it produces can't be held and admired. But the value of this product is priceless and sometimes taken for granted—the guarantee of freedom for our country and the preservation of the American way of life.

The corporation is called U.S. Army Forces Command (FORSCOM), and it's the largest major command in the Department of the Army. It comprises the Army component of U.S. Atlantic Command. FORSCOM supervises the training of more than 741,000 active and reserve component soldiers to provide a strategic, power-projection ground force capable of responding rapidly and successfully to crises worldwide. Its impact on the local economy is significant. Military and civilian personnel in FORSCOM headquarters put more than $400 million in salaries and contracts into the Atlanta economy every year. Forged in 1975 as a result of a restructuring of the entire U. S. Army after the Vietnam conflict, FORSCOM's three-quarter-million people have gone to every hemisphere to ensure peace and security.

FORSCOM's headquarters, located at Fort McPherson on the boundary of the cities of East Point and Atlanta, is housed in a 356,000-square-foot command and control complex and is the workplace for 1,800 military and civilian employees. FORSCOM's corporate reach, however, goes far beyond the Atlanta area. It has subsidiaries in 48 states and Puerto Rico, employing more than 741,000 people—active Army, Army Reserve, Army National

Guard, and Army civilians—to ensure that FORSCOM's motto, "Freedom's Guardian," is carried out around the world. This motto is FORSCOM's pledge that its soldiers will sacrifice, perhaps even at the cost of their lives, to protect America's freedom wherever and whenever duty calls.

At any particular time, FORSCOM has about 15,000 to 20,000 soldiers and civilians working away from their homes. While the soldiers are often deployed to far corners of the world, these forces enjoy high visibility and respect wherever they are sent in support of the country's national security interests.

FORSCOM people have what it takes to get the job done anywhere in the world. They find solutions, fix problems, and if necessary, fight and win the nation's wars. Their commanders and

▶ Forces Command was formed in an overall reorganization of the Army in 1975. The FORSCOM headquarters was established at Fort McPherson in Patton Hall, until Marshall Hall (shown above) was built.

◀ FORSCOM's motto, "Freedom's Guardian," is carried out around the world and is FORSCOM's pledge that its soldiers will sacrifice, perhaps even at the cost of their lives, to protect America's freedom wherever and whenever duty calls.

Part of that Reserve Component is led by a major subordinate command of Forces Command, also headquartered at Fort McPherson: the U.S. Army Reserve Command (USARC). U.S. Army Reserve forces are prepared to support FORSCOM's combat power by providing specialists in such technical skills as medical treatment, civil affairs, engineering, construction, transportation, maintenance, and supply.

And when they are federalized, U.S. Army National Guard units within the continental United States are incorporated as combat soldiers into the overall FORSCOM battle plan.

Whether it is Operation Desert Storm in southwest Asia, Operation Uphold Democracy in Haiti, or Operation Joint Forge in Bosnia, FORSCOM soldiers are wherever the action is around the world. FORSCOM units provided greatly needed support after Hurricane Mitch; fought forest fires in the Southeast and the West; built dikes to keep back flood waters along the Missouri and Mississippi Rivers; and provided engineering, radar, and surveillance support to U.S. counter-drug agencies.

leaders are dedicated to meeting a mission that would challenge any CEO.

FORSCOM is a team of teams, providing ready forces to meet the operational requirements of our nation. It trains, mobilizes, deploys, and sustains land military forces worldwide; develops and cares for people; optimizes available resources; and improves quality installations from which it projects and supports the force.

A significant part of FORSCOM is its Reserve Component forces, outnumbering Active Component forces by three to one. The Army National Guard and Army Reserve provide those citizen-soldiers, who are more essential than ever before as U.S. Army Forces Command has restructured and downsized since the end of the Cold War.

The history of U.S. Army Forces Command clearly supports its corporate image of heroes: brave, powerful, far-reaching. These are America's sons and daughters, some of whom have died fighting for freedom and democracy. They have fed hungry children with tenderness and care. They help people in war-torn parts of the world put their lives back together.

The entire FORSCOM family—active Army, Army Reserve, and Army National Guard, their family members, and civilian employees—is proud to be part of the Atlanta community and is dedicated to serving as "Freedom's Guardian." ❦

Taracorp, Inc.

Atlanta-based Taracorp is ranked among the top ten producers of quality solders in the world and is the only company specializing in lead-free solders. Even more remarkable, the company has consistently ranked at the top since its inception in 1884.

Taracorp originated as Seitzinger's, Inc. in Atlanta. Later, the Taratoot family purchased the operation and changed the name. For decades, the company produced high-quality lead products to serve many a U.S. industry. From nuclear transportation casts, to plumbing solders, to roofing and radiation shielding, and alloys for the automotive battery industry. It also ranks as a sports leader in the reload cartridge industry for sport shooting. Taracorp has protected and served a country constantly on the move.

In 1998, Taracorp focused its energy and talents exclusively on the production of lead-free solders. The company poured funding into research and development to design products that could meet the exacting specifications of very precise markets with materials that were more environmentally friendly. This move was made as a matter of perfection and dedication on the part of the company, as Taracorp had already achieved excellence in environmental protection for its lead-producing plants.

With the introduction of a line of water-soluble flux, Taracorp solidified its position as the industry leader in the production of lead-free solder and related products. Taracorp Imaco boasts the first facility in the United States dedicated exclusively to the manufacture of lead-free solder. The plant, located in Winston-Salem, North Carolina, produces Taramet Sterling, Dutch Boy, and other lead-free products under rigid quality control standards. The brands produced are familiar logos found on most hardware, building supply, and professional/industrial supply stores nationwide. The brands are favorites among professionals who demand high quality and performance.

Taracorp's national sales offices are strategically located to provide maximum service and convenience to customers. As an ESOP company, the principals and staff are wholly dedicated to superior product production, delivery, and customer support.

Today, under the leadership of Louis J. Taratoot, chairman and CEO, and James M. Taratoot, president and COO, Taracorp is an industry leader with an unsurpassed record of achievement in product development, customer satisfaction, product quality, and environmental concern. ❖

▶ **Taracorp is ranked among the top ten producers of quality solders in the world and is proud to be based in Atlanta.** Photo by Ron Sherman.

Interdenominational Theological Center

As the new millennium approaches, part of the nation waits in anticipation and part shudders in apprehension. The '90s have taxed the country in ways none could have predicted before, escalating to the unfathomable children-killing-children sprees in the country's schools. Some Americans are anxious to simply close this chapter in history, while others look forward to change inherent in a new era.

In order to put fear and troubles in the past and instill hope in our future, many believe that there must be a renewal of American society, a restoration of morals, hope, and sense of community. But given the many differences in race, culture, religion, gender, and ages, it is a formidable task few are willing to take on.

The Interdenominational Theological Center (ITC) is one of those few. Founded in 1958, the ITC is a unique ensemble of six denominational seminaries—United Methodist, Church of God in Christ, Christian Methodist Episcopal, Presbyterian Church USA, African Methodist Episcopal, and Baptist. Now in its fourth decade of service, the ITC educates and trains one of every ten African-American students enrolled in Master of Divinity degree programs offered by the 200 accredited member schools of the Association of Theological Schools in the U.S. and Canada. The ITC also reaches the public in unprecedented numbers from pulpits the world over.

It is this unity of a diverse group of denominations and their incredible reach among the masses that offers so much hope to a nation in search of both a method and a vehicle to begin the restoration of American society. The ITC and its graduates are uniquely positioned to recreate the ties that bind in a society that has forgotten the concept of neighbor. The need is just as great now as it was in the 1960s, when the ITC served as the first home of the Martin Luther King Jr. Center For Nonviolent Social Change.

Located in Atlanta, the ITC is one of the six campuses of the Atlanta University Center, the largest consortium of African-American higher education in the world. Individual seminaries of the ITC date back as far as 1867. Students come to the ITC from 27 states and 13 foreign countries representing most of the major religions in the world, including Islam. The ITC's alumni serve as college presidents, professors, government officials, community leaders, chaplains, and pastors, as well as bishops and other denominational officers.

Beyond its scholarly teachings and community service, the ITC also trains professionals in church management and is building the

nation's first national database of African-American churches and members—complete with donated computers to link each congregation to all the others. The new system will enable widespread and instant communication nationwide—the first organized communication system of its kind and a major factor in immediate response time to prevent or heal tragedies in any community.

ITC has formed a number of partnerships between religions, big business, and governments over the past decades to strengthen communities. As more of these partnerships form, the ITC's role will increase. Ultimately, healing a society of its many ills will require many forms of medicine. But underneath it all lies the universal need for compassion, understanding, acceptance, and neighborly love. ❧

◄ The Interdenominational Theological Center (ITC) is home to the James H. Costen Center, a modern lodging, hospitality, and meeting facility. The Costen Center was one of the media headquarters during the 1996 Summer Centennial Olympic Games in Atlanta.

◄ The Interdenominational Theological Center, a unique consortium of six seminaries, is one of the six campuses of the Atlanta University Center, the largest consortium of Black higher education in the world.

267

REV. MARTIN LUTHER KING, JR.
1929 — 1968
Free at last, Free at last
Thank God Almighty
I'm Free at last

CHAPTER SIX
1960-1970

❦

At the beginning of the 1960s, the issue of desegregation was of utmost importance to Atlanta. The city's business community was aware of the criticism leveled at Little Rock and other cities where segregationists had the upper hand. Fearing economic development would suffer if Atlanta was lumped in the same group, Mayor Hartsfield worked hard at keeping desegregation efforts moving forward while keeping publicity that might spark a white backlash to a minimum.

Photo by Ron Sherman

It was during these years, Atlanta awarded itself the title of the "City Too Busy to Hate," a slogan picked up by the national media.

▲ The Atlantan who truly brought international recognition to the city was Martin Luther King, Jr., whose commitment to non-violent resistance made him the leading figure of the civil rights movement. In 1963 he led a massive march on Washington and delivered his most famous speech, the "I Have a Dream" address. In 1964 he was awarded the Nobel Peace Prize. King was assassinated in Memphis in 1968. As many as 200,000 mourners marched through downtown Atlanta as his coffin—drawn by mules—was transported from Ebenezer Baptist Church to Morehouse University. Today, King's gravesite is often visited, and memorials to the great leader can be found throughout the city. Pictured above, Daddy and Coretta Scott King, 1977, photo by Ron Sherman. MLK funeral procession photo courtesy of the Atlanta History Center. Monument photo by Ron Sherman

At the same time, though, black Atlantans were becoming disenchanted with the go-slow approach. A new generation of black leaders—some of them still college students at the Atlanta University complex—was at hand and they weren't interested in carefully calibrated advances.

The Hartsfield approach held when it came to public transit. After a small public sit-in, Hartsfield arranged for a token arrest that would throw the issue into the court system. Two years later, in 1959, the courts desegregated the transit system to little public fanfare.

He wasn't so lucky when it came to the city's retail stores. The target was Rich's, the city's oldest and most beloved retailer. Rich's was a paradox. It extended credit liberally to blacks and whites, and employees addressed all customers as "Mr." and "Mrs." But the store restrooms and restaurants were segregated. The campaign of public sit-ins and demonstrations launched by college students greatly frustrated Hartsfield and Richard Rich—the grandson of founder Morris Rich.

By now Hartsfield was at the end of his political career and Ivan Allen, Jr., son of the man who had chaired the Forward Atlanta campaign of the 1920s, was handed the task of mediating the confrontation.

After little or no progress in resolving the issue, Allen decided to piggyback on another statewide desegregation controversy: the schools.

The first black students had been admitted to the University of Georgia by court order in 1959. Although they suffered considerable personal humiliation and abuse from fellow students, the state's segregationists had been essentially outflanked and no Georgia politician was ever photographed standing in a schoolhouse door.

When the General Assembly threw in the towel and passed a law in effect desegregating the state's public schools en masse, Allen saw his opportunity. He offered the demonstrators a deal: Back off until after the start of the 1961 school year and within thirty days department stores and lunch counters would fully desegregate. The deal was accepted—in large part thanks to intervention by Martin Luther King, Jr.—and both the schools and stores were desegregated smoothly. Georgia Tech desegregated

uneventfully in 1961 and the city's movie theaters followed
shortly thereafter.

His success at brokering orderly change fueled Allen's determination to run for mayor and he won election handily after
Hartsfield retired.

Hartsfield's last hurrah in office was cutting the ribbon at the new
airport terminal, an $18 million, 11-story tower. Significantly, the
new terminal no longer carried the word "municipal." Atlanta was
starting to recognize itself as a metropolitan area. Indeed, the city
would grow significantly in just about every way during the 1960s.

One of Allen's desires was to bring professional sports to
Atlanta. The city had a minor league baseball team, the Crackers,
but the business leadership didn't want to be minor league in anything. In 1963 the owner of the Kansas City Athletics offered to
move to Atlanta as soon as the city could build him a stadium.

Allen quickly agreed and chose a 60-acre tract next to the
interstate that had been recently cleared by an urban renewal program. As Allen noted, it was land the city didn't own intended for

a stadium the city had no money to build. The hero of the story was Mills Lane, the freewheeling head of C&S Bank. Lane stepped in to guarantee the financing and the stadium Atlanta-Fulton County Stadium was rushed to completion in just fifty-one weeks. Although the Athletics were ultimately denied permission to move, Allen enticed the Milwaukee Braves to move south and professional sports came to Atlanta for good in 1966.

That same year, the National Football League awarded the city a franchise, purchased by insurance executive Rankin Smith for $8.5 million.

It took a horrific tragedy at the beginning of the decade to bring the city's anemic arts facilities into similar focus. In 1962 the cream of the city's arts patrons had embarked on a month-long tour of European museums. Departing from Paris to return to Atlanta, their plane crashed on the runway, killing 106. The tragedy tore an enormous hole in the city's social fabric. Almost immediately, efforts to memorialize the dead through the building of a performing arts center began. With the help of an anonymous gift from Coca-Cola's Robert Woodruff, construction of a theater, symphony hall, and art school began on Peachtree Street in Midtown. Today, the Woodruff Arts Center is still the center of Atlanta's arts scene.

The early 1960s also saw the Chamber of Commerce revive the Forward Atlanta campaign. As it was in the 1920s, the three-year advertising campaign was successful in attracting new jobs and industry and extended for another three years. After the extension, it became a permanent part of the Chamber. Forward Atlanta also added one other thing to the Atlanta landscape in the early 1960s: a publication, named *Atlanta Magazine*, designed to promote the city. It was in the magazine's pages, around 1964, that Atlanta was first labeled an "international city," a boast that proved more easily printed than accomplished.

The Atlantan who was truly bringing international recognition to Atlanta was Martin Luther King, Jr. King's commitment to non-violent resistance made him the leading figure of the civil rights movements. In 1963 he led a massive march on Washington and delivered his most famous speech—the "I Have a Dream" address. In 1964 he was awarded the Nobel Peace Prize.

Nevertheless, King was never fully embraced by the city power structure. Still, the Nobel Peace Prize could not be ignored and there was a gala civic dinner held in early 1965 to honor him. Carried live on national radio, the dinner was a public event

▲ As part of the new "modern" downtown, workmen spent the early 1960s dismantling the last of the overhead electric wires that had powered the trackless trolley. Almost as soon as they finished, plans were being made for a new rapid transit system that would include the current bus system but also add subways and surface rail lines. The new system was the Metropolitan Atlanta Regional Transit Authority, or MARTA for short. Construction on the east-west rail line began in 1971. The north-south line opened in the mid 1980s. Photos by Ron Sherman.

▲ In 1962, the cream of the city's arts patrons were killed in a plane crash in Paris, returning from a month-long tour of European museums. Efforts to memorialize the dead through the building of a performing arts center began almost immediately. With the help of a gift from Coca-Cola's Robert Woodruff, construction of a theater, symphony hall, and art school began on Peachtree Street in Midtown. Today, the Woodruff Arts Center is still the center of Atlanta's arts scene. Photos by Ron Sherman

reminiscent of the *Gone With The Wind* premiere twenty-five years earlier.

When King was assassinated in Memphis three years later, Atlanta was once again in the spotlight. As many as 200,000 mourners marched through downtown as his coffin—drawn by mules—was transported from Ebenezer Baptist Church to Morehouse University.

As part of the new "modern" downtown, workmen spent the early 1960s dismantling the last of the overhead electric wires that had powered the trackless trolleys. Almost as soon as they finished, plans were being made for a new rapid transit system that would include the current bus system but would also add subways and surface rail lines. The new system was the Metropolitan Atlanta Regional Transit Authority, or MARTA for short. By 1968 backers had crafted a $377 million bond issue to begin construction but it failed to garner black support at the polls and failed.

One of the most noticeable business trends was new construction downtown. Since 1930, only one large office building had been built downtown. The positive national publicity the city's peaceful desegregation efforts were receiving and a strong national economy promoted a sense of optimism that translated into a desire to modernize. During the decade, fifteen new buildings of more than twenty stories were started downtown, the tallest of which was the 41-story headquarters of First National Bank.

► One of the most notice-
able business trends was
new construction down-
town. During the decade,
fifteen new buildings of
more than twenty stories
were started downtown,
the tallest of which was
the 41-story headquar-
ters of First National
Bank. The one-million-
square-foot Merchandise
Mart was built in 1961
by an ambitious young
architect/developer
named John Portman, a
Georgia Tech graduate.
Photos courtesy of Georgia
State University Special
Collections

Construction of the tower at the Five Points corner where Jonathan Norcross operated his general store cost the city the Peachtree Arcade, but nobody seemed to notice.

One of the earliest examples of the downtown building boom was the one-million-square-foot Merchandise Mart built in 1961 by a ambitious young architect/developer named John Portman. Portman was a Georgia Tech grad and was unusual in that few architects had the wherewithal to develop their own designs.

In 1967 Portman opened the Hyatt Regency hotel on Peachtree Street. The hotel featured a towering central atrium and the feature was a sensation that brought Portman international accolades. Portman's idea was to replicate Rockefeller Center's mix of retail and office space on Peachtree Street. He was remarkably successful, building a half-dozen office towers clustered around a below-ground shopping mall on the northern edge of downtown. To move pedestrians, he connected the buildings with enclosed walkways, some as many as twenty stories above street level. The walkways were considered very progressive at the time, although they drew much criticism in later years. Portman named the complex Peachtree Center, and over time it would draw the center of downtown northward from Five Points.

While so much of the new downtown construction was going up along the spine of Peachtree Street, another ambitious young developer, Tom Cousins, was pioneering new territory to the west. Primarily a residential homebuilder, Cousins was offered "air rights" over the tangle of railroad tracks west of the Spring Street viaduct. He started by building an elevated parking deck over the tracks but his plans for the area were so grandiose that it would be the 1970s before they began to take shape.

Other developers were starting to make marks outside the traditional downtown boundaries. Fueled by the new interstate highways, they were pushing out into the suburbs. One of the country's first suburban office parks—low-rise buildings in a campus-like arrangement with plenty of parking— was built along Interstate 85 at North Druid Hills Road on what had once been a dairy farm. It proved quite successful—and much duplicated—and was the first indicator that strong rivals to downtown's business pre-eminence would surface in the coming years.

Still, even in the 1960s there were few shopping centers outside downtown. One of the earliest was Lindbergh Center, a conventional shopping strip on the edge of Buckhead that opened in the

late 1950s. A more elaborate example was Lenox Square, set square in the middle of Buckhead on the site of a former country estate. It boasted more than fifty stores and some six thousand parking spaces on seventy-four acres. Originally an open-air development, Lenox Square was covered in the late 1960s and became Atlanta's first modern mall. Although future malls were all tied to nearby interstate highways, Lenox Square proved to be the catalyst in future years for an explosion of new upscale office and retailing development in sleepy Buckhead.

The end of the decade brought sighs of relief. The city had emerged from the end of the desegregation process largely unscathed. Its reputation for progressiveness had won it national plaudits, which had translated into a healthy economy and a downtown building boom. Professional sports had put Atlanta into the ranks of "big league" cities. The predominantly white business community, which had put its weight behind racial moderation, had reason to be pleased with itself. ❧

◄ John Portman, the Georgia Tech graduate who built the Merchandise Mart, opened the Hyatt Regency Hotel on Peachtree Street in 1967. The building was notable for its towering central atrium, a feature that was a sensation and that brought Portman international accolades. Photo by Ron Sherman

◄ It was Portman's idea to replicate Rockefeller Center's mix of retail and office space on Peachtree Street. He was remarkably successful, building a half-dozen office towers clustered around a below-ground shopping mall on the northern edge of downtown. To move pedestrians, he connected the buildings with enclosed walkways, some as many as twenty stories above street level. Photo by Ron Sherman

▶ Fueled by the new interstate highways, developers were pushing out into the suburbs. One of the country's first suburban office parks—low-rise buildings in a campus-like arrangement with plenty of parking—was built during this decade. Today, office parks are the norm throughout the U.S.
Photo by Ron Sherman

▶ Mayor William B. Hartsfield's last hurrah in office was cutting the ribbon at the new airport terminal, an $18 million, 11-story tower.
Photo by Ron Sherman

◄ Accessibility to and from
Atlanta increased in the
1960s with the arrival
of the Interstate highway
system. Today, the 75/85
connector makes Atlanta
accessible to the nation.
Photo by Ron Sherman

▲ A new concept that was born as the interstates brought more people to live in the suburbs was the shopping center. One of the earliest was Lindbergh Center, which opened in the late 1950s. The Stewart Lakewood Shopping Center was added to suburbia in 1963. Shopping centers were the precursor to the mall. Lenox Square, set in the middle of Buckhead, was an open-air shopping center boasting more than fifty stores and some six thousand parking spaces on seventy-four acres. In the late 1960s, Lenox Square was covered to become Atlanta's first modern mall. Historic photo courtesy of Georgia State University Special Collections. New photo by Ron Sherman

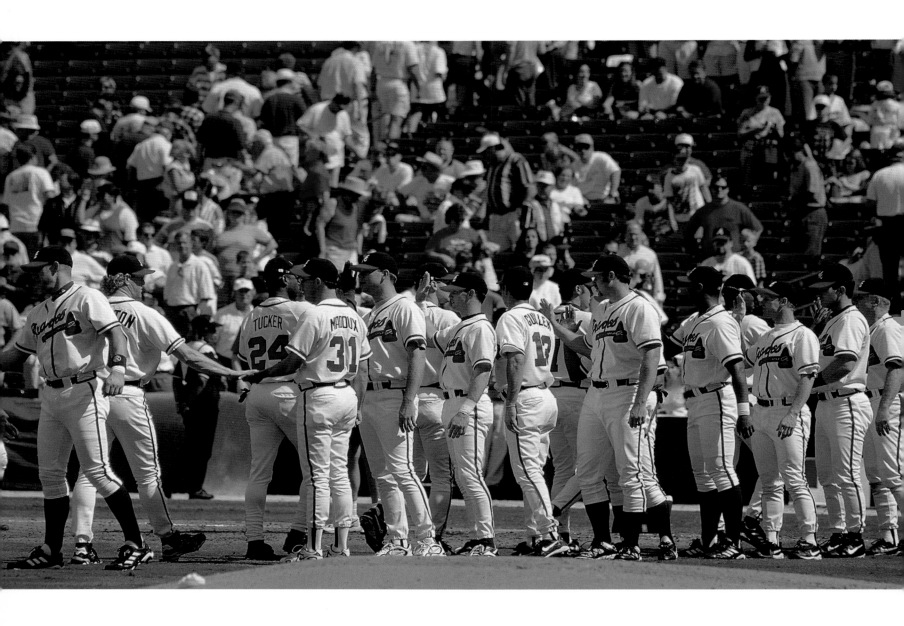

◄ When Ivan Allen Jr. became mayor of Atlanta in 1961, he wanted to bring professional sports to Atlanta. The city had a minor league baseball team, the Crackers, but the business leadership didn't want to be "minor league" in anything. In 1963, Allen selected a 60-acre tract of land next to the Interstate for the construction of a stadium, and Mills Lane, the head of C & S Bank, agreed to guarantee the financing. Fulton County Stadium was rushed to completion in just fifty-one weeks, and Allen enticed the Milwaukee Braves to move south in 1966. That same year, the National Football League awarded the city a franchise, purchased by insurance executive Rankin Smith for $8.5 million, and Atlanta had its Falcons football team. In 1999, coach Dan Reeves led the Falcons to an NFC championship. In 1968, developer Tom Cousins added professional basketball with the purchase of the St. Louis Hawks. Photos by Ron Sherman. Historic photo courtesy of the Atlanta History Center

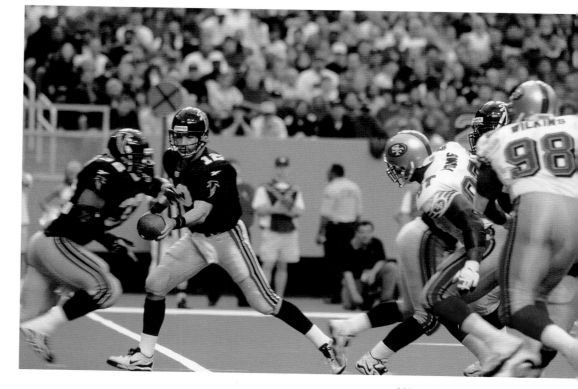

Hewlett-Packard

► The HP Atlanta Business Center is home to 2,100 employees who serve customers in the United States and HP sales and support organizations in the United States, Canada, and Latin America.

In 1939 Bill Hewlett and David Packard had no inkling that they were building an international empire on little more than a handful of good ideas. Nor could they have imagined the technological wonders Hewlett-Packard (HP) would produce in the 1990s and through the new millennium. They were simply on an adventure of discovery and an innovative pursuit of solutions for a changing world.

By 1959, HP had opened its first manufacturing plant outside of Palo Alto, California, in Boblingen, West Germany. *Fortune* magazine included HP on its list of the largest U.S. industrial corporations for the first time in 1962, the same year HP came to Atlanta.

The list of innovative works that led HP to fame and fortune is intimidating in its expanse. Product highlights include signal generators and radar-jamming devices for the Navy in 1943; the first microwave spectrum analyzer in 1964; the company's first computer in 1966; a noninvasive fetal heart-rate monitor in 1967; a highly accurate portable cesium-beam standard used to synchronize international time standards in 1964; and the world's first programmable scientific desktop calculator in 1968.

The 1970s and '80s brought more innovations at even faster rates: the HP laser interferometer in 1971; a handheld calculator that made the slide rule obsolete in 1972; a 64-channel cardiac ultrasound product in 1980; the first laser printer fast and inexpensive enough to use outside a central computer room in 1980; a silicon chip with 600,000 transistors; first major wide-area commercial network and e-mail in 1982; Signal Data Network for monitoring multiple hospital patients from a central station in 1982; thermal ink-jet technology for high-quality, low-price personal printers in 1984; and the HP LaserJet, now the world's most popular personal desktop printer, in 1984.

The 1990s brought forth even more advancements: the HP color scanner and plain paper color printers in 1991; the smallest, lightest portable personal computer weighing less than three pounds in 1993; and the world's brightest LEDs in 1994. In 1997,

► Dave Packard (left) and Bill Hewlett developed an innovative audio oscillator in a Palo Alto, California, garage in 1939 used to test high-quality audio frequencies. HP's oscillator improved on existing oscillators in size, price, and performance.

HP developed a laser jet printer capable of producing the equivalent of 1,200 dots per inch at full engine speed; it also exchanges information with other devices without the use of a PC. Other key accomplishments that same year include another industry first in the HP Omnibook 3000 laptop; a single diagnostic ultrasound system that can perform all applications without compromise; the high-performance, scalable V-class servers; joint strategies with Microsoft and Intel to simplify integration; new HP Photo Resolution Enhancement and ColorSmart technologies; and the industry's leading 3-D graphics solution—HP Visualize fx.

Today, HP is one of the 19 largest companies in the U.S. and one of the world's largest computer companies. Nearly 70 percent of its business is generated outside the U.S. in more than 120 countries. The HP Atlanta Business Center is home to 2,100 employees who serve customers in the United States and HP sales and support organizations in the United States, Canada, and Latin America. The facility houses the largest of 34 customer response centers. It also contains three education centers that provide customer training and various HP administrative and support organizations.

Hewlett-Packard products open a world of opportunities and brings the world home to millions of people. More than computers, more than a myriad of technological gadgetry, Hewlett-Packard is a living icon of "expanding possibilities" and the American Dream. ✺

Rosser International

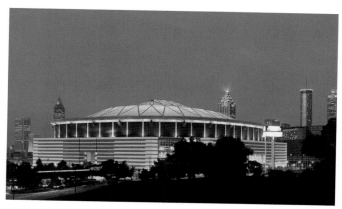

During its 50 years of providing architectural, engineering, and planning services, Rosser International, Inc. has made a significant impact on the structures of Atlanta and in cities throughout the nation.

Consistently ranked in *Engineering News Record's* Top 300 Design Firms, Rosser International is headquartered in Atlanta, Georgia, with offices in Savannah, Puerto Rico, and Cairo, Egypt. With a staff of 250 design professional and support personnel, the firm has completed projects throughout the United States and various parts of the world.

Projects

Travel around Atlanta and you will see Rosser International's architectural and engineering projects throughout the city. Rosser has worked with many of Atlanta's most notable companies, including The Coca-Cola Company, BellSouth, Delta Air Lines, and Turner Broadcasting Company. Some of Atlanta's prominent structures are the product of Rosser's Sports Division—including Turner Field Baseball Stadium and the Georgia Dome Football Stadium. During the 1996 Olympic Games, the firm worked on 17 separate venues that remain in service today.

Problem Solving

Rosser's major contribution to its clients is to create innovative solutions to complex projects. Using a process that involves all the stakeholders of a project, Rosser works to understand and gain consensus of needs. One of Rosser's clients has commented, "All of the firm's representatives have shown true dedication, integrity, and a strong desire to accommodate the needs of the users of the facility."

Diverse Services

No matter what kind of building is needed, Rosser's specialized divisions work with clients to achieve lasting, exciting, and economical solutions. Company divisions include the following:

Sports: Creation of notable collegiate arenas and stadia through-

out the nation, including the Bud Walton Arena at the University of Arkansas and the Pyramid Arena in Memphis, Tennessee.

Criminal Justice: Recognized nationally and internationally for expertise in designing prisons, jails, court complexes, and youth facilities. The Criminal Justice Division has designed facilities in 46 states.

Aviation: Developing large commercial and military hangars and aircraft test and support facilities throughout the United States.

Military: Designing barracks complexes, command centers, and support and training facilities for all military branches of the Department of Defense.

General Practice: Creating corporate office designs, hospitality, and broadcast facilities.

Engineering: Preparing sites and buildings through civil, landscaping, and building engineering, including structural, mechanical, electrical, fire protection, and plumbing design.

Complex Projects

Severe damage by tropical storm Alberto in June 1994 flooded 25 of the 28 buildings on the campus of Albany State University by up to 12 feet of water. Under the direction of Rosser Program Management, 18 architectural and engineering firms and four general contractors programmed, planned, and negotiated the installation of a temporary campus. This temporary campus was put in place in only eight weeks, in time for the September 21 opening of "Unsinkable Albany State." The entire rebuilding program was completed over a three-year period within its budget of $145 million.

Future

As Rosser moves into the next century, the firm will continue to grow and adapt, with more specialized services, unusual teaming arrangements, and new project delivery systems. Though change is inevitable, its core service will remain—creative solutions tailored to specific needs. ◖

◄ Rosser International's Sports Division was part of the team that designed The Georgia Dome, one of Atlanta's most prominent structures.

◄ The Fulton County Justice Center is just one of Rosser's Criminal Justice Division designs.

Golder Associates

Its work is done underground and underwater, in a world no one sees. Beneath the cities, deserts, mountains, jungles, rivers, lakes, and oceans of 110 countries, from Algeria to Zimbabwe, Golder Associates is working on hydroelectric power projects, highways, rapid transit, dams, tunnels, oil and gas pipelines, irrigation and off-shore drilling, mining and mine waste disposal, global searches for oil and water, and the restoration of severely contaminated industrial sites.

"We believe in customizing the services in our tool box to fit the clients' needs," says Principal and Senior Consultant William Brumund. "We draw from our 80 offices around the world, putting the right skills together for each project, so our clients get the best service."

Originally a consulting engineering firm specializing in the geotechnical field, over half of the firm's worldwide business has been in the environmental field since the mid-70s. Today, Golder is a multinational "multi-niche" company, with expertise in a wide range of disciplines, including soil and rock engineering, engineering geology, hydrology, water resources, computer modeling and civil engineering, and many different environmental disciplines. Golder Associates blends traditional techniques with emerging technologies. It pioneered the application of soil nailing (steel spikes that tie the earth together), and its accomplishments in site restoration and high-level nuclear waste management have become standards of the industry.

In 1973 Golder Associates approached Brumund, then a professor at Georgia Tech, to open Golder's Atlanta office. From 1985 to 1996, Brumund served as the firm's CEO, and Atlanta became the world headquarters from the mid-1980s to the present. "We knit together a vibrant group of professionals," Brumund recalls. The firm's business volume increased over ninefold, and the number of employees increased from 350 to over 1,900.

Among many projects close to home, Golder has maintained a 30-year relationship with the Kaolin Industry, helping it cope with groundwater control, wetlands, mine stability, and the disposal of mine wastes. The firm also designed the foundation for the Egleston Children's Hospital and has worked on numerous projects for MARTA. "We designed an arched tunnel system under I-285 to the Indian Hills Station," says Brumund, explaining how the tunnel was constructed a breath-holding six feet under the interstate highway.

Golder won three awards for its Dalton, Georgia, reservoir project, including an award for the uniqueness of its concept—storing floodwater and releasing it when needed, instead of building a conventional dam—which minimized the impact on adjacent wetlands. The company is currently designing the DeKalb County Scott Candler reservoir, which will have a capacity of 300 million gallons of water, and is scheduled to be completed in 2003.

One of the world's largest and most trusted specialist consulting firms, Golder's 1998 worldwide revenue was in excess of $187 million. Golder Associates is 100-percent employee owned, and among its 1,900 employees are Rhodes scholars, worldwide experts, creative scientific innovators, and former faculty from the world's top scientific universities.

Whether creating a foundation for the Smithsonian's National Aeronautics and Space Museum, building innovative ice islands to stabilize offshore drilling platforms in the Arctic, or designing infrastructure for Gwinnett County, Golder applies the same high standards. "We pride ourselves in providing resourceful, responsive project teams that focus on client needs," Brumund says. "Establishing trust and credibility is the key to our business." ◉

▶ Golder is a multinational "multi-niche" company, with expertise in a wide range of disciplines, including soil and rock engineering, engineering geology, hydrology, water resources, computer modeling and civil engineering, and many different environmental disciplines.

▶ Golder Associates' work is done underground and underwater, in a world no one sees.

EDS

The industry leadership position that the information technology giant EDS enjoys today is a direct result of its Atlanta roots. In 1966, with a staff of five people, EDS (Electronic Data Systems) managed financial operations for Economic Opportunity Atlanta, a federal antipoverty pilot program. With very little capital, and even fewer resources, EDS earned a reputation for being the best at automating financial systems for government and private sector clients. Three years after its inception, the Atlanta office's client base included United Family Life Insurance, The Lovable Bra Company, and Blue Cross Blue Shield of Atlanta.

"Atlanta really offers a natural business synergy for EDS," says EDS Atlanta President Dennis Stolkey. "The 'can-do' attitude of our first Atlanta staff exists within our workforce today and is common in Atlanta's business community. We like it here because the people consistently demonstrate their ability to solve problems. From the development of business solutions, to meeting needs in the community, our employees and citizens always find a way to get things done."

Today, EDS has more than 2,000 employees in Atlanta providing information technology support to 32 clients. Worldwide, the company has more than 110,000 employees and serves clients in 47 countries in such industries as manufacturing, aerospace, health care, finance, insurance, food, retail, travel, transportation, energy, and communications. EDS provides information technology services for BellSouth Telecommunications, General Motors, and the Georgia Department of Medical Assistance. The company also has many clients at the state and local level of government, as well as at the national level.

EDS's long-standing commitment to the Atlanta community is as much a part of its corporate culture as its outstanding business expertise. All over Atlanta EDS

employees are feeding the hungry, participating in walk and run-athons for charitable organizations, and leading the next generations through the changing and ever-widening exploration of technology. One example of this is the CyberEDS lab in the northwest section of the city. CyberEDS is a collaboration between EDS and the Georgia Chapter of the Rainbow/PUSH Coalition. The EDS volunteers staff the lab after school and on weekends, sharing their expertise so students and members of the community can use the Internet to do research and take advantage of the resources the World Wide Web has to offer. Thanks to this program, hundreds of Atlanta's inner-city students and their families enjoy the use of a state-of-the-art computer lab, Internet access, and instruction on using the World Wide Web.

One way that EDS is preparing for the new millennium is by adding value through electronic business, which connects enterprises to new capabilities such as electronic payment and Internet commerce. As a result, its clients are realizing the advantages of digital supply chains that are significantly faster, more robust, and more profitable than traditional chains. This means that the companies no longer have to warehouse huge quantities of data. Instead, EDS's Internet capabilities allow them to have push-button access to any data they might need.

EDS is committed to being a great place to work, a trusted business partner, and an attractive investment. "The prospects for EDS's future are indeed compelling," said Richard H. "Dick" Brown, EDS chairman and chief executive officer. "This is a company rich with assets—a strong client list, global capability, a solid balance sheet, and, best of all, a workforce that's built a legacy of leadership in this business. I am confident that, with the right strategy and hard work, we can take full advantage of EDS's many strengths and achieve outstanding results for its clients, shareholders, and employees." ✹

◄ All over Atlanta EDS employees are feeding the hungry, participating in walk and run-athons for charitable organizations, and leading children through the changing and ever-widening exploration of technology.

◄ EDS's long-standing commitment to the Atlanta community is as much a part of its corporate culture as its outstanding business expertise.

Harold A. Dawson Company

The Harold A. Dawson Company is one of the most successful development firms in Atlanta and a major player in the booming redevelopment of in-town areas. The company is known for many high profile projects and is one of the leaders in the cutting-edge, mixed-use development phenomena sweeping the nation and Atlanta. The company has developed and built office buildings, shopping centers, and apartment complexes valued at over 400 million dollars, creating hundreds of jobs for Atlantans.

The founder, Harold A. Dawson Sr., is a native Atlantan and a prominent African-American. He has served as president of The National Association of Real Estate Brokers and president of The National Association of Real Estate License Law Officials. His 17 years on the Georgia Real Estate Commission included a stint as chairman. Licensed as a real estate professional in 1957, he became president of Alexander/Dawson Associates in 1963 and founded Harold A. Dawson Company (HADCO) in 1969. In the early days, he dealt in residential real estate, selling thousands of homes to metro Atlantans and developing residential communities and subdivisions. He built the company on an exceptional reputation based on solid relationships, honesty, and integrity. Today, Mr. Dawson Sr. is chairman and chief executive officer.

Harold A. Dawson Jr. joined the firm in 1994 after completing his master's degree at Harvard Business School and gaining experience at Trammell Crow Company in Dallas, Texas, and at Salomon Brothers, Inc. in New York City. Today, he is president and chief

operating officer. Dawson Jr. adds a dynamic approach and financial expertise to the company's marketing strategies, new business acquisitions, joint venture undertakings, and financial strategies. He is recognized as a formidable leader in real estate by many premier publications, including *Business To Business* magazine and *Black Enterprise Magazine*, and is deemed one of Forty Stars Under Forty by *National Real Estate Investor Magazine* in their fortieth anniversary issue. His business and community involvement includes serving on the board of directors of Security First Network Bank.

The sheer entrepreneurial achievement of the company is a great American success story, yet it is equally remarkable to find family succession in today's real estate market, where successful companies are more often merged into corporate hierarchies. Family succession is particularly unique and significant in the African-American community, where a tradition of generational wealth and influence is relatively rare.

The company is influential in shaping the development and redevelopment of Atlanta proper. The new mixed-use development around MARTA's Lindbergh Station features 200 condominiums to be developed by HADCO. The $55-million mixed-use residential and commercial complex called Centennial Hill, a key to the redevelopment of the area surrounding Centennial Olympic Park, carries the mark of HADCO's expertise and dedication to excellence. City Plaza is a prime example of the company's pioneering financing strategies. Each example of the company's development in Atlanta is a physical testament to the family's and the company's desire to build a better city and a brighter future. ❦

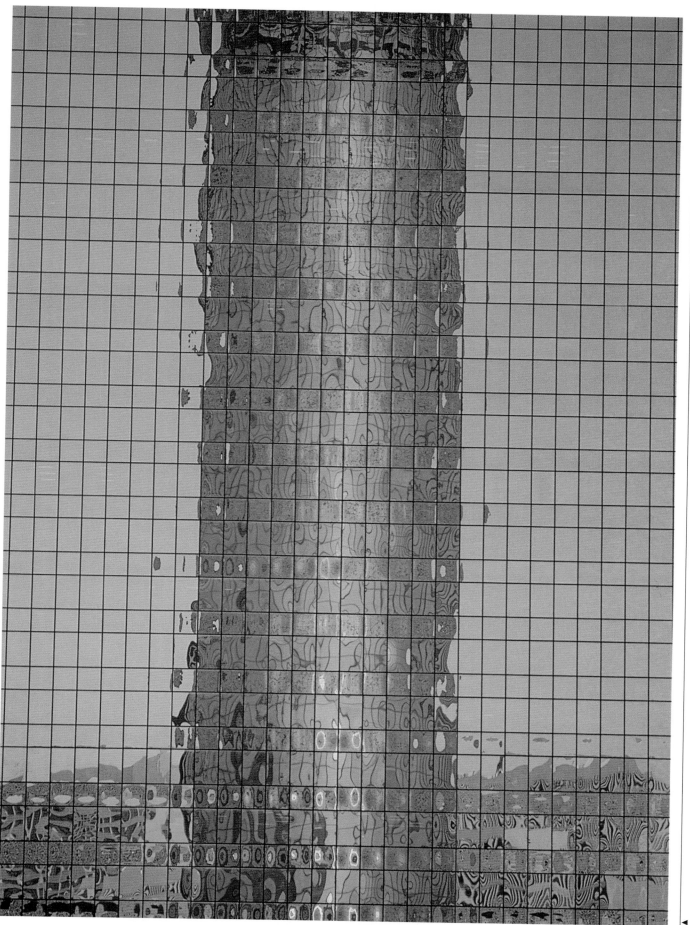

◄ Photo by Ron Sherman.

CHAPTER SEVEN
1970-1980

If Atlanta had a decade that tested its power of positive thinking it was the 1970s. It started out optimistic, with the business community hoping for a continuation of the go-go 1960s, but the local economy was clobbered by a severe real estate recession.

Photo by Ron Sherman

The city's political structure underwent a sometimes rocky transition from white to black control and, most worrisome after a century of uninterrupted growth, the city actually lost population.

The decade began, promisingly enough, with the realization of two long-standing wishes.

One was the construction of a new indoor coliseum, an idea that had been a pet project of Ivan Allen, Jr.'s. In contrast with the 1960s, though, this time the team arrived in Atlanta before the venue was built. Developer Tom Cousins had purchased the St. Louis Hawks professional basketball team in 1968 and wanted a coliseum built over the railroad gulch west of downtown where he had just built a parking deck. Newly elected Mayor Sam Massell worked hard to craft a deal that used municipal bonding authority to finance the building and captured coliseum revenues to guarantee repayment. It was an innovative plan that would be much-copied in the future, and The Omni opened in 1972. In the interim Cousins also purchased a professional hockey team, called the Flames, to keep the building full.

The other municipal dream was a rapid transit system. So far, though, boosters had been unable to persuade voters to finance the building of a rail network to complement bus service. In 1971 they tried again, this time guaranteeing to keep fares at fifteen cents—down from forty cents—for seven years in return for the imposition of a one-cent sales tax. Massell campaigned heavily for the proposal, even hovering above the Downtown Connector in a helicopter and using a bullhorn to address stalled commuters. The referendum passed narrowly—by just 461 votes—and only in the city, Fulton, and DeKalb counties. MARTA quickly purchased the buses of the Atlanta Transit Co. and began construction of the east-west rail line.

The third major civic project of the decade was a brand-new terminal complex for the airport. Ex-Mayor William Hartsfield, the father of aviation in Atlanta, had died in 1971 and the airport was quickly renamed William B. Hartsfield International Airport in his honor. But the new terminal Hartsfield himself had dedicated in 1961 had been rapidly overwhelmed. Both Delta and Eastern had grown into large air carriers and the number of passengers passing through Atlanta had quadrupled since 1960.

Planners opted to build a completely new terminal complex in the middle of the existing runways with four separate, parallel

▲ Newly elected Mayor Sam Massell worked hard to craft a deal for the construction of a new indoor coliseum to house the Atlanta Hawks professional basketball team, brought to Atlanta in 1968 by developer Tom Cousins. Massell used a municipal bonding authority to finance the building and captured coliseum revenues to guarantee repayment. It was an innovative plan that would be much copied in the future, and The Omni opened in 1972. Photo by Ron Sherman

concourses, a high-traffic design that became an industry standard. At more than $400 million, the terminal took several years to construct, but came in on-time and on-budget in 1980. Almost immediately Hartsfield challenged Chicago's O'Hare Airport for the title of the country's busiest airport.

Although boosters were touting Atlanta as an "international city" in the early 1960s, it wasn't until 1971—when Eastern began a daily non-stop flight to Mexico City—that Atlantans could actually fly to an international destination. Delta won its first international routes in the latter half of the decade.

A real estate recession struck Atlanta in the mid-1970s as the national economy slumped. Inflation coupled with interest rates that rose as high as 20 percent knocked the legs out from under overextended developers and lenders.

After the 1960s, it was a rude awakening. Tom Cousins was hit particularly hard. Cousins was the primary rival to John Portman for the title of Atlanta's preeminent developer. Cousins didn't have Portman's international reputation as an accomplished architect, but he had a more modest demeanor and a very strong local power base.

The two had knocked heads over the issue of the location of the Georgia World Congress Center, a state facility intended to service the city's mushrooming convention business. Portman wanted it close to his Peachtree Center and pushed a site next to the newly constructed Civic Center just north of downtown. Cousins maneuvered to get it built near The Omni. Cousins won out and he promptly began construction of a grand office, retail, and hotel complex next door to The Omni, complete with ice skating rink in the middle of the atrium. But the real estate recession made it a struggle for him to finish.

The city's convention business was a bright economic spot in the 1970s. Although the city had had a convention bureau since the 1920s, only recently had meetings and conventions become a significant economic force. With the completion of the $35 million World Congress Center, for a while the country's largest exhibition hall, Atlanta rose to become one of the top three convention sites.

As the convention business grew, there was a need for more hotel rooms downtown. Portman, who had showed the way in the 1960s with his Hyatt Regency,

▶ **Ex-Mayor William Hartsfield, the father of aviation in Atlanta, died in 1971, and the airport was quickly renamed William B. Hartsfield International Airport in his honor. Eastern began a daily non-stop flight to Mexico City in 1971, beginning international air travel from Atlanta. To accommodate the growing air traffic, planners built a new terminal complex in the middle of the existing runways with four separate, parallel concourses, a high-traffic design that became an industry standard. The project came in on time and on budget in 1980, and almost immediately Hartsfield challenged Chicago's O'Hare Airport for the title of the country's busiest airport.** Photos by Ron Sherman

◄ Construction of the
MARTA rail lines began
in 1971 when voters
were finally persuaded
to pass a referendum to
finance the construction.
Today, the MARTA rail-
line system is one of the
most efficient people-
moving systems in the
country. Photo by Ron
Sherman

▶ The city's convention business was a bright spot in the 1970s. With the completion of the $35 million Georgia World Congress Center, for a while the country's largest exhibition hall, Atlanta rose to become one of the top three convention sites. Photos by Ron Sherman

built the tallest hotel in the U.S—seventy-three stories—in 1976. The Westin Peachtree Plaza—a perfectly round cylinder with a spectacular exterior elevator and crowned by a revolving restaurant—stood on the site of the old Henry Grady Hotel on Peachtree Street. The same year Hilton opened a similarly lavish convention hotel only a couple of blocks away.

A controversy over the Fox Theater got some Atlantans thinking about preserving the city's past, something of a new concept in a city usually too busy looking forward to spend any time looking back.

The Fox, which had gotten off to such a rocky start in the 1930s, was experiencing a bumpy old age as well. Despite its lavish decoration, by the 1970s it couldn't compete as a movie house anymore. Southern Bell, which was ready to build a new headquarters building, considered tearing down the theater, a plan that sparked a grass-roots effort to save the Fox. Southern Bell agreed to build next to a planned MARTA station and preservationists went on to raise enough money to renovate the theater. Unfortunately, the coalition that saved the Fox was too late to rescue Terminal Station. The last architectural link to the railroads that created the city, Terminal Station was unceremoniously demolished for a new federal office building at the beginning of the decade.

The end of Ivan Allen's second term as mayor in 1969 marked a major turning point for the city. The percentage of black Atlantans had increased steadily during the 1960s—thanks in part to the city's reputation for racial moderation—until the number of black and white voters were essentially equal. In 1969 black votes put Sam Massell in the mayor's office. Massell promised to bring blacks into city government, and he did. But he was a transitional figure. Black Atlantans were ready to flex their political muscle and put one of their own in City Hall.

The candidate that emerged four years later was Massell's vice-mayor, Maynard Jackson. Only 35, Jackson was a lawyer with deep roots in the community. His grandfather, John Wesley Dobbs, had been a legendary black political leader in Atlanta and his aunt was an opera singer.

The business community was wary of Jackson, but reassured somewhat by his middle-class background. Like Massell, Jackson promised to put blacks in a position to profit from Atlanta's growth. He decreed that black businesses must participate in future public works projects, particularly the new airport terminal. Though the business community gnashed their teeth, they quickly resigned themselves to finding black-owned partners.

Jackson soon had his hands full with crises in public safety and schools. During the 1970s, murder statistics soared. A prominent scientist and his wife attending a convention were killed one night during a street robbery. A cheating scandal involving the police

exam also contributed to a perception that downtown streets weren't safe anymore.

As for the public school system, white students were melting away. The trend had started in the late 1960s and accelerated. By the mid-1970s, the city schools were nearly all black.

The crime issue helped cost the city Underground Atlanta, a collection of dancing and drinking establishments occupying storefronts underneath the downtown viaducts. Opened in the late 1960s to much acclaim, it closed ten years later after a large chunk of the complex was destroyed by MARTA construction.

But the most agonizing manifestation of crime was the missing and murdered children episode that began in 1979. As the number of child murders mounted without a killer being identified, there was intense national interest in the story and something close to hysteria gripped the city. The nightmare finally ended in 1981 with the arrest and conviction of Wayne Williams, but Atlanta's reputation was badly singed.

All during the decade, the city had been slowly losing population, primarily whites. City population peaked at just under 500,000 in 1970 and by the end of the decade the number was closer to 425,000. Jackson had repaired his relationship with the primarily white business community but there was no doubt that

▶ In 1973, Atlantans elected Maynard Jackson as Mayor, a lawyer with deep roots in the community. His grandfather, John Wesley Dobbs, had been a legendary black political leader in Atlanta. Photo by Ron Sherman

▶ As the convention business grew, there was a need for more hotel rooms downtown. Noted Atlanta architect and builder John Portman built the tallest hotel in the U.S.—seventy-three stories—in 1976, the Westin Peachtree Plaza—a perfectly round cylinder with a spectacular exterior elevator and crowned by a revolving restaurant. Photo by Ron Sherman

▶ (opposite) The 1978 announcement by Georgia-Pacific Corp., a wood and paper products company, that it would move its corporate head-quarters and thousands of jobs to Atlanta from Portland reminded people hurt by the economic recession of the 1970s that the city was still strong. Photo by Ron Sherman

the "doughnut" counties surrounding Atlanta—Cobb, Gwinnett, DeKalb, and the northern reaches of Fulton County—were becoming serious competitors for new businesses, jobs, and housing.

Still, the 1978 announcement by Georgia-Pacific Corp., a wood and paper products company, that it would move its corporate headquarters and thousands of jobs to Atlanta from Portland reminded people that downtown wasn't a lost cause. The company built a handsome, 51-story headquarters on a downtown lot once occupied by the Loews Grand Theater on Peachtree Street. The theater, which had been the site of the premiere of *Gone With The Wind*, had been destroyed by fire in 1978. ❦

► From art to fashion to the business of day-to-day life, Atlanta added its own unique style to the decade of the 1970s.

Photos by Ron Sherman

◄ On April 8, 1974, Hank Aaron smacked a fastball over the fence and into the record books, racking up his Home Run No. 715. The feat unseated Babe Ruth as the most prolific home-run hitter of all time. Today, a statue of the baseball great is placed at the Braves' new home, Turner Field.
Photos by Ron Sherman

◄ Former Georgia Governor Jimmy Carter came from obscurity to capture the presidency in 1976 and took a number of Atlantans with him to Washington. The Carter Presidential Center, which sits on a 35-acre hilltop overlooking downtown Atlanta, includes a library and museum of the Carter presidency and the Carter Center, a nonprofit organization devoted to human rights, resolving conflicts, and promoting democracy. Photos by Ron Sherman

Watkins Real Estate Groups

A Georgia native who grew up on a farm in Metcalf, Bill Watkins started his business empire in 1932 with a $300 pickup truck and built it into one of the largest trucking companies in the United States.

The fleet grew to two trucks, then seven, and soon Watkins added freight hauling. As his territory grew, so did his business. By 1941, Watkins had 50 trucks and was hauling war material throughout the eastern seaboard. After World War II Watkins began transporting processed foods, including frozen citrus concentrate, becoming one of the largest carriers of perishable foods in the country in the 1960s. During the late 1970s, Watkins established centralized rating, dispatching, tracing, customized coding, and started on-line billing.

Today, the Watkins family of companies numbers close to 30. Along with two real estate companies, Watkins Associated Developers and Wilwat Properties, other Watkins Associated Industries (WAI) companies include citrus production, window and door manufacturing, Christian Broadcasting, ready mix concrete, seafood processing, bridge building, and insurance.

Inspired by his close friend Bill Cesery's success in the apartment business in Jacksonville, Florida, Bill Watkins founded Wilwat Properties to provide quality rental housing. At that point in his career, Watkins had turned over the management responsibilities of his transportation company to his sons and other key personnel. In 1976, Wilwat Properties purchased the land

that became Tree House Apartments. Their property name, "tree," stands for a commitment to Atlanta's precious urban trees. Since their inception, Wilwat has saved every tree possible on a development site. "We feel that a naturally wooded environment puts people more at ease," says Kim Watkins, vice president of Wilwat and Bill Watkins' youngest son. "You can hardly see the units for the trees." Watkins spent every summer working on his dad's freight docks until he graduated from college and returned to Atlanta to work for Wilwat Properties.

"We start with a topographic survey," Watkins explains. "Our engineer takes that survey and marks every tree bigger than five inches in diameter. We know where the clusters of dogwoods, pines, and oaks are, where to cut, and where to fill to save every possible tree. It's more expensive on the front end, but you have less grass to mow and fewer trees to replant. It makes good economic sense."

The economic growth potential of Atlanta and its region was the main draw to the area. As the Southeast's economic hub, Atlanta's surrounding counties have nearly unlimited growth potential, and growth strongly influences the success of apartment communities. "Everything we've built has been outside the I-285 Perimeter, because our experience is in garden-style apartments," says Watkins. "We need more space, more trees."

Wilwat builds between 300 and 500 units per year. The company is smaller in comparison to some developers, and Watkins likes it that way. "We're fairly small, but good things comes in small

packages. It enables us to go slowly about site selection and continue with improvements to product quality," explains Watkins.

Wilwat has built properties in Douglasville, Norcross, Decatur, Duluth, Lawrenceville, and Apharetta. The company owns sites in Gainesville, Grayson, and Lawrenceville that it plans to develop in the future. The next project is located in Douglasville. One of Watkins' favorite developments is Tree Summit in Duluth. "It's got a lake and nestles into the landscape naturally. It looks like a North Carolina mountain retreat," Watkins says.

Each new community sees new design improvements. "We do surveys with tenants and over the years we've made modifications," says Watkins. "One major change was moving from a contemporary style to a more traditional look."

Interior design changes include vaulted nine-foot ceilings for a more spacious feel, as well as bigger bathrooms, walk-in laundry rooms, and walk-in pantries. The sunrooms and balconies built in the '70s and '80s are now outdoor decks. Since 1988 all of the buildings' units have been fitted with fire sprinklers. They are designed with utmost safety in mind and have proved their worth many times.

Wilwat now builds units with concrete lap siding and brick. Both of these materials are impervious to humid conditions found throughout the Southeast. "Concrete lap siding is a new construction technique for us that has greatly reduced exterior maintenance requirements. It's embossed in a wood-grain, but bugs don't like it and it holds the paint better," Watkins explains. Wilwat also now builds automated entry gate systems to all its communities. These systems prevent arbitrary drive-through traffic and provide residents with more security and peace of mind.

Wilwat has a positive impact on the economy, providing employment for many skilled workers. Each new development requires approximately one hundred subcontractors, from engineers to roofers, concrete finishers to architects.

But the company supports the community with more than jobs and quality, affordable housing. WAI is a company committed to giving, as a Partner in Education with local schools and by its

fund-raising efforts on behalf of the Georgia Council on Child Abuse. Wilwat also joins with the Atlanta Apartment Association for the annual Thanksgiving Can-a-thon food drive, by distributing and collecting bags of canned goods for the hungry. Watkins Associated Industries, through the Watkins Christian Foundation, contributes $3 million yearly to Christian charities and numerous schools and churches in Atlanta, as well as the Union Mission, Salvation Army, and Georgia Sheriffs' Youth Fund.

Watkins continues to grow, with an emphasis on providing the best product in the industry, with a "less is more" philosophy. "We're not here to become the Goliath of the apartment builders. We're the size we want to stay at," Watkins says. "We want to keep our business family-owned; we don't plan to go public. We like keeping it in-house, to keep control of what we're doing. We can comfortably manage 5,000 units.

"We're a small, self-contained company that's proud of what we do, proud of our employees. We'd like to see our family tradition continue, and see it handed down to our children."

Watkins Retail Group is the shopping center leasing, management, and development arm of Watkins Associated Industries, with offices in Orlando and Atlanta. Services include asset and property management, leasing, development, construction management, finance, marketing, and brokerage.

Bill Watkins' friendship with George Jenkins, founder of Publix Supermarkets, led to the development of over 25 Publix-anchored neighborhood shopping centers. Watkins leases, owns, and manages shopping centers throughout Georgia and Florida, including the first Publix-anchored shopping center in Gwinnett County, Georgia.

"We take raw land and visualize a vibrant shopping center, full of

◀ **Tree Creek Apartments, Lawrenceville, Georgia.**

▼ **Tree Creek Apartments, Lawrenceville, Georgia.**

Atlanta

▶ **Sugarloaf Crossings Kids Village, Lawrenceville.**

Crossings in Lawrenceville, with more planned for the future. The multiple awards Watkins has won for landscaping and architectural design reflect the company's appreciation for beauty and quality.

Golden Park Village in the Lake Lanier area and Tree/Summit Village in Berkeley Lake area are under construction in 1999 and WRG plans to expand to even more communities. "We have sites pegged in McDonough and Stockbridge for Publix-anchored neighborhood shopping," Freeman says. "We feel strongly that the south side is underserved."

In 1996, Watkins Associated Developers designed and opened the Abbotts Kids Village Shopping Center in Alpharetta, Georgia, a child-oriented shopping experience that was the first of its kind in the country. "In 1995 we noticed there was nothing around us for good, wholesome activity, no place to buy gifts or have a party," Freeman recalls. "We do retail; it's all we've done since '78, and we love kids. Why not develop a shopping center geared to children?"

Geared to ages 12 and under (children of all ages welcome), Freeman developed his concept with "kid-sultants." The design, which won the 1997 ICSC International Mall Award for Innovative Design and Construction of a new project, has a zany, whacky spirit that includes shop awnings and doors in primary colors, and sidewalks painted with hopscotch, puzzles, and a curvy, wiggly

tenants, that meets the neighborhood's needs, being totally committed to doing it right and not cutting corners," explains Neal Freeman, executive vice president of Watkins Retail Group. In addition to managing the team, Freeman acquires the land, maintains the relationship with Publix, and negotiates and maintains the leases.

With over 20 years' experience, WRG has developed a following of tenants. Lee Freeman, vice president of leasing and operations, states, "You use your best judgment, survey people, communities, and demographics and try to match tenant to consumer. We have strong relationships with tenants we've treated right. From a win-win standpoint, we love to help them be successful. It helps us succeed, too."

▶ **Sugarloaf Crossings and Shopping Center, Lawrenceville, Georgia.**

Jeff Abrams is vice president of Design and Construction, working with architects, engineers, and contractors to give each shopping center a different look. "We do our best to have design elements that are comparable to the surrounding community. We did stacked stone in Alpharetta, granite for Hamilton Mill, and a brick facade in Suwanee," says Abrams.

TreeTrail Village on Indian Trail was the first Publix-anchored center to open in Gwinnett County. When the TreeTrail Village opened, there were tremendous crowds. "The fire marshal had to help; as one person came out, he'd let one in. There was a waiting line for carts," recalls Freeman.

The roster of Publix-anchored shopping centers that WRG either owns, leases, or manages includes Mableton Walk in south Cobb, Abbotts Village in Alpharetta, Peachtree East in Peachtree City, Horizon Village in Suwanee, near the Mall of Georgia, Duluth Station in Duluth, and Sugarloaf

310

track to follow. "We leave sidewalk chalk out and encourage wholesome graffiti," says Freeman. A signpost points directions to all the local schools, and even the retail store signs have a fun spirit about them. The whimsical décor includes comical fish heads, giant flowers with faces, and frogs that spit water into the fountain (all fountain donation coins go to support the Georgia Council on Child Abuse). A tower clock with gloves on its hands points out that there is always "time for kids."

"Since this had never been done, we got to create it as we wished. Seeing the kids, their parents, and grandparents enjoying themselves at the Village gives us tremendous satisfaction," says Freeman, who notes that the company supports the community in other ways, including being Partners In Education with local schools.

The tenants live up to the shopping center's registered motto, Where Kids Rule and Fun is King, and include swim clubs, day care, computer camps, gymnastics and cheerleading facilities, kids' clothing, toys and books, arts and crafts, haircuts for kids, pint-sized furniture, a pediatric center, and a candy store. Later additions included children's interiors, children's shoes, fast-food, and a family photography studio.

The company has expanded the Kids Village concept to include Sugarloaf Kids Village in Lawrenceville, and Mt. Zion Kids Village in south Atlanta.

With offices in both Orlando and Atlanta, the highly successful company looks forward to continuing its development of quality neighborhood shopping centers in the Southeast. ◔

▲ Duluth Station Shopping Center, Duluth, Georgia.

◄ Abbotts Kids Village, Alpharetta, Georgia.

Williams-Russell and Johnson, Inc.

Big cities are often thought of in terms of big buildings and even bigger building projects. Far from being only elements of a skyline or cityscape, these magnificent structures sprung from the imaginations of architects and engineers, the labors of many, and the continuous maintenance and expansions at the hands of planners and organizers. Though the builders', designers', and planners' identities often fade beside the attraction and utility of their end-products, the structures themselves are timeless monuments to the skills of their creators.

Williams, Russell and Johnson, Inc. are creators and caretakers of some of the nation's most noteworthy structural accomplishments. Organized in 1976, the company is a multidisciplined engineering, architectural, planning, program management, and construction management firm. The company provides professional services to public, private, military, and governmental clients. The Atlanta headquarters is surrounded by local projects from Hartsfield Airport and the Fulton County Government Center, to the Georgia Dome and the Lenox Transit Station. Other branch offices in Dallas, Miami, and Nashville are similarly encompassed by extraordinary edifices of both the functional and aesthetic flavors.

The firm's operations are strategically placed to service a broad base of clients throughout the United States and the Caribbean Islands. All told, the many offices of Williams, Russell and Johnson house over 115 employees.

The firm offers a strong combination of management, staff, and project experience necessary to complete projects in a timely and cost-effective manner. As a multidisciplined firm, the company is divided into several functional groups, which include civil engineering, environmental engineering, electrical engineering, mechanical engineering, structural engineering, and architecture

planning, and program and construction management. Within each of these areas, the firm provides comprehensive services from project planning and conceptual design through construction completion. The firm's principal areas of expertise include commercial, municipal, and industrial facilities; environmental engineering services; roadway improvements; rapid transit facilities; and aviation projects.

The Hartsfield Atlanta International Airport Expansion Program represents the culmination of many years of planning and design to produce an advanced aviation facility. Williams, Russell and Johnson is a partner in a three-way joint venture that provides consulting engineering, architecture, and construction management services for the landside and airside improvements at the airport.

The firm's joint venture involvement has been continuous since late 1979 and has resulted in the design and construction of numerous new and improved facilities.

But Hartsfield is not the only aviation project on Williams, Russell and Johnson's list of credits. The firm provided construction management services for the Dallas/Ft. Worth International Airport; the planning, design, and construction surveillance for enplaning and deplaning drives for the Nashville Airport terminal ramps and short-term parking; and the design and construction services to develop a portion of the Opa-Locka Airport into a 294-acre industrial airpark. Opa-Locka Airport is the second busiest general aviation airport in the United States and one of the six airports in the aviation system operated by the Dade County (Florida) Aviation Department. Other stateside aviation projects include the Detroit Airport Air Rescue Firefighting Facility, the Ft. Lauderdale/Hollywood International Airport, the Miami International Airport, lighting rehabilitation at the Orlando Executive Airport, and construction management of the Orlando International Airport's third runway.

Williams, Russell and Johnson was retained by the Virgin Islands Port Authority for the Cyril King Airport Expansion for St.

Thomas and the U.S. Virgin Islands, to provide a complete review of all architectural and engineering services provided by the airport expansion design consultant. The services included the quality controll review evaluation of all schematics, preliminary design, and final design documents and assistance to the Authority during the bidding and construction award period. Other services provided by the firm for this project included, but were not limited to, a review of environmental and safety monitoring, and in-depth functional analysis of all modes of ground and air transportation, as well as pedestrian movements, administrative offices, concessions, drainage, utilities, and other associated functions.

Water and wastewater treatment plants are another specialty of the firm. Williams, Russell and Johnson provided engineering services for the City of Atlanta for the expansion and upgrade of the Utoy Creek Waste Water Reclamation Center. The project had an aggressive schedule subject to a state consent order and state legislation. Design components included new headworks, biological phosphorus reduction process, aeration tanks, secondary clarifiers, filter influent pumping station, effluent filters, ultraviolet disinfection, post aeration, sludge thickening facilities, a new Administration/Laboratory building, and maintenance and storage facilities. Additional water and waste water projects include Fulton county's Little River Wastewater Treatment Plant, the North Area Water Treatment Plant, Atlanta's Hemphill Plant, Finished Water Pumping Station, the Boston Harbor and Dade County, Florida wastewater improvements.

Sports facilities are some of the more spectacular examples of Williams, Russell and Johnson's labors. The Atlanta Olympic Stadium, Turner Field, the Georgia Dome, the Charlotte Coliseum, Philadelphia's CoreStates Arena, Little Rock's AllTell Arena, the Atlanta-Fulton County Stadium parking lot improvements, and the Greensboro War Memorial Coliseum Complex are but a few examples of the firm's works.

As part of a four-way joint venture, the firm provided design and construction administration services to the Atlanta Olympic Stadium. Williams, Russell and Johnson provided all the civil engineering, plumbing, fire protection design for the stadium, and participated in the structural engineering design. The 85,000-seat Olympic Stadium served as the venue for track-and-field events as well as the opening and closing ceremonies.

The same joint venture team that was responsible for the design and construction administration of the Olympic Stadium also prepared construction documents and provided construction administration for the post-Olympic conversion of the stadium into a 50,000-seat baseball stadium. One of the remarkable things

about the conversion was that it took place in less than nine months to accommodate the Atlanta Braves' requirement that the facility be ready for the start of the 1997 baseball season.

The Georgia Dome is the first oval-shaped, cable-supported, translucent-roofed stadium in the world. The seven-level complex is adjacent to the Georgia World Congress Center. The firm provided demolition plans of existing structures and prepared the civil/site engineering and fire protection construction documents for the Georgia Dome.

There are many other projects to the firm's credits, and many more in the works. The firm's creative application of its architectural and engineering disiplines provided services for the Tennessee State University Student Center, the City of Nashville public schools, 650 student Montessori School and the General Tolson Youth

Recreation Center at Ft. Bragg, NC. Williams-Russell and Johnson will meet the new millennium with a mix of groundbreakings and ribbon cuttings as it continues to build the future of mankind through the structures man needs to work, travel, play, and meet. ◐

◄ (Left to right) **Pelham C. Williams, P.E.** serves as CEO and chairman of the board of Williams, Russell and Johnson, Inc. **Charles E. Johnson, P.E.** is the firm's president and COO.

The Home Depot®

The Home Depot is a shining example of a hometown retail Cinderella story. Founded in Atlanta in 1978 by two out-of-work home improvement center executives, Bernie Marcus and Arthur Blank, The Home Depot was a simple idea: a broad range of home improvement products in an economical warehouse format. They hired friendly, knowledgeable employees to offer in-depth expertise and guide the novice remodeler to the right item, from faucets to ceiling fans. Most of the orange apron-clad employees also are stockholders, giving them the incentive that comes from having a personal stake in a company's future.

Guaranteed everyday low-pricing, large assortments, and excellent customer service proved to be a winning combination. By the end of 1999, The Home Depot will be operating more than 900 stores in 45 states, 5 Canadian provinces, Puerto Rico, and Chile. And making stock available to its employees (called associates) has resulted in a home-grown crop of many Home Depot millionaires, and associates famous for company loyalty and exemplary customer service.

The original 1979 store carried about 12,000 different products. Money was so scarce during the start-up there were empty cans of paint stacked behind full ones to fill the shelves. Now the average Home Depot store is 108,000 square feet and stocks approximately 40,000 to 50,000 different kinds of building materials, home improvement materials, and lawn and garden supplies. New stores also include a 16,000- to 28,000-square-foot garden center.

Helpful sales associates still guide homeowners through the intricacies of home improvement projects, from installing ceramic tile to replacing a water heater. Home Depot also is encouraging the next generation of do-it-yourselfers by conducting Kids Workshops™ in Home Depot stores—the first how-to, project-oriented training program for kids. A four-week course, called Home Depot University, teaches customers how to do more in-depth home improvement projects and supplements its clinic program.

Since 1979, The Home Depot has increased sales in the Atlanta market at nearly eight times the compound annual growth rate of the metro area population. Team Depot, an organized volunteer force developed in 1991 to promote community volunteer activities, continues to spread the wealth by giving back to the community. Through Team Depot, the company focuses its unique philanthropic resources in 1999 on affordable housing, at-risk youth, the environment and disaster relief. It assisted Habitat for Humanity and Christmas in April in developing and rehabilitating affordable housing and helped nonprofit organizations such as YouthBuild and KaBoom transform the lives of young people and their communities.

For six consecutive years, the company has been ranked America's Most Admired Specialty Retailer by *Fortune* magazine. Future plans include building 200 EXPO Design Centers℠ throughout North America by 2005. The EXPO Design Center combines the offerings and services of eight designer showrooms all under one roof. Using its proven strategy—huge assortments, competitive prices, and knowledgeable associates—EXPO is an excellent complement to The Home Depot.

The Home Depot stores in Santiago, Chile, are a springboard for future growth in Latin America, expanding its business opportunities to a global market. The company has announced plans to open three stores in Argentina in 2000 and plans to continue its aggressive expansion in Canada. Look for Home Depot to operate more than 1,900 stores by 2003. ❧

◀ **Two Home Depot volunteers install siding on a Habitat for Humanity Home.**

◀ **Bernie Marcus and Arthur Blank rally the troops at the company's 20th anniversary celebration.**

▼ **Expo Design Center-a division of The Home Depot-plans to operate more than 200 stores in North America by 2005.**

Hilton Atlanta & Towers

▶ Hilton Atlanta & Towers is the cornerstone of Atlanta's hospitality community.

In the spring of 1976, America's bicentennial year, Barron Hilton presided at the ribbon cutting ceremony of the Hilton Atlanta & Towers and welcomed the first conventioneers, the Avon ladies. Since then travelers from all walks of life, as well as celebrities such as Elvis Presley, Elton John, Diana Ross, and President Jimmy Carter, have been guests of Hilton Atlanta & Towers.

Hilton Atlanta & Towers is the cornerstone of Atlanta's hospitality community. It recently completed a $28-million total renovation on its 1,224-room hotel and 42 suites, from a new front entrance and lobby with new furnishings and award-winning landscaping, to a refurbished prefunction area and public corridors. All guest rooms and suites, the largest in the city, have new carpet and new bed and bath linens, as well as new wallpaper and accessories. In addition, all meeting and exhibit space has been completely renovated. The Grand Ballroom has new airwalls and, along with all meeting rooms and smaller breakout rooms, is newly carpeted. The most recent addition was the completion of the Convention Registration Area. Designed by meeting planners for meeting planners, this 1,135-square-foot area is designated for groups who wish to simplify their registration procedure. The hotel offers a unique floor plan of its meeting space, referred to as "smart flow." Groups have the ability to host their general sessions, meals, and breakouts all on one level.

Two years ago the Hilton added TeleSuite, a unique service that allows teleconferencing to numerous locations nationwide in an established private suite. Future renovations and additions to the

hotel will include full installation of ISDN lines in all meeting rooms, ballrooms, and breakouts.

In 1999, The Hilton Atlanta & Towers teamed up with Kinko's to open a complete, full-service business center, the first of its kind to open within a U.S. Hilton hotel. "The flexibility for a meeting planner to change its printed programming up to the day before arrival, and to have it all coordinated on-site, is a tremendous benefit. We are pleased to be able to offer this, as well as many other superior meeting services to our customers," said Dick Groves, General Manager.

Included in these additions is *A Point of View,* an upscale jazz lounge with a skyline view, perfect for an after-work drink or a before-dinner cigar and cocktail. Located atop the Hilton Atlanta & Towers, adjacent to *Nikolai's Roof,* the jazz lounge offers a state-of-the-art sound system and a large standing cigar humidor. In addition to serving fine single-malt scotches and cigars, *A Point of View* features live jazz on Wednesday evenings. One of the most unique features of this downtown property is its Tennis and Fitness Center. It

▶ Fine dining is just one of the hotel's many amenities.

includes state-of-the-art cardiovascular equipment, an out-door jogging track, lighted tennis courts, and a full basket-ball court.

An enthusiastic contributor to the local community, the Hilton Atlanta & Towers has helped renovate an aban-doned house for Hospitality Helping Hands, raised money for The March of Dimes, and prepared meals and organized craft time at the Atlanta Day Shelter for Women and Children (a local battered women's shelter). The Hilton has also led an aggressive United Way campaign that, in the past five years, has raised pledges equaling over $100,000.

The award-winning property has been the recent recipi-ent of the Successful Meetings' Pinnacle Award, the Meetings & Conventions' Gold Key Award, and Association Meetings' Inner Circle Award. "Hilton hospi-tality is legendary, and at the Hilton Atlanta & Towers we make it even more special by making it our own," said Dick Groves. ☜

◄ Hospitality is legendary at the Hilton Atlanta & Towers.

◄ The award-winning prop-erty has been the recent recipient of the Successful Meetings' Pinnacle Award, the Meetings & Conventions' Gold Key Award, and Association Meetings' Inner Circle Award.

Healthdyne Information Enterpises

In 1970, Parker H. "Pete" Petit's infant son died from a condition then as unforeseeable as it was tragic: SIDS (Sudden Infant Death Syndrome). Within weeks of his son's death, Petit had designed a physiological monitor for infants, a small portable system to monitor heart and respiratory activity that was simple enough for parents to operate at home. Petit persuaded a couple of engineers at Georgia Tech to help him build a prototype, and that was the birth of Healthdyne, a company that would use technological skill to serve patient care.

By 1976 Petit had obtained a Small Business Administration loan for $100,000, and Healthdyne got the first major order for Infant Monitors from SIDS researchers at the University of Maryland.

The company survived a roller coaster growth path in the wake of nationwide health care reforms and the growth of managed care. Healthdyne has navigated through both challenging and prosperous times with its initial goals intact: to reduce suffering and improve patients' quality of life.

Healthdyne split into three publicly traded corporations in 1996—Healthdyne Technologies, Healthdyne Information Enterprises, and Matria Healthcare, and Petit gave up the CEO role to three other executives. Pete Petit still serves as chairman for two of the companies, Healthdyne Information Enterprises and Matria.

HIE (Healthdyne Information Enterprises, Inc.) was conceived as one of the Healthdyne subsidiary companies in 1994. The common stock was spun out to Healthdyne shareholders in late 1995. Two years later, HIE redefined its strategic direction and became The Integration Solutions Company, providing strategic, tactical, and technical expertise to solve practical software integration problems.

Mergers, acquisitions, affiliations, new business models, and new technology all drive the need for information integration. HIE's products allow companies to have their information systems share data in real time, including those with multiple hardware platforms, operating systems, and applications. HIE is the leading provider of software that enables companies to link their applications, then monitor and manage those linkages as they add to their IT systems.

HIE's enterprise integration technology tools (like integration engines, message brokers, enterprise master person indexes (EMPIs), and data loaders) cope with the wide variety of application-, vendor-, and platform-specific communications protocols necessary to allow information to flow throughout a business.

Hospitals, physician clinics, and other health care environments require a proven and flexible application integration technology that's easy to use. HIE's Cloverleaf® allows information, in the form of messages, records, or transactions, to be easily exchanged, transformed, and routed between different applications simultaneously. Petit explains, "Our tools and services help enterprises leverage the information systems investments they've already made, while integrating new applications and technologies."

HIE combines its strong product with excellent service. Its service team offers integration design, implementation, and maintenance services. Led by subject matter experts, who are also skilled instructors, HIE training brings new people up to speed quickly and enhances the skills of current staff members.

Headquartered in Marietta, Georgia, with additional offices in Dallas; Columbus; London, England; and Essen, Germany; HIE has over 1,200 customer sites, 200 employees, and a distribution network encompassing North America, Central and Eastern Europe, the Asia/Pacific region, the Middle East, and Africa.

"The Atlanta medical community and our universities are conducive to the growth of bio-tech companies. Georgia Tech and Emory are incubators for bio-tech companies," says Petit. "I expect, in the next decade, Atlanta to be one of the foremost centers of medical technology in the country." ❧

Matria Healthcare

Matria Healthcare is a leading provider of comprehensive disease management services, with programs that allow physicians and payers to provide more comprehensive, coordinated, and cost-effective care to women and newborns, and to individuals with the chronic conditions of diabetes, cardiovascular disease, and respiratory disorders.

Matria's original core services were prenatal risk assessment and patient education, preterm labor management, diabetes in pregnancy management, and specialized obstetrical home care. The company's products included the only home uterine activity monitors with FDA premarket approval for early detection of preterm labor.

Today, Matria's pregnancy services focus on acute patients already experiencing preterm labor as well as pregnancies involving high order multiples, which are more often at risk of preterm delivery or the complications of pregnancy. The high order birth rate has grown dramatically in the United States, climbing 20 percent between 1995 and 1996, doubling since 1990, and approximately one-third of all triplet births in the United States receive care from Matria.

In 1998, Matria expanded beyond managing the condition of pregnancy into a broader market that included cardiovascular, respiratory, and diabetic disease management through four business units: Women's Health Division, Gainor Diabetes Division, Quality Diagnostic Services, Inc. (QDS), and Respiratory Management Service (RMS). Additionally, Matria provides information system solutions to physicians and specialists through Clinical Management Systems, Inc. (CMS) and infertility practice management services through National Reproductive Medical Centers, Inc. (NRMC).

An estimated 15.7 million people in the United States have diabetes, and the number of people diagnosed with diabetes in the U.S. has increased six-fold over the past four decades. Matria's acquisition of DMS and Gainor in January 1999 created the nation's first full-spectrum diabetes management provider.

The combined businesses distribute diabetes products and supplies to over 50 countries worldwide, and provide comprehensive diabetes education, clinical interventions, and diabetes management services for self-insured employers and health plans.

Cardiovascular Disease (CVD) is the leading cause of death in the United States and the nation's costliest health problem. Over 57 million Americans, more than one-fourth of the population, have some form of CVD. Matria acquired QDS and is now a provider of cardiac arrhythmia monitoring services.

Chronic obstructive pulmonary disease (COPD) affects 16 million people in the United States and is the country's fourth leading cause of death. Over 15 million people suffer with asthma, which cannot be cured but can be controlled.

Matria markets a comprehensive asthma and COPD management program developed by National Jewish that offers physician and patient education, risk assessment, acuity-based treatment stratification, disease specific care management, state-of-the-art telephone support by medical professionals, and outcome measurement and reporting. Asthma disease management reduces emergency room visits and hospitalizations.

Matria has a strategic partnership with WebMD, an Internet portal for education, communication, and training for physicians, health care professionals, and patients. Initially, this new service will concentrate on obstetrics and gynecology and will expand into the areas of respiratory, diabetes, and pediatrics. Matria's newest service is a web site that allows people to access medical texts and video clips, and immediately telephone a nurse at a Matria call center to follow up on specific questions.

"From our initial focus on high-risk pregnancy and women's health, we have developed into a national organization that is reducing costs associated with a number of chronic diseases, and improving the patient's quality of life," Petit says. ●

◄ **Matria® has emerged as the technology and product innovation leader in the field of cardiac arrhythmia monitoring and surveillance.**

◄ **Matria® nurses assist obstetricians in the management of their high-risk pregnancies by receiving clinical information from the patient's home and remaining in daily contact with the patient.**

Cushman & Wakefield

The Atlanta office of Cushman & Wakefield was established in 1977 as a regional office for the southeastern United States. Specializing in brokerage services, this office grew from five people in 1977 to more than 90 professionals today. Representing clients in leasing, acquisition, disposition, construction, property management, and valuing buildings that shape the Atlanta skyline, Cushman & Wakefield is the preeminent real estate firm in Atlanta, throughout the United States, and around the world.

From the firm's Midtown office in One Atlantic Center, Cushman & Wakefield's real estate professionals provide their clients with expertise and solutions for any real estate need. Recently, the Atlanta office of Cushman & Wakefield was ranked as the top brokerage firm in the city by the *Atlanta Business Chronicle*.

From its inception in 1917, Cushman & Wakefield has helped businesses solve their real estate challenges. Cushman & Wakefield's first major Atlanta assignment was the development consulting and leasing of Georgia-Pacific Corporation's new corporate headquarters facility. Georgia-Pacific was relocating from Portland, Oregon, to Atlanta, Georgia, and they required 685,000 square feet of office space. As its real estate specialist, Cushman & Wakefield helped develop the 1.1-million-square-foot Georgia-Pacific building, as well as lease the excess space. Most recently, Cushman & Wakefield marketed and sold Peachtree Center, a 2.5-million-square-foot office and retail complex which is a downtown Atlanta landmark.

Globally, Cushman & Wakefield manages 325-million square feet and either dominates or is a market leader in all its businesses, including office and industrial brokerage, financial services, advisory services, asset services, corporate services, valuation advisory services, and research services.

Today, Cushman & Wakefield has the diverse talents of 8,500 employees worldwide in 134 offices in 41 countries. With 45 offices throughout the United States and international operations in Europe, Canada, Mexico, South America, and Asia, Cushman & Wakefield provides these services at the local, regional, national, and global level. Purely a service organization, Cushman & Wakefield is not an owner or investor, avoiding potential conflicts of interest that otherwise could occur.

Cushman & Wakefield's primary mission is to help clients succeed by delivering superior real estate services. The firm takes a long-term view of the services it provides by focusing on close client relationships built on trust. These strong working partnerships maximize the understanding of client needs and enable it to formulate real estate solutions that anticipate and respond to those needs. Today, more than ever, Cushman & Wakefield is responding to those needs and continues to meet the everyday real estate challenges of its clients. ☻

► **Representing clients in leasing, acquisition, disposition, construction, property management, and valuing buildings that shape the Atlanta skyline, Cushman & Wakefield is the preeminent real estate firm in Atlanta, throughout the United States, and around the world. Most recently, Cushman & Wakefield marketed and sold Peachtree Center, a 2.5-million-square-foot office and retail complex which is a downtown Atlanta landmark.**

Turner Broadcasting System, Inc.

When Ted Turner purchased an Atlanta UHF station in 1970, all he needed was an audience as big as his ideas. Six years later Turner created the "Superstation" concept by transmitting Channel 17's signal to cable systems via satellite, the first station distributed nationwide. That same year Turner purchased a Major League Baseball team, the Atlanta Braves. The three main ingredients of Turner Broadcasting System, Inc.'s (TBS, Inc.) phenomenal success— entertainment, sports, and cable—were in place.

Olympics, and the 1998 Goodwill Games in New York, as well as track and field, college football, boxing, the 2000 Winter Goodwill Games in Lake Placid, New York, and the 2001 Summer Goodwill Games in Brisbane, Australia.

TBS, Inc. and Royal Philips Electronics are developing Atlanta's new 20,000-seat sports and event facility, the Philips Arena, collaborating on a 20-year agreement valued at over $100 million. "This agreement signals a long-term relationship between two local companies with global constituencies," said Terence F. McGuirk, chairman and CEO of TBS, Inc.. The Philips Arena anchors a 25-acre redevelopment tract in downtown Atlanta, stretching from Centennial Olympic Park to the Georgia Dome and including the CNN Center, TBS, Inc.'s worldwide headquarters.

In 1980 Turner launched CNN, reinventing television news. His 24/7 cable news network, beset with start-up slipups, silenced the scoffers by making history, changing the nature of news from past tense to present live action. CNN has since become the preeminent news source for the global power elite and the dispossessed alike.

The subject of *Time* magazine's 1991 Man Of The Year story, Turner was quoted as saying, "I was the right man in the right place at the right time," adding, "not me alone, but all the people who think the world can be brought together with telecommunications." Today, nearly one billion people have access to CNN service, which continues to expand, making many nations witnesses to history.

Turner raised the professional sports profile of Atlanta, rooting for the Braves through years of lackluster play until they exploded out of the cellar by winning a "worst to first" division championship. The Braves have since won the 1995 World Championship, seven consecutive division championships, and five trips to the last six World Series. The National Basketball Association's Atlanta Hawks arrived in 1977 and have earned trips to the NBA playoffs. Turner's latest sports team addition, The National Hockey League's Atlanta Thrashers, will debut in September 1999. TBS Inc.'s sports line-up includes coverage of the NBA, Atlanta Braves baseball, NASCAR, golf, figure skating, the 1998 Nagano Winter

In 1996 Ted Turner sold TBS, Inc. to Time Warner, Inc., becoming vice chairman of Time Warner. Today, TBS Superstation, which converted to a copyright paid basic cable channel in 1998, is watched by more people than any other cable network. In 1998, localized feeds of the TBS entertainment networks continued to launch within regions of both Europe and Asia. The company now produces 15 localized versions of its entertainment networks outside the United States. Turner entertainment networks are leaders in virtually all key demographic segments.

Competitive, colorful, and eminently quotable, Ted Turner's high stakes risks have reaped substantial rewards, securing his reputation as a visionary who has revolutionized global media. ❧

◄ In 1980 Turner launched CNN, reinventing television news. CNN has since become the preeminent news source for the global power elite and the dispossessed alike.

◄ Competitive, colorful, and eminently quotable, Ted Turner's high stakes risks have reaped substantial rewards, securing his reputation as a visionary who has revolutionized global media.

ABN AMRO Bank N.V.

ABN AMRO Bank is a long-established, multifaceted, and prominent bank of international reputation and standing, ranked among the world's 10 largest banks with $500 billion in total assets.

Founded in 1824, this Dutch-based company established its Atlanta branch in 1977, to better serve its clients in the Southeast market. Its Atlanta presence is part of ABN AMRO's long-standing philosophy of operating locations close to its customers.

Nicknamed "The Network Bank," ABN AMRO's global reach is made possible by the bank's 3,400 branches in 72 countries. The company proudly stands as the U.S. market's largest foreign bank, with over 400 branches and offices, 17,000 employees, more than 2,000 corporate customers, and U.S. assets exceeding $100 billion. Its universal banking approach brings all disciplines—corporate, investment and merchant banking, asset management, and private banking—under one roof for "one-stop shopping."

The sound financial strength of ABN AMRO is confirmed by Moody's long-term debt rating of AA2 and S&P's AA rating.

A distinct advantage of ABN AMRO is its strength in the sectors of trade finance, international cash management, asset securitization, project finance, and treasury. Along with its expertise in general corporate businesses, the bank focuses on 11 core industries: automotive, chemicals and pharmaceuticals, communications, consumer products, diamonds and jewelry, financial institutions, forest products, integrated oil and gas, power and infrastructure, technology, and transportation. A team of ABN AMRO banking professionals, working in centers located in key countries around the world, maintain an in-depth knowledge and understanding of these 11 core industries.

Unique to ABN AMRO is its century-long presence in such major regional markets as Asia-Pacific and South America. It owns the third or fourth largest banks in Brazil, Hungary, and Thailand, all of which provide a full range of corporate and private banking services.

A good corporate citizen in the Atlanta community, ABN AMRO takes pride in providing long-standing financial support to such civic associations as the Atlanta and Georgia Chambers of Commerce, the United Way, the Woodruff Arts Center, and the Atlanta History Center. The company also strengthens its corporate culture through a large scale, in-house program that underscores the importance of the bank's core values of integrity, teamwork, respect, and professionalism.

ABN AMRO's ambition is to be a front-runner in value-added banking, both on a local and worldwide level. This aspiration is based upon the preservation of ABN AMRO Bank's reputation and tradition of high quality, and upon the expertise of its highly motivated and qualified professional staff.

The future is bright for ABN AMRO Bank as it enters the new millennium. Having invested heavily in technology and human resources, the company is rapidly moving to electronic "real time" banking.

As one of the world's truly global banks, it is proud to serve Atlanta locally, yet deliver the world. ☙

▶ The team of ABN AMRO banking professionals maintains an in-depth knowledge and understanding of 11 core industries.

Solarcom, Inc.

Established in 1976 as Sun Data, Inc., Solarcom, Inc. is a leading business and technology solutions provider headquartered in Norcross, Georgia.

Solarcom delivers consulting and integration solutions in the areas of system integration, LAN/WAN, e-commerce, web-enablement, groupware applications, lease/financing services, and has a worldwide wholesale division. The company's multi-platform, multi-vendor product offerings include systems and products from IBM, Sun Microsystems, Microsoft, Cisco, Sprint, Hewlett-Packard, Compaq/Digital, Novell, and others.

During the last eight years Solarcom has expanded its core business from primarily providing equipment to being an independent business consulting, systems integration, and financing solutions company. In 1999, it officially changed its name to Solarcom because services became such a substantial part of the business. "Changing our name to Solarcom conveys our focus of providing comprehensive services and solutions, rather than primarily products and equipment," says Eric Prockow, Solarcom's chairman and CEO. "Turnkey business solutions are the thrust of our business services."

Solarcom houses its Professional Services division in its newest facility in Norcross, which is directly across from its headquarters. This facility also houses the company's Southeast Sales Team, Business Development Group, and National Specialty Team Management Group. The facilities include a product demonstration room that runs multiple system platforms and provides simulated presentations of numerous hardware and software solutions. In

addition, there are two training rooms and a demonstration room featuring Sun Microsystems equipment.

"Our strategic business plan demands a wide range of expertise while leveraging the products and services needed to provide our clients a competitive edge," says Gary Otto, Solarcom's president. "Our extended facilities accommodate Solarcom's expanding team of sales and services professionals."

When clients ask Solarcom about platform hardware, the company's first question is "What business issue is driving this need?" The answer to that question is crucial to ensure a good fit between a client's hardware needs and the demands of its business. When Solarcom understands a firm's fundamental business issues, it can best formulate the right mix of hardware and services that can grow as a business changes.

The Arthur Andersen/Atlanta Journal-Constitution 1999 list of the top 100 Private Companies in Georgia ranked Solarcom at number 25. Additionally, Solarcom placed at number 32 on *Global Technology Business* magazine's annual ranking of the top 50 privately held IT companies in the world.

Solarcom has experienced steady growth since its entry into the comprehensive consulting, design, and implementation services arena by building partnerships with its clients, offering a single point of responsibility for all of its customers' information technology needs.

"We believe that Solarcom's future growth and success are dependent upon helping our clients grow," said Eric Prockow. "We will achieve this mutual growth by designing and implementing tailored, high-value solutions quickly and responsibly with principal focus towards the needs of our clients." ✿

◄ **Established in 1976 as Sun Data, Inc., Solarcom, Inc. is a leading business and technology solutions provider headquartered in Norcross, Georgia.**

◄ **Solarcom has expanded its core business from primarily providing equipment to being an independent business consulting, systems integration, and financing solutions company.**

Business Georgia

In early 1973 a group of community-minded bankers saw the need to create a company, The Business Development Corporation of Georgia, Inc., to specialize in providing financial resources to the ever-increasing number of small businesses in Georgia. Since that time Business Georgia has successfully helped hundreds of small businesses start up and expand operations.

As one of the State's leading small business lenders, Business Georgia believes that proper funding is essential to the viability of young and growing companies. Their mission is to offer financial opportunity to Georgia's entrepreneurs, so that more small businesses can get started, grow, and flourish—stimulating the local economy and creating jobs as they expand.

Business Georgia is fully staffed to market, underwrite, close, and service its programs statewide. The company provides financing to Georgia businesses through conventional loans, the U.S. Small Business Administration (SBA), and the U.S. Department of Agriculture Business & Industry loan program. Business Georgia is a preferred lender under the SBA 7(a) loan program; this distinction is earned by experienced lenders who have consistently demonstrated responsible and prudent credit decisions. The company also manages the Business Growth Corporation of Georgia, a nonprofit company founded in 1984 to encourage the creation of jobs in Georgia. In conjunction with the SBA 504 loan program, the company assists small businesses in the acquisition of long-term fixed assets such as land, buildings, and equipment. Business Georgia is able to help small companies grow

and reach their potential by making loans that might not be available through traditional lending channels.

Business Georgia makes loans to a wide variety of businesses from wholesale and manufacturing companies to day care facilities and retail operations. The company's goal is to reach business owners and entrepreneurs of all gender and racial segments of the population, and they are proud to say that over one-third of their loans have consistently gone to minority or female-owned businesses.

When the company was formed, the staff consisted of a president, a part-time secretary, and the original 25 founding institutions. Today, Business Georgia is owned by 58 Georgia financial institutions, foundations, and public companies represented by 16 directors. Total assets now exceed $27 million, and the company employs a staff of 14 people. Over the last 27 years Business Georgia has approved more than 900 business loans totaling over $290 million, and more than 7,500 jobs have been created or retained in the State by the businesses who were recipients of Business Georgia loans. In 1998, Governor Zell Miller declared May 2, 1998, as "Business Georgia Day" in recognition of its 25th anniversary and its contribution to the small businesses in the State. That same year the company reached its goal of becoming the State's largest SBA lender.

Business Georgia expects the coming years to bring increased business prosperity to Atlanta and the entire State, and the company is well positioned to participate in that expansion. ❧

Long Aldridge & Norman LLP

In 1994, Long Aldridge & Norman expanded its Atlanta practice into Washington, D.C., opening an office there that focused initially on energy law and government affairs. Today, the firm's lawyers located in the nation's capital provide advice and counsel in many other areas of law as well, including all types of intellectual property law, corporate transactions, and litigation.

As the firm has grown, so has its commitment to the community that fostered its growth. Long Aldridge & Norman attorneys have held leadership positions in an array of civic and charitable organizations, among them the Atlanta Union Mission, the Atlanta Ballet, Zoo Atlanta, Central Atlanta Progress, the Atlanta Visitors and Convention Bureau, and The Georgia Conservancy. The firm sponsors significant pro bono legal services as well.

Long Aldridge & Norman attorneys also have held public office, served in the administrations of elected officials, and held political party leadership positions at the local, state, and national level. Among other roles, they have been senior policy advisors and chief aides to the President of the United States, the Governor of Georgia, and the Mayor of Atlanta.

In reflecting on the firm's next 25 years, Chairman Long said, "I only hope they will be as good as the first 25." ❧

◄ Rare in Georgia, peregrine falcons nest on the 51st floor balconies of Long Aldridge & Norman LLP in downtown Atlanta. Photo by Leigh Garner.

When Long Aldridge & Norman LLP celebrated its 25th anniversary in 1999, its founders could look back on a quarter-century of phenomenal growth and look forward to an ongoing commitment to setting new standards of excellence in providing legal services.

In 1974, four Atlanta attorneys joined together to form what has become one of the major business law firms in Atlanta. Today, the firm offers the entire range of legal services clients need in our evolving economic, technological, and political climate. By helping clients in many industries throughout the United States achieve their business objectives, the firm has earned a reputation as one of the nation's leading law firms.

"Atlanta has been the ideal location for us to build a law firm to serve local, regional, national, and international clients," states Clay C. Long, founding partner and firm chairman. "The strength of the economy, the spirit of entrepreneurship, the commitment of Atlanta's business and political leaders to creating a city where businesses thrive have all contributed to our success. I doubt there is another city where, in relatively few years, we could have grown in size and reach the way we have in Atlanta."

Long Aldridge & Norman reaffirmed its long-standing commitment to downtown Atlanta in 1993, when it moved into the city's newest landmark, One Peachtree Center. Just three years later, the attorneys were joined by one of the few pairs of peregrine falcons to nest in Georgia since 1942. The pair has returned to nest on 51st floor balconies of the firm each year, providing some arresting images from offices and conference rooms.

◄ The two-story atrium reception area of Long Aldridge & Norman LLP provides dramatic views of Atlanta and a sampling of the firm's extensive art collection.

Pope & Land Enterprises, Inc.

the present and future value of real estate.

The firm's overall goals are neatly summarized in its mission statement: Pope & Land Enterprises, Inc. is dedicated to creating value for its properties by maximizing opportunities related to the acquisition, development, marketing, management, and disposition of improved and unimproved real estate. The firm is committed to executing all fiduciary responsibilities in an ethical and professional manner as it provides diverse real estate services to clients and projects.

Pope & Land emphasizes teamwork to achieve maximum efficiency, flexibility, and responsiveness in the day-to-day demands of real estate. With in-depth local market knowledge, the company is often able to strategically calculate trends and movements ahead of the curve and to use such information in a meaningful and profitable manner.

The vertically integrated team is charged with the responsibility of taking a project from start to finish with integrity and character. Pope & Land professionals have the creative freedom to cultivate ideas and execute strategies to provide innovative solutions for their respective projects, while bearing full accountability for the outcome of their decisions.

Pope & Land is an opportunity and market-oriented company. The results are some of the most innovative land uses and buildings with unique applications and optimum return on investment. At Pope & Land, results are both measurable and livable. ✎

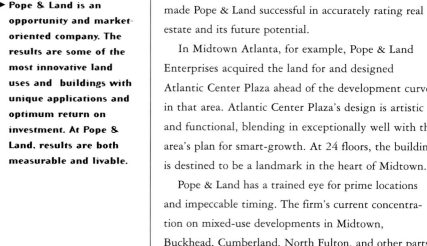

▲ **Headquartered in Atlanta, and incorporated in 1979, Pope & Land has developed numerous notable properties, including Cumberland Center in northwest Atlanta.**

Real estate is as much an adventure as a venture. It takes talent and experience to be able to distinguish between trend and real value, and to invest accordingly. It is this intrinsic knowledge and experience that sets Pope & Land Enterprises apart in the highly competitive field of commercial real estate.

Headquartered in Atlanta, and incorporated in 1979, Pope & Land has developed numerous notable properties. The firm has many remarkable mixed-use projects in Atlanta and throughout the Southeastern United States.

The hallmark of the firm's long history has been stability. The conservative, aggressive nature of the firm has protected both the company's own assets and its clients' assets, while continuing to increase and build value. This attribute alone attracts many clients, but it is stability combined with experience that has made Pope & Land successful in accurately rating real estate and its future potential.

In Midtown Atlanta, for example, Pope & Land Enterprises acquired the land for and designed Atlantic Center Plaza ahead of the development curve in that area. Atlantic Center Plaza's design is artistic and functional, blending in exceptionally well with the area's plan for smart-growth. At 24 floors, the building is destined to be a landmark in the heart of Midtown.

▶ **Pope & Land is an opportunity and market-oriented company. The results are some of the most innovative land uses and buildings with unique applications and optimum return on investment. At Pope & Land, results are both measurable and livable.**

Pope & Land has a trained eye for prime locations and impeccable timing. The firm's current concentration on mixed-use developments in Midtown, Buckhead, Cumberland, North Fulton, and other parts of the Southeast reflects the firm's understanding and timely response to social changes that, in turn, dictate

◄ Photo by Ron Sherman.

The Making of a World Class City

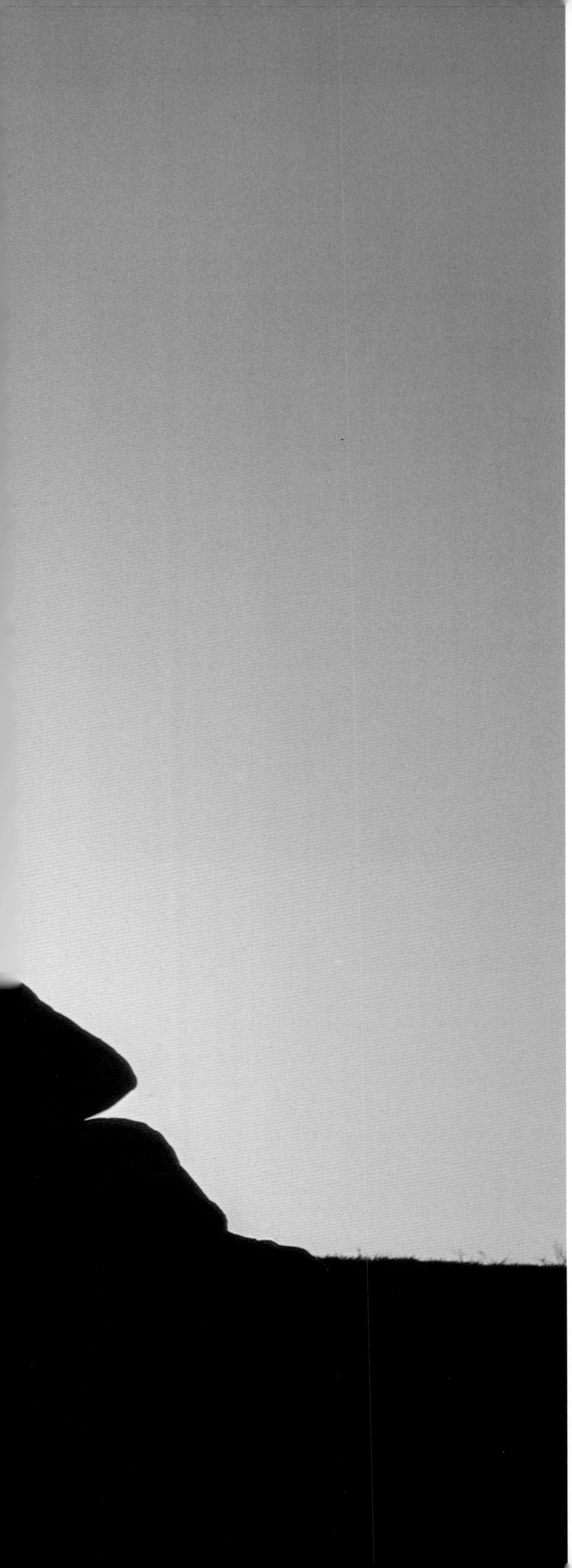

Chapter Eight
1980-1990

On June 1, 1980, Atlanta took its first step into a brave new world of global communication when Cable News Network began its first broadcast in a converted country club on Techwood Drive.

Photo by Ron Sherman

On June 1, 1980, Atlanta took its first step into a brave new world of global communication when Cable News Network (CNN) began its first broadcast. In 1980, the number of homes estimated to be able to receive cable was just 1.7 million nationally, and only twelve thousand Atlantans could watch CNN. Today, almost every home in America has cable television, and CNN is broadcast worldwide.

Photos by Ron Sherman

It was a new product—a 24-hour news television channel—unimagined by most people, but not by its handful of scrappy true believers.

Few people took notice of CNN at first. Unlike most conventional television signals, CNN was delivered to homes by cable, after the signal had first been bounced from Atlanta to a satellite and beamed back down to the ground. In 1980, cable was used primarily to deliver television signals to isolated rural communities. The number of homes estimated to be able to receive cable in 1980 was just 1.7 million nationally and only twelve thousand Atlantans could watch CNN. It hardly seemed recipe for success.

Equally unlikely was CNN's proprietor, a local entrepreneur named Ted Turner. Yet, for a town that relied on a handful of international flights a day for its self-proclaimed status as an international city, CNN would over time bring the city more international recognition than even its most fevered boosters could ever imagine and would make Turner an international celebrity.

Turner was almost impossibly colorful. At 24, Turner was thrust into running a outdoor advertising company by his father's suicide. In the late 1960s, Turner acquired a broken-down television station that broadcast on UHF. Turner programmed the station himself using a mixture of decade-old sitcoms and moth-eaten movies nobody else wanted. He billed WTBS as family-friendly and, to nearly everyone's surprise, it proved popular. Over the years he kept expanding the reach of his signal until it was a national institution known as the Superstation.

In 1976, Turner was approached to buy the Atlanta Braves baseball team, then plagued by poor attendance. Turner said yes. He gave the same answer in 1977 to buying the Atlanta Hawks from developer Tom Cousins. Not only did he keep both teams in Atlanta, but he used their games as inexpensive programming. It was an idea that would be much-copied in the future.

Turner's oddball programming mix—which included as little news as he could get away with—was a ratings success locally. He soon changed his mind about news, though. He believed that cable television would grow and that it would pay him to provide news to their customers. He was right. Cable television exploded in the early 1980s and CNN grew right along with it. Because it was the first—and for many years—only channel of its kind, CNN penetrated the

national consciousness deeply during big news events. Foreign heads of state claimed to be avid watchers. Fidel Castro cut a promotional spot.

As his business empire grew, so did Turner's reputation. An avid sailor, Turner won the America's Cup in an upset in 1977. He closed out the 1980s by marrying actress and political activist Jane Fonda.

The rest of Atlanta was prospering right along with Turner. In the early 1980s, a crippling recession struck particularly hard at the Midwest, sending a steady stream of economic refugees to the Sunbelt and setting Atlanta off on another decade of torrid population growth.

The city became the adopted home of misfits who believed they had new and better ideas and kept Atlanta's reputation as a center for entrepreneurial thinkers alive.

For instance, Bernard Marcus and Arthur Blank were working together at a home improvement store in Los Angeles in the mid-1970s when they were abruptly fired. The two took their idea—Home Depot, a store that sold building materials to do-it-yourselfers—on the road and landed in Atlanta, drawn by the city's growth history. They opened three stores in 1979. Many of the boxes on the warehouse-style shelves were empty because the pair didn't have enough capital to buy a full inventory. Marcus' children gave shoppers one-dollar bills apiece to walk in the door.

By 1980 Home Depot was making a profit and a year later became a publicly traded company. Home Depot quickly expanded into Florida and other states and grew at double-digit pace all

during the 1980s. By the end of the decade it was an industry leader with hundreds of stores and was reporting $3 billion a year in sales. It made fortunes for its investors, too, once splitting its stock three times in a single year.

A third Atlanta dreamer was Dennis Hayes, a Georgia Tech graduate who started a company in his house in 1978. Hayes made modems, a new device for sending data over telephone lines. In 1982, the company only had $12 million in sales but with the advent of personal computers, demand for modems grew wildly. By the

mid-1980s, Hayes' Modem held almost 50 percent of the total U.S. market and annual revenues rose in excess of $120 million. Hayes was the industry standard and soon employed more than 1,000 employees. As more manufacturers jumped into the fray, Hayes share of the market dropped but revenues increased to $1 billion in 1989 and the company was known for its lavish employee parties.

In 1981, Andrew Young was elected to succeed Maynard Jackson as mayor. Young had been a lieutenant to Martin Luther King, Jr., during the civil rights struggle and had served as ambassador to the United Nations in the 1970s for President (and former Georgia governor) Jimmy Carter.

Young was by nature a conciliator and he worked hard to win back the trust of the local business community. He worked hard at revitalizing the downtown area. He hatched a plan to rebuild Underground Atlanta as a shopping and entertainment center that could lure suburbanites and pulled together a public-private partnership to raise the $140 million needed to pull it off. Underground reopened in 1989 to a steady stream of visitors.

Suburbanites came downtown to visit Underground Atlanta, at least at first, but most were happy where they were. Those who came in search of better jobs and lower costs of living mostly settled in the suburban areas of Cobb, Gwinnett, and the northern parts of Fulton County. By the latter half of the decade, Gwinnett County was a fixture on lists of the fastest-growing counties in the United States. Between 1977 and 1987, Cobb's population increased 60 percent and Gwinnett's by 141 percent.

Businesses migrated to the Sun Belt as well. The Chamber of Commerce—which celebrated its 125th birthday in 1985—opened a computerized marketing office early in the decade that provided executives with instant comparisons on the cost of doing business

◄ CNN's proprietor was a young entrepreneur named Ted Turner. He purchased a television station in the late 1960s, broadcasting in UHF. Turner programmed the station himself using a mixture of decade-old sit-coms and moth-eaten movies nobody else wanted. He billed WTBS as family-friendly, and, to nearly everyone's surprise, it proved popular. Today, the station is a national institution known as the Superstation.

In 1976, Ted Turner was approached to buy the Atlanta Braves baseball team, then plagued by a poor record and dismal attendance. Turner said yes. In 1977 he bought the Atlanta Hawks from developer Tom Cousins. He kept the teams in Atlanta and used their games as inexpensive programming. The Braves experienced a rapid turnaround in the early 1990s and became one of baseball's elite teams. Photos by Ron Sherman

in Atlanta and twenty other cities. The aggressive efforts paid off. In 1985, for instance, the Chamber reported attracting 226 new firms to Atlanta. Later, RJR Nabisco, at the time the second-largest consumer products company in the country, moved its headquarters to Atlanta from North Carolina.

The Sunbelt migration quickly drove the metro population past two million early in the decade and—with the help of a turn-around in the national economy—set the stage for a rosy decade that outstripped even the most optimistic economic projections. Between 1983 and 1987, for example, 337,500 new jobs were created in the Atlanta metro area.

The gravitational pull of the rapidly growing suburban areas was inescapable. Both Cobb and Gwinnett counties got large malls, each built next to the interstate but miles outside I-285, that served as de facto town centers. The Gwinnett mall opening was considered an event of such significance that it received live television coverage.

The clearest sign that the population center was moving north was the new development along I-285. Once envisioned as a way to detour trucks outside the city, I-285 soon became a kind of Main Street of the suburbs. The farmland along the road had been bucolic well into the 1970s but now it was sprouting malls, like Perimeter Mall, and low-rise office park developments, like Perimeter Center. To move the rapidly increasing traffic, the state mounted an effort that doubled the number of lanes available.

The demand for suburban office space soared in the 1980s as jobs moved out towards where people lived. In response, suburban office buildings rose upwards and developers began building collections of skyscrapers at developments like Ravinia and Concourse that rivaled anything downtown. Building sites along I-285 became so valuable that groups of neighbors bundled their 1960s-era ranch houses together and sold them en masse to developers.

Commercial developers, who had been relatively quiet during the latter half of the 1970s, came roaring back. So great was the demand for new office space that a number of out-of-state firms, mostly from Texas, set up shop in Atlanta. The industry adopted a mixed-use model of development that combined office, shopping, hotel, and sometimes residential uses. The Galleria, for example, opened in Cobb County in 1981 with an 18-story office building, a 500-room hotel, and a mall. Plus, the property had space for four more office towers.

Even John Portman and Tom Cousins—two developers who remembered when all the office space was downtown—began developing suburban office projects.

From 1983 to 1987—dubbed "The Golden Years"—Atlanta was absorbing roughly 4.5 million square feet of new office space annually. Developers, of course, built more than that. In 1984 alone, plans were announced to build 48 million square feet of office space and eleven thousand new hotel rooms. With other categories of new commercial construction included, the total investment announced for the year was a staggering $10 billion. When the Chamber of Commerce attempted to list all the projects announced in 1984 it took twelve pages of small print. The next year, 1985, the announced total was $12 billion. Not everything announced was built, of course, and many mixed-use developments were to be built in phases over a number of years, but the tide seemed unstoppable.

Housing starts were just as numerous. In 1983, thirty-nine thousand new housing permits were issued, the most in a decade. Simply servicing the newcomers' need for housing, groceries, and entertainment provided a solid economic base.

Nevertheless, the city's banking industry took a major hit in the 1980s. Ever since the Civil War, Atlanta had taken pride in its banks and its position as the leading financial center in a capital-starved region. In that spirit, the state has signed on to an agreement with other Southeast states in 1985 designed to keep Northern banks out of the region. But the agreement backfired. State law had always forbidden Atlanta's banks to operate on a statewide basis and that rule had limited the assets they could amass. States like Florida and North Carolina allowed statewide branching and so built larger banks. In just a couple of years, old-line Atlanta banks like Citizens & Southern and First Atlanta were quickly acquired, not by Northern banks, but by their regional peers.

Not all the economic news took place in the suburbs. MARTA finally opened its north-south line—north through Midtown and south to West End—in the mid-1980s. John Portman opened the 1,674-room Marriott Marquis hotel downtown in the late 1980s and then set about adding two office towers next door.

A long tradition of newspaper competition ended in 1982 when the staffs of the *Atlanta Constitution* and *Atlanta Journal* combined in a joint operating agreement. The papers maintained separate editorial pages.

◄ **In 1981, Andrew Young was elected to succeed Maynard Jackson as mayor. He worked hard at revitalizing the downtown area, and hatched a plan to rebuild Underground Atlanta as a shopping and entertainment center that would lure suburbanites. Underground reopened in 1989 to a steady stream of visitors.** Photos by Ron Sherman

▶ The 1980s was a decade of torrid population growth for Atlanta. Those who came in search of better jobs and lower costs of living settle mostly in the suburban areas of Cobb, Gwinnett, and the northern parts of Fulton County. By the latter half of the decade, Gwinnett County was a fixture on the lists of the fastest growing counties in the United States.

Photos by Ron Sherman

On the cultural front, the big news was the opening in 1983 of the High Museum, a gleaming white, modernistic design.

Atlanta wooed both Republican and Democratic political conventions for 1988, eventually convincing the Democrats to stage theirs inside The Omni, where they nominated Michael Dukakis.

Robert Woodruff, the man who made Coca-Cola an international powerhouse, died in 1985 at age 95. He had remained active in company affairs into the early 1980s. One of this last acts of philanthropy was to give Emory University $100 million of Coca-Cola stock in 1979. During the 1980s, the stock price rocketed skyward under CEO Roberto Goizueta, swelling Emory's endowment considerably and making Coca-Cola an even greater international presence.

The 1980s was a decade of growth, energy, and ambition that was reminiscent of the early decades of the century. According to various polls taken during the 1980s, Atlanta was ranked the best place to live in America; the best place to locate a business; the best place to relocate a business; and the best place to do business. Each was an accolade Henry Grady would have admired. ❦

◄ The clearest sign that the population was moving north was the new development along I-285. Once envisioned as a way to detour trucks outside the city, I-285 soon became a kind of Main Street of the suburbs.
Photo by Ron Sherman

◄ The Chamber of
Commerce, which
celebrated its 125th
birthday in 1985, opened
a computerized marketing
office early in the decade
that provided executives
with instant comparison
on the cost of doing
business in Atlanta and
twenty other cities, in an
effort to draw new
business to the city. Photo
by Ron Sherman

◄ In 1982, the staffs of the
Atlanta Journal and
Atlanta Constitution
combined in a joint
operating agreement.
Photo by Ron Sherman

◄ From 1983-1987—
dubbed "The Golden
Years"—Atlanta was
absorbing roughly 4.5
million square feet of
new office space annually.
Photos by Ron Sherman

◄ Concerns about suburban
sprawl and longer com-
mutes sparked a boom in
new housing downtown
and inside I-285, giving
a boost to the city popu-
lation. Photos by Ron
Sherman

◄ **In 1983, thirty-nine thousand new housing permits were issued, the most in a decade.** Photos by Ron Sherman

▶ On the cultural front, the big news was the opening in 1983 of the High Museum, a gleaming white, modernistic design in Midtown, just next door to the Woodruff Arts Center.
Photos by Ron Sherman

Hilton Atlanta
Northwest/Windy Hill

► Even though the hotel has undergone several changes over time, the Hilton Atlanta Northwest/Windy Hill has remained a popular Cobb hangout almost from the day it was built in 1980.

The hotel underwent its most recent renovation in 1999. At a cost of $4 million, the 222-room hotel transformed into a marbleized, upscale rendition of Hilton splendor. A two-floor concierge level now pampers the individual business traveler and the discriminating tourist. Secure and private, the concierge level provides a separate lounge with food, drinks, room to socialize, and open and spacious meeting areas complete with boardroom tables. There are also special floors and rooms for Hilton Honors guests with upscale amenities.

Guests are treated to oversized rooms with a choice of two double beds, a king bed, or one of three lovely suites. All rooms feature in-room coffeemakers, computer data ports, irons and ironing boards, in room amenities, two phone lines, and complimentary HBO and ESPN.

In the public area downstairs, a new upscale bar and restaurant satisfies even the most demanding palates. A new business center offers all the known technological advances and services of the new millennium and caters to both the individual business traveler and groups. The Hilton Atlanta Northwest/Windy Hill also has its own in-house, full-service audiovisual company. Its function is to provide equipment, along with some videography and editing services, to guests of the hotel. Everything from flip charts and slide projectors and production, to LCD panels and power point presentations are available, allowing guests or meeting groups to make last-minute changes to their own presentations or construct new presentations while the meetings are in progress. The video company is a pleasant plus to wedding parties, business groups, and family reunions, and a unique feature of the hotel.

A postmodern health facility completes the total pamper package for guests. Inside is Nautilus™ equipment, cardiovascular equipment, a whirlpool, an indoor heated pool, and other world-class

Even though the hotel has undergone several changes over time, the Hilton Atlanta Northwest/Windy Hill has remained a popular Cobb hangout almost from the day it was built in 1980. The area known as the Sweetwaters Conference Center today was the lounge area then, and it was definitely the place to be seen and a regular stop for locals and travelers in search of lighthearted fun.

Today, the hotel is renowned for its social bashes. From its extravagant holiday brunches on Thanksgiving, Christmas, and Mother's Day, to its fabulous New Year's parties, elegant weddings, and fantastic weekend events, the Hilton Atlanta Northwest/Windy Hill is still very much a "happenin' place." With 11,000 square feet of meeting space, there is plenty of room for everything from a conventioneer's celebration and a socialite's wedding to corporate training sessions and an intimate gathering for a family reunion. Regardless of the size or type of event, the Hilton easily accommodates them all with equal aplomb.

► With 11,000 square feet of meeting space, there is plenty of room for everything from a conventioneer's celebration and a socialite's wedding to corporate training sessions and an intimate gathering for a family reunion.

amenities. The hotel has an outdoor pool, as well, so that guests can cool off or enjoy the outdoors in the spring and summer.

In all its grandeur, the Hilton Atlanta Northwest/Windy Hill is also a reflection of historic Marietta and Kennesaw. Many of the meeting rooms carry the names of figures, places, and events of local historic significance. Other items from photographs and paintings to the occasional artifact add to the atmosphere of a glorious past and fond memories.

The hotel is also a popular tourist stop and buses are welcomed. Conveniently located just north of the I-75 and I-285 interchange, the hotel is in the northwest section of Atlanta, home of the 1996 Olympic Games, and just five minutes from the Galleria Convention Center, Cumberland Mall, and all of Atlanta's progressive business centers. Downtown Atlanta is only 15 minutes away; the airport is less than 30 minutes from the hotel. Guests at Hilton Atlanta Northwest/Windy Hill are mere minutes from White Water Park, Six Flags, and Stone Mountain. Complimentary shuttle service within a five-mile radius of the hotel is provided for the convenience of guests.

The Hilton Family Plan is an added attraction to individual business travelers, groups, and tourists alike. Under the plan, there is no charge for children, regardless of age, when they occupy the same room as their parents.

Regardless of whether guests stay at the Hilton for business or pleasure, the hotel is dedicated to pampering guests in the style and comfort that has become the Hilton chain's trademark. Guest satisfaction is the sole focus, as the Hilton Atlanta Northwest/Windy Hill seeks to live up to the word "hospitality" in its truest and broadest sense. ❦

◄ Guests are treated to oversized rooms with a choice of two double beds, a king bed, or one of three lovely suites.

◄ Regardless of the size or type of event, the Hilton easily accommodates them all with equal aplomb.

Hunton & Williams

Founded in Richmond, Virginia, in 1901, Hunton & Williams is an international law firm and among the largest in the United States. The firm employs 650 lawyers in 10 U.S. offices, including New York, Washington, Atlanta, and Miami. Overseas, Hunton & Williams lawyers serve clients in London, Hong Kong, Bangkok, Islamabad, Warsaw, Brussels, and Vienna and in more than 80 countries on six continents in all major practice areas. As one of the largest law firms based primarily in the Southeastern United States and the only Southeastern law firm with offices in New York, Washington, and overseas, Hunton & Williams' practice is as diverse as it is sophisticated.

Hunton & Williams' lawyers come from nearly every state and several foreign countries. They are graduates from over 65 law schools—both domestic and abroad—and hold undergraduate and graduate degrees from over 100 colleges and universities. Collectively, they speak more than a dozen languages and are intimately familiar with international business customs. The firm's practice knows few geographic boundaries.

▲ C. L. "Mike" Wagner Jr. is the founding executive and managing partner of the Atlanta office of Hunton & Williams.

Communication among the various offices is facilitated by state-of-the-art technology. Lawyers communicate with one another through firm-wide telephone, electronic mail, and computerized document retrieval and transmission networks. The firm's Internet page is located on the Web at www.hunton.com.

Established in Atlanta in November of 1988, Hunton & Williams' Atlanta office provides legal services in major practice areas, including general corporate matters and corporate finance, both domestic and international; technology-related matters; environmental regulation; labor and employment; tax and employee benefits; real estate; banking; litigation; municipal finance; and health care. The Atlanta office performs significant legal work for numerous public and private companies, including regulated utilities, banks, transportation and delivery service companies, agricultural companies, chemical producers, and machinery manufacturers. The office also performs significant work for governmental agencies and individuals with significant legal needs.

The practice is organized into several distinct but interrelated teams. Each of the firm's lawyers practices on one of these teams and specializes in one or more areas of the law.

The Atlanta finance practice includes the representation of banks and other financial institutions making unsecured and asset-based commercial loans of all varieties, including syndicated and single lender Leveraged Buy-Out (LBO), Managed Buy-Out (MBO), going private, and other acquisition loans, term loans, working capital loans, subordinated loans, and real estate loans. The firm also represents clients making venture capital investments, and has extensive experience in representing financial institutions in loan restructurings and workouts. In addition, the firm counsels several leading foreign banks on U.S. banking regulations and assists them in their commercial lending activities.

An Atlanta team specializes in domestic and multinational commercial arrangements, transactions, and financings for technology product and services businesses, and in information and technology support systems and services for general business operations. The firm is general counsel to several public and private companies in the electronic commerce, Internet access and content, wide and local area network services, on-line information, and software industries. Hunton & Williams is also engaged by the information and technology services departments of several Fortune 500 companies in the on-line services, lodging, and transportation industries.

Corporate lawyers specialize in the increasingly complex areas of corporate structure, finance, venture capital funding, acquisitions, mergers, divestitures, and compliance with securities laws. The firm has acted as issuer's or underwriter's counsel on public offerings of equity and debt. The firm's lawyers have expertise in both federal and state securities laws; work in this area has included providing advice on compliance with the requirements for registration and availability of exemptions from the registration process, proxy statements, annual report and financial disclosure obligations, insider trading rules, resale of restricted securities under Rule 144 and otherwise, issuer stock repurchase programs, and reporting requirements.

The Atlanta office environmental practice complements the firm's environmental practice, which is among the most substantial in the world. Hunton & Williams has developed a strong and dynamic practice with the Environmental Protection Agency's Southeastern Regional Office in Atlanta–EPA Region IV. The firm's experience includes cases brought by EPA Region IV under all major federal environmental statutes in all eight states in Region IV. The firm is also actively involved in every other aspect of environmental law, including permitting proceedings, providing compliance advice and audits, assisting in corporate finance and real estate transactions, appearing before administrative tribunals, defending criminal enforcement activities, participating in rule making, and assisting the litigation practice group in civil litigation and contested cases in federal and state courts.

The Atlanta office also provides a wide range of legal services to foreign companies and individuals doing or seeking to do business within the United States. The firm also assists U.S. companies doing business abroad, particularly in Europe and Asia, on acquisitions, product distribution, technology transfers, and investments. In the Atlanta office alone, there are lawyers who are fluent in Japanese, French, Russian, and Spanish, and firm-wide resources include fluency in every commercially significant world language.

The firm is also fluent in the language of local and state government. The legislative and government affairs practice in Atlanta has worked with and represented clients before the City of Atlanta, Fulton and DeKalb Counties, and the State of Georgia. These activities include legislative monitoring, as well as working with individual legislators on specific issues.

In the practice areas of health care and labor and employment, Hunton & Williams covers the entire spectrum of issues with an emphasis on preventive measures where possible and litigation support services otherwise. Hunton & Williams' litigation practice in Atlanta is multifaceted and provides a wide array of services in complex litigation. The hallmark of the practice is its diversity and ability to handle lawsuits of all types and magnitudes. Whenever necessary, the Atlanta litigation practice draws upon the staffing resources of the firm's more than 175-member Litigation Team, including six fellows of the American College of Trial Lawyers.

The Outsourcing, Public Finance, Real Estate, and Tax and ERISA practice groups in the Atlanta office complete the circle of services needed the most by businesses and individuals in the commercial world. All practice areas are constantly evolving in order to maintain the expertise necessary to meet clients' future needs.

Service to clients is foremost for Hunton & Williams' lawyers, but they also have lives outside the office and are engaged in a wide variety of individual endeavors. The lawyers have served as presidents of national, state, and local bar associations and have chaired important sections and committees of those associations. One of the firm's former partners was president of the American Bar Association, and several have been chairmen of ABA Sections.

Former members of the firm include a retired justice of the United States Supreme Court, a former state governor now serving in the United States Senate, a former university president, the dean of a major law school, and a federal district judge.

Current members of the firm include a former United States ambassador, former governor and attorney general of Virginia, a

◀ Kevin A. Ross is the former managing partner of the Atlanta office of Hunton & Williams.

partner who returned to Hunton & Williams after serving as the first black justice of the Supreme Court of Virginia, a former minority leader of the United States House of Representatives, and a former senior United States District Judge for the Eastern District of Virginia.

Current and former partners and counsel also have served in the management of corporations, including AT&T Technologies, Best Products, Dominion Resources, Ethyl Corporation, General Electric, Long Island Lighting Company, Philip Morris, and Tredegar Industries.

The firm encourages affiliation with cultural and academic institutions. Partners and counsel have served on the boards of art museums, symphonies, and theater groups, and the former president of Washington and Lee University is now at the firm. Hunton & Williams' lawyers have taught in law schools and colleges, and are regularly published as experts on a variety of legal and nonlegal topics. They also serve on the boards of a number of colleges and universities. ❧

Spencer Stuart, Executive Search Consultants

For Spencer Stuart, one of the world's leading retained executive search firms, the city of Atlanta in the twenty-first century is a dynamic place to be. The city's steady economic strength is recognized globally; it is home to more than a dozen Fortune 500 companies and has been ranked as among the best American cities in which to conduct business.

When Spencer Stuart opened its Southeast office in Atlanta in 1981, the city's growth was only beginning. As an emerging city, it was a natural location for the Chicago-based firm, which already had 22 offices globally and domestically. After all, Atlanta was a burgeoning business center and was ready for representation by a top-notch global search firm.

Before locating in Atlanta, Spencer Stuart—led by founder Spencer R. Stuart—had been conducting executive searches for companies with offices all over the world. Beginning in 1956, the firm's search assignments had taken the staff to nearly 30 countries in just two years, and the company had identified qualified executives for top management positions among Danes, Swiss, Germans, English, French, and Italians, as well as Americans and Latin Americans. Spencer Stuart's initial clients were mostly American corporations in pharmaceuticals, cosmetics, food, machinery, construction equipment, and banking.

Spencer Stuart eventually opened offices in London, New York, Zurich, and Mexico City, and over the next decade, the firm expanded its network of offices into Frankfurt, Paris, Dusseldorf, Brussels, and Sydney. It now has 50 offices in 24 countries worldwide—throughout Asia, the Americas, and Europe—and conducts more than 4,000 executive searches annually.

In addition to recruiting top level executives across all industry and functional areas, Spencer Stuart also has a well-established practice dedicated to the selection of nonexecutive directors for corporate boards. Spencer Stuart's boardroom clients now range in size from worldwide multibillion-dollar companies to high-potential start-ups.

In the Southeast, the firm's core industries include aviation, board services, high-tech, consumer goods and services, financial services, and life sciences.

Aviation

Spencer Stuart's Global Aviation Practice is a world leader in the recruitment of senior level executives for airlines, aerospace, airports, and associations. The practice was created to serve the world's leading aviation organizations and has completed more than 250 aviation sector searches over the last decade. In Atlanta, the aviation practice was recently responsible for recruiting the senior management team for Delta Air Lines.

In addition to its corporate aviation sector work, Spencer Stuart's Global Aviation Practice is the firm of choice for leading industry associations such as IOTA, ATA, and ACI. This cross-industry work provides consultants with unmatched access to industry leaders.

High Technology

No industry in the world experiences change at a faster pace than high technology. It follows that every high technology company is unique in size, stage of growth, technical disciplines, strategic objectives, and executive needs. Yet all companies share a stake in the expanding global market and a need for leadership capable of managing the challenges of a new century.

▲ Spencer Stuart has a strong international presence with over 50 offices in 24 countries worldwide staffed with more than 270 of the best-trained and most highly regarded search consultants in the profession. Photo by Daemon.

The partnership has worked. Atlanta's diverse business community and its corporate needs fit perfectly with Spencer Stuart's wide range of practices: expertise that ranges from technology, aviation, and financial services to consumer goods, transportation, logistics, and health care. Since 1981, the firm has secured executive level talent for some of Atlanta's most important companies, including Delta Air Lines, Coca-Cola, Bell South, and EQUIFAX. In addition, some of Spencer Stuart's most exciting work is within the network of Atlanta's young, high-tech start-ups.

Spencer Stuart's high-tech consultants all have previous line operating and/or management consulting experience in a high technology industry. With Atlanta's emerging high-tech community, this practice will continue to be one of the more important as we start the twenty-first century.

Board Services

For more than 20 years, Spencer Stuart has been widely acknowledged as the preeminent search firm for recruiting directors of corporate boards. In 1998, the firm conducted nearly 300 director searches for a diverse group of clients, ranging from established Fortune 500 companies to spin-off companies that are developing boards for the first time.

Spencer Stuart's Board Services Practice is experienced in identifying qualified outside directors as well as providing counsel to chairmen, CEOs, and nominating committees on important board issues. To complement this personal network, Spencer Stuart's Quality Executive Search Tracking (QUEST) system has a Boards Database that contains nearly 8,000 profiles of board member prospects, updated on a daily basis.

Consumer Goods and Services

With nearly 90 search consultants working in 20 countries throughout the world, Spencer Stuart's Consumer Goods & Services Practice has a breadth of experience in the industry that translates into firsthand knowledge of specific markets, an appreciation of individual needs, and timely results. The practice concentrates on key segments of the industry, including consumer durables, consumer marketing services, consumer packaged goods, fashion and apparel, food services and hospitality, and retail.

Executives in today's consumer goods industry face a world of constant change and reinvention. Executives with an awareness and understanding of new marketing formats, the savvy to succeed with fewer resources, and the ability to manage change—both from outside and within a business—will be critical to the success of consumer goods companies. Spencer Stuart's track record is strong with regard to helping clients manage these changes effectively.

Financial Services

Comprising 23 percent of Spencer Stuart's worldwide client base, the Global Financial Services Practice is guided by industry specialists who have conducted more than 2,000 executive searches over the past five years. The practice has placed executives in consumer financial services and retail banking, global securities and wholesale banking, insurance, investment management, and real estate.

Throughout the industry, a trend toward integration has been forcing banks and other financial service businesses to rethink their traditional roles. While an increasing number of mergers continue to transform the competitive landscape, many segments of financial services are evolving to keep pace with a global market. The result is new opportunities are emerging for companies that are flexible and willing to venture into new territory.

Life Sciences/Health Care

Spencer Stuart's Life Sciences Practice is a global leader in the recruitment of senior level executives throughout each sector of the health care industry. These include pharmaceuticals, biotechnology, medical equipment and devices, integrated delivery systems, academic medical centers, managed care organizations, and physician groups.

The Life Sciences Practice consists of 37 consultants worldwide, and has conducted nearly 400 general management and board director searches over the past five years.

Serious corporations now understand that competing for talent is serious business, and that a disciplined approach is necessary in order to identify the best talent available. Spencer Stuart offers a systematic approach to investigating the universe of possibilities available to the companies it serves. ❧

▲ Spencer Stuart believes each search assignment is unique and must be tailored to the specific needs of the client. Photo by Daemon.

◀ Spencer Stuart's Atlanta office opened in 1981. Photo by Daemon.

Compaq Computer Corporation

The company has changed dramatically during the past two years, from a vendor of personal computers to a global IT company offering a broad portfolio of products, services, and solutions. Today, it is an enterprise computing company offering Web-enabled solutions to any company of any size on a global scale—a strategic IT partner with the solutions experience and service capabilities necessary to help customers solve the most complex IT problems. Compaq Services has more than 29,000 service and support professionals around the world and 30,000 service partners.

Compaq is going direct with innovative products for small and medium-sized businesses (SMB). The new family of Prosignia notebooks, desktops, and servers are designed specifically for the SMB market. And now they can be ordered direct from Compaq with leasing options, Internet services, customized services, and reseller support. When customers contact Compaq DirectPlus by telephone or over the Internet, choose the configurations they want, and place an order, the systems can be shipped as fast as the next business day.

▲ Compaq offers the most experience and the broadest range of 64-bit computing products, including Alpha and Intel's soon-to-ship Merced chip.

Back in 1982, Rod Canion, Jim Harris, and Bill Murto sketched the design for the first Compaq personal computer in a Houston pie shop. In its first full year of sales (1983), Compaq shipped 53,000 units of its sole product—the Compaq Portable PC—for revenues of $111 million, a U.S. business record.

Today, Compaq Computer Corporation (www.compaq.com) is the second largest computer company in the world and the largest global supplier of computer systems, developing and marketing hardware, software, solutions, and services. Compaq products are sold and supported in more than 100 countries, and the company ranked 42nd in the 1998 Fortune 500.

Compaq arrived in Atlanta early on, attracted by the metro area's growth potential. The company quickly established locations in Alpharetta, Mansell Road, Powers Ferry, and Galleria, which in 1999 employs a total of 2,400 people to provide sales, support, and service. "Atlanta is a major regional business and transportation hub, and Compaq wanted to establish a significant executive presence here," says Tom Baber, Vice President for the southeastern United States. "Compaq is one of the most dynamic and successful companies around. It's a natural match with Atlanta, one of the most dynamic and fast-growing success stories of the South."

An industry leader in environmentally friendly programs and business practices, Compaq supports community organizations that focus on education, health, social services, and the arts. In 1997 Compaq was awarded the World Environment Center's Gold Medal for International Corporate Environmental Achievement. Compaq also participates in the Green Light and Energy Star Design environmental programs.

► Vice President for the southeastern United States Tom Baber feels Compaq is a natural match with the dynamics of Atlanta.

Compaq is also meeting the needs of large and global companies for high-performance, inter-networked solutions. With the acquisition of Tandem and Digital, Compaq now has 29,000 service and support professionals worldwide, which has expanded its ability to deliver enterprise solutions—from the desktop to the data center.

To help customers find solutions quicker, Compaq introduced an

innovative, Web-based knowledge center called activeAnswers. It draws on the expertise of Compaq and its software partners to deliver the information, tools, and methods needed to plan, deploy, and operate enterprise solutions.

Compaq and Microsoft have begun a joint engineering initiative that will adapt key technologies such as clustering and systems management from Tru64 UNIX, OpenVMS, and Tandem's NonStop Kernel, and incorporate them in future releases of NT. This is important because customers will continue to have mixed environments incorporating Windows NT, UNIX, OpenVMS, NSK, NetWare, and other operating systems. By delivering the best interoperability, Compaq believes customers will get the greatest value out of their existing IT investments.

Compaq pioneered the Internet PC with its unique Presario Internet keyboard, which provides easy access to a wide range of Internet services, and has also introduced the world's first broadband Internet home PC. It is pioneering next generation display technology for the home with the FP-700, 15-inch Digital Flat Panel Display, which delivers unsurpassed brightness and clarity.

Compaq offers the most experience and the broadest range of 64-bit computing products, including Alpha and Intel's soon-to-ship Merced chip. The results are impressive and include the innovative work that animators and digital artists are doing with Compaq's Alpha system. The incredible images and effects in movies like *Titanic* and *What Dreams May Come* both relied on Alpha systems.

Compaq is doing more than providing bright displays and fast modems. It is also working with leading cable and telecommunications companies to make ultrafast Internet access available to everyone. It has implemented a broadband Internet access program called "triple play," because it spans three high-speed communications technologies—cable, DSL, and satellite. It is the most comprehensive partnership strategy to provide U.S. consumers with the widest choice of high-speed connections to the Internet.

Compaq's long-term goal is very simple: to help customers get the most out of computing, from the family that is buying its first PC and venturing out on the Internet for the first time, to the small business that is establishing a storefront on the Web, to the company that is building a global inter-networked enterprise.

The Internet is now the number one reason that consumers buy a home computer. That has changed the way Compaq designs its

PCs—from the easy access Internet buttons on Presario keyboards to high-speed broadband modems. The PC is becoming a window to an ever larger world of communication, information, and entertainment, a new way to explore the world—from the neighborhood scale of local area networks to the planetary scale of the Internet.

Compaq predicts the home will have two advanced digital gateways—a data gateway represented by the PC and ready for the next generation of Internet content and a video gateway prepared for the next wave of entertainment. The availability of broadband access and an integrated home network will encourage the development of new Internet devices designed for a wide variety of uses in the home. Using a home network and the Internet will be as easy as using the telephone today. Compaq expects to be the preferred brand in the networked digital home, helping to make on-demand information, business, and entertainment a way of life. ❧

Blimpie International, Inc.

Back in 1964, Tony Conza and two high school friends had $2,500 in borrowed money and a simple idea—sell sandwiches made the way they would fix them at home. Choose only the finest quality meats, cheeses, and toppings, and pile them high for a fresh, tasty, satisfying sandwich.

Conza looked through the dictionary to find the perfect word to describe his submarine sandwich, something descriptive with a touch of whimsy. He chose BLIMPIE®, a name that is now recognized by nearly half of all consumers. It's a word that reflects both his product's satisfyingly generous shape and his company's winning attitude—take sandwiches seriously, not themselves. This idea was the concept behind the company's national advertising campaign, "BLIMPIE. It's a beautiful thing,™" which is based on the premise that BLIMPIE is passionate about sandwiches, whimsical about life.

Today, BLIMPIE Subs & Salads is the second largest submarine sandwich franchisor with over 2,060 locations in the United States and 13 foreign countries. The company is publicly traded on the American Stock Exchange.

The first BLIMPIE restaurant in Atlanta opened in 1973 on the corner of Roswell and Wieuca Road. The greater Atlanta area is now home to 200 BLIMPIE locations, employing over 1,000 people. BLIMPIE restaurants are everywhere—shopping centers, malls, business districts, suburban communities, colleges, hospitals, sports centers, convenience stores, and free-standing buildings. Cool new ways to grab a BLIMPIE include carts, kiosks, and vending machines.

As the company grew, so did the energy and ideas of its management. In 1984, Blimpie International's franchise support headquarters was born in the back room of Atlanta's Powers Ferry Road BLIMPIE restaurant. The opening of Blimpie International in Atlanta was to help support BLIMPIE franchises across the country. The first office had less than five people. Today, Blimpie International employs almost 100 people in three offices (BI Franchise Support, Maui Tacos International, and Georgia Statewide Development) in Atlanta.

Atlanta is also home to the BLIMPIE Business School, a training school which covers all facets of operating the BLIMPIE Subs & Salads business, such as marketing, accounting, hiring policies and procedures, cash management, customer relations, and other critical business matters. Georgia was, and still is, the most densely populated BLIMPIE area in the U.S. outside of the New York area. With its promising economy and outstanding labor pool, Atlanta was the obvious choice for the location of Blimpie International's franchise support headquarters.

Today, Blimpie International is a family of complementary franchised restaurants and brands, including BLIMPIE Subs & Salads, MAUI TACOS™, PASTA CENTRAL™, and SMOOTHIE ISLAND™.

SMOOTHIE ISLAND offers blended yogurt and fruit drinks, while PASTA CENTRAL offers entrees such as lasagna, Chicken Parmesan, and pizza, plus kids' pasta meals in fun shapes. MAUI TACOS serves Hawaiian-style Mexican fare, including tacos, burritos, and salads. It's all part of Blimpie International's strategic transformation into a corporation with a family of new brands, new structure,

► The first BLIMPIE restaurant in Atlanta opened in 1973 on the corner of Roswell and Wieuca Road. The greater Atlanta area is now home to 200 BLIMPIE locations, employing over 1,000 people.

► MAUI TACOS serves Hawaiian-style Mexican fare, including tacos, burritos, and salads.

new initiatives, new programs, new partners, and new customers. The company also operates the nonedible BI Concept Systems, Inc., a professional design and equipment company in Houston, Texas.

Maui Tacos International, Inc., one of Blimpie International's newest companies, opened the doors to its first MAUI TACOS/SMOOTHIE ISLAND location in August 1998. The Dunwoody restaurant's award-winning design has the casual, laid-back look and feel of a Hawaiian ocean-side shack with an old style VW bus in the wall, surfer boards on the ceiling, a concrete floor, and walls covered in distressed wood. Maui Tacos International plans to develop at least 41 more of these restaurants in the Atlanta area alone over the next seven years. The food, a marriage of charbroiled steak, chicken, and seafood marinated in pineapple, lime, and Hawaiian spices, wrapped up burrito and taco style, was originally created by the MAUI TACOS founder, nationally renowned chef Mark Ellman.

Blimpie International strongly believes in supporting the communities that support it. Since 1992 BLIMPIE Subs & Salads has donated a portion of its drink sales to The Boys & Girls Clubs of America (B&GCA, headquartered in Atlanta) as part of their "Buy a Drink, Build A Link" program. A long-term supporter of the Clubs, Blimpie International CEO, chairman, and founder, Tony Conza, chairs the B&GCA's marketing committee and has recruited the help of other successful companies, such as Nike.

BLIMPIE has committed to donate $500,000 to the B&GCA by the year 2000 through various programs at the national and local levels. On a more personal basis, employees donate their time working with local Atlanta clubs. The company has also set up a trust for employee and franchisee donations. For years, Atlanta employees have raised money and sponsored a festive Holiday Party for a local B&GCA club.

In 1998 Blimpie International announced the BLIMPIE Urban Initiative Leadership Development (BUILD) program. It's a pilot program with the Atlanta Empowerment Zone and the City of Atlanta and part of Blimpie International's strong belief in "Doing Well By Doing Good." The program plans for BLIMPIE Subs & Salads to award 200 franchise agreements with the initial fee of $18,000 waived, and 300 more franchises to be offered at a

◄ BLIMPIE sandwiches are made from the finest quality meats, cheeses, and toppings, and piled high for a fresh, tasty, satisfying sandwich.

substantially reduced fee, to qualified, aspiring applicants in areas designated by the Department of Housing and Urban Development as Empowerment Zones or Enterprise Communities. After the launch of this $7.5-million pilot program in Atlanta, the program will be expanded to Detroit before it is rolled out across the United States. In June of 1998, Tony Conza participated with other top business leaders in a forum led by Vice President Al Gore to discuss these new private-public sector initiatives in urban areas. "It's truly a 'win-win' situation. Atlanta wins, future entrepreneurs win, and we win," says CEO Tony Conza. "With our franchise support office based in Atlanta, we feel like this city is our second home. And given Atlanta's long history of community service and corporate and individual volunteerism, we are proud to announce that our first franchises through this program will be established here." Conza adds, "When it comes to BLIMPIE, 'It's Atlanta!' " ❂

Sanderson Industries, Inc.

▶ The firm supplies stamped metal components for both passenger and commercial vehicles. Ford Motor Co., General Motors Corp., Ogihara America Corp., Tower Automotive, and Magna are their primary customers.

▶ Sanderson Industries is one of the major contract manufacturers of stamped metal products and related assemblies in the Southeast.

Sanderson Industries is one of the major contract manufacturers of stamped metal products and related assemblies in the Southeast. Minority-owned and operated, it is headed by founder and Chairman/Chief Executive Officer Walter Sanderson and his son Rory Sanderson, who is president.

The firm supplies stamped metal components for both passenger and commercial vehicles. Ford Motor Co., General Motors Corp., Ogihara America Corp., Tower Automotive, and Magna are their primary customers. Sanderson ships its merchandise all over the United States, as well as to Mexico and Canada. The firm is becoming more international as it is entering the South American and European markets.

In addition to its high-volume manufacturing abilities, the company is a full-service supplier, complete with a CAD engineering office that is capable of providing rapid documentation on designs and feasibility agendas.

The firm's relationship with Ford goes back 35 years to when the company was first founded in Chicago in 1965. In 1989, Sanderson Industries received Ford's prestigious Q1 Quality Achievement Award. In 1998, it also achieved the globally recognized QS900 certification.

Walter Sanderson attributes his firm's success and growth to the philosophy of never-ending improvement. He explains, "This philosophy is a way of doing business at Sanderson Industries. A further

overview can be achieved by examination of our product and service enhancements resulting from our 'continuous improvement management system' (CIMS). At the same time, these achievements are supported by consistent quality and service improvements to our customers while continuing to strengthen our operations and management teams. We presently have a comprehensive training program for all employees and thereby a reinforcement to the never-ending improvement philosophy."

The firm is especially known for its ability to improve quality through the application of statistical methods that focus on defect prevention rather than detection. By reducing the need for redundant testing, inspection, product rework, and material scrappage, productivity and quality are increased. Sanderson notes, "It is our belief that today's highly competitive markets and ever-changing demands for quality and service are signs of a progressive move toward world competition. Our commitment to our customers and ourselves is to produce products that not only meet all the requirements of our customers, but exceed them. Our goals are high, and our intentions are clear—to develop the best quality parts available today."

Sanderson got his start in the industry at the age of 10, when he swept floors in a Fulton, Missouri, machine shop. By the time he was 12, he had more responsibility and earned $12 a week. Sanderson studied mechanical art at Lincoln University in Jefferson City, Missouri, and worked at several manufacturing facilities after graduation until he opened his own plant in Chicago in 1965 with

board anymore—it's all CAD. We send a disc to our vendors and it's pure math data, no blueprints," Sanderson says. "This has happened in the last five years."

Sanderson Industries works closely with the Atlanta community, mentoring students in the Fulton County Boys Association. Involved for a forth year with the Ford Academy of Manufacturing Science (FAMS), Sanderson Industries works with Therrell High School, offering student interns exposure to real-world skills that include project management, computer presentations, industrial maths and sciences, and some of the hottest CAD technologies. "Manufacturing, especially metal stamping and fabrication, is a tremendous career opportunity for young people," Sanderson says. ◗

◀ The Atlanta facility, which ships over 30 million parts a year, operates in two 70,000-square-foot buildings and employs over 175 people.

$25,000 in savings. The company made speakers and other parts for the radio and TV industry. By the end of his first year, the firm had sales of $450,000 and 12 employees. By 1968, the company purchased a larger facility and began producing parts for the telephone industry, as well as parts for Ford's plant in Chicago Heights. The firm was also contracted to produce parts for the National Accelerator Laboratory, now known as Fermilab.

The firm needed additional space again in 1983 because of its growth, at which point Sanderson decided to relocate to another state. After meeting Mayor Maynard Jackson and being courted by officials of the Atlanta Economic Development Corporation, Sanderson chose to relocate to Atlanta in 1985. "Atlanta offered us the best deal and incentives," explains Sanderson. He adds, "The enterprise zone at Atlanta Industrial Park gave us tax relief for the first five years, and our location off of I-285 is good for trucking. Also, I do not miss the weather in Chicago."

The Atlanta facility, which ships over 30 million parts a year, operates in two 70,000-square-foot buildings and employs over 175 people. The company is growing at a rate exceeding 15 percent annually. For this facility to maintain and repair its production tooling, it has a staff of expert tool and die makers and a well-equipped tool shop. Having these facilities in its plant helps to ensure minimum production time loss because of die maintenance.

A full-service supplier, Sanderson has design capability. "We take the client's concept and make it more feasible to manufacture," Sanderson says. Using the latest computer technology, including electronic data interchange (EDI) and computer-aided design (CAD), the company downloads math data directly, eliminating the need for hard-copy drawings in their quoting. "There's no drawing

◀ The firm is especially known for its ability to improve quality through the application of statistical methods that focus on defect prevention rather than detection.

Hartsfield International Airport

▲ **Hartsfield International Airport, 10 miles from downtown Atlanta, covers 3,750 acres. More than 200,000 people, enough to fill the Georgia Dome three times over, pass through Hartsfield daily. Photo by Ron Sherman.**

an option to purchase the land outright for $100,000 (which the city did in 1930). Doug Davis, an aviator, brainstormer, and early Atlanta airport proponent, constructed the first fixed-operation center on airport grounds in 1927.

Today, Hartsfield International Airport, 10 miles from downtown Atlanta, covers 3,750 acres. The Terminal Buildings, Concourses T, A, B, C, D, and the new International Concourse E cover 5.7 million square feet. Within these concourses are 24 international and 146 domestic gates, all connected by a 3.5-mile underground people mover transit system. More than 200,000 people, enough to fill the Georgia Dome three times over, pass through Hartsfield daily.

Hartsfield's airport operation revenues come from landing fees, concession revenues, parking fees, and building and land rentals. The airport is considered to be the largest employment center in the state of Georgia.

Concourse E opened on September 21, 1994. This $300-million investment gave Hartsfield the largest single international concourse in North America. Of the 30 airlines that serve the airport, 14 are international carriers, and each day 103 international flights serve 40 cities in 32 foreign countries.

In the past two years, five new foreign carriers began service to Atlanta, making airlines like Austrian and LAPA as at home here as the more familiar Delta, AirTran, and TWA.

In the summer of 1996, when Atlanta hosted the Centennial Olympic Games, Hartsfield was ready with the largest passenger terminal complex in the world. With a single connection, an international traveler could reach Atlanta from almost anywhere in the world.

Twenty-five all-cargo airlines serve Atlanta, and international air cargo is the fastest growing activity at the airport. With cargo traffic expected to increase by more than nine percent a year, Hartsfield has developed a new 400,000-square-foot south cargo complex, which opened in 1998. It adds one million square feet of airport parking ramps and four 100,000-square-foot buildings. A new runway is under construction, while additional terminals, concourses, expanded parking, and ground transportation access are being proposed.

Hartsfield International Airport was named Best Airport in North America by *Business Traveler International* magazine for the ninth consecutive year in 1997. And in 1998, 73.5 million passengers came through Hartsfield, making it the world's busiest airport. Thanks to Hartsfield, Atlanta has become the financial and commercial capital of the Southeast, a flourishing high-tech industrial center, and one of the three leading conference and meeting sites in the nation. ❧

Since the day a railroad man drove a stake into the ground to mark the site of a transportation hub, the future city of Atlanta was destined to be a center of commerce. With the invention of the airplane, the sky became the limit for the city's economic growth and vitality.

In 1923 William Berry Hartsfield proposed the site of the city's first permanent landing strip, an abandoned race track outside of Hapeville called Candler Field and owned by Coca-Cola magnate Asa Candler. Two years later, the city committed to a five-year, rent-free lease to develop the 287 acres into a crude airfield, with

◄Within the concourses are 24 international and 146 domestic gates, all connected by a 3.5-mile underground people mover transit system. Photo by Ron Sherman.

◄Hartsfield International Airport was named Best Airport in North America by *Business Traveler International* magazine for the ninth consecutive year in 1997. Photo by Ron Sherman.

◄ (Far left) In 1996, when Atlanta hosted the Centennial Olympic Games, Hartsfield was ready with the largest passenger terminal complex in the world. With a single connection, an international traveler could reach Atlanta from almost anywhere in the world. Photo by Ron Sherman.

◄Hartsfield's airport operation revenues come from landing fees, concession revenues, parking fees, and building and land rentals. The airport is considered to be the largest employment center in the state of Georgia. Photo by Ron Sherman.

FINOVA Capital Corporation

The FINOVA Group Inc., through its principal operating subsidiary FINOVA Capital Corporation, is one of the largest and most successful financial services companies in the United States serving midsize businesses. FINOVA's name derives from its people, the "financial innovators" who apply their expertise and knowledge in specific industries and products to tailor effective financial solutions for customers.

FINOVA's strategic focus is to serve the middle market with a broad range of financing products within three complementary business groups—Commercial Finance, Specialty Finance, and Capital Markets. This niche orientation enables FINOVA to provide "one-stop" financing to customers whose businesses span a wide range of industries and continues to win FINOVA recognition as The Capital Source for Midsize Business℠.

Headquartered in Phoenix with business development offices throughout the United States and in London, United Kingdom, and Toronto, Canada, FINOVA serves midsize businesses in several focused market niches. This niche orientation enables FINOVA to provide a variety of innovative financing and capital markets products, generally ranging in size from $500,000 to $35 million.

FINOVA's history goes back more than four decades. During most of that time, the company operated as Greyhound Financial, the equipment-leasing subsidiary of the Dial Corp. In March 1992 Dial spun off Greyhound Financial to its shareowners as an independent New York Stock Exchange Company known then as GFC Financial Corp. In 1995 the Phoenix-based company adopted its current name, The FINOVA Group, Inc., and deemed its principal operating subsidiary FINOVA Capital Corporation.

Strategic acquisitions have played a significant role in diversifying FINOVA's product offering and enhancing financial performance. From 1992 through mid-1999, FINOVA completed 13 acquisitions, each of which has broadened the company's product offering, added critical mass to existing businesses, and/or increased FINOVA's geographic reach. FINOVA will continue to pursue strategic acquisitions throughout 1999 and well into the millennium.

FINOVA's Atlanta office was initially founded in 1976 under the name TriCon Capital. At that time the company generated small-ticket leases up to $1 million. In 1994 FINOVA acquired TriCon Capital and the company evolved into a full-service financial provider to the commercial marketplace. Today, FINOVA's growing Atlanta operation consists of approximately 25 employees based in two Atlanta offices.

FINOVA employees in these offices provide expertise in the following areas:

Business Credit—collateral-oriented revolving credit facilities and term loans for manufacturers, distributors, wholesalers, and service companies.

Commercial Equipment Finance—equipment leases, loans, and turnkey financing to a broad range of midsize companies.

▲ FINOVA's strategic focus is to serve the middle market with a broad range of financing products. This niche orientation enables FINOVA to provide "one-stop" financing to customers whose businesses span a wide range of industries.

► FINOVA's name derives from its people, the "financial innovators" who apply their expertise and knowledge in specific industries and products to tailor effective financial solutions for customers.

Specialty markets include the supermarket industry, corporate aircraft, and emerging growth technology industries.

Corporate Finance—full range of cash-flow oriented and asset-based term and revolving loan products for manufacturers, wholesalers, distributors, specialty retailers, commercial, and consumer businesses.

Health Care Finance—full range of account receivables, real estate, and equipment financing products for the U.S. health care industry.

Distribution and Channel Finance—financing for manufacturers, distributors, value-added resellers, system integrators, retailers, and dealers for the computer and telecommunication industries. Products range from interest-free inventory financing and extended payment programs to accounts receivable financing and term loans.

Rediscount Finance—revolving credit facilities to the independent consumer finance industry, including sales, automobile, mortgage, and premium finance companies.

Realty Capital—commercial mortgage lending and mortgage banking services for all major property types nationwide.

In addition to going above and beyond the norm for its customers, FINOVA is also strongly committed to supporting the communities in which its employees live and work. Through its national Care & Share Program, FINOVA provides significant charitable donations, and employees devote countless volunteer

hours to nonprofit organizations. In Atlanta, Care & Share volunteers have participated in numerous community projects, such as the Salvation Army Angel Tree Program, Special Olympics, and Atlanta AIDS Walk.

FINOVA was recently honored by *Fortune* magazine as one of the "Best 100 Companies to Work for in America." FINOVA debuted on *Fortune's* 1999 list at number 12 for the many innovative benefits and incentives the company provides for employees, such as a college tuition program for children of employees known as the Future Leaders Grant Program. FINOVA also partners with The University of Arizona to sponsor The FINOVA Institute, a mini-MBA program design to educate employees—at every level in the company—about the financial industry. The company also provides stock-option grants to every employee in the company, not just for senior management or executives, and offers employees an on-site concierge service.

Looking ahead, FINOVA will strive to continually expand its services and presence—locally in Atlanta, as well as on a national and international level, to meet the ever-changing financing needs of midsize businesses. ❧

◄ FINOVA's growing Atlanta operation consists of approximately 25 employees based in two Atlanta offices. Receptionist Cora White greets customers with a smile.

◄ George Saintignan of Rediscount Finance provides revolving credit facilities to the independent consumer finance industry, including sales, automobile, mortgage, and premium finance companies.

The Buckhead Coalition

This is a story about a mixed-use community in north Atlanta serviced by one of Georgia's most powerful and prestigious business organizations, a community that started as a small but loyal gathering around a local tavern over 150 years ago. The business was owned by an "outsider," a man from South Carolina named Henry Irby. The area got its name from a hunting trophy that hung over the front door. The place has been called Buckhead ever since.

Much has changed since those early days. Buckhead is even an official part of Atlanta now. It has been for quite some time. But the one thing that hasn't changed is the sense of community, an almost tangible feeling of a unique collective identity. In a day and age where the new millennium is here and neighbors no longer feel like neighbors, Buckhead may be one of the only neighborly niches left in the country.

Not that there's anything quaint or old-fashioned about the place. Quite the opposite. Buckhead sports some of the world's finest dining, celebrity hang-outs, multimillion-dollar houses and condos, sophisticated shopping, and high-tech gurus—in fact, all that is trendy is not only present in Buckhead, but it was also probably here first. Among all this money, pricey real estate, and worldly connections lies the heartbeat of power. Its name is the Buckhead Coalition, but it uses its power mostly to distribute empowerment.

The Buckhead Coalition, like the community itself, is a different kind of animal. It is part Chamber, part Town Hall, part Convention and Visitors Bureau, and yet none of these. It responds to the public but operates privately. Its members are 75 chief executive officers of the area's major firms having a pronounced commitment to the community. Membership fees are $5,000 annually, with additional thousands required as are needed to complete community projects. Money alone won't buy a membership though; this affiliation is by invitation only.

There's enough power in the board room to wield dictates in several major cities around the globe—simultaneously. Yet the group focuses on traffic, parking, public defibrillators, 911 call boxes, combining police and security forces, and supporting arts and charity organizations. In other words, the Coalition is a bunch of neighbors looking out for neighbors.

The Coalition even persuaded other business property owners to join them in a self-taxation program through a Community Improvement District to fund even more improvements. It seems there is nothing they won't do to help out the neighborhood.

No wonder Buckhead is such a popular place. Though trendy, it isn't plastic. Roots and emotions run deep in this section of town where the people so closely identify with one another that they even have their own separate BellSouth business phone book.

Buckhead has often been called Atlanta's second downtown. It provides for almost half of Atlanta's property taxes, the bulk of Atlanta's retail receipts, and most of the job growth. Buckhead isn't competing with the remaining city. Quite the opposite, it's proud to be a part of metro Atlanta. Though a Buckhead address is exclusive, the attitude here is not. The Coalition works diligently and in good faith with governments, associations, and other groups outside of Buckhead.

Atlanta will continue to grow, but even so, Buckhead will always be Buckhead. The sense of community will remain forever a part of the personal identity of those who live there. The words engraved upon their hearts? There's no place like home. ◑

Holder Properties

By all accounts, Atlanta is the economic engine of the southeastern United States. From the inner city to outside of the perimeter highway, growth and change are constants. New corporations are forming, older ones are merging, and others are moving in almost daily. Atlanta is the place to be, the place to play, and the place to prosper. But where in all the hustle and bustle is the right location for any given company in a city as diverse as humankind, with goods and services as plentiful as the air itself?

▲ Holder Properties is actively involved in developing single tenant build-to-suit projects for corporate clients and multiple tenant projects including Prominence in Buckhead, which opened in July 1999.

► Committed to being the premier provider of real estate development and management services. Holder Properties provides the highest quality and value while ensuring the maximum benefit to its investors and clients. An example of this fine work is National Service Industries' headquarters in midtown Atlanta. Photo by Rion Rizzo.

Committed to being the premier provider of real estate development and management services, Holder Properties provides the highest quality and value while ensuring the maximum benefit to its investors and clients. Holder Properties is a local favorite in identifying the right address for many corporate clients. The company's services include feasibility studies, site selection, master planning, land acquisition, zoning coordination, design coordination, development management, debt and equity financing, marketing, leasing, and property and asset management. Holder Properties is actively involved in developing single tenant build-to-suit projects for corporate clients and multiple tenant projects for its own portfolio.

Founded in 1980 and based in Atlanta, Holder Properties offers unique advantages beginning with its privately held status, which, combined with strong equity partners, provides uncommon transaction flexibility. Financial partners include Morgan Stanley Dean Witter, Equity Office Properties Trust, and Westbrook Partners, among others. Corporate clients of the real estate firm also read like a who's who list: Equifax, Wachovia Bank, Turner Broadcasting System, State Farm Insurance, McKessonHBOC, Ryder System Inc., E*TRADE, and MCI WorldCom, among many others.

Beyond its financial stability, reputation, and transaction flexibility, the Holder Properties' advantage is in its in-house expertise and experience earned from successfully developing over 6 million square feet of commercial space in more than 30 buildings, leasing over 1.2 million square feet of office space, and managing more than 2.5 million square feet of commercial space while serving over 250 tenants. Combined with the size and strength of Holder Construction Company, a sister company founded in 1960 and ranked as one of the 100 largest general contractors in the United States, Holder Properties provides the complete spectrum of services needed to develop, lease, and manage commercial real estate efficiently, cost-effectively, and quickly. No other Southeastern developer offers all of these benefits.

Holder Properties employs experts with years of experience in the various real estate fields from civil engineers to architects, landscape architects, construction managers, CPAs, real estate brokers, appraisers, property managers, and market researchers. The team approach addresses the complete real estate life cycle from project conception and feasibility, development and construction, through occupancy and start-up, to ownership and property management. The result is that clients can focus on their primary line of business, while the experts at Holder Properties focus on providing outstanding real estate services and first-rate developments. ❧

AirTouch

Remember what life was like before cell phones? Today, people depend on them more than ever before, not only for business-related purposes, but for life in general.

AirTouch Communications has more than 17 million customers who enjoy the company's high level of wireless service and technology in cellular, paging, and personal communications, and in the near future, global satellite communications.

In the United States alone, AirTouch's cellular and PCS footprint now covers cities in 25 states, reaching a total of 145 million people—over half the U.S. population.

AirTouch Cellular of Georgia, one of the first two companies to offer cellular service in Atlanta, launched its service in February 1987. Today, the company's service spans an extensive coverage area of more than 20,000 square miles throughout 33 counties in Georgia, including metropolitan Atlanta, Cartersville, Hartwell, Madison, Rome, and Washington. AirTouch has the characteristics of the Atlanta area itself—young and energetic, fast-growing and cutting-edge, service-oriented and caring. It is a company that is enormously proud of its people and its community.

The company continues its leadership position, offering superior quality wireless services and products, including AirTouch Digital Service, Prepaid Cellular, Voice Mail, Caller ID, Digital Text Messaging, Mobile to Mobile Calling, National Calling Plan, and Roadside Assistance.

Communication is about more than just price plans and technology. What differentiates AirTouch from its competition is the

company's exceptional level of customer service. It promises "live" customer service 24 hours a day, seven days a week. In addition to taking customers' problems off their hands the first time they call, AirTouch promises to provide a credit for the interruption if a call is dropped. Other customer service features unique to AirTouch include free customer service anywhere in the United States and the flexibility to change to any qualifying plan at any time.

Tim Driscoll, AirTouch Director of the Year in 1997, is Vice President of Sales and Service for AirTouch Cellular of Georgia, one of the top three cellular markets in the country. Driscoll, who lives in Alpharetta with his family, is responsible for the more than 550 AirTouch employees working throughout north Georgia.

AirTouch has built a talented and diverse workforce, and the area's growing position as a new technology center will enable AirTouch to continue its locally based recruitment. In addition to working hard and serving the needs of their customers, the AirTouch people bring their spirit and knowledge into their neighborhoods, offering hundreds of hours of volunteer time in schools, parks, homeless shelters, and in houses of worship.

Through the AirTouch Communications Foundation, the company has made significant annual contributions to the United Negro College Fund, the United Way, and Hands on Atlanta. Additionally, AirTouch is a proud sponsor of WSB's Family2Family program. Spearheaded by the Atlanta-area ABC television affiliate, this year-long community affairs initiative supports numerous family-oriented projects throughout the Atlanta region.

At the forefront of the wireless revolution in communication, AirTouch has successfully balanced growth, profitability, and customer satisfaction. On January 15, 1999, AirTouch and Vodafone Group Plc announced a definitive agreement to merge. The transaction, which closed June 30, 1999, created a global wireless powerhouse with a combined market capitalization of about $110 billion that reaches nearly one billion people in 23 countries on four continents. Serving more than 23 million cellular and PCS customers, Vodafone AirTouch is the largest wireless company in the world. ◐

◄ AirTouch hosts an annual "Take Our Children to Work Day" and provides creative activties such as a design contest where children get to create their own version of a cellular tower.

◄ AirTouch Cellular of Georgia's service spans an extensive coverage area of more than 20,000 square miles throughout 33 counties in Georgia, including metropolitan Atlanta, Cartersville, Hartwell, Madison, Rome, and Washington.

Noro-Moseley Partners

One of Atlanta's oldest venture capital firms, Noro-Moseley Partners, has helped promising Southern entrepreneurs grow their businesses since 1983. NMP finds, acquires, and manages investments in a number of private, diversified growth companies. Ninety percent of NMP's investments are in the Southeast, and over half are located in the metro Atlanta area, where the partners have extensive experience and contacts.

NMP has created four limited partnership funds totaling approximately $262 million in capital, and has invested in over 100 companies, ranging from retailers like Just For Feet to high-tech firms like nFront, a provider of Internet banking services. The firm's current fund, Noro-Moseley Partners IV L.P., together with a related fund, tops $112 million, with an emphasis on telecommunications, information, and medical technology.

Founding Partner Charles Moseley's grasp of the growing importance of the technology industry was evident with his very first investment in 1983, Sawtek, a Florida company that manufactured electronic components. NMP continues its strong support of technology companies, guided by its partners' expertise. Jack Kelly was chief operating officer with Scientific-Atlanta, Inc. Russell French was formerly a partner with King & Spalding. Charles Johnson was a cofounder and CEO of Sales Technologies, Inc., a start-up software company. Alan Taetle was a former executive at MindSpring Enterprises, Inc., and Allen Moseley was previously an investment banker with Robinson-Humphrey Company.

In recent years, Noro-Moseley began to make more early-stage investments because of a growing number of attractive local start-up companies, and the fact that the thriving stock market is supporting technology companies more quickly than it used to. NMP's collective wisdom, experience, and capital has made a significant contribution to Atlanta's ability to attract and sustain cutting-edge technology firms. "As a result, we've played a key role in developing Atlanta as a technology center," says Moseley. "In the past, and even more in the future, that position will serve our state very well."

Venture capital financing is only the beginning of the relationship. Noro-Moseley's involvement in a funded company is almost always more comprehensive. "It's much more than the money. We take young, growing companies and give them the capital, the advice, and the help they need to really grow," Moseley explains. "It's a worthy effort. We all get great satisfaction out of building up these companies."

Prior to forming NMP, Charles Moseley was a senior vice president and director of The Robinson-Humphrey Company, Inc., a major regional investment banking firm. "There were numerous attractive investment opportunities in this region, but no regional venture capital firm," Charles Moseley recalls. "I saw a need." Over the years, NMP has developed extensive contacts with investment bankers, lawyers, accountants, business brokers, entrepreneurs, other venture funds, commercial bankers, and senior business executives—all valuable resources to growing portfolio companies.

A typical day in the life of a successful venture capitalist might begin with a presentation from a company seeking financing. Hours are spent checking into prospective companies or advising existing investments, with many dozens of e-mails and phone calls sandwiched in between. Every Monday Noro-Moseley meets to evaluate "deal sheets," write-ups on companies that have made presentations. Partners also find time to attend board meetings and give talks about venture capital to a variety of groups. Several days each week are devoted to travel, either visiting portfolio companies or assessing new financing prospects, most often to Research Triangle Park, North Carolina.

"We're excited about the rapid pace of development in Atlanta," Moseley says, noting that the Southeast is a growing region expected to have continued above-average economic expansion. "Noro-Moseley has a vested interest in seeing Atlanta's companies succeed." ❦

CIBA Vision

At CIBA Vision, more than 6,000 associates work every day to improve, protect, and preserve the eyesight of people around the world. Through a broad portfolio of contact lenses, lens care products, ophthalmic surgery, and ophthalmic pharmaceutical products, CIBA Vision provides innovative solutions to today's eye care needs and tomorrow's demands.

With worldwide and North American headquarters in Atlanta, CIBA Vision is one of the 30 largest employers in the state of Georgia. Atlanta is home to CIBA Vision's corporate campus, which houses administration, global research and development, and distribution, and its state-of-the art contact lens manufacturing site.

CIBA Vision began as a small start-up company in 1980 and today has grown to be a global leader in vision care. When the company entered the contact lens market in the 1980s, it ranked 27th. Today, with worldwide sales of more than one billion dollars, CIBA Vision is second in the global optics market, sixth in ophthalmic pharmaceuticals, and is the eye care unit of Novartis, one of the largest life science companies in the world.

More than 12 million people in 70 countries enjoy enhanced lifestyles with CIBA Vision's contact lenses and lens care products. And millions more find help and hope with CIBA Vision ophthalmic pharmaceuticals to treat a variety of conditions and diseases of the eye.

CIBA Vision develops, manufactures, and markets a wide range of soft contact lenses, including the Focus® family of daily, weekly, and monthly replacement lenses. CIBA Vision's new Focus® DAILIES® are redefining the daily disposable contact lens marketplace, delivering exceptional affordability, comfort, and convenience. The recent development of Focus® NIGHT & DAY™ lenses marks a major milestone in CIBA Vision's six-year effort to bring to market a true extended wear soft contact lens that can be worn for up to 30 days and nights. Additionally, CIBA Vision was the first manufacturer to market a monthly replacement toric soft contact lens, Focus Toric, and today Focus Toric is the world's best selling contact lens for people with astigmatism.

Caring for contact lenses is made convenient and easy thanks to CIBA Vision's full

line of lens care products. Offering better performance in less time, products such as AOSept®, SOLO-care®, and QuickCare® are designed with the consumer in mind.

Ophthalmic pharmaceutical solutions developed and marketed by CIBA Vision help to prevent and treat specific eye disorders, including glaucoma, inflammation, infection, and dry eye.

The future of CIBA Vision's ophthalmic pharmaceuticals remains strong as the company is leading the way with new therapies for conditions and diseases of the eye that today have no adequate treatment. CIBA Vision, in collaboration with Vancouver-based QLT PhotoTherapeutics, continues the development of Visudyne™ therapy, a potential breakthrough in the treatment of the wet form of macular degeneration (AMD), the leading cause of blindness in people over age 50.

In 1999, CIBA Vision made its entry into the ophthalmic surgical market with the purchase of a complete line of intraocular lens products, including the innovative MemoryLens®, the only pre-rolled, foldable intraocular lens in the world.

As the new millennium approaches, CIBA Vision sees boundless opportunities ahead—opportunities that will revolutionize eye care around the world. The company's commitment to innovation and excellence in its people, processes, and products is truly changing the way you see.

▲ **Atlanta is home to the worldwide and North American headquarters of CIBA Vision, a global leader in vision care.**

◄ **More than 12 million people in 70 countries enjoy enhanced lifestyles with CIBA Vision's contact lenses and lens care products.**

Watson Wyatt Worldwide

With more than 5,000 associates in 90 offices spanning the globe, Watson Wyatt Worldwide is one of the world's leading consulting firms, specializing in employee benefits, human capital management, and human resources technologies.

B. E. Wyatt and his cofounders established The Wyatt Company in 1946 as an actuarial consulting firm dealing exclusively with pension plans. The firm was successful in its niche and clients soon began requesting assistance with group health care plans. By the early '60s, Watson Wyatt had expanded into a well-rounded human resources consulting company providing services in human resources strategy, compensation, and benefits.

Responsive to its clients' needs, Watson Wyatt continued to expand throughout the '80s. The company moved into thriving cities like Hong Kong, London, Madrid, and Sydney. At the same time the bustling economy of Atlanta and the large number of clients located here marked the city as a prime location for another office—and in 1981, the Atlanta office of Watson Wyatt was opened. The Atlanta office, based on the tradition of the Wyatt Company, focused mainly on retirement services, but by the late '80s it developed into a full-service consulting office bringing together two disciplines—people and financial management.

In 1995, The Wyatt Company formed an alliance with R. Watson and Sons, the United Kingdom's premier actuarial and benefits consultancy, to become known as Watson Wyatt Worldwide, a leading actuarial, benefits, and human resources consulting firm.

Today, Watson Wyatt prides itself on the ability to share resources across geographic boundaries. It can provide multinational corporations with experienced professionals to ensure that benefit plans comply with local regulations worldwide while maintaining local, personalized service.

The company's global presence continues to expand with their latest triumph, a new office in Shanghai. Watson Wyatt is the first human resources consulting firm to win approval of a wholly foreign-owned enterprise license from the authorities in the People's Republic of China.

As Watson Wyatt has grown into a global presence, it has kept a local heart, quick to contribute to the community it serves. The company works with Junior Achievement to inspire the business leaders of tomorrow, visiting both public and private classrooms of Atlanta-area schools. The company also contributes funding to Georgia State University's Actuarial Sciences Department and supports the Beebe Institute.

Wholly owned by its active associates, Watson Wyatt inspires a collaborative, multicultural environment that encourages creativity and innovation. From developing a stock option program to implementing a compensation strategy, to developing an employee benefit package and designing automated benefit services, Watson Wyatt is backed by the best and most current research on people and financial management issues.

Watson Wyatt consultants help companies solve complex problems and make their business strategies work. Their collaborative consulting approach starts with ClientFirst™, the process for defining client needs and expectations. "We let the corporations we serve measure our performance according to the criteria they set. They decide what's most important; then we deliver," says Gary Lawson, Watson Wyatt vice president and managing consultant in Atlanta. "Watson Wyatt listens carefully to our clients in order to serve both their present and future needs with custom-designed solutions."

According to Lawson, the future promises a greater emphasis on technology and continued efforts to better serve clients. "We expect to continue the rapid growth of our operation in Atlanta, to build our consulting services and make this one of our strongest centers," Lawson concludes. ◐

▲ **With more than 5,000 associates in 90 offices spanning the globe, Watson Wyatt Worldwide is one of the world's leading consulting firms, specializing in employee benefits, human capital management, and human resources technologies.** Photo by Deborah Celecia. Inc.

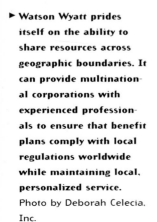

▶ **Watson Wyatt prides itself on the ability to share resources across geographic boundaries. It can provide multinational corporations with experienced professionals to ensure that benefit plans comply with local regulations worldwide while maintaining local, personalized service.** Photo by Deborah Celecia. Inc.

RMT Construction, Inc.

Earl Thomas, sole proprietor of RMT Construction, Inc., deftly juggles big blueprints and big budgets in his Lithonia home office. "I manage construction, building from 10 to 15 large, upscale custom homes per year," Thomas says, with the calm assurance of the consummate professional. "My company is sought after by people who are looking for quality."

Born in Jamaica, Thomas has worked as an architectural engineer, builder, and surveyor since 1968. He made the move from New York to Atlanta when his wife, Dr. Pam Thomas, was recruited by Lockheed to be their medical director. "We've always supported each other's careers," says Thomas, adding with a smile, "and she was tired of the snow." Once in Atlanta, Thomas designed and built his family's home, a luxurious, light-filled two-story brick house in Lithonia, and incorporated his business, RMT Construction, Inc. (named for his children, Ramogi and Monifa) in 1989, with his wife as secretary and treasurer.

The first house he built was unprofitable because of his unfamiliarity with the local market. "It cost me money," Thomas recalls ruefully. "Lumber prices escalated and that hurt me." But Thomas persevered and other jobs came quickly. At one time he was working between five counties: Fayette, Cobb, Coweta, DeKalb, and Fulton. "I decided to specialize in Fayette and south DeKalb," Thomas says. "Atlanta's northside is already congested."

Thomas is determined to bring more upscale living to the south DeKalb area. "DeKalb has got plenty of starter homes, but there aren't enough fine homes," Thomas explains. "People don't want to leave their church, their schools, and their friends. I see a tremendous opportunity for development."

RMT Construction recently completed a house for a professional baseball player in Fayette County, Georgia, RMT's biggest house so far, with over 10,000 square feet. In addition, Thomas has developed two upscale subdivisions, Adrian Oaks and Sandstone Estates. "My work is tangible," Thomas says. "I get a lot of satisfaction when I drive down the streets and can say, 'I built that one, and that one and that one.' "

RMT's clients are professionals who want the best quality work. "My competition tries to underbid; then they run into trouble because they can't handle the expectation level of the clientele. My clients are very, very particular about what they will accept," says Thomas. "I end up being good friends with the majority of my clients because I treat them properly." In fact, all of RMT's work has come through the referrals of satisfied clients and positive word of mouth.

Working constantly, Thomas has even had to turn some potential clients away. "If I expand we may lose quality. I'm trying to do better, not more," says Thomas. "What I'd like to do is bring my son on board. Eventually he'll have enough experience to do construction, and I'll do more of the development."

Today, Thomas builds deluxe, custom houses in the Greater Metro Atlanta areas of southwest Atlanta, Fulton County, Fayetteville, and Lithonia, and routinely manages 100 or more subcontractors ranging from plumbers, electricians, roofers, masons, and landscapers, to framing and trim carpenters, as well as skilled tile and carpet installers. With increasing revenues, RMT construction is looking forward to a prosperous future as Thomas continues to build the best in custom homes. ❧

◀ **Thomas builds deluxe, custom houses in the Greater Metro Atlanta areas of southwest Atlanta, Fulton County, Fayetteville, and Lithonia.**

◀ **With increasing revenues, RMT construction is looking forward to a prosperous future as Thomas continues to build the best in custom homes.**

Business Computer Applications, Inc.

Business Computer Applications, Inc. provides cost-effective information technology solutions to the health care industry. The company also provides automated data processing services to various groups across all industries, including government agencies, large companies, and private institutions.

"Our products help health care providers give better care at lower costs," explains CEO and President Albert Woodard. "Our work promotes better health care, especially for people in urban and rural situations and for those living in poverty."

BCA's software operates successfully in dozens of hospitals, community health centers, and managed care organizations. BCA's Clinic Management System was designed specifically for federally funded community health centers and similarly styled private clinics. BCA's Managed Care Management Information System was developed for Managed Care Organizations and HMOs. BCA's industry solutions include GUI, client-server, and midrange computer legacy products for the medical industry, custom software development, and time and material consulting projects.

BCA's professional service division is the fastest growing aspect of the company. "We have leveraged our technical expertise in medical information technology, making it applicable to multiple industries," says Woodard. Clients include the Centers for Disease Control, University of Texas, TRW, Electronic Data Systems, and IBM.

Business Computer Applications, Inc., a minority-owned and operated corporation headquartered in Atlanta, was founded in 1977 by two information technology pioneers, Albert Woodard and Ricky Cotton.

Woodard, a former seven-year IBM employee, and Cotton, a veteran of the United States Air Force, developed state-of-the-art total software solutions for many different industries. Both men were technically oriented with experience in business systems, and success came quickly. "We made more in the first three months than we did in the last year with IBM and the Air Force," says CEO and President Woodard.

With a customer base that extended from Miami to Los Angeles, the firm moved to

Atlanta in 1985 to take advantage of the city's superior transportation infrastructure. "Atlanta was also beginning to attract technology firms, which gave us access to supplies, equipment, and personnel," Woodard says, noting the excellent recruitment opportunities offered by the colleges of Clark, Atlanta University Center, Mercer, Morehouse, Spellman, Morris Brown, Georgia Tech, and Emory.

The company opened a regional office in Dallas, Texas, in 1996 to provide better support for their customers. "It gave us a way to expand our market west of the Mississippi," Woodard explains.

BCA has been recognized with several local, state, regional, and national awards for excellence in service and quality, including Minority Business of the Year and a National Quality Award, as well as recognition from the Chattanooga Urban League.

The year BCA moved to Atlanta, company revenues were in the $1-million range. The company's revenues in the last fiscal year were $5 million, an 85 percent surge in growth.

"These are exciting times for us, even more exciting than when we started," Woodard concludes. "We're helping to create a healthier population worldwide. Technology is the means to do it, and we are on the cutting edge. Atlanta has been nurturing to BCA and that has been fundamental to our success." ◆

Elite Staffing Services

Atlanta is without a doubt one of the largest growing cities in the world. Though there is much to celebrate, there are a few growing pains to cope with as well. One of the most demanding is finding the right people to power so much growth.

Warm bodies are not sufficient in the sophisticated, high-tech, fast-paced metro Atlanta of today. A careful match of the total person to the job can mean immediate results for a company, whereas a warm body merely fills the seat and can drag production in the opposite direction from company goals. This is why Elite Staffing Services is such an advantage to Fortune 500 companies and smaller companies alike.

Now in its 17th year, Elite has built its reputation on highly customized solutions rather than huge databases. Once an account manager is assigned to a company, that manager works to fully understand the culture and needs of that company. Only then does the real interviewing begin.

Certainly testing, assessment, and background checks are the first step, as they are with any reputable staffing firm. But Elite takes the process many steps further. For example, the account managers are an integral part of the interviewing process in order to match the real person with the company's culture and needs not necessarily spelled out in the job description. From this in-depth examination, comes a list of candidates more uniquely qualified and more closely matched with the company than any simple automated system could ever deliver. The absence of top-heavy bureaucracy also speeds the process.

"We know who we are sending out. Not just the name—but the person," says Leonard Jenkins Jr., chief executive officer. "The risk factor of the human element is largely reduced with our program when compared to the numbers games played in database roulette."

Incorporated in 1983, Elite Staffing Services has two offices in Atlanta and one in Columbus, Georgia. The concentration on

Georgia has allowed the company to identify top talent in the state and reduce relocation costs for companies and new employees alike. Availability is often quicker, as well, when prospects are already in the state.

While Elite is a full-service staffing firm providing permanent and temporary help in the fields of office clerical, professional, and entry level technical, the company is also expanding its horizon to become one of Atlanta's premier sources of information technology workers. This part of the company has become so immensely popular that Elite is in the process of forming a separate company specializing in staffing the "industries of the mind."

Elite's corporate clientele reads like a Who's Who list in the nation: Allstate, AT&T, BellSouth, Centers For Disease Control, Federal Express, Georgia State Bar, Grady, Lucent Technologies, Michelin, Nabisco, SunTrust, and the Veterans Administration, among many others. Their collective satisfaction with Elite Staffing is the best testament to the company's customized services. Over the past five years, Elite Staffing Services has had over 91 percent repeat customers.

As Atlanta continues to grow, Elite will be there to fuel the engine with qualified, talented people uniquely chosen to suit even the most demanding fields. ❡

◀ Under the direction of Leonard Jenkins Jr., Elite Staffing Services is an advantage to Fortune 500 companies and smaller companies alike. Now in its 17th year, Elite has built its reputation on highly customized solutions rather than huge databases.

◀ Elite Staffing, with guidance from Operations Manager Kathy Graham and President and CEO Leonard Jenkins Jr., is expanding its horizon to become one of Atlanta's premier sources of information technology workers.

Weibel & Associates, Inc.

Like monuments to American ingenuity and prosperity, magnificent buildings stretch up to scrape the sky, spread out in huge malls, sprawl out from major cities like tentacles reaching from a core body, and cluster in new areas of commerce. As each of these creations is pondered, designed, built, and sold, the need to assess their true value becomes more and more crucial to owners, buyers, and financiers—especially when there are millions or even billions at stake.

The staff of Weibel & Associates, Inc. has appraised commercial property in over 35 states and throughout Canada. All of the firm's work complies with the Appraisal Institute (MAI), and is in accordance with the Uniform Standards of Professional Appraisal Practice (USPAP), as promulgated by the Appraisal Foundation. Weibel & Associates, Inc. is approved by most financial institutions across the nation and works on a nationwide basis with competitive fees regardless of location. In short, all the credentials are in order, all the number-crunching is sound, and the fees are both affordable and well worth the investment.

Though frequently sought out by financial institutions, law firms, corporations, and investors nationwide, Weibel & Associates, Inc. calls Atlanta home. Founder Clay M. Weibel moved to Atlanta as a child, while wife and co-owner, Susan Thomas Weibel, granddaughter of famous Atlanta artist Steffen Thomas, traces her roots through several generations of Atlantans. The firm was born in 1985 on Atlanta soil.

Clay Weibel, president, has 25 years of experience in real estate, including appraising, consultation, brokerage, and property management and is qualified as an expert witness in U.S. Bankruptcy Court and State Court. His real estate training began with a BBA degree in real estate and urban development from the University of Georgia. He is often called upon as a speaker and instructor by financial institutions to train or update personnel or investors on real estate values and trends.

The professional staff at Weibel & Associates, Inc. all have impressive histories and credentials with many years of experience. Each is trained to assess property and generate reports that specifically address the needs of every client. Weibel & Associates, Inc. is consistently ranked in the top 10 in the annual listings of Atlanta's Top 25 Commercial Real Estate Appraisers published by *The Atlanta Business Chronicle*.

Valuation services, or value estimates, can be based on several concepts, depending on the nature of the client's concern or inquiry. These include, but are not limited to, Market Value, Fair Value, Investment Value, Value In Use, Going Concern Value, and Replacement Value. Assignments may be limited in nature or extensive in scope; either way the professionals at Weibel & Associates are there to serve.

The staff works with sophisticated computer tools, enabling comprehensive discounted cash flow analysis, internal rate of return computations, and sensitivity analysis which consider a variety of variables. Valuation reports are used for mortgage loan underwriting, investment decisions, acquisition, disposition, insurance coverage, tax-related issues, and many other applications.

All Weibel & Associates' reports are carefully formatted for consistency, clarity, and comprehensiveness. Each assignment is undertaken according to the client's purpose and scope, and conclusions are clear, concise, and focused accordingly. The firm is heavily experienced in providing appraisal reviews for HUD, the FDIC, and other lending institutions.

As Atlanta continues to build upon its prosperity and dreams of a bright future, Weibel & Associates, Inc. will be there to root the dreams in reality and the nourishing soil of profits and returns. ❦

▶ **Founder Clay M. Weibel moved to Atlanta as a child, while wife and co-owner, Susan Thomas Weibel, granddaughter of famous Atlanta artist Steffen Thomas, traces her roots through several generations of Atlantans. The firm of Weibel & Associates, Inc. was born in 1985 on Atlanta soil.**

The Mulling Group

As the new millennium approaches, companies find themselves competing in new markets with more opportunities than ever before. They also find those markets are often fluid, changing almost as quickly as each new dawn. It's a challenge to keep up, much less prosper.

Fortunes are made and lost virtually overnight. It is not a time or place for the timid or the outdated. One of Atlanta's best tools for updating and strengthening employees, and for assisting former employees for new opportunities of their own, is The Mulling Group.

Founded in 1986, The Mulling Group is a management consulting firm specializing in outplacement and executive coaching. The Mulling Group helps individuals make the right career selection and realize their potential in all phases of development. Whether a person is making a job change or developing successful management skills, the group's goal is to prepare professionals and their organizations for future growth.

The Mulling Group is a member of Lincolnshire International, which provides consulting services throughout North America, Europe, and Asia. This affiliation allows client companies a more feasible and cost-effective approach to outplacement and executive coaching services in multiple locations.

The Mulling Group's outplacement services combine career search training with ongoing consulting to maximize individual efforts. By assisting candidates as they target their professional skills and interests, are able to focus on more fulfilling career choices. In addition, they learn how to keep abreast of the information age, which assists in their job search and their overall productivity once on the job. It's a win-win situation for everyone involved.

As new markets and products dictate the need for newer, different management practices, The Mulling Group provides the how-to in getting the job done. Executive coaching is in demand from The Mulling Group for this very reason. For some CEOs and other top-level executives, the old way has been around for so long that a new way is hard to identify. The Mulling Group can update and present options that fit individual styles and company goals.

While most companies realize the need for training, especially on the management level, few have the time and resources to follow

up and fine-tune individual development. This is a major plus in using The Mulling Group. Executives become more productive faster under the ongoing care of a Mulling Group training consultant. ❧

◄ The Mulling Group's professionals have diverse experience in a wide range of businesses. They specialize in creating custom solutions for a company's needs in both outplacement and executive coaching. Pictured (seated left to right) are Emory W. Mulling, President; Kay M. Massih, Senior Vice President of Business Development; (standing) James C. Gaskin Jr., Vice President of Consulting; Cheryl M. Dennison, Senior Vice President of Consulting; Karen Preslock, Director of Information Services; Pamela L. Wyatt, Vice President of Business Development; M. Tara Pickens, Vice President of Consulting; and A. Ron Bolt, Vice President of Consulting.

◄ The Mulling Group specializes in creating individualized programs designed to meet each candidate's needs. Emory Mulling works with an outplacement candidate to develop a career search plan.

CHAPTER NINE
The 1990s

❦

*With the advent of CNN, Atlanta
began to make good on its two-decade-
old boast of being an international city.
The white-hot economy of the 1980s had
induced a score of international banks to
open offices in Atlanta.*

Olympic Stadium, Opening Ceremonies, 1996 Centennial Olympic Games.
Photo by Ron Sherman

Japanese banks and investors had arrived in Atlanta near the end of the decade seeking to buy "trophy" skyscrapers. International air cargo operations at the airport increased steadily during the decade and by 1985, one million international passengers were visiting the airport annually.

Still, the idea that Atlanta should apply to host the 1996 Summer Olympic Games was considered laughable. The idea had been born in 1987 in the mind of Billy Payne, a former collegiate football star. Payne had become a successful lawyer in Atlanta but was otherwise unknown.

According to Payne, he was restless, seeking a challenge beyond his narrow business confines. A capital campaign at his church occupied him for a while, but afterward he was at loose ends until the Olympics popped into his head.

As it turned out, the idea of hosting an Olympics had been brought up before, in the 1970s, but the financial fiasco of Montreal in 1976 scared Atlanta off. A decade later, the landscape was different. The 1984 Los Angeles Olympics had shown that corporations would pay handsomely to sponsor the event, leaving

◄ The eyes of the world were upon Atlanta as the city hosted the 1996 Olympic Games on the 100th anniversary of the modern Olympics. Photo by Ron Sherman

◄ Built for the 1996 Olympic Games, Centennial Olympic Park is the centerpiece of Atlanta's downtown revitalization. The park hosts concerts, festivals, and other special events. A unique attraction of the park is the Rings Fountain, at which columns of water spring from the ground, expressly intended to wet its admirers. Photo by Ron Sherman

Payne determined that, if he got that far, Atlanta could privately finance the Games.

At first, Payne was ignored or ridiculed. He finally won an audience with Andrew Young, then finishing up his second term as mayor. Young was as big a dreamer as Payne and the two of them managed to pry enough money out of corporate Atlanta to successfully campaign to be named the U.S. bid city for 1996.

Payne and his miniscule band of early volunteers proved to be shrewd campaigners, even though 1996 would be the 100th anniversary of the modern Olympics and Athens, Greece, the ancestral home of Games, was the sentimental favorite. Atlanta was in very good shape when it came to physical facilities and Young possessed invaluable international contacts. Payne stressed Atlanta's role in the civil rights movement and petitioned the International Olympic Committee members tirelessly.

The two-year effort came down to a September morning in 1990, when tens of thousands of Atlantans crowded Underground to watch a live television hookup from Tokyo. The crowd held its breath collectively then exploded in glee when the announcement was made. It was one of the great moments in Atlanta history.

The scale of the job Payne had won for himself and the city was staggering. The budget for putting on the Games added up to well above $1 billion and, except for security, nearly all of it had to be raised from private sources.

The Georgia Tech campus became the Olympic Village for the fifteen thousand athletes and coaches. The Marriott Marquis hotel

was designated home to Olympics officials and a new Olympic Stadium was constructed next to Atlanta-Fulton County Stadium. Almost all the events were held in the Atlanta metro area except for sailing in Savannah, soccer in Athens, and canoeing in Tennessee.

Nearly all the facilities built expressly for the Olympics were constructed with post-Olympic use in mind. Athlete dormitories were donated afterward to Georgia State University and the Georgia Institute of Technology. Moreover, Olympic Stadium was partly dismantled and reconfigured to become the new home of the Atlanta Braves, who had experienced a rapid turnaround in the early 1990s and become one of baseball's elite teams.

Tens of thousands of volunteers were mobilized to direct traffic, guide tourists, and staff athletic events. Local governments and businesses went into a frenzy of planning to improve streetscapes and figure out how to profit from the Games.

Despite the inevitable snags along the way, the Games themselves went off smoothly for the most part. It was largest Games ever staged, both in the number of athletes who participated and in the number of spectators attending, and the throngs of visitors gave the downtown area a vibrant street life it hadn't seen in decades.

But by the middle of the fortnight, just as things were functioning smoothly, a pipe bomb left in a backpack exploded one night in a packed Centennial Olympic Park, killing one person and wounding 111 others. After consultation the Games were kept open and on schedule and there were no further incidents. Three years later, the perpetrator and the purpose of the bombing were still unknown.

After the years of planning and bustle, Atlanta was somewhat adrift after the Games ended. From an economic standpoint, the 1990s were proving a replay of the 1980s, with the decade opening with a recession followed by years of surging growth.

Housing starts in the metro area were well above the record levels of the 1980s and in several years led the nation. Office and other commercial construction was just as strong as Atlanta continued to attract the young and ambitious. Job growth was at or above the levels of the 1980s.

But there were signs of strain in the city's water and sewer system. A massive sinkhole near a Midtown motel reminded residents that much of the water system was seventy-five years old and increasingly fragile. Water treatment was an issue as well.

Georgians downstream from Atlanta complained increasingly loudly about the water quality of the Chattahoochee River. City officials promised to tighten standards and improve operations.

There were issues of land use as well. Ever since the 1980s, voices had been raised about suburban sprawl and after the Olympics the chorus grew louder. Without natural boundaries to contain growth, there was little to stop developers or citizens from moving farther out in search of more affordable land or a more rural lifestyle. Traffic congestion grew steadily as the population expanded and transportation planners exhausted their ability to widen the existing interstates. In 1998, after studies showed residents drove more miles to and from work than other Americans, Atlanta was tagged as the "next Los Angeles." The federal government made good on a threat to withhold highway funds until the region agreed on a plan to improve air quality.

The decade did see one major transportation project completed. The idea of a road that would connect Buckhead with downtown and the suburbs to the north had been on the drawing boards since the 1950s. The idea was dusted off in the 1980s as Buckhead began to sprout new office towers, entertainment opportunities, hotels, and greatly expanded malls. Known as Georgia 400, the new road plan had a twist: it would be a toll road that would pay for itself over time. After four years of wrangling, it finally won final approval in 1989 and opened in 1993, complete with a MARTA rail line running down its center.

The concerns about sprawl and longer commutes did start a small boom in new housing downtown and inside I-285 and it appeared the city population would show a small increase for the decade.

Besides the Olympic-financed new baseball stadium for the Braves, a new domed football stadium—the Georgia Dome—was opened next to the Georgia World Congress Center in 1992, thus bringing the Super Bowl to Atlanta in 1994. And in 1997, The Omni was imploded after twenty-five years to make room for a new sports arena for the Atlanta Hawks and for a new professional hockey team, the Thrashers.

The late 1980s had not been kind to John Portman. Faced with a debt crisis, he was forced to relinquish control of much of his empire, including Peachtree Center, but his reputation as an architect and visionary was intact and his services remained in high demand in the 1990s, particularly in Asia.

But even during the turmoil, Portman continued to build. He built the Inforum, an attempt to build a mart that would serve the emerging information technology industry. But the building struggled until Olympic organizers filled much of the space, a fortuitous

379

bit of geographic karma. One day Billy
Payne looked out his window at the
blocks of older buildings, surface parking lots and abandoned properties bor-
dering the Georgia World Congress
Center and envisioned an urban park
that would provide a central gathering
place for Olympic visitors. After the
Olympics, the Centennial Olympic
Park would become the catalyst for the
development of a new urban residential
neighborhood around it.

Portman also built the 60-story
One Peachtree Plaza on the very
northern edge of downtown, opening
it during the short-lived real estate
slump of the early 1990s.

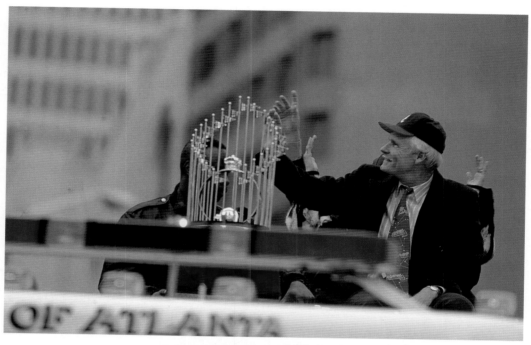

Ted Turner fared much better. Although CNN and the WTBS
Superstation no longer had the cable television field to themselves,
he kept moving ahead. In 1996 he merged his empire with the
Time Warner conglomerate and secured the number two executive
position for himself.

Amid all the rapid growth, there were some noteworthy economic casualties, names that evoked an earlier city.

Eastern Airlines had been associated with the beginnings of aviation in Atlanta. Even though it had eventually moved its headquarters to Miami it competed fiercely with Delta for Atlanta passengers. But it never prospered in the deregulated aviation environment and it suffered from a toxic relationship between its executives and unions and finally shut down in 1991.

The same year, Rich's unceremoniously closed its downtown
store, a legendary facility that could trace its origins to the
arrival of Morris Rich in 1867. The downtown store had been
the last word in Atlanta retailing for most of the century but it
suffered greatly from the rise of the suburbs and the decline of
the central downtown. Underground Atlanta limped through
the 1990s as visitor numbers stagnated. In 1998, the complex
was put up for sale.

But new names arrived to take their place. In 1991 United
Parcel Service, the world's largest package handler, announced it
would move its headquarters from Connecticut to Atlanta. The
courtship and negotiations had been kept secret right until the end
and the announcement electrified the city the same way that the
arrival of Georgia-Pacific had a decade earlier.

In 1993, Bill Campbell, a young City Council member, replaced
Maynard Jackson, who had returned to the mayor's office for a single term, as mayor and then won re-election handily in 1997.

▲ The Atlanta Braves won
baseball's ultimate prize
in 1995, when they beat
the Cleveland Indians in
the World Series. Ecstatic
fans lined the streets to
cheer the Braves—and
their owner, the colorful
media mogul Ted Turner.
Today, fans pack Turner
Field to cheer on
"America's Team."
Photos by Ron Sherman

◄ A new Olympic Stadium
was constructed next to
Atlanta-Fulton County
Stadium to host many
events in the Summer
Olympic Games in 1996.
The stadium eventually
would become the per-
manent home of the
Atlanta Braves, and was
renamed Turner Field.
Atlanta-Fulton County
Stadium was demolished.
Photo by Ron Sherman

► Turner Field, home of the Atlanta Braves, is more than a ballpark—it's total entertainment. The facility boasts the latest in design and equipment, plus a full-service restaurant, a Braves museum, children's activities, a courtyard with a pre-game party, and more. And fans have plenty to cheer about. The Braves have won seven straight divisional titles and more games than any other team in the 1990s, and have played in the World Series four times in this decade.
Photos by Ron Sherman

Despite the growing pains, it was clear that metropolitan Atlanta was the economic engine driving the state of Georgia. The metro area's strong base of business services—lawyers, salespeople, marketers—was increasingly complemented by telecommunication, software, and technology companies. Venture capital firms began to take notice of the growing base of engineering talent flowing out of Georgia Tech and starting new companies, even as one of the first and most successful of Atlanta's high tech companies—Hayes Modem—fell victim to rapidly changing markets and was forced to declare bankruptcy. The old Atlanta story of restless ambition and hard work seemed secure for the new millennium. ✍

◄ The Atlanta Falcons, whose home is the Georgia Dome, were crowned the 1999 NFC Champions. The Dome also hosted Super Bowl XXVIII and the "NFL Experience;" and will be the site of Super Bowl XXXIV. The Dome also hosts collegiate athletic events including the annual SEC Championships for football and basketball; and the Chick-fil-A Peach Bowl. For the 1998-1999 season, the Georgia Dome served as a temporary residence of the Atlanta Hawks professional basketball team. The Hawks' old headquarters, The Omni was imploded and a new stadium, Philips Arena, created to house the Hawks and a new NHL expansion team, the Atlanta Thrashers, who will thrill warm-blooded Atlantans with professional hockey action on the ice. Photos by Ron Sherman

► The Atlanta Ballet's annual holiday production of "The Nutcracker" is a family tradition for thousands of Atlantans. The Atlanta Ballet's origins date back to 1929, making it the oldest, continuously operating dance company in the country. Photo by Ron Sherman

► In addition to its professional productions, the Atlanta Ballet offers classes for children and adults at its Atlanta School of Ballet. Photo by Ron Sherman

◄ **Founded in 1986, the Georgia Shakespeare Festival makes its permanent home on the campus of Oglethorpe University, delighting its audiences with top-notch productions of plays by Shakespeare and other classic authors.** Photo by Ron Sherman

► Stone Mountain is the world's largest exposed granite outcropping and features a carving of Confederate heroes Robert E. Lee, Stonewall Jackson and Jefferson Davis that covers thirty-five acres. During the summer, Atlantans gather every evening to watch a laser light and music show projected on the side of the mountain. While the energetic can walk to the summit, many visitors prefer to take the cable car. Photos by Ron Sherman

▲ Since the late 1960s, Six Flags Over Georgia has meant thrill-riding fun for generations of Atlantans. Photo by Ron Sherman

◄ White Water Park in Cobb County keeps Atlanta's kids cool and wet during steamy Southern summers. Photo by Ron Sherman

► Every spring, Music Midtown brings hundreds of thousands of music fans to Atlanta for a three-day urban festival featuring dozens of bands. Photos by Ron Sherman

▲ The Fernbank Museum of Natural History has seventy acres of preserved forest, a planetarium and observatory, a public laboratory and an IMAX theater. Its Great Hall hosts traveling exhibitions like these dinosaurs from China.
Photo by Ron Sherman

▲ The Atlanta History Center is where the story of Atlanta is told—from its beginnings as a railroad center to its current standing as an international city. On the center's grounds are two historic homes, thirty-three acres of gardens, and a fully staffed library and archives. Photo by Ron Sherman

◄ Designed by world-renowned architect Michael Graves, The Michael C. Carlos Museum on the campus of Emory University is home to fifteen thousand objects, including a world-class collection of ancient Egyptian funerary art, including ten mummies. Photo by Ron Sherman

◄ (opposite) The Atlanta Botanical Garden in Piedmont Park has fifteen acres of landscaped gardens, fifteen acres of hardwood forest, and the spectacular Dorothy Chapman Fuqua Conservatory. The grounds include land that was part of the Cotton States Exposition in 1896. Photos by Ron Sherman

▼ The Callanwolde Fine Arts Center was once the home of Howard Candler, the oldest son of Asa Candler, the founder of The Coca-Cola Company. The mansion is now a center for art education, offering classes to children and adults. Photo by Ron Sherman

► Atlanta's downtown area has experienced a renaissance, and is a hub for everything from education to entertainment to world-class business. The campuses of Georgia State University, The Georgia Institute of Technology, and Atlanta University are at the heart of downtown's new life. Photo by Ron Sherman

► Traffic congestion grew steadily as the city's population increased. The idea of a road that would connect Buckhead with downtown and the suburbs to the north was dusted off in the 1980s as Buckhead began to sprout new office towers, entertainment opportunities, hotels, and malls. A new road known as Georgia 400 was built, and it had a twist—it is a toll road that will pay for itself over time. Photos by Ron Sherman

▶ **Atlanta opens her arms to people of all ages and interests, creating a diversity that adds richness to the fabric of everyday living.** Photos by Ron Sherman

▶ Atlantans don colorful
traditional garb and fanci-
ful gear from "days of
yore" as they participate
in Atlanta's many festivals.
Photos by Ron Sherman

▲ The Atlanta Track Club's Peachtree 10K Road Race, held July 4, boasts 50,000 participants running from Lenox Square Mall in Buckhead to Piedmont Park in Midtown. Photo by Ron Sherman

► Atlanta is constantly growing, and signs of her changing face can be seen everywhere in the city—from the striking contrast of classic architecture against the angled grace of modern skyscrapers, to the ever-present orange cones and "men at work" signs.

Photos by Ron Sherman

◄ Not all of Atlanta's artwork is housed in its many museums. Art is evident in the architecture of the city's classic buildings, such as the Fulton County Courthouse and the Hurt Building, and adorns the city streets in the form of original sculptures and statues. Photos by Ron Sherman

◄ Founded as an evening business school in 1913, Georgia State University has six colleges offering its twenty-four thousand students more than two hundred majors and fifty-one graduate and undergraduate degrees. With its urban campus just east of Five Points, Georgia State is playing a major role in the revitalization of downtown Atlanta. Photos by Ron Sherman

▶ Atlanta Motor Speedway seats 120,000 fans for auto races and other special events. Atlantans have always been fascinated by cars. The area's first racetrack is now the site of Hartsfield Atlanta International Airport.
Photo by Ron Sherman

▲ Sports are as much for playing as for watching in Atlanta, with numerous recreational leagues available to suit a variety of interests and age ranges. Photo by Ron Sherman

◄ Zoo Atlanta offers more than one thousand animals and acres of exhibits designed to mimic lush natural habitats. It has been rated one of the ten best zoos in the country. Special exhibits include the Ford African Rain Forest, the Masai Mara savannah grassland exhibit, and black rhinos. Photo by Ron Sherman

▶ Atlanta is proud of its citizens whose service helped keep America strong. The city hosts special events for veteran's recognition as well as July 4 parades throughout Fulton County. Photos by Ron Sherman

◄ Atlanta is the capital city and seat of government. With the weighty matters of state government upon them throughout the regular session, legislators are ready to celebrate when their work is done for the year. Photo by Ron Sherman

Georgia World Congress Center Authority

▲ The 21-acre Centennial Olympic Park has become a critical catalyst for the revitalization of downtown Atlanta. Its many features, such as the Fountain of Rings, its various events such as performing arts entertainment and festivals, and its functions such as private receptions, reunions, and athletic fund-raisers make it a multipurpose mecca for business and pleasure, for local and out-of-town visitors. Photo by Johnny Cain.

▶ Ranked among the nation's top five such venues, the Georgia World Congress Center hosts a myriad of conventions, consumer/trade shows, and corporate events each year. During the 1996 Centennial Olympic Games, the GWCC hosted seven sporting events and served as the International Broadcast Center.

Atlanta is one of the nation's leading convention and sports centers.

Nestled in the core of Downtown Atlanta, the Georgia World Congress Center Authority operates most of the facilities that led to Atlanta's top ranking in the nation's premier lists of star attractions for visitors—from conventioneers to international tourists. The combined events and attractions of these facilities provide the pulse of the city as it fuels the economy in numbers almost too large to fathom.

Indeed, the Georgia World Congress Center, the Georgia Dome, and the Centennial Olympic Park together comprise one of the largest sports, entertainment, and convention complexes in the world.

Established by the State of Georgia in 1974 to develop and operate the Georgia World Congress Center—and later the Georgia Dome, Centennial Olympic Park, and related facilities—the Georgia World Congress Center Authority's primary objective is to promote and facilitate events and activities that generate economic benefits to the citizens of the state and the city.

The Georgia World Congress Center is the first state-owned and operated major convention center in the United States. Year after year, the Authority is able to sustain operations without public subsidy. General business activities related to GWCC events generate over $2 billion annually in total economic impact. Indeed, hospitality is the second largest industry in Georgia and touches the economy of the entire state in a myriad of ways.

The Georgia World Congress Center is one of the most heavily booked convention facilities in the nation for major conventions, trade shows, consumer shows, and corporate meetings. Events are scheduled well into the year 2017. More than a million guests attend functions at the Congress Center annually; over 125,000 have attended a single event.

Including meeting rooms, galleries, exhibit halls, kitchens, and storerooms, there are more than 52 acres of floor area on multiple levels throughout the Center. The 33,000-square-foot ballroom is on a level equal to that of an 11-story building.

The Congress Center's West Concourse exhibit halls are more than twice as long as Atlanta's highest skyscraper is high. From one end of the halls to the other, the earth curves three-fourths of an inch.

When the World Congress Center opened in September 1976, the facility had 750,000 square feet, 350,000 of which were dedicated exhibit space. A 1985 expansion increased the Center's size by 1.1-million square feet and 290,000 square feet of exhibit space. The Phase III expansion in 1992 increased the facility to 2.5 million square feet and 950,000 square feet of prime exhibit space, making it the second largest convention center in the United States. During the Centennial Olympic Games in 1996, the Congress Center hosted seven sporting events and the International Broadcast Center, adding favorable notoriety to an already famous facility and city.

In 1999 the Georgia General Assembly approved $220 million to fund construction of the Phase IV expansion of the Georgia World Congress Center. With the Congress Center already generating a total statewide economic impact of approximately $2 billion, a PriceWaterhouse feasibility study indicated this expansion would attract 500,000 additional out-of-state visitors, generate $1 billion in economic impact, contribute $53 million in new tax revenues, and sustain up to 19,000 new jobs annually in Georgia.

The expansion will include an additional 450,000 square feet of exhibit space; a 45,000-square-foot ballroom; two fixed-seating lecture halls on the exhibit floor level; 24 flexible-space meeting rooms on the plaza and ballroom levels; and a boardroom in the upper connector.

This architecturally breathtaking building—along with the 4.5-acre landscaped plaza between it and the Georgia Dome—will add an impressive, revitalized look to this stretch of North Side Drive. Construction began in September 1999, and the completed facility is targeted to open in August 2002.

Another facility operated by the Authority is equally famous—the Georgia Dome. Opened in 1992, the world's largest cable-supported, domed stadium in North America has helped establish Atlanta as a first-class host city for international sporting and entertainment events.

Home venue of the NFL's Atlanta Falcons, the Dome has hosted the NBA's Atlanta Hawks, Super Bowl XXVIII in 1994, Super Bowl XXXIV in 2000, and the NCAA Men's Basketball Final Four in 2002 and 2007, and Women's Final Four in 2003. The Dome also hosted basketball, gymnastics, and the finals of team handball during the 1996 Centennial Olympic Games.

The Georgia Dome seats 71,500 football fans comfortably, but also provides flexibility for stadium seating configurations from 20,000 to 80,000. The executive level concourse provides exclusive access to the Dome's 4,600 club seats and 203 executive suites. The 102,000-square-foot floor accommodates a variety of events, including trade shows, concerts, and sporting events ranging from basketball, boxing, and wrestling to motor sports and track-and-field events.

At the roof's center, the Georgia Dome is 275 feet high, as tall as a 27-story building and 50 feet taller than the "Great Gasp" ride at nearby Six Flags Over Georgia. A pair of C-5 transport planes could fit on the Dome floor, and the 8,300 tons of reinforced steel in the building weighs more than the iron and steel used in the Eiffel Tower.

The Georgia Dome routinely hosts more than 2.4 million guests, who spend more than $190 million in "new dollars," which, when circulated, generate a total economic impact of more than $414 million a year. Twenty-million dollars in new tax revenues and 7,130 new jobs were created by virtue of the Dome's existence. These benefits came at no risk to taxpayers—construction of the Dome was financed through tax-exempt industrial revenue bonds issued by the Authority and guaranteed by a private letter of credit.

The third facility of Atlanta's famous trio is the Centennial Olympic Park, considered the greatest physical legacy of the 1996 Centennial Olympic Games. It is a popular civic symbol and community focal point. It reflects well Atlanta's natural and topographic beauty, as well as its reputation as the City of Trees.

The Park features the memorable Fountain of Rings and Light Towers, and an array of water gardens that connect commemorative

plazas all with a quilt theme that shows the interlocking partnerships that are the foundation beneath the Olympic Games, world peace, and the unique features of the City of Atlanta.

The Quilt of Dreams recognizes Billy Payne's quest to bring the Olympic Games to Atlanta. The Quilt of Remembrance recognizes the victims of the explosion during the 1996 Olympic Games. The Quilt of Origins honors the Greeks as hosts of the ancient and modern Olympic Games. The Quilt of Olympic Spirit salutes the 10,000 participating athletes. The Quilt of Nations honors the 197 participating nations of the Centennial Olympic Games.

Centennial Plaza, a dramatic, formal venue, is a 100-by-100-meter civic square that commemorates the 100th anniversary of the modern Olympic Games. The Plaza marks the formal gateway into the park along International Boulevard.

Centennial Olympic Park unifies Coca-Cola Headquarters and the Georgia Tech campus to the north; the Georgia World Congress Center and the Georgia Dome to the west; the hotel and financial district to the east; and CNN Center, Fairlie-Poplar Historic District, Woodruff Park, Underground Atlanta, and Georgia State University to the south. The Park is a handsome backdrop to CNN Center, much as Rockefeller Plaza is for NBC News in midtown Manhattan.

The City of Trees will move through the new millennium like a breeze—the Georgia World Congress Center Authority and its facilities will be there to provide business and recreational opportunities like a comforting shade from the Southern sun. ☙

◀ Opening in the summer of 2002, the latest GWCC expansion will add another 450,000 square feet of exhibit space. It will also offer 25 meeting rooms, two fixed-seating, tiered lecture halls, a new entrance and registration area, separate shuttle bus and taxi drop-off points, and a new 46,000-square-foot ballroom that will overlook a landscaped pedestrian plaza.

◀ The Georgia Dome is the largest cable-supported, domed stadium in North America. With a seating capacity of 71,500 for football, the Dome also offers arena and stadium configurations from 20,000 to 80,000 people. It is the NFL Atlanta Falcons' home field and has hosted Super Bowls XXVIII and XXXIV and the 1996 Centennial Olympic Games' gymnastics, basketball, and finals of team handball. It has been selected as the site for the NCAA Men's Final Four in 2002 and 2007 and NCAA Women's Final Four in 2003. The Dome also hosts major college football and basketball events, concerts, trade shows, and corporate meetings.

Philips Consumer Electronics North America

The now world-famous Philips' shield emblem was born in 1938. Since then, the trademark has become a global icon signifying and identifying Philips products as some of the most innovative and trustworthy in the world.

An international company needs a truly international city to call home. That's why when Philips Consumer Electronics began exploring cities for the relocation of its North American headquarters, the company chose Atlanta.

"When we began in-depth research on the city of Atlanta we discovered that Atlanta offered all that Philips hoped for in a new hometown," says Robert Minkhorst, chief executive officer of Philips Consumer Electronics North America. "We also knew that other Philips divisions had offices across the city." Atlanta proved to be all that was promised, supportive of local businesses, a pro-business culture in the government, a strong high-tech trained workforce, and internationally accessible through the United States' busiest airport—Hartsfield International Airport. In addition, as an international organization, Philips knew they would be in stellar company among the numerous global corporations already based in Atlanta.

After only two years in its new Atlanta offices as of this writing, Philips Consumer Electronics North America is proud of its decision to relocate to the metro area. "The move has more than met our expectations," says Minkhorst.

With its offices firmly established in north Atlanta's Perimeter area, Philips Consumer Electronics North America is settling in its new hometown and anxious to become involved in the community.

Turner Broadcasting System, Inc. and Philips have forged a strategic alliance to share and develop a diverse range of projects and properties between the software and hardware companies, including naming Atlanta's new 20,000-seat sports and event facility,

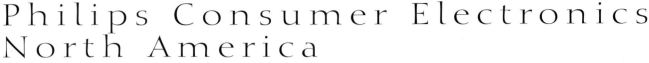

Philips Arena. Executives of TBS, Inc., parent company Time Warner Inc., and Philips outlined the 20-year agreement in February 1999, which is valued in excess of $100 million.

Philips Arena anchors a 25-acre redevelopment tract in downtown Atlanta, stretching from Centennial Olympic Park to the Georgia Dome and including the CNN Center. It is the most innovatively designed facility of its type ever constructed and serves as the home of the NBA Atlanta Hawks and the NHL Atlanta Thrashers. Additionally, it is expected to average more than 200 entertainment events each year. The Philips Arena is a monument to Philips' commitment to become a visible presence on Atlanta's corporate skyline. As the Turner organization, Philips' partner on the new arena, also calls Atlanta home, the division looks forward to more joint marketing opportunities beyond the new Philips Arena, home of the Atlanta Thrashers and Hawks.

Philips technologies and products will be featured throughout the new arena. More than 500 Philips video monitors will be used in the arena and the adjacent CNN Center; video components and lighting sources in public areas of the new facility will be Philips Electronics products; and fans will have first exposure to the latest digital technologies from Philips as they are introduced. In addition, Philips occupies a 10,000-square-foot showcase within the complex designed to enhance the visitors' experience.

Nearly every part of our lives is touched by Philips Electronics—in our homes, hospitals, offices, airports, factories, arenas, and on our streets. Some of Philips' inventions are eye-catching, like the FlatTV, which simply hangs on the wall. Others

are barely visible, like integrated circuits and CD drives.

From the telephone to the television, consumers can find Philips' leading edge products at every turn. The PC video cameras, for example, makes video mail fun for friends, family, and business associates. The company's WebTV Internet terminal brings the universe of cyberspace into the living room.

Established more than 100 years ago as a lamp factory, Philips also holds firmly to its roots, illuminating our world and landmarks like the Eiffel Tower, Big Ben, the Great Sphinx, and even Times Square for the start of the new millennium.

As a worldwide leader in electronics, Philips' growth and diversification has mirrored that of the industry. It is a leading supplier of consumer electronics, lighting products, broadcast television systems, broadband network systems, medical imaging equipment, and a wide range of other products and services.

"With our products we aim to make a contribution to improve the quality of people's lives—enabling them to enjoy the thrill of digital technology, organize their activities more effectively, keep in touch with others, and so on," says Philips President Cor Boonstra.

Every Philips Consumer Electronics North America employee is anxiously looking forward to the new millennium and the opportunities, both business- and community-related, that await in its new hometown and the world at large. The company truly believes its advertising slogan and is working with Atlanta's leaders to "make things better." ◉

Some Philips Fun Facts

- One in every two U.S. households owns a Philips product.

- Five of the world's top 10 PC manufacturers sell monitors produced by Philips.

- More than 60 percent of all telephones in the world contain Philips products.

- Worldwide, more than half the soccer stadiums, nearly one-third of all offices, and 65 percent of the top airports are illuminated by Philips Lighting.

- One in seven television sets worldwide contains a Philips picture tube.

- Each year, about 2.5 million heart procedures (scans and interventional procedures) on X-ray equipment are carried out using Philips technology.

Womble Carlyle Sandridge & Rice, PLLC

Womble Carlyle Sandridge & Rice, PLLC is one of the largest law firms in the Southeast, with approximately 400 lawyers among its ranks, and is one of the most technologically advanced law firms in the nation.

For more than 100 years, Womble Carlyle has been an integral part of the Winston-Salem, North Carolina, business community, where the firm began, representing leading corporations and financial institutions. In pursuit of its dream to service clients throughout the Southeast, the firm has expanded its practice into six thriving market areas—Raleigh, Charlotte, Atlanta, Research Triangle Park, Washington, D.C., and Greenville, South Carolina—with a long-term vision of continued growth in these and other geographic areas.

The first Atlanta office of Womble Carlyle was established in 1993 by two members of the firm's Banking, Finance, and Property practice group, primarily to serve the firm's high profile financial institution clients doing business in Atlanta.

Through mergers with business law firm Parker, Johnson, Cook & Dunlevie in 1996 and intellectual property firm Isaf, Vaughan and Kerr in 1998, along with the dynamic Atlanta economy, this office has developed a full-service law practice with more than 50 attorneys. "Womble Carlyle is extremely bullish on Atlanta," says Steven S. Dunlevie, managing member of the Atlanta office. "We believe it has the growth potential to become the epicenter of the firm in the next decade." In fact, the firm's vigorous growth led it to make a major long-term commitment to Atlanta by moving to more spacious quarters at One Atlantic Center in 1999.

Today, the Atlanta office is a technology hub, with a voice, video, and computer network that seamlessly links all of the firm's offices, permitting lawyers and clients in multiple offices to work together as if at a single location. "Our goal is to be recognized for what we have already become, a super regional law firm covering the mid-Atlantic and Southeast, with national clients and extensive international contacts. Atlanta is key to accomplishing that goal," says Dunlevie.

The firm's emphasis on technology is no accident, because it views technology as a vigorous growth sector. "Electronic commerce is the future. It is simply going to explode," predicts G. Donald Johnson, the Corporate and Securities Atlanta practice group leader. While technology is a priority, Womble Carlyle also offers full service to its clients, including intellectual property, information technology, corporate finance and securities, banking, real estate,

tax, employment law and benefits, health care, environmental law, and business and products liability litigation. Commitment to serving and partnering with its clients is a hallmark of Womble Carlyle's reputation.

For its technology clients, Womble Carlyle helps to secure capital, commercialize, and deploy their technology, and guides growing companies into strategic alliances. "We've taken several software companies from being a gleam in the eye, through several rounds of capital, and then have taken them public," says Johnson.

The strategic merger with intellectual property firm Isaf Vaughan & Kerr, P.C. in 1998 enabled the firm to expand its already eminent position in high-tech law with a strengthened capability for patent prosecution (i.e., patent searching, patent applications, and infringement opinions). "The alliance allows us to better serve our intellectual property clients with the deep resources of a full-service, regionally dominant firm," says James F. Vaughan, one of the founding partners of the former Isaf Vaughan & Kerr.

Womble Carlyle continues to maintain a flourishing banking, corporate finance, and commercial real estate practice, which has long been a mainstay of the Atlanta office. The firm regularly represents borrowers, lenders, issuers, and underwriters in major deals.

"In this office in 1998, we did in excess of $1 billion in mergers and acquisitions and initial public offerings, and another $1 billion in commercial financings and conduit loans," says Dunlevie. Womble Carlyle assisted its client Premier Bancshares, Inc., a Georgia bank holding company, in listing on the New York Stock Exchange on June 1, 1999, in culmination of Premier's six years of growth through capital offerings, mergers, and acquisitions. Subsequently, Premier announced its planned merger with another

Womble Carlyle client, BB&T Corporation, a large regional bank holding company.

Meanwhile, Womble Carlyle continues to help its manufacturing clients grow market share safely and profitably, and enter new markets around the world, protecting and defending their rights and assets in courts across the country. When litigation becomes necessary, the firm has extensive experience in products liability defense, representing manufacturers and distributors in varied industries such as medical, automotive, pharmaceutical, housing, and food.

One of Womble Carlyle's unique technological services is its ClientPlus group, a dedicated team of technology consultants who work exclusively for the firm's clients. "We have lawyers who are also systems engineers—technology lawyers in the truest sense. They know what's going on inside and outside the box and can utilize applications to effect solutions to our clients' problems," Dunlevie explains. This gave Womble Carlyle the advantage when it competed with several other firms for the position of John Hancock Life Insurance Company's regional counsel. One of the deciding factors in Womble Carlyle's win was its computer savvy, especially its document management and assembly capability.

Womble Carlyle not only preaches technology, but the firm also practices it. The offices brim with laptops, state-of-the-art video conferencing equipment, high-tech software, scanners, and desktop faxing, all used to better serve clients. The firm constantly upgrades its systems to take advantage of new developments. In 1996, Womble Carlyle established a secure private web site for Lex Mundi, an international association of 150 independent law firms. The firm also has an Intranet, which allows lawyers and support staff to use Internet technology to distribute information within the secure environment of Womble Carlyle's internal Wide Area Network. The firm has developed Extranets, which enable its lawyers to use Internet technology to communicate and share data with clients in a secure, low-cost, easy-to-use environment.

Womble Carlyle's efforts are not confined to boardrooms and courtrooms. Its lawyers are committed to making a difference in the Atlanta community. As a case in point, last fall, instead of racing to court, attorneys of Womble Carlyle raced through the streets of downtown Atlanta in a Mini Grand Prix, a fund-raiser that benefited the Georgia Chapter of the Arthritis Foundation. And that's only one of the many ways Womble Carlyle contributes to the city. The firm also donates toys, clothes, and money to the Atlanta Children's Coalition, is a partner in the city's Adopt-A-Park program, and underwrites programming for WABE-FM, National Public Radio in Atlanta.

Womble Carlyle attorneys contribute charitable and civic leadership as well, supporting with their time, talent, and resources the Metro Atlanta and Georgia Chambers of Commerce, Woodruff Arts Center, Epilepsy Foundation of Georgia, American Heart Association, Atlanta Symphony Orchestra, Egleston/Scottish

Rite Children's Hospital, Fernbank Museum of Natural History, Georgia Volunteer Lawyers for the Arts, and other worthwhile causes. "Our attorneys are actively involved in local civic, arts, church, and school organizations," says Robert F. Cook, Banking, Finance, and Property practice group leader in Atlanta. "We believe it's important to be a positive influence in the community in which we live and work."

As Atlanta continues to grow as a world-class city, Womble Carlyle Sandridge & Rice is providing fuel and growing with it. The firm offers not only community and professional leadership, but also leading-edge information and communication technology, first-rate legal and business knowledge, and strategic insights into industry and commerce. Atlanta is learning that Womble Carlyle's lawyers mean business. ❧

◄ Bob Cook (Banking, Finance, and Property), Kirk Watkins (Litigation), and Don Johnson (Corporate Securities) direct the primary practice areas of the firm's Atlanta office, whose vigorous growth led to a move in 1999 to more spacious quarters in midtown's One Atlantic Center.

◄ Commercial real estate lawyers Amy Huskins (left) and Carolyn Wilson are active members and past presidents of Commercial Real Estate Women of Atlanta (CREW). Womble Carlyle has won for two consecutive years the CREW-Atlanta Champions Award, and won the 1999 NNCREW National Champions Award. Amy was the inaugural co-recipient of the 1998 CREW-Atlanta Member of the Year Award.

Hughston Clinic

> ► As one of the founders of the sports medicine disciplines, Dr. Jack Hughston has helped lead the world to the realization that the physician must understand how an injury occurred to understand how to treat the injury.

> ► High profile sports figures like tennis greats Andre Agassi, Steffi Graf, and Pete Samprass have all relied upon The Hughston Clinic physicians for their expert care.

The same state-of-the-art medical expertise that helps many of Atlanta's top professional athletes stay in shape is available to everyone in need of orthopedic care at The Hughston Clinic, a nationwide network of health care providers specializing in orthopedics and sports medicine.

Six branches of The Hughston Clinic bring first-rate medical care to the greater Atlanta area, from the centrally located Piedmont Road branch, adjacent to Piedmont Hospital, to branches in Alpharetta, Fayette, Morrow, Gwinnett, and Conyers. These clinics work to prevent and treat injuries and diseases of the musculoskeletal system. They also offer advanced services in the areas of orthopedics and sports medicine.

High profile sports figures like boxer Evander Holyfield, tennis greats Andre Agassi, Steffi Graf, and Pete Samprass, baseball's Bo Jackson, basketball's Dominique Wilkins, and golf legend Jack Nicklaus have all relied upon The Hughston Clinic physicians for their expert care.

And it all started with the vision of one man who wanted to make a difference. Dr. Jack Chandler Hughston's revolutionary approach to orthopedic medicine began during World War II with his entry into the Army Medical Corps. On field duty for 18 months, he spent several months working in orthopedic hospitals.

After his release from the army, Dr. Hughston entered Duke University's Orthopedic Training Program to fight another war—the battle against the devastating effects of the polio epidemic.

Columbus, Georgia, was the treatment center for all the victims of infantile paralysis in south Georgia during the polio epidemic of the 1950s. Dr. Hughston worked long hours, gaining knowledge and experience, and in 1951 he founded the Crippled Children's Clinic, where children were examined, diagnosed, and treated, free of charge. Among his patients were children who were injured while playing sports. The terrible threat of polio diminished after the development of Salk's polio vaccine, and Dr. Hughston began to focus on the treatment of children injured during athletic activities. He thought witnessing the damage the moment it occurred would help him to better treat the injuries. He began to attend university and high school games, watching from the sidelines, and the playing field became his laboratory. Modern Sports Medicine was born.

An advocate for equipment safety, Dr. Hughston encouraged protective devices like the use of the mouthpiece, now standard equipment for amateurs and pros alike, and prevented the destruction of countless smiles. His campaign for the elimination of the "crack back block," (hitting below the waist) has saved thousands from serious knee injuries.

Dr. Hughston soon realized that injuries observed and treated on the playing fields were similar to those sustained by industrial workers in rural factories. The knowledge and expertise he'd gained on the football field also benefited those Dr. Hughston called "Industrial Athletes."

In 1968 Dr. Hughston founded the Hughston Sports Medicine Foundation, a nonprofit research and education center for the study of musculoskeletal wellness. Today, the Hughston Sports Medicine Foundation houses a sports medicine fellowship program and is involved with research in pharmaceutical trials, cartilage replacement techniques, and surgical procedures.

In 1984 construction began on The Hughston Sports Medicine Hospital that serves as the teaching hospital for the Hughston

Sports Medicine Foundation's fellowship program.

Today, Hughston, Inc. is the holding company for the many Hughston organizations. They include Hughston Management Services, a full-service management organization offering health care and management services to physicians and practices throughout the state of Georgia. Hughston Orthopedic Network is a statewide orthopedic network, allowing patients access to the first-rate orthopedics throughout Georgia and the Southeast. The Hughston Managed Care Corporation is a workers' compensation managed care organization, certified by the state board of Workers' Compensation, and provides care to Georgia's injured workers. Hughston Health is a health and wellness facility in Columbus which offers health and fitness training and health assessments. Hughston Sports Medicine Hospital is a Columbus specialty hospital, located on the 52-acre Hughston campus in Columbus, Georgia. The Hughston Clinic, a 53-physician, comprehensive musculoskeletal multispecialty, practices orthopedic sports medicine and occupational medicine. The Hughston Clinic team is made up of sports medicine professionals—orthopedic surgeons, family practitioners, physical therapists, and athletic trainers, all focused on the needs of the communities they serve.

"The Hughston Clinic method is unique not only due to some of the specialized surgical techniques and skills we possess, but also due to the manner in which the sports medicine philosophy is applied to the treatment of any musculoskeletal problem," says Dr. Todd Schmidt, president of The Hughston Clinic's Atlanta group. "In other words, rather than the typical 'If it hurts, don't do it,' we say, 'if it hurts, first put the joint and muscle forces back into balance and fitness.' The body will take care of itself more naturally and physiologically. Then, if necessary, we use surgical skills."

The Hughston Clinic's vision for its future in Atlanta is one of commitment and service. "We want to serve as educators for the maintenance of the musculoskeletal health of our community," says Dr. Schmidt. This includes the ever-increasing numbers of recreational athletes, an aging but still active population that retires from the workplace earlier and continues to enjoy personal physical activities, and an older workforce that presents unique problems of joint and bone health.

The Hughston Clinic looks forward to providing Atlanta with the technical innovation and medical integrity necessary for consistent, cost-effective, quality outcomes. ●

▲ The same state-of-the-art medical expertise that helps many of Atlanta's top professional athletes stay in shape is available to everyone in need of orthopedic care at The Hughston Clinic, a nationwide network of health care providers specializing in orthopedics and sports medicine.

Motorola Energy Systems Group

In 1928 Paul Galvin founded Motorola, Inc., a company named to characterize the new age that was ready to mix music and motion. The innovative creation of the car radio made Galvin his fortune and started a global communications giant.

Today, Motorola is a Fortune 50 company that has become one of the world's leading providers of wireless communications, semiconductors, and integrated electronics systems. Its major equipment businesses include cellular telephones, two-way radios, paging and data communications, personal communications, automotive and industrial electronics, defense and space electronics, and computers.

Motorola's Integrated Electronic Systems Sector (IESS) is a leading provider of electronic systems for customers who integrate them into their products. IESS designs and manufactures electronic solutions for the automotive, communications, imaging, manufacturing systems, computer, consumer, and industrial markets.

Motorola Energy Systems Group

Located outside of Atlanta, in Lawrenceville, Georgia, is one business of IESS, Motorola Energy Systems Group (ESG). ESG is one of

the world's largest providers of integrated energy systems for portable electronics. It makes battery packs, charging systems, power supplies, and accessories. What differentiates ESG from its competitors is that it leverages a broad range of technologies and systems expertise to deliver integrated energy systems—from the wall to the host. Motorola's integrated energy systems are in many of today's leading brand-name mobile phones, notebook and palm computers, and other portable electronic devices.

"We decided to make our worldwide headquarters in Atlanta primarily because 70 to 80 percent of our employees said they would relocate if we chose Atlanta," said Jerry Blanton, corporate vice president and general manager, Energy Systems Group. "In 1994, 123 Motorolan families relocated to the metro Atlanta area, and over 5 years, more than 95 percent have stayed. I believe the [employees'] enthusiasm for relocating to Atlanta was directly tied to the quality of life here."

ESG brought 70 years of production experience, manufacturing capabilities, and research and design competencies to Georgia. Its areas of technical expertise include benchmarking, performance and safety, Underwriters Laboratories Certification, and battery cell technology.

ESG hires highly skilled, educated, and experienced people in design engineering, manufacturing engineering operations, research, and quality control who deliver a depth of electrochemical and electronics integration know-how. In addition, it hires sales and marketing professionals with an understanding of industry needs. Motorola is an Equal Employment Opportunity/Affirmative Action Employer. Globally, ESG employs about 4,500 people at five research, design, and manufacturing facilities in Lawrenceville, Georgia; Harvard, Illinois; Penang, Malaysia; Dublin, Ireland; and Tianjin, China.

"Atlanta is more than just the functional headquarters for Energy Systems Group. It is also the ESG headquarters for the future. Here we will design the future products that will benefit our customers, employees, and communities," said Jerry Blanton.

Motorola's Consumer and Retail Business Radio Division

Another Motorola entity—with local presence—is Motorola's Consumer and Retail Business Radio Division (CRBR). CRBR creates cutting edge two-way radios that improve productivity, efficiency, security, and individual communications for businesses and families everywhere. In early 1997, the sales, marketing, and worldwide distribution for CRBR relocated its headquarters to Suwanee, Georgia.

"The CRBR family is excited to call Atlanta home and looks forward to contributing to the lives of the residents and the growth of the community," said Mike Fraser, vice president and director of operations of the CRBR Division.

Motorola's two-way radio technology has been making a difference in people's lives, all over the world, since 1940. This impact began with the creation of the first portable, FM two-way radio— the "walkie-talkie" backpack—which was vital to battlefield communications during World War II.

In addition, two-way technology has been critical to the success of NASA programs. In 1962, on its flight to Venus, Mariner II carried a Motorola transponder that provided a radio link spanning 54 million miles. Two years later, with similar equipment, images of Mars were relayed back to Earth aboard Mariner IV. And in 1969, astronaut Neil Armstrong's first words were relayed from the moon to the Earth using a Motorola transponder.

Today, in Atlanta, Motorola's Talkabout and Spirit Professional Two-Way Radios enhance people's daily lives and business productivity. Talkabout Radios help families and friends, all over the city, stay in touch. Whether it be during a bike trip on Stone Mountain, a tour of the Coke museum, or while keeping track of the family at the Mid-Town Music Festival, Talkabout Radios make communication easy and bring peace of mind. The

◄ Motorola Spirit GT (Group Talk) professional two-way radios help businesses enhance their daily productivity.

Spirit Professional Two-Way Radios are designed to enhance the job-site communications of Atlanta's bustling business community. Local restaurants such as Rio Bravo, local retailers such as Home Depot, and local construction companies such as Dixie Construction all use Motorola products every day.

"The CRBR division is committed to providing the people of Atlanta with innovative new products that will not only stimulate local economic growth, but will also simplify and better their everyday lives," said Mike Fraser.

Motorola Atlanta is comprised of several divisions. Collectively, each division contributes to the community through education, diversity, and community relations programs. Motorola has made a commitment to support programming that positively impacts the quality of life in Atlanta. And Motorola has been able to follow through on its commitment by contributing to such organizations as Junior Achievement, the Atlanta Hispanic Chamber of Commerce, and Hands on Atlanta.

For the Centennial Olympic Games and the Atlanta Paralympics, Motorola contributed state-of-the-art voice and data communications equipment that were crucial to the successful coordination of events.

Motorola is a neighbor, as well as a multinational, with sales that topped $28.4 billion in 1998.

◄ Motorola TalkAbout two-way radios are used by families throughout the Atlanta area.

Heidelberg USA, Inc.

offices coordinate the process, while locally based service technicians and technical consultants keep in close contact with the customers worldwide.

Heidelberg USA, Inc. was formed with the merger of Heidelberg West, Inc., headquartered in San Francisco, and Heidelberg Eastern, Inc., based in New York. It was decided to establish headquarters for the combined organization in Georgia on 28 acres in a Kennesaw office park. "It is easier to merge two cultures in neutral headquarters," explains Hans Peetz-Larsen, CEO of Heidelberg Americas, which is the parent company of Heidelberg USA and consolidates the company's management operations in the United States, Canada, and Mexico. "Atlanta is strategically well located. We are an international company, and through Hartsfield Airport we have easy and convenient access to the whole world." Peetz-Larsen further cites the relatively good state of Atlanta's infrastructure, the favorable housing costs, lower tax rates, and moderate utility costs as part of Atlanta's enticements.

Peetz-Larsen also believes that Atlanta's amenities help to attract first-rate employees. "When you offer Atlanta as base, there's little or no hesitation. They say, 'When's the next plane?'" On a personal note, the CEO appreciates Atlanta's pleasant quality of life. "It's a good place to raise a family," says Peetz-Larsen, whose family has lived here since 1994.

▲ In a quietly efficient office park in Kennesaw, the North American operations of Heidelberger Druckmaschinen AG, the world market leader in products and services covering all facets of the print process, is redefining printing.

▶ Hans Peetz-Larsen serves as the Americas CEO.

In a quietly efficient office park on Gutenberg Drive, the North American operations of Heidelberger Druckmaschinen, AG, the world market leader in products and services covering all facets of the print process chain, is redefining printing. Headquartered in the Kennesaw facility is Heidelberg's North American Regional staff and the home office of Heidelberg Americas Inc., as well as Heidelberg USA, Inc., the Sales and Service provider for the United States.

Originally a supplier of printing presses, Heidelberg has taken the initiative and expanded beyond putting ink on paper by broadening its products and services. Today, as a systems vendor and adviser for printers worldwide, Heidelberg covers the entire spectrum of printing needs, from prepress and press to postpress. It's like the orange, the press, and the juice—instead of supplying only the press, Heidelberg now offers all three.

As part of this strategy, Heidelberg acquired the Sheridan Systems Division of AM International in 1996 and the Linotype-Hell Company in 1997. Those acquisitions provided Heidelberg with expanded presences in the prepress and postpress segments of the graphic arts business. Recently, Heidelberg acquired Kodak's Office Imaging division and formed a joint venture with Kodak to provide digital printing solutions to the industry.

When it comes to service, Heidelberg's international network of Regional offices support their clients with one of the largest sales and service organizations in the world. The tech centers and sales

Before they moved south, Heidelberg set up an "Atlanta room" in their New York office that featured Atlanta's daily papers as well as information provided by the Atlanta and Cobb County Chambers of Commerce, school system, realtors, and banks. "We relocated 90 people from New York and San Francisco in September of 1994 and at the same time provided an additional

140 jobs in the local community," says Senior Vice President of Administration, James Carlson. One of Atlanta's pluses is old-fashioned Southern hospitality. "Our relocated employees commented on how people were extremely friendly, welcoming, and gracious," Carlson recalls.

Heidelberg's sleek, 157,000-square-foot headquarters currently houses 430 employees and a spotless state-of-the-art showroom. The showroom hums with activity, and the air has the faint, delicious smell of a new book.

The offset printing presses in the showroom range from the smallest model, about the size of a sawed-off VW bug, to a sleek gray machine as big as a hook and ladder fire engine. The top-of-the-line press has automation that enables it to monitor every pixel, each dot of color, with precision, whether it's copy number one or copy number 100,000.

That level of efficiency and precision is part of Heidelberg's strength, along with its impeccable reputation. The company is characterized by industry insiders as offering the "Mercedes" of printing presses, but Heidelberg's range is even wider.

"We cater to the whole printing industry," emphasizes Niels M. Winther, CEO of Heidelberg USA. "We make thoroughbreds, yes, but we also make workhorses."

Winther describes Heidelberg presses as coming in all sizes and capabilities, and ranging in price from $50,000 to $5 million. "The smaller presses suit quick print operations, the kind of neighborhood print shop that makes business cards and invitations," Winther explains.

Heidelberg offers everything they might need—prepress equipment, the printing press, the paper cutter, and paper-folding machines sized to fit their requirements. Once the small business grows and begins to develop corporate clients and establish their own sales force, Heidelberg can help them upgrade to a four-color process press and related equipment that can create sales spec sheets, brochures, and other printed products geared to the markets they serve.

Heidelberg's largest format equipment is right for customers targeting high quality printing jobs for advertising companies and clients with high volume production and annual report requirements. Atlanta has a number of world-class printing companies serving such needs. "We start a personal relationship with individuals and are ready to help them when they need to add to their capabilities," says Winther.

Heidelberg also believes in the importance of investing in the community. One example of its generosity is the annual $10,000 contribution Heidelberg is giving Kennesaw State University for education over the next decade. The company is likewise strongly committed to cultural causes, providing support to the Woodruff Arts Center, the Cobb County Symphony, and the Kennesaw Civil War Museum.

"Supporting the arts is a priority," says Heidelberg Americas CEO Peetz-Larsen, who believes that a flourishing arts community is an intrinsic part of the definition of a world-class city.

Heidelberg is prepared to lead the industry into the next millennium. Peetz-Larsen makes the point that the Agricultural Age took thousands of years to evolve; the Industrial Age took three hundred years to develop; but the advances of the new Information Age are measured in months, if not weeks.

The twenty-first century is the Communications Age. People can now communicate faster and more often than ever before. As a result, the quantity of information is growing all the time. New communication technologies are leaving their mark on the print products market and posing new challenges for the printing industry.

In a study Heidelberg conducted, the company looked at the entire global graphic arts markets: printing, computer output, copiers, everything that required paper consumption. Every imaginable factor was taken into account. In the end the conclusion was that printing will continue to grow. "We are positioned to deal with everything to do with the printed sheet. We're systems providers, sellers of solutions."

Peetz-Larsen concludes, "Within the printing equipment industry, our company is, by a substantial margin, number one in the world. As the technology leader, Heidelberg will continue to play a major role in shaping the future of the graphics industry." ☙

▲ (Top) **James Carlson is Heidelberg USA Senior Vice President of Administration.**

▲ **Niels M. Winther is Heidelberg USA president and CEO.**

Corporate Enviroments

▶ Corporate Environments
is one of the top woman-
owned businesses in the
Atlanta market. Pictured
are (left to right) Karen
Hughes, president; John
Harris, chairman; and
Janet Miller, executive
vice president.

John Harris bought Corporate Environments, a locally owned, full-service contract furnishings and office systems company, in 1990. He grew the company rapidly using a simple, effective strategy. "We'd do anything. We'd bid on one chair when we were trying to establish ourselves. We were small, flexible, owner-involved, and we made it our mission to support the architect and design community," Harris recalls. His enthusiasm, determination, and flexibility soon brought distinction to the company. One of Corporate Environments' early efforts for the Atlanta law firm Sutherland Asbill turned out so well that the prestigious furniture manufacturer Knoll used it in its marketing materials.

In 1993, Harris bought Ball Stalker, which had furnished Atlanta offices for more than 30 years and was the only other competitor that carried the high-design Knoll furniture line. Corporate Environments' sales doubled overnight, and the expanding company became Knoll's exclusive dealer in Atlanta, while continuing to represent many other manufacturers that offer high-quality furnishings. Simultaneously, Knoll & Corporate Environments were awarded the United Parcel Service headquarters project. "That order was several years' worth of work," Harris recalls. "They checked us out carefully. They knew we could handle it." Between 1990 and 1997, the number of employees grew from 8 to more than 100, and the company had revenues of $39 million in 1997.

In 1998, Harris decided to make a change. "I wanted less stress, more fun," Harris says. After rejecting other corporate suitors,

Harris accepted an in-house offer and sold his majority interest in Corporate Environments to Karen Hughes, vice president of finance, who teamed up with Janet Miller, vice president of sales and marketing. The deal made Corporate Environments a top woman-owned business in the Atlanta market.

"Corporate Environments is the best group of people. It's our second family," says Hughes about their decision to buy the company she knew so well. "No one else could have taken over and left it essentially unchanged," Hughes says. Miller adds, " Corporate Environments was already a successful company when we bought it. We loved what Corporate Environments stood for—integrity and commitment to excellence. Everyone works hard, has fun, and believes in what we're doing. We wanted to protect that and build on the foundation John created."

"Karen and Janet have taken the company over, given it their flavor, and are taking it to the next level," says Harris, who still owns 15 percent and remains at the company as chairman. "Part of my mission is to make sure they don't fail."

Today, 80 percent of the business comes from 50 to 70 customers, an impressive client list that includes UPS, The Coca-Cola Company, and Turner Broadcasting System, as well as Georgia-Pacific and many other top Atlanta-area corporations.

"We have a good relationship with the design community. We work with them, instead of competing against them," explains company President and Co-owner Hughes. They recommend us, put their reputation on the line, because they can depend on us to get the job done. We may not be the lowest bid, but we've proven that we can perform. The UPS corporate campus is really what turned the corner," Hughes continues. "The size and complexity of the

▶ Knoll & Corporate
Environments were
simultaneously awarded
the United Parcel Service
headquarters project.
UPS photo courtesy of TVS
Interiors/Brian Gassel.

job was huge. It amounted to what we had done in annual volume the previous year. We worked on it for a year before we installed the first piece of furniture."

Corporate Environments has successfully handled a wide range of formidable projects. "We've been working with TBS for about five years. We've done newsrooms in New York, Washington, D.C., Los Angeles, and Atlanta. It was quite a task, because CNN is on-air all the time, so the installation was very challenging," Hughes says. Corporate Environments managed the job by working off hours during commercial breaks. The Delta Crown Room, located in an airport that never closes, and the EPA downtown Atlanta installation

during the Olympics also proved challenging.

"We've also done a couple of mansions in Buckhead, several restaurants, and Coca-Cola's retail store in Las Vegas," Chairman Harris recalls. "There's an incredible amount of business with the growth of this town."

Today, Corporate Environments customizes its service to the level of each company's needs, whether it be once a month or five days a week. The company offers its customers dedicated crews available to move workstations, add case goods, or make any other needed changes. "Managing not only our customers' product needs but also their service needs is an important part of our business," says Hughes.

Executive Vice President Miller agrees. "Our customers are faced with constant changes: technology, reorganization, and real estate issues. Our role is to stay on top of what's happening so we can be a resource to help companies make smart decisions about their facilities."

Corporate Environments has established a unique hot line phone/fax number for immediate client response, which directly connects clients with a Customer Satisfaction Representative whose only objective is to pursue a client's issue to a satisfactory resolution. "We look carefully at our clients' business, what they need, and how can we help them do their job easier," says Hughes.

Corporate Environments has been listed on *INC's* 500 fastest growing private companies in America list three times in the last decade. Corporate Environments is Atlanta's second-largest office furniture dealer, as well as the fifth-largest Women-Owned firm, according to *Atlanta Business Chronicle's* lists published in 1999. And in 1997, Corporate Environments opened an office in Nashville—Synergy Business Environments.

A formidable competitor in the contract furniture industry, Corporate Environments is optimistic about the future. "Our strength is our experience and ability to remain flexible. Every customer is different," Miller says. "We're here to stay. We're committed to being a responsible member of the Atlanta business community and look forward to the growth and success of this city." ❧

◄ **Corporate Environments has successfully handled a wide range of formidable projects, including the Atlanta Development Authority.** ADA photo courtesy of Mary Mobley Johnson Interiors/Brian Robbins.

◄ **Eighty percent of Corporate Environments' business comes from 50 to 70 customers, an impressive client list that includes The Coca-Cola Company and many other top Atlanta-area corporations.** The Coca-Cola Company photo courtesy of Knoll. Inc.

Goode Van Slyke Architecture

oriented. We're both strong designers who have different approaches. This mix allows us to be more flexible and creative, while adhering to strict budgets and schedules."

Van Slyke focuses on design, technical quality control, and project management. "We educate the client on the project, including all the facts. We make sure the budget is appropriate to the project and keep the client informed," says Van Slyke,

▲ Christopher Goode and Paul Van Slyke, two imaginative architects, working with the courage of their design convictions, have designed such buildings as the HPER Facility.

Christopher Goode and Paul Van Slyke believe that significant, innovative architecture is important to Atlanta's future success. These two imaginative architects, working with the courage of their design convictions, have already handled award-winning projects with a cumulative construction value of $165 million, making Goode Van Slyke Architecture a leader in resourceful, ingenious design.

Christopher Goode, born in Nuremberg, Germany, received his degrees from North Carolina State University and the University of California at Berkeley. A project architect and designer for 13 years before founding GVSA in 1996, Goode has always been fascinated with new construction. "Growing up in North Carolina I used to watch houses and commercial buildings come together," Goode recalls.

Born in New York, Paul Van Slyke was awarded degrees from Georgia Tech after additional studies at the école des Beaux Arts, Paris, and the Architectural Association in London and Cambridge University. "I come from a scientific background," says Van Slyke. "I love the expression of architecture coupled with the science of structure."

The two young architects met through mutual friends, and decided to become colleagues. "We're a lot alike in personality and character," Goode says.

Goode is involved in all major decisions within the firm, concentrating on quality control, design, and business development. He meets with clients throughout the design process, solves client problems, and reviews the results. "Architecture is an organized art form, and I am an organized person," Goode explains. "Paul's a little more technical, production oriented, and analytical. I'm more marketing

▶ Van Slyke focuses on design, technical quality control, and project management. An example of the firm's work is the Dorothy C. Benson Senior Multi-Purpose Complex.

who has worked on many different types of projects, including health care, educational, libraries, commercial, industrial, and residential. "We sell the process, not an off-the-shelf product. We already have a strong background with public-sector clients and we are building clientele in the private sector: loft projects, mixed-use, and corporate offices. We're really flexible, designing everything from a $1.2-million custom home to a $25-million mixed-use development."

The partners decided early on to build their future in Atlanta. "When I went to school here I recognized a lot of success," Van Slyke recalls.

Goode agrees. "I wanted to do big architecture and Atlanta was the strongest city. If an architect wants to do projects of significant scale, Atlanta is one of the target cities."

Ask these architects about their favorite projects and Goode doesn't hesitate. GVSA's recent design of the $14-million Health, Physical Education, and Recreation Facility at Albany State University required the utmost flexibility, so that as many functions as possible could occur simultaneously. The large open areas called for a sophisticated structure, and the high humidity and chemical content in the pool atmosphere meant complicated HVAC systems, while the specialized sports equipment and scorekeeping equipment needed extensive coordination, and the computer and health

performance laboratories required networking coordination.

"It's rare for a firm to win a commission this complex early on," Goode explains. "This project set the tone of what our firm is capable of." The result—a remarkably adaptable, clever design that includes a three-court gymnasium that can be converted into a 4,000-seat arena or a 4,800-seat convocation center. Classes and recreational small craft exercises take place in the stretch pool, while NCAA competitions are facilitated by a floating, movable bulkhead. Varsity functions are grouped together in the building and include eight locker rooms, weight training, and state-of-the-art rehabilitation and training facilities. "A fun place to be is a fun place to design," says Goode.

Restoration and renovation projects developed by GVSA have meticulously preserved historic buildings while enabling maximum use of the interior space.

GVSA's work on the Savannah Civil Rights Museum involved the reuse of a building that is on the National Historic Landmark Register. Because of the constraints associated with Historic Landmark designation, the firm designed the project on its computers in three dimensions, rather than the conventional two dimensions. The 3D images enabled the firm to "virtually" tour the client through the building before construction began. GVSA's innovative design for the Savannah Civil Rights Museum was featured on NPR radio and *NBC Nightly News*.

The firm is fully computer-automated, a distinct advantage when GVSA participated in the Look of the Games program for the 1996 Olympic Games. Of the 12 Atlanta firms involved, GVSA was the only firm to use a completely computer-driven process, which was part of the original project requirements. Photos of the University of Georgia's stadium and coliseum were scanned into the computer, graphic images were created in a drafting program, and an assembly of computer images was imported to form the construction documents.

Another one of GVSA's groundbreaking design concepts is Price

Middle School in south Atlanta (30 percent renovation and 70 percent new construction). "We talked to the community, the teachers, and the students, and redesigned the school from the inside out," Goode explains. "We designed the building as an envelope to fit around the people." The GVSA architectural design for Price Middle School is intended to serve as a model for Atlanta's middle school system.

Other projects include a teleconference center for the CDC's Atlanta headquarters, an addition to the Georgia Tech computer center designed 100 percent via computer, a hypoallergenically safe lab addition for the Ecology Department at the University of Georgia, and the Dorothy C. Benson Multi-Purpose Senior Complex.

The partners are a community-minded presence in metro Atlanta and one of the sponsors for the 1997 Special Olympics. Goode has also been involved in Friends of Zoo Atlanta, and Van Slyke received the volunteer of the year award from the Southern Region Breakthru House. GVSA is currently supporting Forrest Hills Elementary School as sponsors in DeKalb County's Partners in Education Program.

"The Southeast is a great area for emerging businesses, a great place to stake your claim," says Van Slyke. "I expect Goode Van Slyke Architecture to do interesting projects that challenge the firm's capabilities," Goode adds. "We have a vision for Atlanta's future." ❦

◄ Another one of GVSA's groundbreaking design concepts is Price Middle School in south Atlanta (30 percent renovation and 70 percent new construction).

▼ Goode Van Slyke Architecture likes to take on interesting projects that challenge the firm's capabilities, such as the Rich Center addition at Georgia Tech.

Holiday Inn Downtown

▲ The entryway of the Holiday Inn Downtown features a domed entrance graced with a beautiful chandelier, warm mahogany woodwork, and marble floors.

▶ Holiday Inn holds each hotel to the highest of standards so that patrons are comfortable at any of thousands of locations worldwide.

In the beginning, the hotel was opened in 1986 as the Ibis Hotel by foreign investors. Catty-cornered from the Ibis stood the old American Hotel, the first hotel to be integrated in the South. But downtown Atlanta had deteriorated, the face of it worn down by the familiar troubles of an inner city.

The Ibis was purchased by the current owners, Crown American Hotels based out of Johnstown, Pennsylvania, in 1989. They changed the Ibis into a Comfort Inn. In pre-Olympic Atlanta the blocks surrounding the hotel were filled with warehouses and old garages. On one side of the hotel stood the bus station. It was, quite simply, the bad part of town. Nonetheless, Comfort Inn provided a safe haven for travelers with its clean rooms and affordable rates.

When the Olympics came and went, downtown Atlanta changed forever. The warehouses, garages, and bus station disappeared from the scene. The Centennial Olympic Park was built one-half a block from the Comfort Inn. It became safe to walk the short distance from the hotel to The CNN Center and The World Congress Center. And the city kept its volunteer Welcome People on the streets to guide visitors and add a sense of security.

The Georgia Dome also opened, home of the Atlanta Falcons, and the Atlanta Braves moved from Fulton County Stadium to Turner Field. The old Omni Coliseum was torn down and Philips Arena was built to house the Atlanta Hawks basketball team and the Atlanta Thrashers professional hockey team.

In response to the lasting changes, Comfort Inn became the Holiday Inn and underwent a multimillion-dollar renovation. Now the entryway features a domed entrance graced with a beautiful chandelier, warm mahogany woodwork, and marble floors. The rooms feature elaborate phone systems with data ports and beautiful appointments. Meeting rooms are designed for flexibility to accommodate the many groups and exhibitors that frequent the hotel.

While meetings and events are underway, families of the conventioneers walk to the CNN Center or the World of Coca-Cola for a tour, or to Centennial Olympic Park and Underground Atlanta. These excursions are often followed by a trip to nearby Planet Hollywood or Hard Rock Cafe.

Atlanta has much to offer and features many a distinctive landmark and attraction. It is also home to some of America's greatest names in the world of business: Coca-Cola, Delta . . . and Holiday Inn. The most recognized hotel name in the world, Holiday Inn is a part of the Bass Hotels and Resorts family that grew and prospered right here in Atlanta. It is, therefore, appropriate that downtown Atlanta be complete with its first and only Holiday Inn.

Holiday Inn has changed over the years. Gone are the old U-shaped, two-story buildings with a pool in the center that used to dot the expressways of America. Today, Holiday Inn holds each hotel to the highest of standards so that patrons are comfortable at any of thousands of locations worldwide. Deviation among franchise owners is not tolerated.

So it is that Holiday Inn is as revitalized and energized as downtown Atlanta. It is fitting that while both have changed, the two belong to each other and represent a history rich in tradition and accomplishment. ◐

Nextel

Nextel Communications Inc., based in Reston, Virginia, has built the largest guaranteed all-digital wireless network in the United States. Nextel covers thousands of communities, serving 92 of the top 100 U.S markets with more than 9,600 dedicated team members throughout the country. In addition, through Nextel International Inc., Nextel has wireless operations and investments in Canada, Mexico, Argentina, Brazil, the Philippines, Peru, Japan, and Shanghai, China.

Founded in 1987 as Fleet Call, Inc., the company changed its name to Nextel Communications Inc. in 1993. Nextel's 1999 agreement with SpectraSite Communications, Inc. to purchase its 2,000 towers and build 1,700 new towers within the next five years supports an aggressive nationwide expansion of the Nextel National Network.

"Our subscriber base at the end of second quarter 1999 had approximately 3.5-million digital subscriber units in service. This phenomenal growth is a result of the quality, value, and simplicity that we provide to our customers," says Nextel Chairman and Chief Executive Officer Daniel F. Akerson.

The 1996 Summer Centennial Olympic Games in Atlanta was a significant milestone in Nextel's history and the launch of the Atlanta market. Nextel had 5,000 phones in operation in Atlanta during the Olympics, the company's first, large-scale test of its products and technology. "Nextel experienced tremendous success. Everything tested out perfectly," says Marty Lock, Nextel's southeast area president. "Multiple key corporations used Nextel during the event. Other companies had problems with their communication technology, but not Nextel. Our system and phones performed magnificently."

The Nextel National Network provides customers with guaranteed all-digital cellular service, text/numeric paging, and Nextel Direct Connect™, their two-way radio feature. Nextel Direct Connect allows the user to speak with one or up to 100 individuals for a fraction of the cost of cellular. All cellular charges, after the first minute, are rounded to the nearest second. The Nextel National Network, the first all-digital wireless network, also offers no roaming charges.

Nextel uses iDEN® (integrated digital enhanced network) wireless communications technology developed by Motorola. The state-of-the-art sound and transmission technology means crisp and clear high-quality voice communications, improved privacy to protect calls from being overheard, and call security.

One way Nextel prepared for the millennium was by teaming up with Microsoft to create Nextel Online℠. Before the year 2000, Nextel Online will offer e-mail, calendar functionality, address book contacts, and access to Web-based stock quotes, weather, news, and sports. These services are being designed and deployed so that Nextel customers will be able to access them in combination with a range of other devices, including personal digital assistants (PDAs), palmtop computers, PCs, and Windows CE operating system-based devices. "Microsoft and Nextel will deliver the next generation of wireless services to enable people everywhere to stay in touch with the information they need, regardless of location," said Bill Gates, chairman and CEO of Microsoft.

"The combination of Nextel's integrated data network and Internet-ready phones will provide our customers with the ability to access information and applications that are important to them, wherever they are," said Dan Akerson, chairman and CEO of Nextel Communications. "This is the ultimate last mile, and we are delivering it wirelessly." ◑

▲ Nextel Communications Inc. has built the largest guaranteed all-digital wireless network in the United States, covering thousands of communities and serving 92 of the top 100 U.S markets with more than 9,600 dedicated team members throughout the country.

◀ New Nextel i1000plus™ Internet-Ready Phone.

Powertel, Inc.

Powertel, Inc., headquartered in West Point, Georgia, provides digital wireless personal communications services (PCS) in the southeastern United States.

Powertel's management team has extensive experience in the industry and deep Southern roots. Chairman of the Board of Directors, Campbell "Cam" Lanier III, a fourth-generation Georgian, is the founder of ITC, a holding company for telecommunications-related service companies that includes Powertel. His great-grandfather, J. Smith Lanier, brought the first telephones to West Point, Georgia, in 1896. Allen E. Smith, Powertel president and chief executive officer, was formerly with SouthernNet and helped establish Powertel in 1993. Their business goal is to provide affordable, superior-quality wireless service throughout the South. They are well on their way, with service in 34 operational markets and along major connecting highway corridors spanning seven states.

Powertel's PCS licenses encompass a territory of approximately 263,000 contiguous square miles with a population of approximately 24.3 million people, the largest contiguous digital PCS network in the southeastern United States. With more than 1,600 operational base stations, customers can use Powertel's PCS service from Jacksonville, Florida, to Memphis, Tennessee, a trip covering 713 miles through four states.

Powertel's clever execution of its regionally focused strategy—the creation of a seamless PCS footprint including the population centers and key corridors of the Southeast—has made its reputation shine. Powertel snapped up Atlanta in 1996 when GTE Wireless put the market on the block, but

decided not to launch Atlanta, the largest metro area in its territory, until it could assure customers strong coverage throughout the region, not just in Buckhead.

The company has continued to rapidly build out its PCS network and launch additional PCS services on schedule. "We continue to build a successful business in a very exciting and competitive industry," said Allen E. Smith, Powertel president and chief executive officer. "Our subscriber growth validates our philosophy of providing high-quality, affordable wireless services with no hidden surprises."

For its success in 1997, *Wireless Week*—one of the industry's leading trade newspapers—named Powertel as the recipient of its PCS "Carrier Excellence Award."

Powertel PCS uses some of the most advanced digital technology ever created—Global System for Mobile Communications (GSM). GSM is far more advanced than traditional analog cellular technology and offers integrated voice, high-speed data, paging, fax, and short message service, all from one network and through one handset. This proven technology, now being used in over 130 countries with approximately 230 million subscribers, will ultimately provide customers with the ability to use Powertel's service across much of the United States and throughout a large part of the world.

"The real challenge is ahead now," says Smith. "We need to continue to execute, to be able to stay in touch with customers and the market, and be able to outperform our competitors."

TWD, Inc.

When asked about his experience in working for Senator Sam Nunn, Thomas Dortch, former State Director and founder of TWD, Inc., had this to say: "You had to go prepared, so working with him [Nunn], you learned that the details were very important. You do your homework, that's part of the mentoring that came over the years with Nunn. But that's the thing a lot of folks didn't know about him. His position was, 'I don't ever want to do anything in the Senate that I wouldn't want done to me or for me.' He was always concerned with impact. That was always important. Those of us who were ever touched by Nunn, we learned the importance of hard work and long hours . . . but the reward was the success of knowing you helped people. That's the focus of my company now. Sure, I look at my bottom line, but the other part is I have fun doing it. I help a lot of people."

During his many years with Nunn, Dortch spent hundreds of hours helping businesses deal with the huge defense agencies in the procurement arena. His efforts resulted in many a new millionaire. His day often revolved around helping businesses make headway in the turbulent and obscure federal waters.

Founding TWD was a natural extension of the duties he loved most in the public sector. Dortch and the TWD, Inc. staff spend most of their energy and time helping people meet people, and teaching them to maneuver through federal, state, and local government red tape. Accessing key contacts for clients is another daily activity for the firm.

In short, TWD is an information/relationship brokerage firm. It is a popular source for many a Fortune 500 company plagued with questions of how, where, and who to get what from in a convoluted world of high-tech and power frenzies. "It's a matter of staying involved, staying connected with the community, of understanding that business is about people. Communities, good employees, and contacts exist only when companies and individuals reach out. TWD helps guide that reach," says Dortch.

Clients of TWD include former Senator Sam Nunn, King & Spalding, Browning Ferris Industries, Miller Brewing Company, Aetna Retirement Services, the U.S. Department of Defense, The 3M Company, Diaz-Verson Capital Investments, Inc., Computer Services Corporation, the Village Foundation in Washington, D.C., and the Georgia Association of Minority Entrepreneurs, among its numerous state, national, and international companies.

Politics are still a big part of the business reality. Personally, Dortch has over 24 years' experience in political campaigns ranging from a stint as associate director in 1974 for the State Democratic Party, to deputy campaign director for the 1992 and 1996 Clinton/Gore presidential campaigns, U.S. Senator Max Cleland's campaign, and many others. Certainly not all of TWD's clients are Democrats, but none argue the unique success Dortch has lent to the campaigns on which he has served, nor with the political savvy that only time in the inside trenches can render. ◐

Thomas Dortch served former U.S. Senator Sam Nunn for 16 years in numerous senior staff positions, wrapping up his illustrious public career as the State Director of Georgia from 1990 to 1995. As director, Dortch held one of the most powerful political positions in the state under the direction of the nation's most powerful senator. One year before Nunn decided to retire, Dortch moved into the private sector, where he founded TWD, Inc. Even so, Dortch still serves his country in a variety of ways, including a Presidential appointment to the nine-member board of the Office of the National Drug Control Policy that oversees an annual $2-billion budget in an effort to reduce drug abuse in the United States.

▲ Dortch has over 24 years' experience in political campaigns ranging from a stint as associate director in 1974 for the State Democratic Party, to deputy campaign director for the 1992 and 1996 Clinton/Gore presidential campaigns.

◀ TWD, founded by Thomas Dortch, is an information/relationship brokerage firm. It is a popular source for many a Fortune 500 company plagued with questions of how, where, and who to get what from in a convoluted world of high-tech and power frenzies. Photo by Black Berry Photography.

Corey Entertainment

The Corey name means different things to different people in Atlanta. To some, the name conjures up an image of Billy Corey and his political, social, and business prowess. For others, the first thought is of Corey Advertising, an icon in the world of advertising. Still others think of the latest Corey enterprise, Corey Entertainment, a national provider of promotions in regard to turnkey solutions for corporate events, the amusement industry, promotional campaigns, festivals, and special events. No matter which image immediately comes to mind, most agree that the Corey name means results.

Corey Entertainment is a fascinating blend of innovative and fantastic solutions for the world of corporate entertaining. Three main divisions provide distinct services that can be used independently or simultaneously at any event.

the knowledgeable staff can deliver and set up for a completely hassle-free corporate party, promotion, trade show, product launch, team building exercise, hospitality event, picnic, or other customized activity.

Corey's New Events Facility is located in downtown Atlanta just blocks from the Georgia World Congress Center and all the Convention hotels. Corey Entertainment, America's number one game rental company, can stage an event at either of these locations or from hundreds of others throughout the United States.

The Amusement Division of Corey Entertainment substantially invests every day in the latest gaming and amusement technology on the market. The division currently operates hundreds of games at colleges and businesses, ranging from the simply engrossing to the latest in virtual reality games. By offering a wide selection of games, successful revenue sharing plans, excellent customer satisfaction, and superior service, the division has grown over the last twenty years into the South's largest game rental supplier.

Corey's Customized Internal Automation System dramatically increases efficiency. Documented revenue reports, computerized security systems, skilled technicians, a fleet of service vehicles, and two-way digital communications are just a few reasons why Corey's Amusement Division is a leader in the industry.

Corporate Events brings unlimited interactive games and entertainment solutions to corporate events held anywhere in the nation. From the imaginations of a highly creative staff, and from the depths of a huge warehouse of innovative products, Corporate Events can entertain, motivate, or promote virtually anything. The multimillion- dollar inventory includes all the latest in high-tech simulator games and old favorites like pool tables, pinball machines, and large-scale inflatable games. The specialists in Corporate Events are equipped to handle any job, any size, anywhere in the country. A fleet of Corey vehicles and

The third division, Corey Promotions, is king of outdoor events. Corey Promotions has supplied many of the largest outdoor events in the southeastern United States, including festivals, concerts, art shows, weddings, corporate events, commercial/retail events, and sporting events with tents and accessories. "Under the tent" accessories range from lights, flooring, and sound systems, to tables, chairs, heaters, and air-conditioners. Other accessories include a wide variety of unique high-impact, cold-air balloons (up to 3 stories high), skytracker lights, and banners, among others.

Though these divisions all hold honors and titles of "best" in their own right, Corey Entertainment services do not stop there. Clients can use Corey Entertainment to handle every detail from event planning to site selection to outfitting to catering and invitation printing, to ensure an unforgettable, successful, and hassle-free event of any kind anywhere. Clients are free to choose all services or any combination or a single service to aid annual and one-of-a-kind events.

Let the games begin. ☜

Hitachi Electronic Devices, (USA) Inc.

Hitachi, one of the world's leading global electronics companies, has been a presence in the United States since 1959. Hitachi is Japan's largest electronic producer with estimated 1998 revenues of $69 billion U.S. dollars. The company employs more than 330,000 people worldwide, with thousands located in the Atlanta area. Several Hitachi group companies have chosen Atlanta as headquarters for their U.S. operations, including Hitachi Electronic Devices (USA) and Hitachi Telecom (USA) Inc. Other Hitachi subsidiaries in the Atlanta area include Denon Corporations (USA), Hitachi Koki U.S.A. Ltd., Nissei Sanyo America Ltd., Sunrise Air Service Inc., and Hitachi Transport System (America) Ltd.

These Hitachi companies manufacture and market a wide variety of products, including consumer electronics, telecommunications equipment, power tools, computers, semiconductors, heavy machinery, power generation, and power and industrial equipment. Other Hitachi subsidiaries provide transportation, warehousing, and travel agency services.

and state governments, and a diverse and highly qualified labor force. In addition, Atlanta provides a variety of cultural events and other activities that can be enjoyed year-round in a near perfect climate.

Hitachi generously contributes to several of Atlanta's community organizations, charities, and schools. Each of the Hitachi companies has an independent Community Action Committee (CAC). The CACs meet monthly to coordinate and pool resources in order to support larger projects. Each local CAC works to identify the critical needs of the community, promote employee awareness and community involvement, and support community projects by funding, in-kind donations, and volunteer service. The Hitachi Foundation of Washington, D.C., provides matching funds.

In Atlanta Hitachi companies support the United Way, Habitat for Humanity, the Muscular Dystrophy foundation, and an inner-city tennis program, among others. Another way Hitachi supports Atlanta schools is by sending employees and expatriates into the local classrooms to educate students about Japan. Hitachi also provides equipment needed by the schools and funds for the purchase of electronic equipment, including computer monitors, televisions, VCRs, and CD players.

Hitachi's strong support of education includes the *Cool Science Show for Kids.* Dinosaur hunts, galaxy gazing, and virtual environments are just a few things kids can experience when they tune in. The television show sponsored by Hitachi offers teens interesting and exciting ways to learn about the world they live in. Another Hitachi sponsored series, *The Mississippi: River of Song* on the PBS network, explores the richness and vitality of American music at the close of the twentieth century. ❧

▲ Each of the Hitachi companies has an independent Community Action Committee (CAC). The CACs meet monthly to coordinate and pool resources in order to support larger projects.

◀ Hitachi is a proud sponsor of the Southern BG 12's Tennis Tournament.

Although operated independently, these companies continually interact and complement each other, providing the high quality of service that is part of Hitachi's reputation as one of the world's foremost corporations.

Atlanta was chosen by these Hitachi companies as the ideal location to conduct business because the city provides excellent proximity to customers and global access through Hartsfield International Airport, as well as a thriving economy, strong local

ChoicePoint Inc.

ChoicePoint is a company poised to deliver on the virtues of the information age. The company's mission—to provide people and businesses with the intelligence they need to make smarter business decisions—has its roots in a strong and dynamic history. The company began in Atlanta as Equifax's Insurance Services Group, providing insurance carriers and brokers with information tools to make better evaluations of policyholders.

Since its spin-off in 1997, ChoicePoint Chairman and CEO Derek Smith has extended the company's expertise into industries and business applications that require what he refers to as "actionable intelligence"—information a customer can use to make smarter decisions.

"Everyone experiences thousands of choicepoints in their life; some critical, others routine," explains Smith. "Helping individuals and enterprises gain access to intelligent information to improve their decision making when they reach a choicepoint is what we are all about."

ChoicePoint has actively sought out new opportunities, technologies, industries, and business partners. The company that once served the insurance industry exclusively now boasts a client roster that includes the who's who of Fortune 1,000 companies. In addition, the company is one of the leading solution providers to the public sector, serving federal, state, and municipal government and law enforcement agencies.

Accordingly, ChoicePoint operates in several market arenas—business and professional services, the public sector, and insurance, both life and health and property and casualty. The company provides pre-employment background screening and drug testing management services to private businesses and public companies, integrated information services for law enforcement agencies tracking fugitives and government agencies searching for parents with

delinquent child support payments, and provides screening services for health care companies and Medicare and Medicaid agencies, as examples. ChoicePoint's custom solutions include web-based property and casualty insurance information order and retrieval, physician verification services, vendor screening, and legal due diligence.

In addition to its commitment to serving customers, ChoicePoint has made a commitment to community involvement. The ChoicePoint Foundation, established in 1998, supports programs in four areas with a specific focus on children: humanitarian efforts, disease and health improvement, education, and safety. The force behind this involvement is the combined effort of ChoicePoint employees, who volunteer countless hours to support numerous causes. Employees actively participate by volunteering, making financial contributions, suggesting appropriate organizations to support, or requesting matching funds for causes they personally support.

ChoicePoint is the leading provider of actionable intelligence that helps businesses, governments, and individuals make smarter decisions. ChoicePoint Chairman Derek Smith believes the company's strength lies in its ability to identify, retrieve, store, analyze, and deliver the right information for customers. He believes there is a significant growth opportunity for the company to leverage these skills in their existing and new markets. ❧

HABITAT FOR HUMANITY
IN ATLANTA, INC.
Funding Provided By
ChoicePoint, Inc.

New South Construction Company, Inc.

Doug Davidson's lifelong interest in construction began at home. "My dad was an engineer and I was always around design and construction areas growing up," Davidson recalls. After working summer jobs in construction from high school through college, Davidson went straight to work for a construction company after graduation and founded New South Construction Company Inc., a midsize commercial general contractor, in 1990. During its first year of operation, New South billed a total of $4.2 million and added 30 employees. Projects included renovation work for the Coca-Cola Company and Delta Air Lines, tenant work for Prentiss Properties, and the Coweta County Jail.

One of the young company's projects was a $2-million gymnasium for Woodward Academy. "We built a relationship as we built that gym," Davidson explains. Today, current projects under construction for Woodward by New South Construction total $18 million. Other early clients included UPS, Southern Mills, and Ford Motor Company. Two of New South's interesting, one-of-a-kind jobs were the Rowing Venue for the Olympic Games and the main entry to Six Flags.

The success of New South Construction is not the result of a marketing department out calling on prospective clients with smoke and mirrors. Instead, the marketing department consists of the principals, managers, and supervisors working on each job and with each client. New South's first project for Coca-Cola was a small and difficult one, involving the replacement of crumbling concrete beams in a heavily trafficked area. New South Construction tackled the job with enthusiasm, high quality management skills, and dedication to doing the job right. That project has led to a 10-year relationship with Coca-Cola. "A client like that opens a lot of doors," says Davison.

The main source of the growth of New South Construction over the past nine years has been repeat business and referral work from previous clients. Once a project is completed, clients gain confidence in New South's ability to complete larger, more complex projects. Referrals from satisfied clients also lead to many new project opportunities.

Referrals from members of the Druid Hills Golf Club, impressed by New South's work on their club, led to contracts to build the Emory Alumni House and Ansley Golf Club. From private schools, churches, and country clubs, to corporate facilities for Coca-Cola, Delta, and the Ford Motor Company, "We go the extra mile," says Davidson. "We look at the project we do today as the marketing for the next big job." Ranked number 41 on the *Atlanta Business Chronicle's* list of fastest growing private companies in 1998, and winner of numerous industry awards, New South Construction supports the American Cancer Society, Cystic Fibrosis Foundation, and Scottish Rite Hospital, among many other charities and Little League teams. Davidson is also on the board of directors of the Associated General Contractors of Georgia. Although New South Construction has grown from a $4-million company to a $55-million company in nine years, it remains client-driven rather than revenue-driven. "We will continue to grow, but we will never outgrow our commitment to client satisfaction and quality work," says Davidson. "Our goal is to earn and keep the respect of the Atlanta business community as a top-notch quality contractor." ✪

▲ **Six Flags Over Georgia's entrance mall development in Austell, Georgia, was built by New South Construction.**

◄ **In Norcross, Georgia, New South Construction built the Upper School Building for the Wesleyan School.**

The North Highland Company

The North Highland Company is an independent management and technology consulting firm dedicated to helping clients enhance revenue, improve productivity, control costs, and increase quality and competitiveness.

Founded in Atlanta in 1992, North Highland grew at a moderate pace for its first five years. However, a 1997 decision to give employees ownership in the company helped fuel some dramatic results: a growth in staff from 21 employees to nearly 200 in 1999, and equivalent revenue growth during the same period. A second office opened in Orlando, Florida, in early 1998, a third office in Nashville, Tennessee, opened July, 1999, and a nationally known customer support consulting firm merged its operations into North Highland's in 1999.

▲ From customer service and call center solutions to business intelligence and knowledge management, North Highland gives clients a competitive advantage by providing the tools needed to turn information into strategy.

▶ The North Highland Company is an independent management and technology consulting firm dedicated to helping clients enhance revenue, improve productivity, control costs, and increase quality and competitiveness.

Officers and principals at North Highland have from 10 to 30 years' experience in consulting. Their knowledge of diverse industries means they understand the environment in which businesses operate and the needs of customers.

North Highland's client list includes the American Cancer Society, BellSouth, Chick-fil-A, Georgia-Pacific Corporation, Home Depot, Melita International, Turner Broadcasting, ZooAtlanta, and a number of departments and agencies of the State of Georgia.

Among the performance-improving services North Highland provides are business process management, information technology management, organizational change management, strategic planning, project management, supply chain management, call center development, business intelligence and data warehousing, knowledge management, manufacturing and distribution industry services, and health care services.

Working in partnership with clients, North Highland uses these services to help design and implement solutions that fit each organization's culture and industry environment. Because North Highland has local people working with local companies, they respond quickly when needed.

Applying value chain analysis, North Highland steers organizations through the opportunities and threats posed by competitors, government actions, international market forces, new technology, and other factors outside their organization's control.

Changing business processes to adapt to these conditions can create new opportunities and services. An Atlanta-based government agency applied these techniques and cut their purchasing lead time in half. A major building products supplier used North Highland's proprietary value chain analysis with a new marketing strategy to brand products differently, change logistics channels, and apply electronic commerce to strengthen supplier-customer relationships.

North Highland also provides project managers that give objective, comprehensive input into all phases of the project management process. For one client, they provided an acting Chief Information Officer and several key project managers. This team developed a custom technology solution that allowed the client to complete its initial public offering a year earlier than its industry competitors.

A company's customer service phone center or internal help desk is a critical part of the business. North Highland can evaluate a call center and recommend new methods and technology to improve service and cut costs. "The Snapshot™ diagnostic tool is rapidly becoming the industry standard for evaluating effectiveness and efficiency of both inbound and outbound call centers," says North Highland Company founder and president, David Peterson.

From customer service and call center solutions to business intelligence and knowledge management, North Highland gives clients a competitive advantage by providing the tools needed to turn information into strategy.

"We use these methods every day in real business situations," says Peterson. "We apply technology where it has bottom-line

benefits. We use business process improvements to create value. At North Highland our business goal is to help your business run better." ◐

Porter Novelli

Who created the "Food Guide Pyramid"? The same people who launched the Cabbage Patch doll craze, made Princess Cruises synonymous with "The Love Boat," got Americans to eat "5 A Day" fruits and vegetables, galvanized teens to reduce tobacco use in Florida, and helped make the Philips Arena a household name in Atlanta.

Who did this and much more? Porter Novelli, the third largest public relations agency in the world.

Porter Novelli is "one of the few agencies where creativity permeates every practice," according to *Inside PR*, an industry publication.

Porter Novelli Atlanta, founded in 1997, has quickly established itself as a major force in the local marketplace. The agency specializes in health care, technology, consumer products, and social marketing.

Porter Novelli today continues the commitment of its founders to "do well by doing good," partnering with nonprofit and public sector clients as well as corporations. Founded in 1972, the agency has 14 offices throughout the United States and operations in over 60 countries.

Porter Novelli is known for its marketing-based approach—for delivering results that are grounded in its clients' business objectives. The agency believes in integrated communications—combining public relations and other disciplines (which can include advertising, investor relations, public affairs, etc.) to achieve clients' goals.

The agency believes that exceeding clients' expectations—always delivering results that are exceptional and measurable—is the path to continued growth. Delivering exciting ideas and strategic programs that motivate clients' target audiences, consistently and over the long-term, is Porter Novelli's approach.

"If it's brand-building you're worried about, Porter Novelli is likely to be close to the top of the short list of agencies," per *Inside PR*. The agency works with many Atlanta clients, including the Woodruff Arts Center, on compelling and consistent brand identity.

Porter Novelli professionals are the heartbeat of its practice. In Atlanta, the team averages 14 years' experience in TV and print journalism, marketing, public relations, advertising, fund-raising, speech writing, and public affairs. Porter Novelli Atlanta is young at heart, with a touch of gray around the temples.

The majority of Porter Novelli's Atlanta-based clients draw on the agency's global organization and expertise. Others focus on the Southeast or nationally. Whatever the market, Porter Novelli Atlanta is here to help clients achieve their growth objectives. ✎

◄ **Porter Novelli Atlanta, founded in 1997, has quickly established itself as a major force in the local marketplace. The agency specializes in health care, technology, consumer products, and social marketing.**

◄ **Porter Novelli is known for its marketing-based approach—for delivering results that are grounded in its clients' business objectives.**

ENTERPRISE INDEX

Corey Entertainment
1935 Sixth Street
Chamblee, GA 30341
Phone: 770-216-8200
Fax: 770-216-8221
www.coreyentertainment.com
Page 432

Corporate Environments
1636 Northeast Expressway
Atlanta, GA 30329
Phone: 404-679-8999
Fax: 404-679-8950
E-Mail: Information@corporate
   environments.com
www.corporateenvironments.com
Pages 424-425

Crawford & Company
5620 Glenridge Drive
Atlanta, GA 30302
Phone: 404-847-4112
Fax: 404-847-4028
E-Mail: drew-maenza@us.crawco.com
www.crawfordandcompany.com
Page 236

Cushman & Wakefield
1201 West Peachtree Street,
Suite 3300
Atlanta, GA 30309
Phone: 404-875-1000
Fax: 404-875-4637
www.cushwake.com
Page 320

Delta Air Lines
Post Office Box 20706
Atlanta, GA 30320
Phone: 404-715-2600
www.delta-air.com
Page 238

EDS
3715 Northside Parkway,
Suite 800, Building 100
Atlanta, GA 30327
Phone: 404-812-2000
Fax: 404-812-2943
www.eds.com
Page 289

Elite Staffing Services
230 Peachtree Street, NW, Suite 2125
Atlanta, GA 30303
Phone: 404-577-4511
Fax: 404-577-2963
E-Mail: corp@elitestaff.com
www.elitestaff.com
Page 371

Equifax
1550 Peachtree Street
Atlanta, GA 30309
Phone: 404-885-8000
www.equifax.com
Pages 126-127

**The Esthetic Dental Practice of
   Goldstein, Garber, Salama
   & Gribble**
1218 West Paces Ferry Road, Suite 200
Atlanta, GA 30327
Phone: 404-261-4941
Fax: 404-261-4946
E-Mail: goldsteingarber@goldstein
   garber.com
www.goldsteingarber.com
Pages 94-97

Federal Home Loan Bank of Atlanta
1475 Peachtree Street, NE
Atlanta, GA 30348
Phone: 404-888-8000
Fax: 404-888-5354
www.fhlbatl.com
Pages 104-105

FINOVA Capital Corporation
400 Northridge Road, Suite 1100
Atlanta, GA 30350
Phone: 770-641-3550
Fax: 770-641-3551
E-Mail: dhoffer@finova.com
www.finova.com
Pages 360-361

The Flagler Company
2126 DeFoors Ferry Road
Atlanta, GA 30318
Phone: 404-351-0007
Fax: 404-351-3662
E-Mail: tflagler@flaglerconst.com
www.flaglerconst.com
Page 208

Georgia-Pacific Corporation
133 Peachtree Street, NE
Atlanta, GA 30303
Phone: 404-652-4000
www.gp.com
Pages 124-125

Georgia Power Company
241 Ralph McGill Boulevard, NE
Atlanta, GA 30308
Phone: 404-506-6906
Fax: 404-506-2441
E-Mail: rablaloc@southernco.com
Pages 62-65

Georgia State University
University Plaza
Atlanta, GA 30303
Phone: 404-651-2000
www.gsu.edu
Pages 100-101

**Georgia World Congress Center
   Authority**
285 International Boulevard, NW
Atlanta, GA 30313
Phone: 404-223-4200
Fax: 404-223-4211
E-Mail: lstevens@gwcc.com
www.gwcc.com
Pages 412-413

Golder Associates
3730 Chamblee Tucker Road
Atlanta, GA 30341
Phone: 770-496-1893
Fax: 770-934-9476
www.golder.com
Page 288

Goode Van Slyke Architecture
280 Elizabeth Street, Suite A-002
Atlanta, GA 30307
Phone: 404-523-5525
Fax: 404-523-5935
E-Mail: architects@gvsa.com
www.gvsa.com
Pages 426-427

Grady Health System
80 Butler Street, SE
Atlanta, GA 30335-3801
Phone: 404-616-4307
www.gradyhealthsystem.org
Page 175

Harold A. Dawson Company
600 Peachtree Street, NE, Suite 3700
Atlanta, GA 30308
Phone: 404-347-8030
Fax: 404-347-8040
E-Mail: main@hadcoinc.com
www.hadcoinc.com
Page 290

Hartsfield International Airport
Post Office Box 20509
Atlanta, GA 30320
Phone: 404-209-1700
Fax: 404-209-2942
E-Mail:
   miguel.southwell@atlanta-airport.com
www.atlanta-airport.com
Pages 358-359

Healthdyne Information Enterprises
1850 Parkway Place
Marietta, GA 30067
Phone: 770-423-8450
Fax: 770-423-8440
www.hie.com
Page 318

Heidelberg USA, Inc.
1000 Gutenberg Drive
Kennesaw, GA 30144
Phone: 770-419-6500
Fax: 770-419-6665
E-Mail: webmaster-@heidelbergusa.com
www.heidelbergusa.com
Pages 422-423

Heidrick & Struggles, Inc.
303 Peachtree Street, NE; Suite 3100
Atlanta, GA 30308
Phone: 404-577-2410
Fax: 404-577-4048
www.heidrick.com
Pages 130-131

Hewlett-Packard
20 Perimeter Summit Boulevard
Atlanta, GA 30319
Phone: 404-648-0000
www.hp.com
Page 286

Hilton Atlanta Northwest/Windy Hill
2055 South Park Place
Atlanta, GA 30339
Phone: 770-953-9300
Fax: 770-953-9315
E-Mail: odomkim@hotmail.com
www.hiltonatlantanw.citysearch.com
Pages 346-347

Hilton Atlanta & Towers
255 Courtland Street NE
Atlanta, GA 30303
Phone: 404-659-2000
Fax: 404-221-6301
www.atlanta.hilton.com
Pages 316-317

Hines Interests Limited Partnership
Five Ravinia Drive
Atlanta, GA 30346
Phone: 770-206-5300
Fax: 770-206-5325
www.hines.com
Pages 262-263

Hitachi Electronic Devices, (USA) Inc.
6200 The Corners Parkway, Suite 300
Norcross, GA 30092
Phone: 770-409-3000
Fax: 770-409-3028
www.hitachi.com
Page 433

Holder Properties
3333 Riverwood Parkway, Suite 500
Atlanta, GA 30339
Phone: 770-988-3131
Fax: 770-988-3105
www.holderproperties.com
Page 364

Holiday Inn Downtown
101 International Boulevard
Atlanta, GA 30303
Phone: 404-524-5555
Fax: 404-524-0218
E-Mail: holidayatl@mindspring.com
www.holiday-inn.com/atldowntown
Page 428

The Home Depot®
2455 Paces Ferry Road, NW
Atlanta, GA 30339-4024
Phone: 770-433-8211
www.homedepot.com
Pages 314-315

Hughston Clinic
Corporate Headquarters:
6262 Veterans Parkway
Post Office Box 9517
Columbus, GA 31908-9517
Phone: 1-800-331-2910
Atlanta Region:
105 Collier Road, Suite 1030
Atlanta, Georgia
Phone: 404-352-1053
Fax: 404-350-0840
Pages 418-419

Hunton & Williams
Bank of America Plaza, Suite 4100
600 Peachtree Street, N.E.
Atlanta, GA 30308-2216
Phone: 404-888-4000
Fax: 404-888-4190
E-Mail: info@hunton.com
www.hunton.com
Pages 348-349

Interdenominational Theological Center
700 Martin Luther King Jr. Drive
Atlanta, GA 30314
Phone: 404-527-7700
Fax: 404-614-6382
E-Mail: bevjones@itc.edu
www.itc.edu
Page 267

Jones, Day, Reavis & Pogue
3500 SunTrust Plaza
303 Peachtree Street
Atlanta, GA 30308
Phone: 404-521-3939
Fax: 404-581-8330
E-Mail: counsel@jonesday.com
www.jonesday.com
Pages 122-123

Kaiser Permanente
Nine Piedmont Center
3495 Piedmont Road, NE
Atlanta, GA 30305-1736
Phone: 404-364-7000
Fax: 404-364-4794
E-Mail: beverly.thomas@kp.org
www.kpga.org
Pages 108-109

King & Spalding
191 Peachtree Street, Suite 4900
Atlanta, GA 30303-1763
Phone: 404-572-4600
Fax: 404-572-5700
www.kslaw.com
Pages 162-163

Lockheed Martin Aeronautical Systems
86 South Cobb Drive
D/84-10
Marietta, GA 30063-0264
Phone: 770-494-4411
www.lmasc.com
Pages 90-93

Long Aldridge & Norman LLP
303 Peachtree Street, NE, Suite 5300
Atlanta, GA 30308
Phone: 404-527-4000
Fax: 404-527-4198
E-Mail: atlanta@lanlaw.com
www.lanlaw.com
Page 325

MARTA
2424 Piedmont Road, NE
Atlanta, GA 30324-3330
Phone: 404-848-5000
www.itsmarta.com
Pages 78-81

Matria Healthcare
1850 Parkway Place, 12th Floor
Marietta, GA 30067
Phone: 770-767-4500
Fax: 770-767-7769
www.matria.com
Page 319

Mercer University
Cecil B. Day Campus—Atlanta
1400 Coleman Avenue
Macon, GA 31207
Phone: 912-752-2700
1-800-837-2911
E-Mail: mercerinfo@mercer.edu
www.mercer.edu
Page 200-201

Metro Atlanta Chamber of Commerce
235 International Boulevard, NW
Atlanta, GA 30303
Phone: 404-880-9000
Fax: 404-586-8416
E-Mail: info@macoc.com
www.metroatlantachamber.com
Pages 160-161

Morrison Management Specialists
1955 Lake Park Drive, S.E., Suite 400
Smyrna, GA 30080
Phone: 770-437-3300
Fax: 770-437-3343
www.iammorrison.com
Pages 58-61

Motorola Energy Systems Group
1700 Belle Meade Court
Lawrenceville, GA 30043-5854
Phone: 770-338-3319
Fax: 770-338-3557
E-Mail: nancy.klentak@motorola.com
www.motorola.com/esg
Pages 420-421

The Mulling Group
10 Glenlake Parkway, Suite 100
Atlanta, GA 30328
Phone: 770-395-3131
Fax: 770-395-3133
E-Mail: emorymulling@mulling.com
www.mulling.com
Page 373

NCR
2651 Satellite Boulevard
Duluth, GA 30096
Phone: 770-623-7000
www.ncr.com
Pages 168-169

New South Construction Company, Inc.
1132 West Peachtree Street
Atlanta, GA 30309
Phone: 404-443-4000
Fax: 404-443-4100
E-Mail:
  info@newsouthconstruction.net
www.newsouthconstruction.net
Page 435

Nextel
6575 The Corners Parkway
Norcross, GA 30092
Phone: 770-825-9000
www.nextel.com
Page 429

Noro-Moseley Partners
4200 Northside Parkway, Building 9
Atlanta, GA 30327
Phone: 404-233-1966
Fax: 404-239-9280
E-Mail: info@noro-moseley.com
www.noro-moseley.com
Page 366

Nortel Networks
5405 Windward Parkway
Alpharetta, GA 30004
Phone: 770-708-5000
www.nortelnetworks.com
Pages 74-77

The North Highland Company
550 Pharr Road NE, Suite 850
Atlanta, GA 30306
Phone: 404-233-1015
Fax: 404-233-4930
E-Mail: resumes@north-highland.com
www.north-highland.com
Page 436

Oglethorpe University
4484 Peachtree Road, NE
Atlanta, GA 30319
Phone: 404-261-1441
Fax: 404-364-8500
E-Mail: info@oglethorpe.edu
www.oglethorpe.edu
Page 174

Philips Consumer Electronics North America
64 Perimeter Center East
Atlanta, GA 31164
Phone: 770-821-2400
www.philipsusa.com
Pages 414-415

Pope & Land Enterprises, Inc.
3225 Cumberland Boulevard, Suite 400
Atlanta, GA 30339
Phone: 770-980-0808
Fax: 770-984-8630
E-Mail: lkelly@popeandland.com
www.popeandland.com
Page 326

Porter Novelli
1040 Crown Pointe Parkway
Atlanta, GA 30338
Phone: 770-280-8080
Fax: 770-280-8081
E-Mail: kbremer@porternovelli.com
www.porternovelli.com
Page 437

Portman Holdings
303 Peachtree Street, NE, Suite 4600
Atlanta, GA 30308
Phone: 404-614-5252
Fax: 404-521-1725
E-Mail:
    portmanholdings@mindspring.com
www.portmanholdings.com
Page 260

Powertel, Inc.
1233 O.G. Skinner Drive
West Point, GA 31833
Phone: 706-645-2000
Fax: 706-645-9523
www.powertel.com
Page 430

PricewaterhouseCoopers LLP
1155 Peachtree Street
1100 Campanile Building
Atlanta, GA 30309
Phone: 404-870-1100
Fax: 404-888-4927
www.us.pwcglobal.com
Pages 106-107

RMT Construction, Inc.
4058 Sandy Lake Drive
Lithonia, GA 30058
Phone: 770-593-9035
Fax: 770-593-0021
Page 369

Rich's
Corporate Headquarters:
223 Perimeter Center Parkway
Atlanta, GA 30346
Phone: 770-913-4000
www.federated-fds.com
Pages 170-171

Rosser International
524 West Peachtree Street NW
Atlanta, GA 30308
Phone: 404-876-3800
Fax: 404-888-6861
www.rosser.com
Page 287

Sanderson Industries, Inc.
3550 Atlanta Industrial Parkway
Atlanta, GA 30331
Phone: 404-699-2022
Fax: 404-696-3956
E-Mail: contact@sndsn.com
www.sandersonindustries.com
Pages 356-357

Selig Enterprises, Inc.
1100 Spring Street, N.W., Suite 550
Atlanta, GA 30309-2848
Phone: 404-876-5511
Fax: 404-875-2629
Page 237

Solarcom, Inc.
One Sun Court
Norcross, GA 39097
Phone: 770-449-6116
Fax: 770-448-7726
E-Mail: marketing@solarcom.net
www.solarcom.net
Page 323

Southern Company
270 Peachtree Street
BIN 908, Suite 1500
Atlanta, GA 30303
Phone: 404-506-5000
www.southernco.com
Pages 66-69

Spencer Stuart, Executive Search Consultants
3424 Peachtree Road, NE
Monarch Tower, Suite 1100
Atlanta, GA 30326
Phone: 404-504-4400
Fax: 404-504-4401
www.spencerstuart.com
Pages 350-351

State University of West Georgia
1600 Maple Street
Carrollton, GA 30118
Phone: 770-836-6418
Fax: 770-836-4659
E-Mail: admiss@westga.edu
www.westga.edu
Page 209

SunTrust Bank
25 Park Place
Atlanta, GA 30302
Phone: 404-588-7711
www.suntrust.com
Page 173

Sutherland Asbill & Brennan LLP
999 Peachtree Street, NE
Atlanta, GA 30309-3996
Phone: 404-853-8000
Fax: 404-853-8806
E-Mail: info@sablaw.com
www.sablaw.com
Page 205

TWD, Inc.
230 Peachtree Street, Suite 530
Atlanta, GA 30303
Phone: 404-521-1115
Fax: 404-525-6226
E-Mail: twdpres@mindspring.com
Page 431

Taracorp, Inc.
3490 Piedmont Road, NE, Suite 1311
Atlanta, GA 30305
Phone: 404-233-1971
Fax: 404-233-4536
E-Mail: helpdesk@taracorp.com
www.taracorp.com
Page 266

Trammell Crow
Five Concourse Parkway, Suite 1600
Atlanta, GA 30328
Phone: 770-698-2200
Fax: 770-698-2222
www.trammellcrow.com
Pages 114-115

Troutman Sanders LLP
Bank of America Plaza, Suite 5200
600 Peachtree Street, N.E.
Atlanta, GA 30308
Phone: 404-885-3000
Fax: 404-885-3900
www.troutmansanders.com
Pages 120-121

Turner Broadcasting System, Inc.
CNN Center
Post Office Box 105573
Atlanta, GA 30348-5573
Phone: 404-827-1700
www.turner.com
Page 321

U.S. Army Forces Command
1777 Hardee Avenue, SW
Ft. McPherson, GA 30330
Phone: 404-464-7276
Fax: 404-464-5628
www.forscom.army.mil
Pages 264-265

United Parcel Service
55 Glenlake Parkway, NE
Atlanta, GA 30328
Phone: 404-828-6000
www.ups.com
Pages 102-103

The Varsity
61 North Avenue
Atlanta, GA 30308
Phone: 404-881-1706
Fax: 404-874-3989
www.thevarsity.com
Page 207

Wachovia Corporation
191 Peachtree Street, NE
Atlanta, GA 30303
Phone: 404-332-5000
www.wachovia.com
Page 172

Watkins Real Estate Groups
1946 Monroe Street
Atlanta, GA 30324
Phone: 404-872-8666
Fax: 404-872-8806
Pages 308-311

Watson Wyatt Worldwide
4170 Ashford Dunwoody Road, NE,
    Suite 432
Atlanta, GA 30319
Phone: 800-654-9676
Fax: 404-256-3549
www.watsonwyatt.com
Page 368

Weibel & Associates, Inc.
3778 LaVista Road, Suite 200
Tucker, GA 30084
Phone: 404-320-2390
Fax: 404-320-2394
E-Mail: weibel@mindspring.com
Page 372

Williams-Russell and Johnson, Inc.
771 Spring Street, NW
Atlanta, GA 30308
Phone: 404-853-6800
Fax: 404-607-8890
www.wrjinc.com
Pages 312-313

Womble Carlyle Sandridge & Rice, PLLC
One Atlantic Center
1201 Peachtree Street, Suite 3500
Atlanta, GA 30309
Phone: 404-872-7000
Fax: 404-888-7490
E-Mail: sdunlevie@wcsr.com
www.wcsr.com
Pages 416-417

WORLDSPAN®
300 Galleria Parkway, N.W.
Atlanta, GA 30339
Phone: 770-563-7400
Fax: 770-563-7004
E-Mail: info@worldspan.com
www.worldspan.com
Pages 116-117

Yancey Bros. Co.
Corporate Headquarters:
330 Lee Industrial Boulevard
Austell, GA 30168
Phone: 770-941-2300
Fax: 770-819-5570
E-Mail: adpromo@yanceybros.com
www.yanceybros.com
Pages 82-85

BIBLIOGRAPHY

Agnew, Lea and Joanne Haden-Miller. *Atlanta and Its Lawyers*. Atlanta: Atlanta Bar Association, 1988.

Frederick Allen. *Atlanta Rising*. Atlanta: Longstreet Press, 1996.

Galphin, Bruce and Norman Shavin. *Atlanta: Triumph of a People*. Atlanta: Capricorn Corp., 1982.

Garrett, Franklin. *Atlanta and Environs*. New York: Lewis Historical Publishing Co., 1952.

Shavin, Norman. *Days in the Life of Atlanta*. Atlanta: Capricorn Corp., 1987.

Webb Garrison. *The Legacy of Atlanta*. Atlanta: Peachtree Publishers Ltd., 1987.

ACKNOWLEDGEMENTS

My own journey through the history of Atlanta started, as does everyone's, with the definitive work of Franklin Garrett and continued through the popular histories written by Norman Shavin, Bruce Galphin, Webb Garrison, Frederick Allen and others. Thanks also to the Chamber of Commerce for making their publication archives available and to Community Communications for the opportunity to learn more about where I live.

Finally, I couldn't have participated in this project without the generous support and understanding of my family and, especially, my wife, Lizanne Thomas.

David Black, *Author*

INDEX